Southern History

Volume 3/1981

Southern History is an academic yearbook covering work in progress on the historic counties of Cornwall, Devon, Somerset, Gloucestershire, Wiltshire, Dorset, Berkshire, Surrey, Hampshire and the Isle of Wight, Kent and Sussex, and the Channel Islands. Many of its contributions will demonstrate the use of new methods in interpreting local sources, which should encourage considerable further work; although the emphasis is primarily historical, papers will be welcomed from related disciplines where they are germane to the study of localities or Southern England as a whole.

Publication is annual, normally in the spring of each year. Prospective authors are asked to write to the editor, with a brief outline of their proposed submissions, and asking for a copy of *Notes for Contributors.*

Southern History

SOUTHERN HISTORY

A Review of the History of
Southern England

Volume 3/1981

Edited by
J. R. Lowerson

Reviews editor
W. N. Yates

ALAN SUTTON
HUMANITIES PRESS

First Published in Great Britain 1981
Alan Sutton Publishing Limited
17a Brunswick Road
Gloucester
GL1 1HG

First published in the
United States of America 1981
Humanities Press Inc.
Atlantic Highlands
New Jersey 07716

British Library Cataloguing in Publication Data

Southern History
   Vol. 3
   1. Great Britain—History—Periodicals
   942.2'005   DA20

   ISBN 0-904387-65-8 (CASE)
   ISSN 0-904387-66-6 (PAPER)
   ISSN 0142-4688
   ISBN 0-391-02316-0 (HUMANITIES PRESS)

Typesetting and origination
by Alan Sutton Publishing Limited
Printed in Great Britain
By Redwood Burn Limited, Trowbridge

Contents

Notes on Contributors   8

Editor's Preface   10

Roman Hampshire: a strategy for research
D. E. Johnston   13

Medieval Jewish persecution in England: the Canterbury
pogroms in perspective
D. Cohn-Sherbok   23

London and the provinces: the association between the
capital and the Berkshire county gentry of the seventeenth
century
C. G. Durston   39

Royalist strategy in the south of England, 1642–1644
M. D. G. Wanklyn   55

The distribution of wealth in the Vale of Berkeley,
Gloucestershire, 1660–1700
J. P. P. Horn   81

Water communications to Margate and Gravesend as coastal
resorts before 1840
J. Whyman   111

Agriculture and land use in Cornwall *circa* 1840
R. Kain and H. Holt   139

'An undoubted jewel': a case study of five Sussex country
houses, 1880–1914
P. Blackwell   183

Inter-war housing policy: a study of Brighton
P. Dickens and P. Gilbert   201

6   Contents

Book Reviews

John Lowerson, *A Short History of Sussex* (T.P. Hudson)   233

Peter Brandon, *A History of Surrey;* Barbara Carpenter Turner, *A History of Hampshire* (John Webb)   234

J.V.S. Megaw and D. D. A. Simpson, *Introduction to British Prehistory* (Bryony Orme)   235

John Collis *et al, Winchester Excavations II 1949–1960* (Colin Platt)   237

David Johnston, *Roman Villas* (D. J. Rudkin)   239

David Johnston, *An Illustrated History of Roman Roads in Britain* (D. J. Rudkin)   240

Medieval Settlement, ed. P. H. Sawyer (Richard Avent)   241

The South Saxons, ed. Peter Brandon (D. J. Rudkin)   243

J. C. Sladden, *Boniface of Devon; The Greatest Englishman,* ed. T. Reuter; D. Kepp, *St. Boniface and His World* (D. H. Farmer)   244

M. Gelling, *The Early Charters of the Thames Valley* (E. O. Blake)   246

K. J. Barton, *Medieval Sussex Pottery* (D. J. Rudkin)   247

Proceedings of the Battle Conference on Anglo-Norman Studies 1978, ed. R. A. Brown (Frank Barlow)   248

Frank Barlow, *The English Church 1066–1154;* J. C. Dickinson, *Ecclesiastical History of England: The Late Middle Ages* (Nigel Yates)   250

The 1235 Surrey Eyre I, ed. C. A. F. Meekings and David Crook (P. D. A. Harvey)   251

Lacock Abbey Charters, ed. K. H. Rogers (Dom Frederick Hockey)   252

The Register of the Common Seal of the Priory of St. Swithun, Winchester, 1345–1497, ed. J. B. Greatrex; *New Forest Documents, 1244–1334,* ed. D. J. Stagg (Dom Frederick Hockey)   253

The Churchwardens' Accounts of St. Michael's Church, Chagford, 1480–1600, trans. F. M. Osborne (W. M. Jacob)

Charles Phythian-Adams, *Desolation of A City* (R. A. Higham)   254

R. Machin, *The Houses of Yetminster* (Deane Clark)

Guide to the Parish and Non-Parochial Registers of Devon and Cornwall, 1537–1837, comp. Hugh Peskett (W. M. Jacob)   258

Theo Brown, *The Fate of the Dead* (Robert Dunning)
G. R. Quaife, *Wanton Wenches and Wayward Wives* (Barry Stapleton) 259
Brian Austen, *English Provincial Posts, 1633–1840* (John Whyman) 261
The Somersetshire Quarterly Meeting of the Society of Friends, 1668–1699, ed. S. C. Morland (Geoffrey Nuttall)
A. F. Scott, *The Early Hanoverian Age, 1714–1760* (James Thomas) 264
Reactions to Social and Economic Change, 1750–1939, ed. Walter Minchinton (R. C. Riley) 265
The Ansford Diary of James Woodforde II 1746–6, ed. R. L. Winstanley (W. M. Jacob) 266
Mark Chatfield, *Churches the Victorians Forgot* (W. M. Jacob) 267
J. F. C. Harrison, *The Second Coming: Popular Millenarianism, 1780–1850* (W. R. Ward) 268
H. M. Brown, *The Catholic Revival in Cornish Anglicanism;* Michael Sparrow, *One Hundred Not Out* (Nigel Yates) 269
David Roberts, *Paternalism in Early Victorian England* (Neil Hamilton) 270
John Hoare, *Sussex Railway Architecture* (John Lowerson) 271
E. W. Gadd, *Victorian Logs; Trowbridge in Pictures, 1812–1914*, ed. Michael Lansdown and Michael Marshman; Christopher Hibbert, *London: The Biography of A City* (Sarah Peacock) 272
James Cronin, *Industrial Conflict in Modern Britain* (Neil Hamilton) 273
F.A. Youngs, *Guide to the Local Administrative Units of England, Southern England* (Nigel Yates) 274
Cornwall Record Office: A Brief Introduction to Sources (M. J. Hoad) 274

Annual Review of Periodical Literature 276

Notes on Contributors

Mr D. E. Johnston is tutor in Archaeology in the department of Adult Education, University of Southampton and lecturer in Roman Archaeology in the department of Archaeology. He graduated from Cambridge and has written numerous research papers, particularly on mosaics. He edited *The Saxon Shore* (1977) and is the author of *Roman Villas* (1979) and *Roman Roads in Britain* (1979). His study of prehistoric monuments will appear in *The Channel Islands: an archaeological guide* (1981). He is the editor of *Bulletin of Experimental Archaeology*.

Rabbi Dan Cohn-Sherbok is a lecturer in Jewish Studies and chairman of the Board of Theology at the University of Kent at Canterbury.

Dr C. G. Durston read Modern History at Oxford and completed a doctoral thesis on seventeenth century Berkshire at Reading. He is lecturer in history at St. Mary's College, Strawberry Hill.

Dr M. D. G. Wanklyn is lecturer in History, Wolverhampton Polytechnic. He read History at Manchester. He has written articles on military history, the coal and iron industries and an unpublished Ph.D. thesis on 'Landownership and allegiance in Shropshire and Chester at the commencement of the First Civil War.' He edited *Landownership and power in the regions* (1979).

Mr J. P. P. Horn lectures in History at Brighton Polytechnic. He has published papers on the social origins of English emigrants to colonial America and is currently compiling a comparative study of local society in seventeenth century England and the Chesapeake.

Dr J. Whyman lectures in Economic and Social History at the University of Kent at Canterbury. He is a member of the editorial board of *Southern History* and *Archaeologia Cantiana* and on the council of the British Record Society.

Dr R. J. P. Kain lectures in Geography at the University of Exeter. He currently directs a three year Social Science Research Council funded project to compile an Atlas of Agriculture in England and Wales from the Tithe Surveys *circa* 1840.

Miss H. Holt worked for two years as a research assistant on the project and is now preparing an Exeter doctoral dissertation on nineteenth century livestock farming.

Miss P. Blackwell is a graduate of the University of Western Ontario and completed an M.A. at the University of Sussex. She works in university administration in Canada.

Dr P. G. Dickens read Architecture at Cambridge, held a fellowship at Fitzwilliam College and now lectures in Urban Studies at the University of Sussex. He works currently on housing and the state in Britain and Sweden.

Mr P. Gilbert, a Jerseyman, read Modern History at Oxford and completed an M.A. in Social Work at the University of Sussex. He is now a senior social worker with West Sussex County Council.

Editor's Preface

This is an important year for *Southern History* in two senses. Firstly, we have reached our third issue and can fairly claim to have become established as a learned journal; certainly the flow of papers offered demonstrates that both young and established scholars feel there is a place for such a regional journal. Secondly, the closure of our first publisher, Dawson, has been weathered and we are pleased to move to an emerging force in publishing, particularly in local studies, for what we hope will be a long association.

There are still obvious imbalances in the overall pattern of work being done in our region and there is a clear need for an extension of work on the medieval and early modern periods using the battery of investigative techniques and conceptual analysis which have developed in recent years. The bulk of work presented, or in progress, tends to fall into two categories – the local or the county. English historical and related studies have quite a considerable distance to go before the region is clearly developed as an operating concept. Clearly it would be unreasonable to expect 'the south' to be a region *in toto* for much of its history – it largely functions as such in more recent centuries as an alternative to 'the north'. Nor are the modern planners' multivariate notions of the regions often of much use to the historian in our area. Within our main coverage, based for clarity and convenience on the geographical counties which existed before 1974, there has obviously been a number of regions at different chronological points and for different contemporary purposes. In the same way, certain sub-regions have long been recognised; one, the Vale of Berkeley, is the subject of a paper in this volume. But research still tends to be problem rather than place specific, except in the case of some local histories. This is, perhaps, inevitable but the plundering of locales solely for illustrative purposes often tends to weaken both the general picture and understanding of the changing nature of English provincial society. The debate is by no means confined to this country – witness the long arguments in France over Braudel's use of the Mediterranean as an analytical base.

Regional journals have an honourable history on the continent, particularly in France where they have been more closely identified with a powerful provincial resistance to centralised culture than could have been the case in the much more physically compact English framework. *Annales du Midi* appeared circa 1890, to be followed in 1910 by *Revue du Nord*. *Annales de Bourgogne* began in 1929 and *Annales de l'Est* and *Annales de Normandie* came in the years of reconstruction just after World War II. The English produced *Northern History* in 1966 and *Midland History* in 1971, although the latter's vicissitudes have slowed its contribution to overall growth. We joined them in 1979. Although all are based on specific institutions, with the support of others, none are 'house journals', either for their own body or for those within their region; the range of interests and scholarship is far wider than the local support. All carry an uneasy but stimulating mixture of the local, the regional and the problematic as sources of inspiration for their contributions. In that respect, all regional journals in this country occupy a difficult position between the Scylla of national (or international) publications and the Charybdis of county bodies, often with long and honourable publishing records, who need historical material desperately to counterbalance the heavy, usually subsidised, dependence upon archaeological reports. The editors of both sides have tended to view the regional newcomers with some suspicion, both because of the as yet incompletely substantiated claims to new intellectual boundaries and also because they might syphon away good contributions. particularly from the local journals. Certainly, a wider readership (and often a more critical one) can be offered in the regional press to the ambitious researcher on local topics, and there are many papers which do need precisely this but which are on the whole inadequately provided for either by the conservatism of some national journals or by their commitment to certain very limited trends in the intellectual disciplines. The regional publications in England must in the long term occupy rather more than a halfway stage between the other two interests. They are part of a steady shift, not necessarily in entire intellectual interests, but in patterns of emphasis. It will be some time before the full significance of this becomes apparent and this is not the best time to launch on major new ventures but we hope for a steady growth.

J. R. Lowerson

Roman Hampshire: A strategy for research

D. E. JOHNSTON

The post-war years have seen a quickening of the sense of urgency in archaeology, almost to neurotic proportions at times; and a realisation that, however sensitive we may think we are to patterns in time and the movement of events, those events can still take us by surprise. Forty years ago we were utterly unprepared for the opportunities that war-time bombing would offer for urban research; but more recently we have been equally slow to realise that the opportunity would occur again in a different form, as the dying centres of our historic towns become due for renewal and redevelopment. Meanwhile, in the countryside, our archive of research material has been disappearing at such a rate that it might well be totally exhausted by the end of the century.

The crisis reaction to this was the creation of 'Rescue', both as a concept and as a reality in the form of a new Trust for British archaeology, pledged to cope with the crisis and at the same time to make the public aware of it. Since those heady days of the early 1970's panic has given way to calmer reflection, the economic squeeze has slowed down the rate of destruction, and archaeologists have become more hard-headed and professional. So we can pause for a while to contemplate the curious theoretical legacy of the crisis period.

Crises have a habit of polarising our thinking into opposites that are not always very helpful — we are all familiar, for example, with the way a threat to a building or site seems to offer us a choice between the stereotypes of 'progress' and 'preservation'. So in archaeology there have been those who sought to make us choose between 'rescue' and 'research' as criteria for the spending of public money — or even for the application of our own time and efforts, which are equally finite. Superficially, this distinction has much to recommend it, as it separates those sites that one must excavate now (or lose for ever) from those that can be left for posterity; the fallacy, however, can be demonstrated by a Hampshire situation that could be matched in almost any part of the country. The line proposed for the completion of the M3 is a 12-mile section through, among other things, a zone of dense Romano-British settlement some three miles north of Winchester. To treat the motorway route simply as a linear site would produce meaningless and even misleading results. In practice, a general study of the whole area by air photography and fieldwork has made possible a choice of specific sites for excavation along the route — the selection of research priorities in a rescue situation. Here and elsewhere the rigid distinction between research and rescue is seen to be unhelpful; rescue is simply research archaeology under duress.

The crisis is still with us, of course, but less acutely; the need for selection was forced on us long ago by financial constraints, and the need to agree on 'priorities' is still urgent. The opportunity for long-term planning produced a large number of 'Implication Surveys' in which the implications of redevelopment were worked out in financial estimates and recommendations for action; expectations thus raised have sometimes remained unfulfilled, but generally the single author of a Survey has been replaced by a Committee to implement its recommendations. Only too often, however, the Committee seems to have become a substitute for direct action, and the proliferation of Surveys and 'Surveys of Surveys' has caused some dismay. In 1974 the Hampshire Archaeological Committee was formed to coordinate and initiate research and to advise on how public money should be allocated. Five such county committees are represented on the Wessex Archaeological Committee, which now has its own professional Unit to implement its policy of excavation. At both regional and county levels shaping a policy involves balancing priorities, and at a Hampshire conference in 1978 a number of us were invited to review the archaeology of the county, period by period, and to make recommendations for the future. The reviews will appear elsewhere:[1] in this paper I am concerned to explore the thinking behind my suggestions for the Roman period.

I assume that we shall be actively searching for evidence; what kind of evidence, and what questions shall we ask of it? 'Archaeological evidence in its simple form can never answer historical questions . . . We must ask historical questions of historical sources, and never get the two mixed up' warns Dr. Richard Reece.[2] His illustration is carefully chosen; the absence of coins in the decade AD 400-410 on a site can be wrongly interpreted as desertion of that site. In fact, the supply of coins had dried up and the absence is normal for sites of this period. Desertion becomes a historical fact only when the coin evidence is shown to be peculiar to that site *and* can be 'calibrated' against another site that shares the peculiarity but has the added advantage of a historical explanation safely chronicled in historical sources. This is true enough: but surely what the example illustrates is not so much the limitations of the evidence as inadequate research? For if we knew nothing about the coin pattern of the period, the desertion idea would be a reasonable inference; provided that we distinguish hypothesis from fact, we can ask whatever questions we like of our evidence.

One could, moreover, challenge this narrow use of the term 'historical' if it is limited to particular events that definitely happened. The history that we are writing from material of both kinds includes not only narrative but much else beside — much that will never be susceptible to proof as fact. I feel that it is important to stress this here, as we must feel free to ask historical questions of our archaeological evidence; the price of this freedom is the responsibility for distinguishing clearly the nature of the answer.

When we turn to Roman Hampshire, our first question illustrates this point nicely. It is: what was the ancient unit most closely comparable to modern Hampshire, and how do we define it? In other words, are we obliged to limit our activities to the County? To take the second version first: if we are thinking of priorities in spending public money, then the county boundary must be the limit. And the same constraint should apply to a county organisation like the Hampshire Field Club or the County Museums Service, though in the case of a site or archaeological zone that crosses the boundary a joint responsibility for its welfare is clearly an urgent priority. An important example of this is Silchester, whose walled area accounts for a salient in the county boundary. The town site has long been in Hampshire, but the finds from excavations remain in Berkshire. Even so, this is only part of the problem, for the *territorium* of Silchester, as yet undefined, remains divided. The proper unit for study is the town and its administrative region taken together, and this must mean cooperation across the county boundary. Recent fieldwork around the town by the Calleva Field Study Group has pointed the way in this.

In our quest for an ancient unit to correspond with our modern county, we might turn to the ancient political geography of this part of Britain. Our sources tell us that before the conquest this was the territory of the Atrebates.[3] Subsequently, the reorganisation of tribal areas into administrative districts or *civitates* divided this region between the Atrebates and the Belgae, Silchester being the capital of the first and Winchester of the second. An additional complication is the possibility that Cogidubnus' new kingdom, the Regni of Sussex, might have extended north-westwards as far as Silchester[4] — at least, until the extinction of the kingdom at the end of the first century. We should expect these boundaries to have been precisely defined in Roman times for financial and administrative purposes. Defining them from archaeological material alone is probably impossible, and we can do no more than guess. Exactly half way along the Roman road linking the two *civitas* capitals stands the Wheatsheaf Inn, the site of a Roman building and associated settlement. It has been suggested that this might have been a temple marking the boundary.[5] Searching for such boundaries might seem a waste of time without documentary help; but what was of great concern to a Romano-Briton should be of concern to us, too. And to say that this is beyond the scope of arti-factual evidence may not be true, either; for one essential fact of Romano-British life was undoubtedly the bureaucratic control of the individual and the associated paperwork (of which very little has survived in Britain), which in turn affected the economy at the local level, and this in turn should leave some artifactual evidence. An individual farmer would be registered either in Silchester or Winchester, and his farm would have an 'orientation' in that direction, and that would be the market for produce and the source of essential supplies. If we could characterise the products supplied by the two sources, such as pottery, or bricks and tiles, we might be able to define a spatial pattern that would otherwise remain pure guesswork. It would be pedantic to enquire whether the question is 'archaeological' or 'historical': the answer may not be strictly a historical fact, but it would certainly be a helpful hypothesis. This particular piece of research would be sophisticated and time-consuming, with no guarantee of success. But the quantity of material recovered from Romano-British sites in Hampshire should make it worth attempting.

There is another version of this regional approach that introduces a chronological dimension. We do not know at present how long the two civitates, the Belgae and Atrebates, continued to exist as valid entities. We do know, however, from our documentary sources that from about AD 213 Britain became two provinces, with our region forming part of *Britannia Superior* whose capital was London. A further subdivision, however, in 284 put us in a new province, *Britannia Prima*, whose capital is understood to have been at Cirencester.[6] Silchester was now in an interesting position, between the two provincial capitals of London and Cirencester. Our estimate of the boundary is extremely speculative but as far as we know Silchester was in Prima and like the rest of our region was now tributary to Cirencester in place of London. This change of 'orientation' would doubtless have had some influence on the regional economy, perhaps in public spending on roads and communications, arrangements for collection of tax and the movement of produce from farms and villas. The four (and later, five) provinces of Britain formed a single Diocese, whose Treasury and administration was in London; was the produce of our Hampshire fields moved via London to the northern garrisons, or used to maintain the field armies and coastal defences of the south and west — or even shipped overseas? The Cirencester connection may perhaps be reflected in the activities of the 'Central Southern Group' of mosaicists[7] who are best regarded as an offshoot of the Cirencester workshops but based possibly on Silchester and seeking new business in an area of increasing affluence; interestingly, their works so far identified are confined largely or entirely to the province of Prima. However, without supporting evidence from properly documented situations for 'calibration' we would be unwise to read much historical significance into this.

Accepting, then, that we are thinking of a wider region of which Hampshire forms a major part, what are the questions that we should be asking?

Our first must concern the conquest of AD 43. The documentary evidence[8] is limited to references to the 'capture' of the Isle of Wight and to largely unlocated hillforts and battles in the south. What was the pre-Roman political temperature among the southern Atrebates, and what was the impact of the Roman invasion? If it is thought improper to answer these questions from archaeological evidence, we can substitute three specific questions: was Danebury refortified and taken by storm? Was there a naval base at Bitterne? Was there a road westwards from Bitterne through the New Forest, and if not, why? At Danebury, Professor Cunliffe's interpretation of some of the skeletal evidence as battle casualties may be tenuous, but his identification of anti-Roman refortification is more plausible.[9] The behaviour of the roads suggests that the army might have passed that way, turning inland towards Cirencester, and if the coastal road was indeed omitted through the New Forest, that could imply simply that the fleet was thought a more satisfactory lifeline.[10] At Bitterne, Flavian occupation is proven, the harbour a near certainty, the Claudian depot a mere guess.[11] Our factual knowledge of the countryside and the two towns in the first century AD is extremely scanty, for Hampshire; in Sussex, by comparison, the documentary and archaeological evidence combines to give us a picture of pro-Roman sympathy and collaboration followed by rapid Romainsation in both countryside and town. The pattern is unlikely to be repeated in Hampshire. But we must look for it; and either the evidence for it or the fact of its absence can be calibrated against the Sussex situation.

When we turn to the economic development of the region, we find there is much to do; much, moreover, that is not peculiar to Hampshire, but concerns the whole of lowland Britain. Our theoretical framework has two principal elements — the development in Britain of a 'state society' and the pressure on native agriculture and industry to produce a surplus. What was the provision for the consumption or disposal of this surplus? This can be answered in the case of pottery from the New Forest[12] and Alice Holt,[13] but is more difficult for other produce. In theory, the answer could be extracted from faunal and environmental material, principally animal bones, seeds and soil analyses. It could be possible to assess the likely crops and their yield, allowing for the probable loss of fertility over four centuries and using the discovery that some chemicals do persist in the make-up of soil as indicators of its previous history. In practice, we now have the personnel and facilities in Southampton University for this research to be pursued. We are moreover making some progress in the analysis of certain settlements and their productivity,[14] and also in the pattern of villa estates, especially those groups that appear to have a focal villa as a collection point.[15]

The MARC 3 study of the area north of Winchester is the only study to give us an integrated picture of the Romano-British landscape in Hampshire, with settlements, villa(s), fields, roads and tracks. It gives us the physical relationships, and a chronology is emerging from excavation. If the relationship of the one probable villa and three other masonry structures to the rest is not particularly illuminating, the relationship to Winchester certainly is, and the Director, Mr P.J. Fasham, has allowed me to offer an interpretation of it. There appears to be a zone some three miles deep to the north of the city, cultivated but free of settlement. These fields could have been worked from the city. Beyond that is an arc of more or less continuous native settlement with villas beyond that again. A unique discovery in this zone is a series of long fields, 70m wide, whose regularity betrays the hand of the official surveyor; what was the legal and administrative status of this area, and how far did it extend? A similar settlement-free zone may have existed to the south of Winchester, too, but the picture is unclear and probably distorted by the large estate of the Twyford villa. Silchester seems to have had an utterly different pattern; the dearth of villas of decurion status has long been noted[16] but recent field-work and air photography has shown a considerable density of settlement within a radius of about 1½ miles. So the problems of the relationships of villas, settlements and towns are far from solved in Hampshire — or anywhere else, for that matter.

It has been suggested that our Romano-British material in Hampshire, if responsibly interpreted, could be of help outside the Roman period. A model of an urban society with a strong rural component and strong supporting data could well be useful for the understanding of later, medieval, society. In this connection, a recent study of small towns in Hampshire includes a consideration of the Romano-British origins of many,[17] and the same researcher is considering the nucleation of late Roman settlements and their relationship with medieval villages.

The question of 'continuity' at both ends of the Roman period is still unresolved. Excavations in Winchester, and particularly at the Lankhills cemetery[18] have told us much about the latest urban phases, and a link with the sub-Roman building in the final phase of the nearby Sparsholt villa is possible. Meanwhile, the forthcoming study of the transformation of the Twyford villa estate into the medieval parish should set an example for future villa studies. At the beginning of the period, continuity from Iron Age farm to Roman villa is by no means common, and it may be rare; elsewhere I have advanced the hypothesis of the third-century revival of defunct villas and the creation of new ones.[19] This is a hypothesis that must be tested against new evidence.

To bring the discussion down finally to the strictly practical, it is tempting to offer a 'shopping list' of priorities for fieldwork and excavation. This is impossible, for several reasons. For one thing, it is hard to compare the merits of long-term and urgent claims, and for another much of the work is done by professional archaeological units, each with its own set of priorities. Most importantly, however, public money is devoted to rescue excavation, and this is inevitably on a 'catch-as-catch-can' basis. In other words, our choice is often made for us; sometimes, however, we are offered a choice of research priorities in a rescue situation and an overall policy is helpful in guiding our choice. Occasionally, advice is sought — as in the recent case of a local archaeological society looking for a simple site for a training excavation. Such offers can generally be fitted into an existing scheme for research. Finally, therefore, let me emphasise that the day of pure research and fieldwork has by no means passed. I hope that in this paper I have indicated some lines on which such research could profitably be pursued.

Acknowledgements

This paper originated in one of the series of seminars on 'Strategies for Hampshire Archaeology' in the Department of Archaeology at Southampton University. I am grateful to those colleagues from Hampshire and adjoining counties whose contributions to the discussion have been incorporated into the present text, and who have allowed me to discuss their discoveries with them. A brief summary of these conclusions was subsequently included in a review of recent work to a conference sponsored by the Hampshire Archaeological Committee and the Adult Education Department of the University. This present paper is not, however, a statement of official policy, and the responsibility both for the ideas in it and their treatment is mine.

David E. Johnston

Notes

[1] S. Shennan et al. (eds) *The Archaeology of Hampshire* (forthcoming).
[2] in D.E. Johnston (ed) *The Saxon Shore* C.B.A. Res. Rept. 18, 1977.
[3] A.L.F. Rivet *Town and Country in Roman Britain* (1964).
[4] G.C. Boon *Calleva: the Roman Town of Silchester* (Newton Abbot 1964), 43-4.
[5] A.L.F. Rivet *op. cit.* 140.
[6] J.C. Mann 'The Administration of Roman Britain' *Antiquity* 35, 1961, 317-20 esp. p. 319.
[7] D.E. Johnston 'The Central Southern Group of Romano-British Mosaics' in Munby, J. and Henig, M. (eds) *Roman Life and Art in Britain* B.A.R. 41, 1977.
[8] Suetonius, *Vespasian* iv.
[9] B.W. Cunliffe 'Danebury: First Interim Report' *Antiq. Journ.* 51, 1971, 240-52 esp. p. 251.
[10] D.E. Johnston *Roman Roads in Britain* (1979) p.40.
[11] M.A. Cotton and P. Gathercole *Excavations at Clausentum, Southampton, 1951 - 1954* HMSO 1958.
[12] M.G. Fulford *New Forest Roman Pottery: Manufacture and Distribution, with a Corpus of the Pottery Types* BAR 17, 1975.
[13] M.A.B. Lyne and R.S. Jefferies *The Alice Holt/Farnham Roman Pottery Industry* C.B.A. Res. Rept. 30, 1979.
[14] P.L. Murphy *Early Agriculture and Environment on the Hampshire Chalklands c. 800BC - AD 400* Unpublished M.Phil Thesis, Southampton University, 1976.
[15] e.g. Stroud. cf. S. Applebaum 'Roman Britain' in H.P.R. Finberg (ed) *The Agrarian History of England* I.ii (Cambridge, 1972), p.176–7.
[16] G.C. Boon *op.cit.*

[17] M.F. Hughes *The Small Towns of Hampshire* H.A.C. 1976.

[18] G. Clarke *Pre-Roman and Roman Winchester pt.2. The Roman Cemetery at Lankhills* Winchester Studies 3 (Oxford 1979).

[19] in M. Todd (ed) *Studies in the Romano-British Villa* (Leicester 1976) p.71–92.

Medieval Jewish Persecution in England: the Canterbury pogroms in perspective

D. COHN-SHERBOK

Introduction

For over a century and a half during the medieval period Jews in England were subjected to discrimination, persecution, massacre and eventually expulsion. In the main both Christian and Jewish historians who have written about this period have attempted to show that Jews were always in the right. The evidence against Jews, they have argued, was invariably insufficient, and in most cases charges were preposterously absurd. The difficulty with such claims, however, is that they are essentially subjective reactions, often made without any documentary basis. In the case of persecution in Canterbury, however, a Latin "Starrum" issued by the Jewish community points to the fact that the Jews themselves appear to have been partly responsible for the disaster that befell them. This particular instance thus suggests that, contrary to the claims of various historians, in certain cases Jews may have not been altogether blameless for the sufferings they endured.

Whether Jews were settled in England before the Norman conquest or not, it is certain that a Jewish immigration into England took place early in the reign of William the Conqueror.[1] In the economy of Norman England Jews were well-fitted to take the place of the middle class; due to the laws of the Church directed against usury, it was left to them to enter upon commercial undertakings such as money-lending, commercial speculation, and even ordinary commerce.[2] Of necessity Jews kept themselves distinct and apart from the general community. Their appearance and gait marked them as aliens, and none of them engaged in occupations in which they might find Christian colleagues. They took no part in the defence of the country, nor in the preservation of peace. They were excluded from the Guilds, and they had no role in local government. Further, the religious laws of the Jews did not permit them to eat food similar to Christians, nor to partake of food prepared by non-Jews. All these differences combined to render the Jews strange and suspect.[3]

During the reign of the first three Norman kings the Jews appear to have suffered neither persecution nor annoyance.[4] However, during and following the reign of Henry I, the Jews were subjected to various sorts of harrassment. In 1146, for example, Jews in Norwich were accused of kidnapping, torturing and crucifying a young child. Incensed at this outrage the populace of Norwich attacked the Jewish community, killing several members and causing others to flee.

Despite such occasional tragedies and the rising tide of anti-Semitic feeling, the period that ended with the death of Henry II was the golden age in early Anglo-Jewish history. Stephen prevented any imitation of crusading barbarities in his Kingdom, and under his successor, Henry II, with the exception of occasional financial oppression, the Jews enjoyed the widest liberty. The generally satisfactory situation of the Jews of England, however, was not destined to endure; in 11& came the first act of serious anti-Jewish legislation which was followed by a century of massacre. In that year it was enacted that 'no Jew shall keep with him mail or hauberk, but let him sell or give them away, or in some oher way remove them from him'.[5] Thus were the Jews left unarmed and unprotected.

In 1189 at the time of Richard I's coronation the Jews of London were severely attacked, losing their homes and their lives. The coronation ceremony took place in Westminster Abbey and was followed by a banquet in the neighbouring palace. Among those who made their way to Westminster to take part in this event was a deputation of the leading Jews of the kingdom, bearing costly presents for the king from whom they hoped for a continuation of the favour that his predecessors had conferred upon them. Though debarred from entering the Church, these Jews mingled with the crowds that assembled at its gates. For some reason,[6] one or two Jews were pushed through the gates, and the guards, on perceiving this, beat them and drove them out. The populace outside, composed largely of attendants of the nobles partaking in the ceremony inside the Abbey, attacked the Jews; every Jew to be found was beaten and many were killed. The houses of those Jews who escaped were also attacked, but since they were too strong to be broken into, the straw roofs were set on fire, and in many instances the houses were burnt together with their inhabitants. According to A.M. Hyamson, 'rapine, murder and plunder became the order of the day'[7] and the rioting continued from midday on Sunday until two o'clock on the following afternoon.

The Jews caught in this tumult were in some cases given a choice between death and baptism by their assailants. Some remained loyal to their faith and were martyred; others accepted baptism. The elderly Benedict of York, for example, chose baptism, but the next day was summoned by the king. When questioned he replied that, although having accepted baptism in order to escape death, he was a Jew at heart. Turning to the Archbishop of Canterbury, the King inquired how Benedict should be dealt with. Replying testily, the Archbishop decreed: 'If he will not be a servant of God, let him be a servant of the devil',[8] thereby allowing him to return to the Jewish fold.

Following the disaster in London, anti-Jewish outbreaks arose almost simultaneously in all parts of the country. At Dunstable it is reckoned that the Jews escaped massacre by accepting Christianity in a body.[9] At Lynn the Jewish community was attacked because Jews broke into a church to kill a fellow Jew who had converted to Christianity.[10] Hearing of this outrage the foreign crew of a ship lying in the harbour burnt the houses of the Jews, murdering any they could find. Loaded with booty stolen from their victims the sailors returned to their ship and sailed away.

'On the following day', according to a contemporary account, 'a certain Jew, a distinguished physician, who was friendly and honoured by the Christians, for the sake both of his art and of his own modesty, commenced to deplore the slaughter of his people rather strongly, and as if prophesying vengence, aroused the still smouldering rage. The Christians soon seized him and made him the last victim of Jewish insolence'.[11]

On March 7, 1190 a similar uprising occurred at Stamford. According to the same chronicler, 'a number of youths who had taken the Lord's sign to start for Jerusalem came together from different provinces. . . Considering, therefore, that they could be doing honour to Christ if they attacked his enemies, whose goods they were longing for, they boldly rushed upon them. . . Some of the Jews were slain, but the rest escaped with some difficulty by retreating to the Castle. Their houses were pillaged and a great quantity of money captured. . . '.[12]

Of all the massacres between 1189-1190 the events at York were the most terrible. After the outbreak of fire in the city, an attack was made on the house of the wealthy Jew Benedict; the house was sacked, its contents plundered, and Benedict's widow, children and friends killed. Fearing further calamities, the Jewish population deserted their houses and retreated to the castle. Huddled together, utterly friendless, and without food, the Jews called a council inside the castle. The words of the spiritual leader of the community, Rabbi Yomtob of Joigny are recorded by William of Newbury: 'God to whom none shall say, 'Why dost Thou so?' (Eccles. viii 4; Dan v 35), orders us to die now for the Law. And behold our death is at the door. Unless, perchance, which God forbid, you think of deserting the sacred Law for this brief space of life, and choose a fate harder than any death of honest and manly minds, namely, to live as apostates at the mercy of impious enemies in the deepest dishonour. Since then we ought to select the easiest and most honourable form of death. For if we fall into the hands of the enemy we shall die at their will and amidst their jeers. And so since the life which the Creator gave us, He now demands back from us, let us willingly and devoutly render it up to Him with our own hands and let us not await the help of hostile cruelty by giving up what He demands. For many of our people in different times of tribulation are known to have done the same, preferring a form of choice most honourable for us'.[13]

Thus, the members of the community sacrificed themselves for the love of God; Joce, a leader of the community cut the throats of his wife and children with a sharp knife. The other heads of the families imitated his example, and then slew one another, until at length Rabbi Yomtob and Joce alone remained alive. Joce was killed by his companion, who finally slew himself.[14]

Despite a short respite from such atrocities during the reign of King John, various Jewish communities were besieged and sacked during the first half of the thirteenth Century. In 1230, for example, the Jews of Norwich were accused of abducting a child of five, probably the son of converted Jew, and circumcising him. Taking action against the Jews, the father brought them to court. The exact date and result of the trial are not known, but in 1214 some of those on trial were hanged after having been dragged to the gallows tied to the tails of horses. At the time of this affair, the Jews of Winchester also suffered persecution on account of an alleged ritual murder in that city (in 1232).[15]

In 1255 the blood accusation underwent a revival. The popular story of the martyrdom of Little St. Hugh of Lincoln entered into the folk songs of the nation, and was even referred to by Chaucer in his *Canterbury Tales.* As told by Matthew Paris: 'The Jews of Lincoln stole a boy of eight years of age, whose name was Hugh; and having shut him up in a room quite out of the way, where they fed him on milk and other childish nourishment, they sent to almost all the cities of England where the Jews lived, and summoned some of their seat from each city to be present at a sacrifice to take place at Lincoln, for they had, as they stated, a boy hidden for the purpose of being crucified. . . In accordance with the summons, a great many of them came to Lincoln, and on assembling they at once appointed a Jew of Lincoln as judge, to take the place of Pilate, by whose sentence, and with the concurrence of all, the boy was subjected to diverse tortures'.[16] This boy was then crowned with thorns, marked with stigmata, pierced in the side, crucified, and then thrown down a well. Eventually the Jew in whose house the child had been playing confessed that the ritual murder of the child was true and that almost every year Jews crucify a boy as an insult to the name of Jesus. Found guilty by various juries a number of Jews from Lincoln were sentenced to death.[17]

The opening of the Civil War was the signal for the plunder of the Jews. Even before the first blow was struck the Jews of Lincoln were attacked. In 1262, the King, having broken with the barons, took refuge in the Tower, and the other party with their army occupied the city. A dispute between a Jew and a Christian resulted in the sacking of London Jewry; seven hundred of its inhabitants were slain.[18] Similar disasters occured in Worcester (1263), London, Northampton and Canterbury (1264), and Lincoln and the Isle of Ely (1266). In 1278 Edward proposed to reform the currency; his first step was to imprison all the Jews in the country and have their houses searched. Found guilty of tampering with the coinage, two hundred and ninety three London Jews were hanged.[19]

The persecution of English Jewry which had lasted for over a century and a half ended with the expulsion of the Jews from the kingdom. On the 18th of July 1290 writs were issued announcing the expulsion of the Jews to take effect on the Feast of All Saints of that year. About sixteen thousand Jews who had been restricted to seventeen towns departed from England, leaving behind their property which passed into the hands of the King.

For some time both Christian and Jewish scholars who have dealt with this period have argued that Jews were invariably innocent victims. At the end of the nineteenth century, for example, W. Rye in a paper read at the Anglo-Jewish Historical Exhibition proposed 'to show that wherever we are able to gather any details of the circumstances under which the affairs (Jewish persecution) took place, we find that the Jews seem to have been in the right, and that the evidence against them was in all cases obviously insufficient, and in most cases preposterously absurd'.[20]

In a similar vein M. Margoliouth in *The History of the Jews* points to the groundlessness of charges levelled at the Jewish community. 'Crimes of every description,' he writes, 'many of a nature the most absurd and groundless were laid to their charge, and the severest penalties inflicted for them. Tumults were, on the most frivolous pretences excited against them; their houses were pillaged and burned, and hundreds of them were massacred by the populace'.[21]

Regarding blood accusations, M. Margoliouth emphasises how difficult it is for the modern reader even to imagine such events: 'Englishmen now regard such tales as but the vestiges of a period long passed by; they listen to them with a smile as belonging to the "olden time", and because such ridiculous calumnies are no longer brought up against the Jews in this highly favoured and enlightened country, they may think it ill-timed to rake up such acts of fanatics of the dark ages'.[22] According to H.P. Stokes these accusations are 'patently inventions'.[23] Similarly, A.M. Hyamson writes in regard to the supposed martyrdom of St. William of Norwich that 'this martyrdom was the first of a long series of similar crimes laid to the charge of the Jews in all parts of Christendom without the slightest evidence in support'.[24] Again, regarding the alleged martyrdom of St. Hugh of Lincoln, J. Jacobs notes: 'I have been surprised to find in conversation with Christian friends, who have not the slightest taint of anti-Semitism, how general is the impression that there must be something at the bottom of all these charges, and perhaps for their sakes it might be desirable to point out how impossible it is for Jews as Jews to use human blood or human sacrifices in any way as part of their religious rites'.[25]

Repeatedly historians stress the innocent sufferings of Jews during this period. A.M. Hyamson, for example, writes that they were 'harried and oppressed, tortured, tormented, fined, plundered, mutilated, struck not only in their own persons, but also in those of their loved ones . . . the limit was at length reached with these children of endurance, whom history has hardened on the anvil of persecution and in the face of relentless and apparently endless oppression'.[26] In his discussion of medieval Canterbury Jewry M. Alder similarly remarks that 'the loss of their inhospitable home in England was but one episode in Israel's tragic history, and the picture I have endeavoured to set before you . . . of the lives of the men whose home had been in the county of Kent depicts in the darkest colours the pitiable lot of Anglo-Jewry as a whole in those unhappy days'.[27] Defending the Anglo-Jewish community for its courage in the face of such misfortunes V. Lipman states that 'we must remember also their devotion to their ancestral faith, their loyalty to it in circumstances of difficulty and hatred, and the occasions on which so many were ready to face martyrdom for its sake'.[28]

Given that Jews were blameless for the disasters that befell them, how is one to explain the cause of their sufferings? Various writers have offered a variety of explanations. J. Trachtenberg, for example, in *The Devil and the Jews*, argues that Jewish persecution during the medieval period was brought about because of a mass subconcious image of the Jew. 'In this region of the subconcious', he writes, 'we shall uncover the source of many a weird notion of the horned Jew, or the Jewish thirst for Christian blood, of the Jew who scatters poison and disease broadcast, or a distinctive Jewish odour, of Jews practicing black magic and blighting their surroundings with the evil eye . . . here we shall uncover the spring of the general conviction that prompts Jew hatred: of the Jew as an alien, evil, anti-social, and anti-human creature, essentially sub-human, indeed, and therefore unanswerable for the supreme crime of seeking to destroy by every subversive technique the fruits of that Christian civilization which in his heart of hearts he despises and abhors'.[29]

J. Parkes in 'Church and Synagogue in the Middle Ages' indirectly criticizes the Church for fostering such an imaginary mythology. 'The frenzied mobs,' he writes, 'which in city after city, county after county, sacked Jewish quarters and massacred their inhabitants drew their force from the imaginings of men like themselves, more than from the pronouncements of popes, bishops or councils. But it was the language of popes, bishops, councils and theologians which made their imaginings possible'.[30]

In this connection several scholars have pointed to religious prejudice as a central motivating factor. According to J. Jacobs, 'so far as the common people were against the Jews, it was not as usurers, but as miscreants and heretics, and it is only in times of religious excitement, as during a crusade, that we find popular attacks on the Jews'.[31] In addition scholars have argued that the Jews' reluctance to convert to Christianity gave rise to intense anti-Jewish feeling. A.M. Hyamson, for example, notes that Jews 'were regarded as a somewhat incongruous element in the population, but hopes were felt for its absorption, by means of a conversion to the dominant faith. The hopes of the clergy for such a result were, however, not realized . . . the attitude of the clergy in consequence gradually changed. . . The votaries of medieval Christianity were also exasperated by the critical incredulity with which the Jews received the pretended miracles and the adoration of images which to so great an extent accompanied medieval Christian worship'.[32]

In addition to religious prejudice, scholars have argued that economic factors led to Jewish persecution as well. According to C. Roth 'about 1130 the London Jews were accused of killing a sick man, who perhaps had gone to one of them for a medical treatment . . . like most vicissitudes of Jewish life (this) was turned to the advantages of the Exchequer. The London community was fined the enormous sum of £2,000. . . The timeliness of the accusation from the point of view of the Exchequer was such as to make one suspect that the coincidence was not altogether accidental'.[33] With regard to the York massacre A.M. Hyamson makes the same point: 'With few exceptions these barons were all indebted to the Jews, and the destruction of the records of their indebtedness must have seemed an easy method of settling their accounts'.[34]

According to Hyamson the prosperity of the Jews evoked envy and resentment on the part of the gentile populace. 'The continued property of the Jews,' he writes, 'had . . . added to the feelings of suspicion and hatred that had been aroused among the people, the additional one of envy. Not only were the Jews still alien in race and religion, strange and hardly comprehensible; they were yet further separated from the people among whom they dwelt by the acquisition of wealth, which the people must have regarded as coming from themselves'.[35]

Other writers have focused on the violence of the times to explain the persecution of the Jews. S. Levy, for example, in his study of Leicester Jews, points out that 'Simon de Montfort, the famous protagonist in the Barons War and the fight for parliamentary institutions, followed in the traditional ways of his mother. Armed with the recollections of his childhood, he readily succumbed to the cruel spirit of the times, easily yielded to the demands of Leicester bigots, and in 1231 granted a charter to his faithful burgesses, giving them liberty entire to banish the Jews from Leicester'.[36]

From this survey of scholarly opinion about medieval Jewish persecution in England, we can see that a wide variety of writers have for one reason or another viewed the Jews as blameless victims of gentile intolerance. Indeed, according to some scholars, the innocence of the Jews is proved by the fact that when persecuted, they appealed to the authorities for justice. W. Rye, for example, maintained that in every case 'it was the Jews, and not their accusers who were the first to appeal in a proper and legitimate way to the civil authorities. In such appeals there seems . . . the strongest proof of the conscious innocence of the crimes attributed to them — *mens conscia recti*'.[37]

While it may be that Jews were often innocent victims of persecution resulting from psychological, religious, social and economic factors, due to a lack of documentary evidence it is extremely difficult, but not impossible, to establish that this was entirely so. In the case of medieval Canterbury a Latin 'Starrum' issued by the Jewish community in 1266 suggests, on the contrary, that the Jews may not have been altogether blameless for the misfortunes they suffered in 1261 and 1264.

The Jews of Canterbury were occupied in money lending at a very early date, and on the basis of their contribution to Richard the Lion Hearted in 1194 as recorded in the Northampton Donum,[38] it is evident that they were quite wealthy. By the beginning of the thirteenth Century the Jewish ghetto of Canterbury was firmly established near the King's Bridge. Among the approximately twenty houses[39] built by Jews was the house of Jacob the Jew who, according to documents in the Canterbury Cathedral Archives,[40] purchased three plots of land for a total of £15 4s, plus a cloak worth 13s 4d along with a yearly rental of 6s 4d.[41] Other rich Canterbury Jews included Isaac le Gros and Isaac Senex who together contributed a total of £69 out of the £1803 paid by all English Jews to redeem Richard the Lion-Hearted in 1194 when he was captured by Leopold, Duke of Austria.[42]

At the close of the Angevin period the Jews in Canterbury probably numbered over one hundred;[43] between 1216 and 1240 their number increased considerably. These Jews, like those who preceded them, engaged in money-lending as well as the buying and selling of land and houses. Benjamin the son of Meir, for example, had the distinction of being one of a quintette of Kentish money-lenders who is frequently mentioned in the records.[44] Benjamin included among his partners such Jews as Samson,[45] Cresse,[46] Vivard the son of Isaac,[47] and Benjamin Crispin.[48]

The Latin and Hebrew deeds of this period give us a detailed account of the purchase and sale of houses by Canterbury Jews. The earliest Hebrew deed is dated 6 Ellul 1230 and states that Elias the son of Berechya sold a house in the Jew's street with the adjoining land to his brother Isaac for the sum of 100 shillings.[49] About 1230

Peytivino the son of Jose bought a messuage in the parish of St. Mary of the Castle in which stood the old Norman castle.[50] In this period, as M. Adler notes, 'the large number of Jewish owners of houses is remarkable, and points to the fact that many houses changed hands several times. No restrictions were imposed upon the acquisition of houses by Jews, who obtained them both from Church and lay vendors with full hereditary rights in perpetuity'.[51]

Between the years 1240 and 1266 the records supply us with the names of the majority of adult male Jews who resided in Canterbury. The business dealings of some of those listed are recorded in various documents. About the year 1239, for example, Friar Alan de Wye Rufus, acting on behalf of the Cathedral, leased the house of Jacob the Jew to Aaron the son of Jose of Leicester[53] who also owned a house he had obtained from Isaac of Sittingbourne[54] as well as a third house.[55] The financial transactions of Salle the son of Jose were on a very large scale, his clients living in all parts of Kent and also in London, where a man once owed him £5 as rent of a house Jose possessed there.[56] Isaac the son of Isaac was a prominent money-lender who, in a certain *shtar*,[57] surrendered a debt of 40 shillings owing to him from two men. Moses the son of Aaron resided in the stone house next to the King's Exchange (next door to Jacob the Jew's house)[58] and was the richest man in the local Jewish community of the day; the bonds that were found in the *Archa* in 1290 under his name showed that some dozens of local Christians were indebted to him for supplies of corn valued at £93 10s.[59]

In 1261 and 1264 this relatively large and prosperous[60] Jewish community suffered two pogroms. In 1261 an attack was made by both clergy and laymen upon the Jewish community of Canterbury living in a small ghetto near the Cathedral.[61] The Calendar of Patent Rolls for 28 December 1261 records the calamity that took place: 'The King on behalf of the Jews (of Canterbury) has received a grievous complaint that certain persons, as well clerks as lay of the said (sic) city, lately came by night to the houses of the said Jews in that town, broke the doors and windows of their houses with axes, brought fire to burn their houses, and afterwards beat some of the Jews'.[62] In 1264 a more serious outrage was committed against the Jews when Gilbert de Clare, Earl of Gloucester, one of De Montfort's adherents who were now in open rebellion against King Henry, captured Canterbury and sacked the Jews' quarter.[63] According to Gervase, the monkish chronicler of the city, almost all the Jews were destroyed or expelled.[64] Two years later the Jews who survived issued an extraordinary treaty of self-protection: 'The community of Jews in Canterbury who are bound in this *shtar* realize through this *shtar* that they have judged and have entered into an opinion that no other Jew from another place other than Canterbury will remain in this place, that is to say any liar, improper person, and slanderer. And if it should happen that someone should come to remain there through the permission of our Lord the King, the whole of the aforementioned community agrees to give to our Lord the King that which Salle the son of Jose, Abraham the son of Leo, and Vivus of Winchester, whose seals are placed on this *shtar*, shall lay upon the same community so that that person may be disqualified by the King from residing there. And if there be someone of the aforesaid community who opposes the expulsion of this same Jew who is a liar, an improper person, and a slanderer or who has got a writ from the King as aforementioned, let him be expelled with the other. And these are the seals of the Jews in the aforementioned *shtar*: Master Moses, Salle the son of Jose, Abraham the son of Leo, Jacob the son of Miles, Benedict the son of Isaac, Leo the son of Abraham, Isaac the son of Abraham, Benedict the son of Cresse, Isaac the son of Isaac, Meir the son of Edra, Samson the Elder, Solomon the son of Isaac, Josceus the son of Solomon, Aaron the son of Salle, Josceus the son of Abraham, Moses the son of Abraham, and Jacob the son of Josceus.[65]

While we have no documents that explain the circumstances which led to the drafting of this treaty, we do know that in the same year three Canterbury Jews, Benedict of Bedford, Leo the son of Solomon, and Samson the son of Jose,[66] who did not sign this treaty, purchased the royal consent to leave Canterbury. It may well be that questionable conduct on the part of these three men led to the drafting of this document. Yet, it is improbable that such misconduct in and of itself would have caused the community to take such drastic measures. What is more plausible is that the community, fearing for its survival, issued this document because it recognized within its own midst the potential cause of further persecutions. Thus, it is likely that the pogroms of 1261 and 1264 occurred as a reaction to illicit business transactions on the part of Jews concerning either money-lending or property negotiations, and that the Canterbury Jewish community, aware of continuing danger, attempted to insure itself against contamination from Jews who were liars, improper persons and slanderers, and thereby eliminate the possibility of further calamities.

This suggestion is supported by complaints as well as legal actions known to have been levelled against certain Canterbury Jews during this period. About the year 1174, for example, Peter de Blois, the archdeacon of Bath, wrote a letter to the Bishop of Ely complaining about the Jews of Canterbury from whom he had borrowed money when he was attached to Canterbury Cathedral. 'Drawn by extreme urgency,' he wrote, 'I am going to Canterbury (i.e. from Bath) in order to be crucified by the perfidious Jews, who torture me by their debts and afflict me with their usury. . . I pray that you will remove this cross from me, and take upon yourself the payment of £6 that I owe Samson the Jew, and, by this act, turn my debts into a cause of profound gratitude to you'.[67] In the earliest entry on the Pipe Rolls, fines were levied upon a number of Canterbury Jews including Berechya (Benedict) for having transgressed the law with regard to usury. Isaac, the brother of Benedict, was punished and ordered to pay twenty marks because he was said to have committed perjury before the King's court. Concerning the wealthy Jew, Salle the son of Jose, it is recorded that in 1253 a special tallage was levied upon his private possessions;[69] Salle did not pay within the time allotted to him, and the Sherriff of Kent was instructed to give him and his wife a note of expulsion from the realm.[70]

Thus while it is not possible to establish conclusively that the persecution of Canterbury Jews in 1261 and 1264 was a response to illicit business transactions on the part of Jewish financiers, it does seem highly probable that this was the case. The fact that the community issued an extraordinary treaty of self-protection in 1266 boycotting Jews of questionable character from entering into their midst, and possibly expelling three of its members at the same time, suggests that the community was deeply concerned about its future survival. We know, however, that such a treaty was ineffectual, because in 1279 three of Salle's sons, Jose, Abraham, and Aaron as well as Solomon of Stamford were hanged on the gallows for coin-clipping,[71] and the community, like all other English Jewish communities, was doomed to expulsion in 1290.

Conclusion

From what we know about medieval Canterbury it seems likely that unsavoury financial dealings on the part of Jewish money-lenders may have inflamed the hostility of gentile laymen and clerics in 1261 and 1264, and this would explain why the Jewish community took such remarkably drastic steps in 1266 to insure that no Jew of an unfavourable reputation would be allowed to live in its midst.

Thus in this instance the Jews cannot be regarded as completely blameless for the suffering that was inflicted upon them. While it may well be that Jews were often innocent victims during the medieval period, the events in Canterbury suggest that in certain cases Jews themselves may have been partly responsible for the misfortunes they endured.

Notes

[1] A.M. Hyamson, *A History of the Jews in England* (London, 1907), 8.

[2] *Ibid.*, 10.

[3] *Ibid.*, 12.

[4] *Ibid.*, 12.

[5] J. Jacobs *The Jews of Angevin England* (London: 1893), 75.

[6] A.M. Hyamson (*op. cit.*, 35) suggests it was 'due to the jostling of the crowd, aided by the eagerness of the Jews to see something.'

[7] *Ibid.*, 36.

[8] *Ibid.*, 38.

[9] W. Rye 'The Persecution of the Jews in England' *Papers Read at the Anglo-Jewish Historical Exhibition 1887* (London: Jewish Chronicle, 1888). 143.

[01] *Ibid.*, 143-144.

[11] The account of William of Newbury, i. 308 ed. Howlett, included in J. Jacobs, *op. cit.*, 115-116.

[12] *Ibid.*, 115.

[13] J. Jacobs, *op. cit.*, 125.

[14] A.M. Hyamson, *op. cit.*, 45-46.

[15] A.M. Hyamson, *op. cit.*, 70.

[16] *Ibid.*, 81.

[17] *Ibid.*, 84.

[18] *Ibid.*, 88.

[19] *Ibid.*, 96.

[20] W. Rye *op. cit.*, 137.

[21] M. Margoliouth *The History of the Jews* (London: 1851), 63.

[22] *Ibid.*, 67.

[23] H.P. Stokes, *Studies in Anglo-Jewish History* (Edinburgh: 1913), 97.

[24] A.M. Hyamson, *op. cit.*, 23.

[25] J. Jacobs, 'Little St. Hugh of Lincoln, Researches in History, Archaeology, and Legend', *JHSE Transactions 1893-1894* (London) 93.

[26] A.M. Hyamson, *op. cit.*, 76-78.

[27] M. Alder *JHSE Transactions 1911-1914* (Edinburgh, 1915), 58.

[28] V. Lipman, 'The Anatomy of Medieval Anglo-Jewry', *JHSE Transaction 1962-1967* (London: JHSE, 1968), 79.

[29] J. Trachtenberg, *The Devil and the Jews* (New York: 1961), 6.

[30] J. Parkes, 'Church and Synagogue in the Middle Ages' *JHSE Transactions 1945-1951* (London: 1952), 31-32. *1951* (London: The Jewish Historical Society of England, 1952), 31-32.

[31] J. Jacobs 'The Typical Character of Anglo-Jewish History' *JHSE 1896-8* 131.

[32] A.M. Hyamson, *op. cit.*, 25-26.

[33] C. Roth *History of the Jews of England* (Oxford: 1941), 8.

[34] A.M. Hyamson, *op. cit.*, 47.

[35] *Ibid.*, 15.

[36] S. Levy 'Notes on Leicester Jewry' *JHSE Transaction 1902-1905*, 37.

[37] W. Rye, *op. cit.*, 137.

[38] M. Adler, 'The Jews of Canterbury' (A paper read before the Jewish Historical Society on March 27, 1911), 74.

[39] M. Adler, *op. cit.*, 22.

[40] *Charta Antiqua*, no. C770, C762, C763, C764.

[41] See W. Urry, 'The House of Jacob the Jew'.

[42] Northampton Donum, 1194 — Canterbury and Kent, as recorded by M. Adler, *op. cit.*, 74.

[43] M. Adler, *op. cit.*, 29.

[44] *Close Rolls* of 1228, 67; 1231, 6, 467; 1233, 350; 1233, 351, 357; 1235, 131.

[45] *Close Rolls*, 1233, 357; 1235, 131.

[46] *Close Rolls*, 1233, 350-351.

[47] *Close Rolls*, 1231, 6, 467.

[48] *Close Rolls*, 1228, 67.

[49] *Shetaroth*, 312.

[50] Chartae Antiq., C.C., C779.

[51] M. Adler, *op. cit.*, 34.

[52] M. Adler op. cit., 77-78: Abraham the son of Samuel, Abraham the son of Salle, Abraham the son of Leo, Aaron the son of Jose of Leicester, Aaron the son of Salle, Bonenfant the son of Cresse, Bonavie, (a) Benjamin the son of Meir, (b) Benjamin the son of Meir, Benjamin the son of Isaac, Benedict and sons, Elias, Aaron and Isaac Delecross the son of Genta, Hayim the son of Yom Tob, Isaac Bigelin, Isaac the son of Salle, Joseph the brother of Samson, Joseph the son of Samson, Isaac the son of Abraham, Isaac the son of Zerach, Isaac the son of Samson, Isaac the son of Jacob the son of Molkin, Jacob the son of Dieulesaut, Jacob the son of Jacob, Joseph the son of Joshua, Jacob the son of Isaac, Jehozadok the son Jehozadok (Rabbi), Jose the son of Salle, Joseph the son of Moses, Leo the son of Solomon, Meir the son of Isaac, Moses the son of Joseph, Moses the son of Aaron, Moses the son of Salle, Moses the son of Jacob, Menahem the son of Joseph, Moses the son of Abraham, Moses the son of Samson, Samson the son of Joseph, Samson the son of Isaac, Salle the son of Joseph, Samuel the son of Benjamin, Samuel of Ospring, Samuel the son of Meshaullam Halevi, Samuel the son of Samson, Samuel the son of Aaron Mokin, Samuel the son of Isaac, Vives of Winchester, Yom Tob the son of Isaac, Zerach the son of Meir, Abraham the son of Isaac.

[53] *Shetaroth*, 342; See also Cathedral Archives, Letter Book II, No. 4.

[54] *Charter Rolls*, 1257, 470.

[55] J.M. Rigg, The Calendar of the Plea Rolls of the Exchequer of the Jews, ii, 201, 232.

[56] *Charter Rolls*, 1262, 39.

[57] *Shetaroth*, 336. (A *shtar* is the Hebrew term for a document.)

[58] *Shetaroth*, 342.

[59] See bonds listed by M. Adler, *op. cit.*, p. 79-83.

[60] In 1194 it came third in order of pre-eminence after London and Lincoln (in contributions to the Northampton Donum). See M. Adler, *op. cit.*, 74.

[61] See M. Adler, 'The Jews of Canterbury' (A paper read before the Jewish Historical Society on March 27, 1911), 22-24 for a description of the Jews quarter, and W. Urry, 'The House of Jacob the Jew' (1953), 15 for a detailed map of this area.

[62] *The Calendar of Patent Rolls*, 1258-1266, 229.

[63] M. Adler, *op. cit.*, 40.

[64] Gervase, Chronicle, ii, 235: 'Sed et in civitate Cantuaria hoc eodem tempore omnes fere Judaei destructi sunt et exulati'. M. Adler disputes Gervase's claim on the basis of the treaty of 1266 which was signed by a number of Canterbury Jews. 'It is evident', Adler states, 'That the eighteen names do not include the whole of the community.' M. Adler, *op. cit.*, 47. Since we know from other records of the

existence of other members of the community at this time, Adler is no doubt correct that this list is not complete. However, the fact that this list includes only these names suggests that after the second pogrom, the community may have been much smaller than before. It should be noted that Gervase did not maintain that all Jews had been killed or expelled, only some. Thus, though Gervase's report may be distorted, it does seem likely that he was right in stating that this second persecution resulted in a number of deaths.

[65] M. Adler, *op. cit.*, 77; 'Communitas Judeorum Cantuarie, qui sigillantur in hoc starro, recognoverunt per starrum suum, quod juraverunt et intraverunt in sentenaciam, quod nullus alius Judeus de alia villa preter quam de Cantuaria manebit in eadem villa, scilicet, homo mentitor, inidoneus et accusator; et si ita evenerit quod aliquis venisset ad manendum ibidem per breve Domini Regis, extunc concessit tota predicta communitas ad donandum Domino Regi id quod Salle, filius Joscei, Abraham, filius Leonis, et Vives de Wintonia, similiter in hoc starro sigillati, ipsam communitatem falliabunt, et idem Rex deponat ipsum qui tale breve impetrabit; et si sit aliquis de predicta communitate rebellis ad deponendum ipsum Judeum qui mentitor, inidoneus et accusator extiterit, vel eum qui breve. Regis impetraverit, ut predictum est, idem deponatur cum eodem. Et sunt Judei in predicto starro sigillati: Magister Mosseus; Salle, filius Joscei; Abraham, filius Leonis; Jacobus, filius Miles; Benedictus, filius Isaac; Leo, filius Abrahe; Isaac, filius Abrahe; Benedictus, filius Cresse; Isaac, filius Isaac; Meir, filius Edra; Sampson, presbiterus; Salomon, filius Isaac; Josceus, filius Salomonis; Aaron, filius Salle; Josceus, filius Abrahe; Mosseus, filius Abrahe; et Jacobus, filius Joscei.' Though M. Adler notes the existence of this document, he does not connect it with the persecutions of 1261 and 1264.

[66] J.M. Rigg, *op. cit.*, I, 134.

[67] Peter Blesensis, *Opera*, ed. Giles, ii, 96, Epistola clvi.

[68] Joseph Jacobs, *The Jews of Angevin England*, 82, No. 48.

[69] J.M. Rigg, *Select Pleas*, 29.

[70] *Ibid.*, ii, 49, 70, 236. For some unknown reason, Salle managed to escape this punishment.

[71] *Charter Rolls*, ii, 1279, 212.

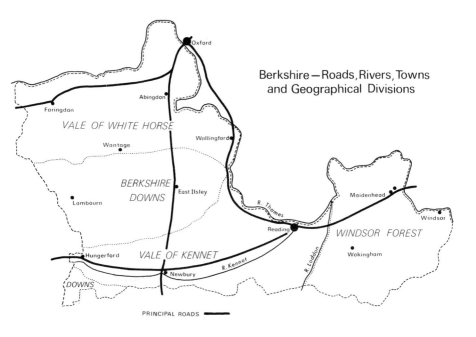

Berkshire—Roads, Rivers, Towns
and Geographical Divisions

Oxford

Abingdon

Faringdon

VALE OF WHITE HORSE

Wantage

Wallingford

BERKSHIRE
DOWNS

East Ilsley

Maidenhead

Lambourn

R. Thames

Windsor

Reading

WINDSOR FOREST

Hungerford

VALE OF KENNET

Wokingham

R. Kennet

R. Loddon

DOWNS

Newbury

PRINCIPAL ROADS ━━━

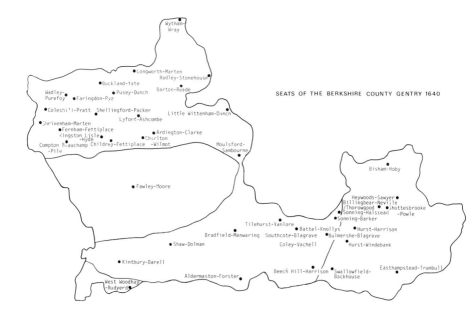

Wytham-
Wray

Longworth-Marten
Radley-Stonehouse

Buckland-Yate

Barton-Reade

SEATS OF THE BERKSHIRE COUNTY GENTRY 1640

Wadley-
Purefoy

Pusey-Dunch

Faringdon-Pye

Coleshill-Pratt Shellingford-Packer

Little Wittenham-Dunch

Lyford-Ashcombe

Shrivenham-Marten

Fernham-Fettiplace

Ardington-Clarke

Kingston Lisle
-Hyde

Charlton

Compton Beauchamp Childrey-Fettiplace -Wilmot
-Pile

Moulsford-
Sambourne

Bisham-Hoby

Fawley-Moore

Heywoods-Sawyer
Billingbear-Neville
/Thorowgood   Shottesbrooke
Sonning-Halstead   -Powle
Sonning-Barker

Tilehurst-Vanlore
Bradfield-Manwaring Southcote-Blagrave

Battel-Knollys
Bulmershe-Blagrave

Hurst-Harrison

Shaw-Dolman

Coley-Vachell

Hurst-Windebank

Kintbury-Darell

Aldermaston-Forster

Beech Hill-Harrison Swallowfield-
Backhouse

Easthampstead-Trumbull

West Woodhay
-Rudyerd

London and the Provinces: The Association between the Capital and the Berkshire County Gentry of the Early Seventeenth Century

C.G. DURSTON

The number of recent studies of the English localities during the sixteenth and early seventeenth centuries began in the mid nineteen-sixties with the appearance of Professor Alan Everitt's work on the county community in Kent.[1] Up until that time, it had been widely assumed that all the important political developments could be understood by focusing attention on Whitehall or the Palace of Westminster, and events in the provinces had been largely ignored. Everitt, however, demonstrated that the county was the seventeenth century Englishman's 'country' and that most of the political events which affected him or were shaped by him could be profitably studied in a county context. Similar studies for counties in other regions which appeared after Everitt's work, in particular Dr J.T. Cliffe's work on Yorkshire, Dr J.S. Morrill's on Cheshire and Dr A. Fletcher's on Sussex,[2] confirmed a number of his findings about local society in the early seventeenth century and, as a picture of provincial society emerged, the impression was given that local communities throughout the country shared a number of basic characteristics. It was generally agreed that the county communities were insular and xenophobic, that their governing oligarchies were stable and deeply rooted in their local area, that provincial opinion was conditioned as much by local as by national issues, and that national political allegiance was inexorably tied up with power struggles within the shires.

However, it has more recently been suggested by Peter Clark that this emphasis on counties some considerable distance from London may have distorted 'our general view of the English provinces in this period'.[3] Until recently, the work on Kent was the only detailed study of local society in a Home County, and Everitt and C.W. Chalklin had convincingly argued that the community in Kent corresponded to the other more outlying regions in its insularity and the stability and continuity of its power structure.[4] However, subsequent briefer investigations of the south east have suggested that the Kentish picture was not typical of this region,[5] and this suggestion has been confirmed by a detailed study I have recently completed on the local community in Berkshire,[6] in which I have tried to show that in a number of significant respects the situation was quite different from Kent. In particular, while Kentish society appears to have been little affected by the nearness of London, in Berkshire the proximity of the rapidly expanding capital was a major influence upon the local community, with the result that Berkshire society was far from introverted and that power in the shire changed hands continually and often rapidly.

The eastern end of Berkshire was only twenty miles, or about a half-day's ride from London, and the main West Country road from the capital ran the whole length of the shire from Maidenhead in the east to Hungerford in the west. Windsor had long been a royal residence, and the Stuart court hunted regularly in the Berkshire walks of Windsor Forest. In addition, by 1640 the prosperity of the county had for many years depended heavily upon the marketing of its agricultural produce at London. The capital was already receiving considerable amounts of grain down-river from Oxfordshire and Berkshire at the beginning of Elizabeth I's reign,[7] and subsequently the size and importance of this trade increased steadily. When the flow of grain was cut off by the Royalist governor of Reading during the civil war there was real concern in both London and Reading,[8] and some of Reading's inhabitants claimed that the stoppage was costing the town at least £2000 'in ready money' each week.[9]

All these observations point to the closeness of the link between Berkshire and London. Perhaps the best way, however, to illustrate the influence of the capital upon the county community is to examine in detail the important group of county or magisterial gentry families which, in the absence of any strong indigenous noble influence, dominated the local community on the eve of the civil war. This county group contained thirty-eight families, or about one-eighth of the total of 300 gentry families in the county at this time.[10] The central feature which characterized them and marked them out from the remaining lesser or parochial gentry was that, whereas the influence of the lesser gentry was by and large restricted to the parishes where they resided and the immediate area surrounding, the county gentry were all capable of exercising some measure of influence over the affairs of the county community as a whole. This influence was produced by, reflected in, and operated through their possession of a landed estate in the shire, their involvement in a web of friendship and kinship connections both within the shire and with important figures outside, and their exercising of important county administrative office, i.e., the magistracy and the shrievalty.

Lay social groupings in seventeenth century England were not rigid castes; rather their composition was responsive to changes in the material circumstance of individuals and families, the most common variables affecting this for the gentry being financial standing, the pattern of family descent, cousinage connections and attitude to the established religious system. Between 1500 and 1640 the impact of these variables produced marked fluctuations in the fortunes of many Berkshire families and as a result the membership of the county gentry group changed continually and rapidly. Only just over half of the county families for 1640 had occupied a similarly elevated position in 1600, and only four of them in 1500.[11]

One further result of this evolving pattern of circumstance was that, far from being homogeneous in terms of status, the Berkshire county group contained internal gradations of importance and power. At any given time one can find examples both of families who were increasing their status relative to their fellow county families, and of those whose position was declining. Right at the top of the social ladder in 1640 were families like the Dunches of Little Wittenham, the Forsters of Aldermaston, the Harrisons of Hurst, the Knollys of Battel, the Martens of Longworth and the Stonehouses of Radley. These were clearly the most important families in the shire, predominant politically, economically and socially. At the other end of the scale were families like the Powles of Shottesbrooke and the Wilmots of Charlton, both of which had achieved county status only very recently, and whose influence was relatively limited. Again, while the fortunes of the Dunches, Martens, Windebanks and others were clearly waxing in the period before 1640, others, such as the Hydes of Kingston Lisle and Darells of Kintbury, had suffered considerable progressive decline in status during this period, and in the case of the Darells this decline was sufficiently advanced by 1640 to threaten the family's position in the county group itself. E.P. Thompson had warned those who attempt studies of social groupings that like any other relationship it [class] is a fluency which evades analysis if we attempt to stop dead at any given moment and anatomize its structure.[12]

When the situation was developing as quickly as it was in Berkshire in the early seventeenth century, this difficulty must be borne in mind; however, if caution is exercised, such study need not necessarily be rendered entirely unprofitable.

*   *   *   *   *

The length of time that a governing county group had resided in a shire was bound to be an important influence over both its character and its relationship with the county community it controlled. The families that constituted the county gentry group in Berkshire in 1640 were very recently settled in that shire. Only eight of the thirty-eight (21 per cent) were settled as rural landholders in the shire before 1500; another sixteen (42 per cent) had entered between 1500 and 1600; and the remaining fourteen (37 per cent) had settled there only after 1600. How this situation compares with that for the leading gentry in other counties for which work has been done can be seen in the table below. The figures are percentages for the leading gentry in each shire.[13]

	Pre 1500	1500-1600	Post 1600
Berkshire	21	42	37
Buckinghamshire	35	33	32
Cheshire	85	[......... 15 ....]	
Essex	16	50	34
Hertfordshire	10	47.5	42.5
Kent	75	[......... 25 ....]	
Norfolk	42	44	14
Suffolk	32	32	36
Suffolk	32	32	36
Sussex	77	[......... 23 ....]	

Clearly the Berkshire county group was far less deeply rooted in its shire than its counterparts in Cheshire, Kent, Norfolk and Sussex; it was also somewhat more recently settled than equivalent groups in Suffolk or Buckinhamshire, but of slightly longer establishment than the leading gentry in Essex or Hertfordshire. Already the impression is given that the county gentry possessed the most shallow roots in those counties nearest to London. However, before investigating where these newcomers originated from, we need to consider how room was made for them.

Prior to the dissolution of the monasteries in the fifteen-thirties, Berkshire had contained two wealthy abbeys, at Reading and Abingdon, as well as a number of smaller religious houses, and thus a considerable amount of land in the county fell into lay hands at the dissolution. In fact, however, only five of the thirty-eight county families for 1640 had either initially established or considerably enlarged their Berkshire estates with monastic land.[14] Thus while the dissolution was undoubtedly a contributing factor in the infiltration of the new families, both in respect of these specific cases and in its effect on the land market in general, it was neither the principal cause nor an essential pre-requisite of the process.

More importantly, the space which allowed newcomers to take up residence as landowners in Berkshire was created by the decline or disappearance of a number of prominent county families. The Norreys of Wytham, the Parrys of Hampstead Marshall, the Wardes of Hurst, the Essexes of Lambourn and the Untons of Wadley were all powerful Berkshire families in the sixteenth century, but they were to suffer from financial difficulties or the extinction of their male line and would disappear from the shire before 1640. In addition, a number of families which did still remain within the ranks of gentry landowners in 1640, nevertheless owned much smaller estates by that stage than they had during Elizabeth I's reign. Successive heads of the Fettiplace, Darell, Forster, Hyde and Englefield families had presided over the alienation of a considerable number of manorial estates between 1560 and 1640; Sir William and Sir Humphrey Forster in particular had between them parted with nine manors in Berkshire during the period 1600 to 1640.[15]

This rapid transfer of lands was noticed by at least one con temporary observer. In his *Worthies of England*, published in 1662, Thomas Fuller remarked

> the lands in Berkshire are very skittish and often cast their owners which yet I impute not so much to the unruliness of the Beasts as to the unskilfulness of the Riders. I desire heartily that hereafter the Berkshire gentry may be better settled in their saddles so that the sweet places in this county may not be subject to so many mutations.[16]

While it is difficult to state with any certainty why there should have been such a marked trend towards estate disintegration in Berkshire, it is possible that the normal problems experienced by gentry landowners throughout the country more often resulted in alienation in Berkshire because of pressure applied by the land-hungry wealth of London. Whatever the reason for the break-up, however, the result was that the average territorial holding of the gentry in the early seventeenth century was small,[17] and that space was created for an influx of new landowners.

*   *   *   *   *

What then were the social and geographical origins of the thirty county families which entered Berkshire after 1500?[18] One family, the Nevilles of Billingbear, was directly descended from a noble family, and another twenty can be definitely identified as off-shoots from established gentry families resident in other parts of the country. Of the remainder, only five had definitely been of below gentry status prior to their settlement as rural landholders in Berkshire. Thus the appearance of these families in Berkshire was more the result of a linear migration of established landed families than of any dramatic movement up or down the social scale.[19]

With respect to the circumstances surrounding the initial acquisition of Berkshire land by these thirty families, the salient point is that no fewer than twenty-one of them had preceded their entry with an interim period of residence at London. With the capital expanding at a tremendous rate between 1500 and 1640 and offering great opportunity for the accumulation of wealth, many of the new Berkshire families were founded by the younger sons of pre-existing gentry families who had been set up in a career at London and had subsequently acquired a landed estate within easy reach of the capital.

In the case of fourteen of the families, the first member of the family to settle in Berkshire had previously pursued a successful career as a courtier or civil servant.[20] In another five cases the first entrant had previously been engaged in some commercial enterprise,[21] and in the last two cases the career involved was the law.[22] As for the other nine families which had had no contact with London, six had inherited Berkshire lands or married into gentry families there while resident elsewhere in the provinces, one was initially involved with the cloth trade at Newbury, one originated from a Berkshire township and acquired land through service for the ecclesiastical hierarchy, and the last simply purchased Berkshire property and moved its main residence there.[23]

The twenty-one London families achieved county status in Berkshire not as a result of a long association with the local community but because their wealth, social status, and good connections acquired outside the county guaranteed them swift elevation to the top of local society. Sir Edmund Sawyer, the revenue auditor, purchased land in 1623 and was appointed to the county bench of justices in 1624;[24] William Trumbull senior acquired Easthampstead in 1628 and was appointed a justice in March 1628/29.[25] John Thorowgood settled at Billingbear in 1630 and was appointed to the bench in 1632;[26] Sir Thomas Manwaring took up residence at Bradfield in the mid sixteen-thirties and was added to the bench in March 1637/8;[27] and Lawrence Halstead was granted Sonning in 1628 and appointed a justice in the mid sixteen-thirties.[28] A number of other county gentlemen who had settled only very recently in the shire, i.e. Edward Wray, Sir Peter Vanlore, Sir Robert Pye, John Packer, Sir Henry Pratt and Sir Benjamin Rudyerd were not active as county justices before 1640, one reason for this being their heavy commitments outside the shire. Nevertheless they have been considered members of the Berkshire county group because their wealth, territorial holding in the shire, and influence at London gave them a social parity with any other leading family in Berkshire, and they therefore possessed the capability of influencing the political life of the whole county community. While their relative lack of active involvement in county administration might perhaps exclude them from the ranks of the county gentry in some other counties, in Berkshire they constitute an important element of the county's governing élite.[29]

The newcomers in general and those appearing after 1600 in particular, 'jumped the queue' of indigenous Berkshire families of longer standing with aspirations to county status which might well have been achieved elsewhere in the country. Thus, unlike many other counties where the governing oligarchy evolved naturally out of the body of the indigenous county community over a number of centuries, in Berkshire this oligarchy was to a great extent grafted onto the local community by outside pressure, principally from London. As a result the outlook of the group reflected this association with London, as well as the newer association with Berkshire.

*   *   *   *   *

Evidence of the influence of the capital over the Berkshire county gentry and of their resultant 'cosmopolitanism' can be found not only in their origins and family traditions, but also in their interests and involvements on the eve of the civil war. Unlike in Kent, where Everitt found that the vast majority of the leading gentry owned land only in their own shire,[30] twenty-seven of the thirty-eight

Berkshire families possessed property outside the county. Altogether forty-nine manors in eleven different counties, some as far afield as Yorkshire and Lincolnshire, were held by Berkshire county gentlemen in 1640.[31] Thirteen of them owned property at London; this usually consisted of one or two residences only, but Sir Henry Pratt owned extensive property there, estimated to have a rent value of £700 annually in the sixteen-forties.[32]

Individual members of a number of families also continued to be involved in professional or business activities in London. Six county gentlemen were still active as central office-holders during the sixteen-thirties, Sir Francis Windebank as secretary of state, Sir Robert Pye and Sir Edmund Sawyer as exchequer officials, John Packer as a clerk of the privy seal, William Trumbull junior as a clerk of the signet, and Sir Benjamin Rudyerd as surveyor of the Court of Wards. Another six were involved in commercial enterprise. Sir Henry Pratt and Lawrence Halstead were both important London cloth merchants operating on a very large scale. Sir John Backhouse was heavily involved during the sixteen-thirties in the administration of the New River Company, which was responsible for the cutting of a canal to bring water to the capital from Hertfordshire; he owned nine of the company's thirty-six shares and began to receive dividends after 1633. Other shareholders included Richard Neville of Billingbear and John Packer of Shellingford. Sir Francis Knollys was involved with the activities of the Virginia Company. A further four gentlemen, John Harrison of Beech Hill, Sir Thomas Manwaring of Bradfield, Anthony Barker of Sonning and Sir Henry Marten of Longworth were engaged in legal work.[33]

The presence within the Berkshire governing élite of so many individuals who maintained a regular contact with metropolitan society and whose fortunes were heavily dependent upon their activities at London was bound to strengthen the connection between the governors in the county and the powerful circles in the capital. Influential figures like Sir Francis Windebank and Sir Edmund Sawyer could hold down important administrative office at London and at the same time participate actively in local affairs as justices of the peace. In fact, during the sixteen-thirties, Sawyer liaised frequently with Windebank and between them these two attempted to keep Charles I's privy council informed of events and attitudes in the shire.[34]

This close contact between the London authorities and members of the governing élite in Berkshire can also be observed during the sixteen-forties when the proximity of the capital allowed the

Berkshire parliamentary committeemen to take an active part in county administration and also put in regular appearances in the Commons. Unlike Kent and Cheshire where only a small percentage of active parliamentary committeemen were also M.Ps.,[35] in Berkshire seven of the nine 'core' committeemen sat at Westminster at some stage between 1642 and 1648.[36]

The impression that the Berkshire ruling oligarchy was less insular or introverted than élites in some other parts of the country is also confirmed by a study of the marriage connections developed by the forty-five county gentlemen. Only twelve of the forty-nine identifiable marriages contracted by these men were with families resident in Berkshire.[37] Many of the remaining thirty-seven brides dwelt in shires adjacent to Berkshire, but some lived as far afield as Monmouthshire, Shropshire, and in one case the Netherlands.[38] As marriage into a landed family was generally preferred, only six of the brides belonged to London families without county estates, but in a number of other cases the contact between families which led ultimately to inter-marriage was initiated through acquaintance developed at the capital. For example, Richard Neville of Billingbear married Anne daughter of Sir John Heydon of Norfolk, Charles I's lieutenant of the Ordnance; both families had a tradition of central government officeholding, and the paternal grandfathers of both Richard and Anne had been implicated in Essex's revolt in the fifteen-nineties.[39] The Whitmore family of Shropshire, into which Sir Edmund Sawyer the revenue auditor married, retained what Dr Pearl has called 'important London connexions', and Sir William Whitmore, Sawyer's father-in-law, was still engaged in commercial activities there in the early seventeenth century.[40] Several members of the Leicestershire Harrington family, into which Sir Benjamin Rudyerd married, held crown office under Charles I,[41] and Sir Henry Pratt's father-in-law, Sir Thomas Adams of Wisbech, Cambridgeshire, was a master of the Drapers Company and, like Pratt, an alderman of the city of London during the sixteen-thirties.[42]

*   *   *   *   *

This study has attempted to show that unlike their counterparts in some other parts of the country, the Berkshire county gentry were far from insular or introverted, but rather were in continual contact with gentry society beyond the borders of their own shire, and in particular upheld a close association with London, the most dynamic political, economic and cultural centre in the kingdom. This association was reflected both in their roots, for many of them acquired the wealth which enabled them to establish themselves in Berkshire through a bureaucratic, commercial or legal career in London, and also in their preoccupations, for many too still possessed residences at the capital and were engaged in a variety of business, professional or political activities there.

There was perhaps one important political repercussion of this situation. During the sixteen-forties, a number of those Berkshire county gentlemen who supported Parliament were able to remain active as parliamentary committeemen and continue to direct county affairs throughout the decade. By contrast, in Cheshire and Kent the county gentry had, as early as the middle of the civil war, effectively surrendered power to activists of a lower social position.[43] It might be suggested that this retention of power by the Berkshire county gentry was to some extent attributable to the fact that they were an especially new and outward-looking ruling élite, well aware of developments at London and thus more likely to exhibit a wide spectrum of views concerning the conflict between Charles and his parliament. Certainly Henry Marten, a staunch republican and a committeeman of great influence and popularity in Berkshire, is one striking example of a county gentleman well attuned to the more radical ideas emanating from the capital.[44]

Clearly though, both by origin and outlook, many of the leaders of Berkshire society in the sixteenth and early seventeenth centuries must be considered infiltrators from London. Kentish society had not been influenced to this degree by the capital, a fact which Everitt attributes partly to the relative inaccessibility of that shire.[45] Dr. Holmes' preliminary look at Essex and Hertfordshire,[46] however, suggests that these counties on the other hand were similar to Berkshire, in that there too local society became dominated by 'new gentry' from the capital. Only further detailed work will fully establish whether the Berkshire county group was *sui generis*, or whether it corresponded to ruling oligarchies in most of the south-eastern counties, and thus formed part of a distinct Home County region within which the burgeoning London of the sixteenth and early seventeenth centuries had a major and lasting influence upon the shape of provincial society.

Notes

[1] A.M. Everitt, *The Community of Kent and the Great Rebellion* (Leicester, 1966). For more recent work on Kent, see Peter Clark, *English Provincial Society from the Reformation to the Revolution. Religion, Politics and Society in Kent, 1500-1640* (Sussex, 1977).

[2] J.T. Cliffe, *The Yorkshire Gentry from the Reformation to the Civil War* (1969), J.S. Morrill, *Cheshire, 1630-1660, County Government and Society during the English Revolution* (Oxford, 1974), A. Fletcher, *A County Community in Peace and War: Sussex, 1600-1660* (1975).

[3] Clark, *English Provincial Society*, p.411, n.5.

[4] Everitt, *Kent*, pp.33-45, and C.W. Chalklin, *Seventeenth Century Kent* (1965) pp.192-6.

[5] In his work on East Anglia, Dr Clive Holmes discovered that the leading gentry of Essex, Hertfordshire, Norfolk and Suffolk were far less deeply rooted in their local areas than their Kentish counterparts — *The Eastern Association in the English Civil War* (Cambridge, 1974) p.231. Dr. A.M. Johnson came to similar conclusions for the gentry in Buckinghamshire — 'Buckinghamshire, 1640-1660' (unpub. M.A. thesis, Univ. of Wales 1963) p.10. Both of these works, however, concentrate on the political developments in these counties and deal only briefly with social structure.

[6] C.G. Durston, 'Berkshire and its County Gentry, 1625-1649' (unpub. Ph.D. thesis, Univ. of Reading 1977).

[7] Professor F.J. Fisher, 'The Development of the London Food Market', *Economic History Review*, 1st ser. V (2) (1935) p.50.

[8] The trade was suspended during the winter of 1643/4 and was resumed in the early summer of 1644, after parliamentary forces had captured Greenland House and Reading. At the end of May, the *Parliament Scout* reported

'That poor town [Reading] no doubt is in as much joy that they have trade again with London as Antwerp was when the Staple of English cloth returned to them . . . they rang bells and made bonfires for joy.' B(ritish) L(ibrary) Thomason Tracts E.49.33.

And in July, a report in the *Kingdom's Weekly Intelligencer* read

'Though they at Oxford do boast of relieving Greenland House yet it is yielded unto Major General Browne, and his soldiers maintain a garrison in it, which is of great concernment to the city for by that means great quantities of provisions may be conveyed by water into London from Oxfordshire and Berkshire'. B.L. E.2.11.

[9] B.L. Harleian MSS. 6804, ff.162-4. The information is taken from a report to Sir Edward Walker at Oxford outlining the reasons why the townspeople at Reading were reluctant to raise a regiment of auxiliaries to defend the town for the king. Admittedly, whoever suggested this particularly high figure had some incentive to exaggerate, but it would not have been in their interests to suggest a totally implausible sum.

[10] The families were Ashcombe of Lyford, Backhouse of Swallowfield, Barker of Sonning, Blagrave of Southcote and Sonning, Clarke of Ardington, Darell of Kintbury, Dolman of Shaw, Dunch of Little Wittenham and Pusey, Fettiplace of Childrey and Fernham, Forster of Aldermaston, Halstead of Sonning, Harrison of Hurst and Beech Hill, Hoby of Bisham, Hyde of Kingston Lisle, Knollys of Battel, Manwaring of Bradfield, Marten of Longworth and Beckett, Moore of Fawley, Neville of Billingbear, Packer of Shellingford, Pile of Compton Beauchamp, Powle of Shottesbrooke, Pratt of Coleshill, Purefoy of Wadley, Pye of Faringdon, Reade of Barton, Rudyerd of West Woodhay, Sambourne of Moulsford, Sawyer of White Waltham, Stonehouse of Radley, Thorowgood of Billingbear, Trumbull of Easthampstead, Vachell of Coley, Vanlore of Tilehurst, Wilmot of Charlton, Windebank of Haines Hill, Wray of Wytham, and Yate of Buckland.

As seven of these families contained more than one individual who enjoyed county status, there were in fact forty-five county gentlemen in 1640. Durston, thesis, vol.II contains detailed dossiers on each of these families.

[11] This situation contrasted markedly with Cheshire about which Morrill has written: 'In the fifteen-forties John Leland drew up a list of what he termed the thirty-five chiefest gentlemen in Cheshire. On the eve of the civil war twenty-five of these families were still represented on the Commission of the Peace'. Morrill, *Cheshire*, p.3.

[12] E.P. Thompson, *The Making of the English Working Class* (1965) p.9.

[13] They are taken from Johnson, thesis, p.10, Everitt, *Kent*, p.36, Everitt, 'Suffolk and the Great Rebellion, 1640-1660', *Suffolk Records Society Publications*, III (1960) p.20, Morrill, *Cheshire*, pp.3-4, Holmes, *The Eastern Association*, p.231, and Fletcher, *Sussex*, p.25. Dr Holmes uses the dates 1485 and 1603 as dividing lines and his figures refer specifically to families of the gentlemen included in the 1642 commissions of array for Essex, Hertfordshire, Suffolk and Norfolk. Dr Morrill's figures concern pre- and post-Reformation settlements, and Dr Fletcher's refer to the forty-five families of county status from 1580 to 1640.

[14] These families were the Blagraves, Dunches, Hobys, Reades and Stonehouses. They did not always acquire the land direct from the crown, but in all cases it had come into their possession by 1560. See Durston, thesis, II, pp.22, 44, 79, 158, 185.

[15] For more details, see Durston, thesis, II, pp.32-6, 51-63, 84-8.

[16] Thomas Fuller, *The History of the Worthies of England* (1662) p.112. This fragmentation was still evident in the early nineteenth century. In 1809 William Mavor wrote

'but great landowners are rare either among peers or commoners. We see several handsome seats with land not exceeding 100 acres. In the parish of Winkfield consisting of 10,000 acres the largest is under 400 acres, nor is this moderate distribution unusual in many of the parishes of Berkshire'.

W. Mavor, *A General View of the Agriculture of Berkshire* (1809) pp.49-50.

[17] The average size of the estates held by county gentlemen in Berkshire in 1640 was only three manors, and as many as fifteen of them owned only one complete manor in the shire.

[18] Of the eight others which had settled before 1500, three, the Fettiplaces, Vachells and Hydes had resided in the county since the thirteenth century, but the other five, the Clarkes, Darells, Moores, Sambournes and Yates had only appeared during the fifteenth. Two of these eight, the Darells and the Moores, had married into important Berkshire families, and another two, the Fettiplaces and Yates, had previously pursued successful commercial enterprises. Adam Fettiplace was active as a merchant at Oxford in the mid-thirteenth century and John Yate was trading as a staple merchant at Calais at the end of the fifteenth century. The backgrounds of the other four families are unclear.

[19] The place of origin has been ascertained for twenty-seven of the thirty. Lincolnshire, Yorkshire, Herefordshire, Norfolk, Oxfordshire, Kent and Hampshire had provided two families each, and Cumberland, Staffordshire, Lancashire, Cheshire, Middlesex, Wiltshire, Gloucestershire and Buckinghamshire, one each. Two families had previously resided in one of the boroughs in Berkshire and two had lived for many years at London. The remaining family originated from the Netherlands.

[20] These families were the Dunches, Hobys, Knollys, Nevilles, Packers, Powles, Pyes, Rudyerds, Sawyers, Stonehouses, Thorowgoods, Trumbulls, Windebanks and Wrays. William Dunch, an auditor of the mint for Henry VIII and Edward VI and esquire of the body to Elizabeth I, purchased in the mid-sixteenth century a number of Berkshire manors previously the property of Abingdon Abbey. Sir Philip Hoby, son of William Hoby of Leominster, was Henry VIII's master of the ordnance in the north in the fifteen-forties, and he too acquired monastic land in Berkshire after the dissolution. The Berkshire lands of the Knollys family were acquired originally by Sir Francis Knollys the Elizabethan privy councillor. Henry Neville, a prominent courtier during Edward VI's reign, received a grant of Billingbear Park in 1552. John Packer, clerk of the privy seal and secretary to the Duke of Buckingham, purchased Shellingford manor in Berkshire in 1620, and Richard Powle, registrar of the Chancery court, purchased Shottesbrooke manor between 1580 and 1600. Sir Robert Pye, auditor of the receipt in the Exchequer under James I and Charles I, bought Faringdon manor in 1622, and Sir Benjamin Rudyerd, surveyor of the Court of Wards, purchased West Woodhay in 1634. Sir Edmund Sawyer, a revenue auditor,

purchased Heywoods manor in 1623 and George Stonehouse, clerk of the Green Cloth in the mid-sixteenth century, purchased Radley manor at the beginning of Elizabeth's reign. Sir John Thorowgood was employed as secretary to the Earl of Pembroke during the 1620s; in 1630 he received the wardship of Richard Neville of Billingbear Berkshire from the earl, and he shortly afterwards married Richard's widowed mother and took up residence in the county. William Trumbull senior, a clerk of the privy council for Charles I, received a grant of Easthampstead Park from the king in 1628. Thomas Windebank, a signet clerk during Elizabeth's reign, purchased Haines Hill before 1593. Edward Wray, a groom of the bedchamber to James I, acquired extensive property in Berkshire in 1623 on his marriage to Elizabeth Norreys, daughter and heir of the lately deceased Francis Norreys, Earl of Berkshire.

For more details of all these families, see Durston, thesis, II, pp.43-50, 78-83, 89-95, 116-29, 135-39, 151-56, 162-68, 176-200, 216-27.

[21] These were the Backhouses, Blagraves, Halsteads, Pratts, and Vanlores. Thomas Backhouse of Whiterigg, Cumberland, apprenticed his son Nicholas at London in the mid-sixteenth century and by the fifteen-seventies Nicholas was prominent as a merchant in the city. Nicholas' son Samuel acquired Swallowfield manor in Berkshire in 1582. Robert, a younger son of Ralph Blagrave of Uttoxeter, Staffordshire, was a prosperous London merchant during the reign of Henry VIII. Robert's son John inherited property in Berkshire, acquired after the dissolution by his mother's second husband William Grey. At the end of the sixteenth century Lawrence Halstead, a younger son of John Halstead of Rowley, Lancashire, was apprenticed to the Merchant Adventurers in London. During the early part of the seventeenth century he was one of the most important cloth traders in that company and in 1628 he obtained a grant from Charles I of Sonning manor in Berkshire. Henry Pratt, son of Francis Pratt of Ryston, Norfolk, was also established in a commercial career at London towards the end of Elizabeth's reign and by the sixteen-twenties was a prominent member of the Merchant Taylors company; in 1620 he purchased Newton manor and in 1626 Coleshill manor in Berkshire which became his main county seat. Peter Vanlore was born in Holland in 1547. Before 1578 he had established himself as a jewel merchant at London and he subsequently amassed a considerable fortune supplying jewellery to the courts of Elizabeth and James I. He purchased Tilehurst manor in Berkshire in 1604 and during the next twenty-three years acquired a further eight manors in the county, both by purchase and annexation when creditors defaulted on debts. For more details see Durston, thesis, II, pp.7-13, 21-26, 64-70, 140-45, 207-11.

[22] These were the Manwarings and Martens. Thomas Manwaring, son of George Manwaring of Ightfield, Shropshire, studied at the Inner Temple from where he was called to the bar in 1626. Subsequently he resided in the capital and pursued a successful career as a lawyer there. In the mid sixteen-thirties he married the widow of Sir Edward Stafford of Bradfield, Berkshire and took up residence in the shire. Sir Henry Marten's background is somewhat obscure. After studying at Oxford he entered Doctors Commons at London in 1595 and by the sixteen-twenties was the most powerful civil lawyer in the country, acting as a judge of the Admiralty Court, High Commission and the Prerogative Court of Canterbury. From 1599 onwards he invested much of his legal wealth in the purchase of Berkshire land, and by the sixteen-thirties owned one of the largest individual estates in the county. Durston, thesis, II, pp.96-109.

[23] These nine were the Ashcombes, Forsters, Harrisons, Purefoys, Reades, Wilmots, Barkers, Dolmans and Piles. For details of their individual cases, see Durston, thesis, II, pp.1-13, 37-42, 58-64, 71-77, 130-4, 146-50, 157-61.

[24] *V(ictoria) C(ounty) H(istory) of Berkshire*, ed. William Page and Rev. P.H. Ditchfield, Vol. 3 (1923), p. 174, P(ublic) R(ecords) O(ffice) Crown Office Docquet Books C.231/4 f.168.

[25] *Deputy Keeper of the Public Records 43rd Annual Report*, App.I, pp. 58, 95. P.R.O. C.231/4 f.266, C.193/13/12.

[26] P.R.O. C.231/5 f.85.

[27] *V.C.H. Berks.*, 397, P.R.O. C.321/5 f.283.

[28] *Deputy Keeper of the Public Records 43rd Annual Report*, App.I, 112. Halstead's name is included in the list of Berkshire justices for 1635 - P.R.O. C.193/13/12, but according to the government's entry book he was only appointed in March 1636/7 - C.231/5 f.236.

[29] Members of most of these families occupied important local administrative office in the sixteen-forties and sixteen-fifties. For details see Durston, thesis, I, pp.173-85.

[30] Everitt, *Kent*, p.42.

[31] The county gentry between them owned twenty manors in Oxfordshire, six in Hampshire, four in Wiltshire, Kent and Hertfordshire, three in Buckinghamshire and Yorkshire, two in Somerset and one in Bedfordshire, Lincolnshire and Northamptonshire.

[32] Those owning London residences were Sir John Backhouse, Humphrey Forster, Lawrence Halstead, Sir Henry Marten, Henry Moore, John Packer, Sir Henry Pratt, Sir Robert Pye, Sir Benjamin Rudyerd, Sir George Stonehouse, Sir John Thorowgood, Sir Peter Vanlore and Sir Francis Windebank, see Durston, thesis, II, pp.10, 61, 68, 98, 107, 113, 141, 155, 165, 188, 194, 211, 220. For a rental of Sir Henry Pratt's London property, see Leeds University Brotherton Library, Loder-Marten MSS. Box 37 (unfoliated - top sheet).

[33] For more details and references for all these individuals, see their family dossiers in Durston, thesis, II.

[34] In 1636, for instance, Sawyer, who had been accused in the shire of conspiring to over-assess the county for Ship Money, wrote to the council informing them of all the various ways in which the government's chief opponents in the shire, Sir Francis Knollys and Sir Thomas Vachell, had been obstructing the crown's wishes over the previous ten years. These obstructive activities included hindering the collection of forced loan money and contributions towards the repair of St. Paul's cathedral, and refusing to assist the carriage of timber for the navy as well as objecting to Ship Money — P.R.O. State Papers Domestic, S.P. 16. 341/50, Petition of Sawyer to the Council. For more details of the pre-war politics in Berkshire, see Durston, thesis, I, chapter II: 'The Growth of Resistance, 1625-1642'.

[35] Everitt, *Kent*, p.145, Morrill, *Cheshire*, pp.82-9.

[36] Durston, thesis, I, pp.185-6. Edmund Dunch and Henry Marten sat as M.Ps. for Wallingford and Berkshire respectively between 1640 and 1648 (though Marten was suspended for three years after 1643). Along with Tanfield Vachell, elected for Reading in 1645, they were responsible for liaising between Westminster and Berkshire during the war. They were later joined by Robert Packer, Sir Francis Pile, William Ball and Daniel Blagrave.

[37] This contrasts markedly with marriage connections developed elsewhere. In Cheshire two-thirds of all marriages contracted by the gentry between 1590 and 1642 were with gentry of the same county and for the same period 48 per cent of all marriages contracted by the county gentry were with members of other county gentry families. In Kent two-thirds of the gentry married locally. Morrill, *Cheshire*, pp.4, 16, Everitt, *Kent*, p.42.

[38] Six of the brides came from London and six from Hampshire. Gloucestershire and Oxfordshire provided three each: Middlesex, Kent, Buckinghamshire and Herefordshire two each: and Suffolk, Worcestershire, Wiltshire, Norfolk, Monmouthshire, Cambridgeshire, Somerset, Leicestershire, Shropshire, Essex and Antwerp one each.

[39] Durston, thesis, II, pp.117-21, and G.E. Aylmer, *The King's Servants* (1961) pp.289-91.

[40] Valerie Pearl, *London and the Outbreak of the Puritan Revolution: Government and National Politics 1625-1642* (1961) pp.306-07.

[41] Aylmer, *King's Servants*, pp.286-7.

[42] Pearl, *London*, pp.292-3.

[43] Everitt, *Kent*, pp.146-55, Morrill, *Cheshire*, pp.82-9.

[44] For more detail on Marten, see Durston, thesis, I, Chapter IV, *passim*; II, 100-09, and C.M. Williams, 'The Political Career of Henry Marten' (unpub. D.Phil. thesis, Oxford Univ. 1954), *passim*.

[45] A.M. Everitt, 'Kent and Its Gentry, 1640-1660. A Political Study' (unpub. Ph.D. thesis, London Univ. 1957) p.27.

[46] Holmes, *Eastern Association*, p.231.

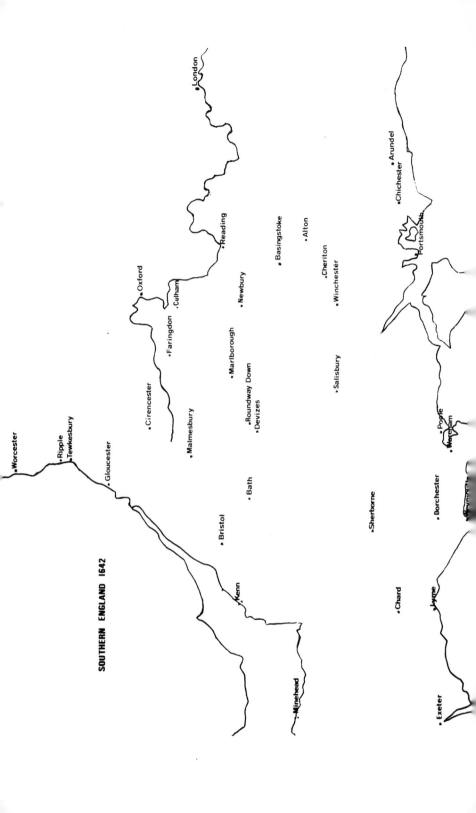

SOUTHERN ENGLAND 1642

Royalist Strategy in the South of England 1642-1644

M.D.G. WANKLYN

After decades of neglect the military aspects of the English Civil War have once more become a respectable field of investigation for professional historians. This is indicated by the stream of books, theses and articles written during the past fifteen years, but as a whole the studies show a distinct bias towards peripheral topics like local administration, neutralism and the impact of the war upon the county communities.[1] There have, admittedly, been a number of useful biographies of Parliamentary generals which give proper weighting to their military as well as their political careers,[2] and a small number of satisfactory accounts of the major battles and sieges.[3] There has, however, been hardly any attempt to re-examine either the narrative framework of the war or the hypotheses about strategy to be found in the works of S.R. Gardiner written almost a century ago. Indeed it is significant that the most recent book to be published entitled *The Civil War* not only dispenses completely with military narrative, but also makes no real effort to explain the outcome of the First Civil War, which must surely be regarded as the main historical problem of the mid sixteen-forties.[4]

This lopsided approach of contemporaries to Civil War studies has had a number of unfortunate consequences. In the first place Gardiner's errors have become encapsulated in military narratives of the war like flies in amber. For example, book after book places Lord Goring's army at Farnham in Surrey rather than at Fareham in Hampshire on 9 January 1645,[5] even though commonsense alone ought to have suggested that, at that stage in the war, the capture of one of the leading Parliamentary garrisons guarding the southern approaches to London would have caused far more of a reaction in Parliament and the Press. Secondly, in almost every discussion of the outcome of the Civil War, impressive accounts of the administrative strengths and weaknesses of both sides are combined with quite erroneous statements about military and naval affairs. Conrad

Russell, in what is otherwise a most judicious assessment of the reasons for Parliament's victory, maintains that the king received no support from foreign powers.[6] Yet in February 1643 the Dutch fleet under Admiral Tromp provided an armed escort for the great convoy of arms and ammunition the queen had collected on the Continent. If this convoy had been destroyed or captured by the Parliamentary ships which were lying in wait for it, there is little doubt that the Royalist cause would have collapsed during the summer through lack of ammunition.[7] It also ignores the fact that the capture of ports like Weymouth, Exeter and Dartmouth by the king's forces in the autumn of 1643 ensured that supplies of munitions from Dutch, French and Spanish sources entered Royalist controlled areas virtually unhindered till as late as the winter of 1645/6.[8] Similar criticisms can be directed against recent work by D.M. Loades, I. Roots and G.E. Aylmer,[9] but the lack of interest in, and command of, the purely military aspects of the war amongst professional historians is most apparent in Professor Kenyon's recent book on the seventeenth century in the *Pelican History of England* series. His account of the conflict contains three serious errors of fact and one of interpretation, which is perhaps scarcely surprising as he dismisses the study of the campaigns as 'of little concern save to military historians'.[10] Nevertheless his mistakes will be repeated by generation after generation of school children and students in their essays and examination scripts.

Finally, in spite of Sir Charles Firth's convincing demonstration that Lord Clarendon's writings were deliberately biased against generals like the Palatine princes and Lord Goring,[11] the *Autobiography* and the *History of the Great Rebellion* are still treated by many historians as if they provide an accurate and disinterested account of the conflict. Also the text of both works is liberally besmattered with factual errors. In a few cases these are an accidental result of the lapse of time between the civil war itself and the date at which much of the writing was done, but there is no doubt that on occasions Clarendon deliberately suppressed evidence he had at his disposal and sacrificed accuracy and balanced judgement on the twin altars of self-righteousness and self-justification.[12] On other occasions, for example in his description of the opening of the 1644 campaigning season and of the raising of the royal standard at Nottingham, hindsight and the desire to produce a dramatic effect result in a distorted impression of the state of the king's affairs at particular points in time. The purpose of this article is to question the stock generalisations, largely based on Clarendon and Gardiner, and to begin the process of reassessing Royalist strategy.

As the Civil War spluttered into life in the high summer of 1642, it was central southern England rather than the south-east or the south-west which attracted the attention of the king and his military advisers. Thickly populated, at a safe distance from London (the centre of Parliament's military preparations), and with a strong episcopalian element amongst its resident nobility and gentry, it must have seemed an ideal recruiting ground for the Royalist army. Moreover Colonel Goring, the governor of Portsmouth, had promised to deliver his garrison with its large arsenal of arms and ammunition into the king's hands at the most propitious moment.[13] Prompted by these considerations, the Royalist council of war sent the marquis of Hertford from York early in July to supervise military operations in central southern England.[14] Although Hertford had little military experience, it was hoped that, as a great landowner of royal descent with a reputation as a moderate in politics, his prestige and authority would command great support and help to discourage the supporters of Parliament. Clarendon dismisses Hertford as an indolent intellectual and Sir Ralph Hopton, his chief military adviser, blames him at times for indecisiveness, but the marquis proved a successful commander in the field with the happy knack of taking the right decisions in times of crisis.[15]

The marquis's orders were to recruit as many men as possible and to establish a connection with Colonel Goring, but he was not to advance on London till the arrival of the main field army from the north.[16] However, enthusiasm for the Royalist cause proved, at best, lukewarm even in those areas where Hertford's estates were situated. Moreover the enemy set siege to Portsmouth early in August with forces far in excess of those he was able to muster.[17] For several weeks there was stalemate. The forces of Parliament under the earl of Bedford were not strong enough to dislodge Hertford from his base at Sherborne Castle, but at no time did he manage to muster enough troops to take the offensive. However, the surrender of Portsmouth (5 September) forced the marquis and his advisers to reconsider their strategy. The Parliamentary troops previously engaged in the siege were advancing towards Sherborne to reinforce Bedford, but there was no chance of Royalist troops arriving from the north after the retreat of Sir John Byron's regiment of horse from Oxford on 10 September.[18] It was therefore decided to abandon southern England completely and to try and effect a rendezvous with the main Royalist army which was beginning to take shape in the north Midlands. Hertford, with the infantry, crossed into South Wales via the port of Minehead, and as a result the Somerset regiment was able to join the king in time to take part in the battle of Edgehill and the abortive march on London.[19] Other regiments from Wales under the marquis's personal command, arrived at Oxford, the new Royalist headquarters, early in the new year.[20]

The cavalry, on the other hand, were not so fortunate. As the ships at anchor in Minehead harbour were unsuitable for transporting horses, they were ordered, in a spur-of-the-moment decision, to retire into Cornwall under Hopton's leadership. This was the only part of the south-west to have shown any real sympathy towards the Royalist cause, and during the winter Sir Ralph was able to raise a force of about 2000 infantry. Even so, he blamed Hertford for ordering the retreat to Minehead rather than attempting to capture Bristol.[21] However the criticism is ill-founded. There was some measure of Royalist sympathy in the city in the spring of 1643, but this seems to have been a consequence of the war, which had deprived the merchants of their lucrative trade with the towns of the middle and upper Severn valley. Evidence suggests that in the autumn of 1642 the city favoured Parliament as the council felt secure enough to send volunteers to expel Hertford's men from Somerset.[22]

The king's decision to establish his headquarters at Oxford (November 1642) seems at first glance rather foolhardy as the city was almost entirely surrounded by enemy territory, but it was well placed to serve as an assembly point for newly-raised regiments coming from Wales, the Midlands and the South-West, as well as being a useful forward base from which to launch an attack on London. It is not, however, surprising that during the winter of 1642/43 strenuous efforts were made to improve Oxford's security by conquering the area to the south and west of the city. Garrisons were established at Abingdon, Wallingford and Reading, but attempts to establish a permanent presence at Cirencester and at Malmesbury were less successful.[23] Large raiding parties of brigade strength made the Royalist military muscle felt as far away as Basingstoke and the outskirts of Gloucester and Bristol.[24] Also the king's supporters in Kent, West Sussex, Surrey and Hampshire, emboldened by the approach of the main field-army, openly declared their allegiance and seized a number of important towns, but these uprisings were ill-planned and badly executed.[25] The handful of cavalry and dragoon regiments sent to their support were needlessly squandered in the defence of Chichester and Winchester against vastly superior forces commanded by Sir William Waller,[26] but, as the uprisings were inspired and, to some extent, supported by the king,[27] they can be seen as the first sign of a deliberate policy to occupy the area to the south of London which was so vital to the Parliamentary war effort.[28]

By the end of March, however, the area to the north of Oxford had become the main centre of Royalist military activity as local Parliamentary armies tried to block communications between the king's headquarters and the provincial commands. Prince Maurice was sent into the Welsh Marches, with a small force of cavalry and dragoons, to stop the triumphant progress of Sir William Waller, Parliament's newly appointed lieutenant-general of the West, who had recently switched his attention to the lower Severn valley.[29] Prince Rupert, on the other hand, led a small army into the North Midlands with the object of blasting a corridor through which troops and supplies could be brought to Oxford. Ammunition was in particularly short supply and the king was anxious to obtain the bulk of what the queen had brought to the north of England from the Continent in February.[30] In mid April, however, the earl of Essex's army set siege to Reading, and the two princes were ordered to return to Oxford immediately. Neither had fully accomplished his mission, but they both obeyed the king's command, a sharp contrast to their behaviour later in the war.[31]

Reading fell on 27 April. This breached Oxford's outer defence ring and the king had serious thought about abandoning his base and retreating to the West Midlands. Moreover the main field-army had expended almost all its ammunition and was in no position to fight a battle with the earl of Essex, but on the advice of Prince Rupert he put off the decision in the hope that ammunition would arrive from the north before Essex was ready to advance on Oxford.[32] As a precaution the infantry regiments were placed in a fortified camp at Culham, near Abingdon, which effectively blocked the southern approaches to Oxford. The cavalry, however, were employed in a more mobile capacity. Sir John Byron's brigade ravaged the country between Wilmslow and Buckingham in the hope either of inducing Essex to divide his forces or of attracting the attention of the Parliamentary troops in Northamptonshire which might otherwise have been used to intercept the first great consignment of arms and ammunition which had begun its journey southwards on 8 May.[33] Prince Maurice on the other hand, was sent back into the Welsh Marches. Waller had taken advantage of his absence to capture Hereford, and by 9 May Maurice was quartered once more at Worcester. The most adventurous plan, however, was for the marquis of Hertford to return to Wiltshire and Somerset where a group of local landowners, sickened by the excesses of the Parliamentarians, were ready to lend their full support to a Royalist recruiting drive. It was also intended that the marquis's cavalry escort should link up with the powerful body of infantry which Sir Ralph Hopton had managed to raise in Cornwall 'for their mutual advantage'.[34]

Hertford's new expedition was to transform the military situation in the south of England, but its background, nature and timing have never been fully investigated. Some authorities claim that it was a response to Hopton's great victory over the earl of Stamford at Stratton, near Bude, on 15 May, but the Royalist ordnance papers and other sources show that preparations for the expedition had started fully a week before the battle took place, and twelve days before the news of the victory reached Oxford.[35] In fact the proposal that Hertford should return to central southern England first seems to have come under serious consideration before the siege of Reading. On 15 April the marquis's commission as lieutenant-general of the six counties was reaffirmed.[36] Four days later, Parliamentary troops from Somerset set out to occupy Sherborne, having received information from captured correspondence that Hertford had already left Oxford. Finally a number of letters captured amongst the baggage of the Cornish army after its defeat at Sourton Down (26 April) contained orders for Hopton to lead his troops into Somerset to co-operate with a force of cavalry under the marquis's command.[37]

The need to prevent the capture of Reading and subsequent concern about the defence of Oxford against the earl of Essex must have caused a postponement. Indeed the garrison at Malmesbury, an important staging post, had to be withdrawn,[38] but once the king's infantry were safely quartered at Culham, and once it had become fully apparent that Essex had no intention of delivering an immediate attack on Oxford, the plan was revived, albeit in a most cautious manner. The western gentlemen, escorted by three regiments of horse belonging to the main field-army, left Oxford on about 11 May, but it is significant that Hertford himself did not depart till eight days later, by which time the safe arrival of the munitions convoy from the north had made the king's position at Oxford more secure.[39] Even so, it seems that Hertford had the strictest orders to return should the military situation in the Thames valley deteriorate to any appreciable extent.[40]

A second misconception surrounds Prince Maurice's appointment as lieutenant-general of cavalry. Some authorities maintain or imply that the prince was involved in the western expedition from the start, but a list of ordnance dated 8 May shows that this was not the case.[41] As has already been shown, Maurice was ordered to return to the Severn valley early in May. On 13 May 'Prince Maurice His Highness's horses' were quartered at Worcester, and on 16 May he arranged to meet a mass levée of the county at Pitchcroft, just outside the city.[42] His commission as lieutenant-general under the marquis of Hertford is dated 17 May, a week after the commencement of recruiting operations in Wiltshire, and it does not seem that he was able to join the marquis till 20 May when he arrived at Salisbury with his own regiment of horse and another, Sir James Hamilton's, which had been raised for the defence of Worcestershire.[43] This decision by the Royalist council of war to transfer troops from the Severn valley to the southern theatre of war could only have been the result of some major shift in the military balance of power. Clarendon maintains that Hopton's victory at Stratton was the determining factor, but news of the battle did not reach Oxford till three days after the issuing of the commission.[44] Clarendon also maintained that the prince's promotion from colonel of horse to lieutenant-general was a reward for his 'great courage and vigilance'. Certainly Maurice's victory over Waller's forces at Ripple Field on 13 April had shown that he was capable of handling a small army in battle, but it does not explain why the commission was dated 17 May rather than a week or so earlier.[48] Elsewhere Clarendon states that Rupert was anxious for his brother to command the western expedition rather than Hertford of whom he was jealous, but it seems that Rupert's real concern was that he had not been consulted about the composition of the expedition.[46] Moreover arguments between the king's military advisers do not explain why it had become necessary to move troops from the Severn valley into Wiltshire at that particular time. The two or three new regiments of horse raising in Wiltshire, together with the three the marquis had brought with him from Oxford, would surely have formed a large enough protective screen for the recruiting operations, especially as evidence suggests that volunteers did not appear in large numbers till after Hertford had fixed his headquarters at Salisbury (20 May).[47]

In my opinion the key to the whole problem is to be found in a letter written by Sir Edward Nicholas to Prince Rupert on 12 May which stated that Maurice's orders, on his return to Worcestershire, were 'to pursue Waller whichsoever way he goeth'.[48] Early in May there had been strong suspicions in Royalist quarters that Waller was about to leave the Severn valley area, with the intention of either attacking Oxford in conjunction with the earl of Essex's army, or of marching into Devonshire to assist the earl of Stamford against the Cornish. Such rumours persisted for some time after Maurice had received his commission: at one time, for instance, Sir William was said to be approaching Malmesbury; on another occasion he was supposed to be already at Cirencester.[49] Even today Waller's movements during the second and third weeks of May are difficult to ascertain, but on about 7 May he left Hereford, which he had recently captured, and moved his headquarters to Gloucester where his army seems to have remained for about three weeks. However, evidence strongly suggests that he himself paid a visit to the south Gloucestershire/north Somerset area before 22 May. On 19 May a letter of Sir Walter Earle shows that Waller was somewhere within a day's ride of Dorchester,[50] whilst a letter from the Parliamentary committee in Somerset to the governor of Bristol dated 22 May suggests strongly that Sir William had recently been at Bath.[51] His journey may have been occasioned by news of Stamford's defeat at Stratton, but he may have simply been holding discussions with members of the county committees in the southern part of his command in the hope of solving his army's perpetual problem, shortage of infantry.[52] Also he probably wanted to assess for himself the scale of the threat to Parliament's control of the West Country posed by Hertford's operations in Wiltshire.

News that Waller himself was in the Bristol/Bath area would have been just the kind of information to convince the Royalist council of war that Sir William was about to move his army out of the lower Severn valley area. In the past he had made his reputation by destroying concentrations of raw recruits,[53] and so Hertford's operations in Wiltshire must have seemed his most likely target. It was therefore imperative to send reinforcements before the marquis was overwhelmed by one of the 'Night-Owl's' famous surprise attacks. If, however, the Parliamentary commander's intention was to march towards Oxford or to advance into Devonshire to help the earl of Stamford against the Cornish, the forces of Maurice and Hertford combined would be strong enough to pose a serious threat to his flank whichever course he took. In such circumstances Maurice's promotion to lieutenant-general would serve to prevent disputes over command as the earl of Carnarvon, who at that time commanded the marquis's cavalry, was almost certainly the senior colonel.[54] Moreover Maurice was the only Royalist commander with experience of fighting Waller, and indeed of defeating him in battle.

Whatever reasoning lay behind the council of war's decision, there is no doubt that Maurice's soldiers were convinced that Waller's army was moving south. On 18 May or 19 May, when a party of them reached the outskirts of Malmesbury, they noticed some Parliamentary cavalry in the distance 'which they took to be Sir William Waller'.[55] Their fears, however, were groundless. Having made arrangements for a rendezvous of the western forces at Bath, and having calmed the fears of the western officers and gentry with promises that he would attack the marquis of Hertford at Salisbury, Waller rode back to Gloucester; but first he intended to lead his army northwards for an attack on Worcester. This was a clear case of insubordination as the earl of Essex had sent him orders to march into Wiltshire to attack Hertford's levies.[56] Waller, however, was convinced that the king's position at Oxford was untenable, and that he would eventually have to retreat to Worcester; but if Parliamentary forces could capture Worcester before his departure, Charles would be trapped in the Thames Valley and forced to surrender. Moreover, as Worcester was only defended by local troops who could not be expected to withstand a determined assault, the city ought to fall as easily as Hereford had done in the previous month. Finally the capture of Worcester would enable him to remove the garrison at Tewkesbury which would add 1000 horse and foot to his army.[57] As for the southern part of his command, it would have to fend for itself for ten days or so. Waller probably gambled on Hopton's setting siege to Exeter (as he had done twice before after victories in Cornwall), and on Hertford's remaining in Wiltshire so as to give support to the king's main army if Essex advanced on Oxford, but for once Sir William made a disastrous miscalculation. Worcester proved strong enough to beat off attack, whilst the power vacuum created in the south by his departure and by the defeat at Stratton enabled the two Royalist generals to join forces at Chard on 4 June, thus creating an army strong enough to threaten Parliament's control over the whole of south-west and south-central England.[58]

Once they had sorted out problems of command, Hertford and Hopton saw their first priority as the need to clear Somerset of the enemy and then to capture Exeter.[59] This clearly reflected the determination of the officers from Devon and Cornwall to 'secure the west', but when Waller and his army suddenly appeared at Bath on 8 June the council of war saw the necessity of obeying Maurice's initial orders and determined 'to follow Waller whichsoever way he goeth'.[60]

The ensuing campaign, which culminated in the destruction of Waller's army at Roundway Down, has been described in meticulous detail elsewhere.[61] It was followed by the siege of Bristol, a combined operation involving both the Oxford army and the western army. Once Bristol had surrendered (27 July), Hopton, who had been badly injured by the explosion of a waggonload of gunpowder some weeks earlier, remained in the city as lieutenant-governor to Prince Rupert with orders to refresh and recruit those regiments of the Oxford army which had suffered most severely in the assault.[62]

Some authorities claim that there was a fortnight's delay in military operations after the capture of Bristol caused by unseemly quarrels between the king's generals over questions of strategy and command,[63] but this was not in fact the case. The King had decided that Prince Maurice should replace the marquis of Hertford as the field-commander of the Royalist forces in the west of England by 27 July at the lastest, and the western army had left the Bristol area within a week of the surrender of the city.[64] Maurice's orders were to reduce the remaining enemy garrison in Devon and Dorset as speedily as possible, and then to rejoin the main field-army.[65] The suspension of military activities only affected the Oxford army and was occasioned solely by the need to wait for a message from the northern command. The king was anxious to invade the Eastern Association, but after the casualties his army had suffered at Bristol he was too weak to do so without the active co-operation of the marquis of Newcastle and the army of the north. The news that Newcastle refused to contemplate such a move till after he had captured Hull was not received till 10 August, whereupon the council of war immediately adopted the only sensible alternative strategy (given the numerical superiority enjoyed by the forces defending London) and set siege to Gloucester. The major reason for this decision was to allow a breathing space during which the army could be recruited. Also, once the city had surrendered, the king's forces would be further strengthened by the addition of regiments previously engaged in containing the Gloucester garrison. Moreover the capture of Gloucester would revive the economy of the Welsh borders, and thus enable the king to collect sufficient taxes and provisions to maintain a large army in the Thames valley area.[66]

For many years the movements of the king's armies in the south of England in 1643 have been seen as part of a grand strategy known as the trident or three-fold attack on London. According to S.R. Gardiner, who first suggested the idea, Charles's intention was to use the main field army to keep the earl of Essex in check in the Thames valley, whilst his armies in Cornwall and Yorkshire pushed forward on the flanks to smother the enemy between them.[67] Subsequently other historians proposed a more complex scenario: the northern and western armies were to cut the Thames below London, whilst the king's forces marched down the Thames valley for a final confrontation with Essex.[68] This explanation of the king's strategic plans for 1643 is accepted without question in a number of books which have been written during the last decade,[69] including the most recently published textbook of the seventeenth century.[70] Other writers, whilst admitting that the evidence for the trident plan of attack is rather sparse, claim that it is an acceptable hypothesis on the grounds of inherent military probability.[71] Only M. Ashley and R.N. Dore dismiss the trident strategy completely, but neither attempts to evaluate the evidence or to suggest a counter-hypothesis.[72]

The trident plan is undoubtably open to criticism on a number of grounds. In the first place it does not make much military sense. If the king's intention had been to attack London from three different directions, the earl of Essex, operating on 'interior lines', could have thrown the bulk of his forces against one prong and then against another as the opportunity offered. Thus the forces of Parliament, even though they might be weaker than those of the king, could destroy their opponents in detail by achieving local numerical superiority.[73]

Secondly the documentary sources which describe, or are supposed to describe, the three-fold attack on London are very few in number (though it is unfair of Dore to claim that they do not exist at all).[74] They are also inferior types of evidence, at best second or third-hand reports of decisions taken by the Royalist council of war. One of Gardiner's sources, for example, is a letter of advice written from the Netherlands which was intercepted by the Parliamentary authorities before it even reached the king. It also relates to the strategy to be pursued in the 1642 campaign, not that of 1643.[75] The other source is, however, more pertinent. It is a letter written by the Venetian ambassador in January 1643 recounting an interview with a man called Herne who claimed to be a royal emissary. Ashley makes light of Herne's report on the grounds that his only previous claim to fame was that he had taught the queen's maids how to dance,[76] but this is an unhistorical comment. Far stranger messengers have been used in time of war simply to avoid arousing enemy suspicions.

The more elaborate versions of Gardiner's hypothesis draw on additional source material, namely reports of captured Royalist correspondence printed in the London newspapers in early June 1643,[77] but the newspaper reports are of questionable value as evidence of the king's strategic plans. In the first place, as the writers of the letters are not mentioned by name, it is impossible to ascertain whether they contained direct or indirect evidence of decisions taken by the Royalist council of war. Secondly, since the original letters do not survive, there must be some doubt as to their provenance. During the Civil Wars newspaper editors on both sides were quite capable of dressing up vague rumours as fact in order to curdle the blood of their readers. Finally the editors themselves had doubts about the reliability of the information they were putting before the public. One of the later reports, for instance, described the northern prong of the trident, by which forces under the queen's command were to advance into Suffolk and Essex, as 'not likely'.[78] There is, however, a possibility that the reports were based on royal letters found amongst the papers of one of the participants in Sir Nicholas Crispe's plot, a scheme to bring about a Royalist uprising in London, which was uncovered at precisely the time the newspapers were printed.[79]

But the most damning argument against the trident strategy is not that the source material is of dubious value, or that it makes little strategic sense, but rather that Gardiner and those that followed after him completely misread the most important piece of evidence, the Venetian ambassador's letter. This states quite clearly that the northern and western armies were *not* to advance directly on London via East Anglia and the south-coast counties. Instead they were to march to Oxford for a rendezvous with the main field-army. Then the king would divide his armies in such a way as to block the Thames above and below the capital whilst the Royalist cavalry scoured the countryside. Thus London would be cut off from its sources of food and fuel, and the citizens reduced to such straits that they would overthrow the Parliamentary leadership by force.[80]

Other, more reputable sources also suggest very strongly that the conjunction of provincial forces with the king's army in the Oxford area played a central role in Royalist grand strategy for much of 1643. On several occasions during the spring and early summer, instructions were sent to the marquis of Newcastle to march south for a rendezvous with the main field-army, and 4000 troops were sent to the Royalist headquarters in May and July as escorts for munitions convoys.[81] In the *Great Rebellion* and the *Life* Clarendon stated on four separate occasions that Hertford and Hopton were to lead their army to Oxford.[82] Sir Samuel Luke's agents told a similar tale, and when Prince Maurice returned to the west in early August 1643 his instructions were to return as quickly as possible 'so his (the king's) armies might unite for some other purpose'.[83]

But did an advance by the provincial armies into Kent, Sussex and East Anglia play no part in the king's strategic plans for 1643? After the capture of Bristol, as has already been stated, there was a short-lived plan for Newcastle's army to advance into East Anglia, but in co-operation with the main field-army. In mid-August the king sent orders that Newcastle should carry out the attack on his own, but this was also rejected.[84] As for the southern prong, Clarendon, in the *Life*, stated that before the marquis of Hertford left Oxford there was some excited talk of raising a new army which 'should never join with the king's army, but capture Portsmouth and then advance into Sussex and Kent', but close examination of the text suggests a date after Hertford and Hopton joined forces.[85] Other sources also suggest a later date for the scheme. In late June and early July six gentlemen from Kent and Sussex received commissions to raise regiments of cavalry.[86] On 15 July William Constantine, the recorder of Poole, who had recently changed sides, urged his fellow-townspeople to surrender, or else the Royalist forces besieging Exeter would storm Poole on their way to London. Towns nearer to the capital had already been occupied, he claimed.[87] Two days later Edward Ford of Up Park, one of the new colonels, wrote to his neighbour, Thomas Cotton of Warblington, urging him to persuade the well-affected in the western part of Sussex to contribute horses, arms and money to the Royalist cause.[88] At about the same time Ford himself was levying troops in Berkshire 'for special service'.[89]But in the summer of 1643 the king had no regiments to spare for a thrust into the south-east, even when a serious revolt broke out in Kent in mid-July.[90] The earl of Essex's army still posed a threat to Oxford and to the second great convoy of arms and ammunition, which had left Newark on 1 July under the queen's personal command, whereas Hertford and Hopton were fully occupied in containing Waller's forces for most of June and early July.[91] Thereafter the sieges of Bristol and Gloucester were of paramount importance. Nevertheless, if Gloucester fell and the king's forces began to march eastwards, the despatch of a brigade of cavalry into Kent and Sussex officered by native gentry might spark off another revolt. At the very least it would pose a threat to the capital's supplies of food and fuel. It may have been a coincidence that early in September three of the six new regiments were serving under the command of the earl of Crawford, who had been in charge of troops sent to Chichester in the previous year,[92] but it is surely significant that when the regiments of Sir Nicholas Crispe and Richard Spencer were surprised by Parliamentary troops at Cirencester a few days later, the officers and men captured claimed that Kent was their next destination.[93]

But the siege of Gloucester dragged on thanks to bad weather and the steadfastness of the Parliamentary garrison. This was undoubtedly a disappointment to the king and his military advisers, who had hoped for a quick success, but there is no real reason for regarding the siege as a strategic mistake. Some historians echo the opinions of Sir Phillip Warwick, Richard Bulstrode and Richard Atkyns that the king ought to have advanced on London after capturing Bristol[94] but, as has already been stated, the Royalist army was too weak in infantry to risk attacking the earl of Essex's army in a prepared position, especially if he was supported by the City of London trained-bands, as at Turnham Green in November 1642.[95] Moreover, during the course of the siege, the main field-army received between four and five thousand additional troops, mostly infantry, from Bristol, Wales and the border counties.[96] Finally, as Parliament also appreciated the strategic importance of Gloucester, the king's officers began to see the city in a new light, namely as a bait for enticing the earl of Essex away from the London area and forcing him to fight a battle in a situation which favoured the Royalist.[97] But the ensuing campaign revealed quite clearly that Charles's main field-army was still too weak to get the better of the Parliamentarians drawn up in a good defensive position. When Essex appeared on the western fringes of the Cotswolds with an army reinforced by six regiments of London trained-bands, the Royalists decided to retreat northwards in the hope of luring him into unenclosed country where they could make the best use of their superiority in cavalry.[98] Essex chose to return to London by a more southerly route, but when the king's forces managed to catch him at Newbury, he found time to draw up his army in a position protected by hedges and steep slopes. After suffering heavy casualties and expending almost all their ammunition, the Royalists retreated and the Parliamentary forces returned to London without having to fight another battle. In the widest sense, however, the failure of the king's army to defeat Essex in the Newbury campaign was Charles's own fault for not having sufficient strength of will to command the marquis of Newcastle either to join him at Gloucester, or to cause a diversion by advancing into the Eastern Association. The decision to send Maurice back into the west country is much less questionable as the Cornish infantry, after their heavy losses in the storming of Bristol, would have added little to his strength had they remained with the main army.[99] Moreover, if Clarendon is to be believed, the soldiers would probably have mutinied if ordered to advance further east before Plymouth and Exeter had been reduced. [100]

After the battle of Newbury the king's council of war changed their strategy of centralization to one of dispersal. Detachments from the royal army were sent to places as remote as Pembrokeshire and Chester, with the object of increasing the area of the country under Royalist control. Most of the new strategic initiatives affected the midlands and the north, but for much of the winter a strong force of càvalry was stationed in the Cotswolds in the hope of capturing Gloucester through starvation or intrigue, whilst Sir Thomas Aston's regiment of horse was sent into Dorset to help contain the enemy garrison at Poole.[101] But the most ambitious project involved the western army. Lord Hopton was to use the marquis of Hertford's corps, stiffened by troops from Ireland and from the Oxford army, to clear Dorset, Wiltshire and Hampshire of the enemy and then to 'point forward as far as he could go towards London'. To this end he was appointed field-marshal-general of the south-east, which gave him supreme command over the counties of Kent, Surrey and Sussex.[102] Prince Maurice, in the meantime, was to assist him by raising forces in the counties further west, and also to reduce Plymouth and Dartmouth, the last enemy garrisons in Devonshire.[103] These operations probably do not indicate a fundamental change in the direction of Royalist military thinking. Admittedly the Newbury campaign *was* followed by bitter arguments and recriminations amongst the king's advisers, but at the same time there were cogent reasons for dispersing the main field-army during the winter season, to ensure that it was in the peak of condition for the start of the 1644 campaign. The Oxford area contained too many garrisons to provide adequate food and fodder for a large army.[104] If it remained there throughout the winter, its strength would ebb away through disease and desertion. On the other hand, if substantial sections were involved in operations in the provinces, those that remained would be well provided for and the rest, if successful, would return with large numbers of recruits for the spring campaign.

The new policy of decentralisation meant that for the first time in the war an advance into the counties to the south and east of London was of prime strategic importance to the Royalist high command, but the military situation was not as favourable as it had been in July and August. The local Parliamentary leadership had largely recovered its morale,[105] and Sir William Waller, having recruited a new army in the London area, was preparing to set out from Farnham to recover the territory he had lost in the Roundway Down campaign.[106] Moreover Hopton seemed to have lost both his confidence and his flair. He blamed the king for expecting him to do too much with the limited resources placed at his disposal, but there can be little doubt that the disasters his army suffered at Alton (13 December) and Arundel (6 January) were very largely of his own making. He underestimated the skill and cunning of Sir William Waller; he failed to exert sufficient control over his subordinates; and he managed to organize his army's winter quarters in such a way that the various detachments were too far apart to give one another assistance in the event of a surprise attack.[107] Hopton's forces were saved from complete destruction by a heavy fall of snow which rendered military operations impossible for the rest of January and much of February, but he had lost almost 2000 men, mostly infantry, in the space of less than a month. Not surprisingly he had also lost the confidence of the Royalist high command.[108]

The king's strategic plans for the 1644 campaigning season are difficult to ascertain as they were so quickly overtaken by events. According to Sir Samuel Luke's spies, the talk at Winchester was of Hopton and Maurice joining forces. Part of the western army was then to keep Waller in check whilst the other advanced into Sussex and Kent.[109] Royalist sources do not suggest as clear-cut a plan as this, but Maurice was appointed lieutenant-general of the south-east in February, which made him Hopton's immediate superior.[110] This, together with the fact that the prince's corps was ordered to march eastwards leaving Plymouth still in Parliamentary hands,[111] suggests that the western army was to be recruited for a move into Sussex and Kent, rather than simply being absorbed by the Oxford army; but in mid March Royalist strategic planning was thrown into confusion by the unexpected news that Waller was about to set out from winter quarters near Arundel to renew his attack on Hopton. Moreover the Parliamentary general had received almost 2000 additional cavalry from the earl of Essex whose army was stationed to the north-west of London. This was a direct result of the Royalist policy of decentralisation. With much of the king's horse quartered in the Cotswolds as a threat to Gloucester,[112] Essex knew he was in no danger of attack from Oxford and therefore could afford to reinforce Waller's offensive in the south.

As Maurice and his corps were still in Devonshire, and as Hopton could no longer be trusted with independent command, the earl of Forth, Lord General of all the king's forces, was sent to Winchester to take charge of operations against Waller. He brought with him substantial reinforcements from the Oxford army, but these were not sufficient to match the reinforcements Waller had received from the earl of Essex.

Nevertheless Forth and Hopton advanced to meet the enemy. Also, even though Waller had taken up a strong defensive position near the village of Cheriton, they decided that attack was the best policy. The ensuing battle (29 March) was an uninspring slogging match in which the generals on both sides seem to have lost control of their subordinate officers early in the day. Henry Bard, who had vowed before the battle that he would show his northern musketeers were as good as the Cornish, began the series of disorganised and fruitless attacks which ended in the Royalists being forced back beyond their starting position by sheer weight of numbers. Even so Hopton found little difficulty in engineering the escape of the king's forces under the cover of night.[113]

Historians have followed contemporary writers like Clarendon and Sir Edward Walker in seeing the battle of Cheriton as an important turning point in the civil war, because it forced the king's armies to assume a defensive role in the 1644 campaign,[114] but this is a mistaken view. The casualties suffered by the Royalists were light in comparison with almost every other major battle in the war, and in comparison with the losses sustained during the winter campaign.[115] Also Waller derived no strategic advantage from his victory. The Parliamentary cavalry carried out raids as far afield as Andover, Salisbury and the outskirts of Dorchester, but Sir William's only permanent gains were two minor garrisons near Southampton. By 12 April he had retreated to Farnham under the threat of a major Royalist counter-attack. The king's main field-army and Hopton's corps, which had by that time joined forces near Marlborough, outnumbered his own army by a considerable margin.

To make matters worse, the London trained-band regiments under his command had decided to return home.[116] The Royalists advanced to Newbury and then to Reading in the hope of persuading Sir William to fight, but he refused to leave Farnham till the earl of Essex's army was ready to take the field.[117] When Essex did move from his winter quarters in mid May, the two Parliamentary generals had about 20,000 men in the Thames valley area to the king's 13,000.[118] It was this numerical disadvantage (which owed almost nothing to the defeat at Cheriton) that forced the Royalist high command to opt for a defensive strategy in the summer of 1644.

In Clarendon's opinion the small size of the king's field army was the result of what had been happening in the marquis of Newcastle's command. In February 1644 Prince Rupert had been sent into the Welsh Marches to raise reinforcements for the Oxford army, but declining Royalist fortunes in Lancashire and Yorkshire forced him to march north instead.[119] This argument raises a number of questions which fall outside the scope of the present article, but one thing is indisputable. If Rupert had led his troops to Oxford, Parliament would have ordered the Eastern Association army to join forces with the earl of Essex, and this would have given the Parliamentary commanders in the Thames valley an overwhelming numerical advantage over the king.[120] Indeed, if Rupert had not marched north, it is difficult to see how the Royalist council of war could have formulated a practicable strategy for the 1644 campaigning season.

The real reason why the king was unable to contend on equal terms with Essex and Waller was the wayward behaviour of Prince Maurice, and Charles's strange reluctance to bring him to heel. The prince's army, about 600 strong, had left its winter quarters near Tavistock towards the end of March. It included experienced troops like the so-called 'Old Cornish' regiments which Hopton had raised in 1642, and if it had joined with the main field-army or operated in conjunction with it, the king would have had at his disposal about as many soldiers as Essex's and Waller's armies combined.[121] Maurice, however, on his own initiative, decided to lay siege to the little fishing port of Lyme. The king's council of war acquiesced in what initially appears to have been a moment of weakness,[122] but, taking into account the military situation in the south in mid April 1644, an attack on Lyme probably appeared both desirable and practicable, provided that the town could be quickly forced to surrender. The Parliamentary garrison there had suddenly become more active in disputing Royalist control over west Dorset and east Devon;[123] and with Waller's army quiescent at Farnham and Essex's still in winter quarters near Aylesbury, there was no immediate need for Maurice to hurry eastwards. Also, the ease with which Wareham had fallen earlier in the month may have convinced the king's council that the siege of Lyme would only be a week's work.[124] Moreover Charles may have seen the advantage of keeping a strong force in Devon and Dorset for a little longer in order to protect the queen. Henrietta Maria was about to leave Oxford for safer quarters at Exeter.[125] If Waller managed to capture her in a surprise attack, she would be impeached for plotting with the Catholic rebels in Ireland, and Charles would probably have to sue for peace in order to save her life. A month later, however, Maurice was still before Lyme, whilst the King's army was being driven back towards Oxford by Essex and Waller.[126] Faced by the worst military situation since August 1642, the king ordered Maurice to march to Bristol for a rendezvous with the main field-army,[127] but the prince refused to abandon the siege. In the ensuing campaign the two Royalist armies were only saved from destruction by the mistakes of their enemies. Thus it was the siege of Lyme, not the battle of Cheriton, which marked the decisive break in the civil war in the south. From then onwards the Royalists were almost exclusively concerned with defending what they had won in the 1643 campaign.

Professor Aylmer has stated that a major reason for the failure of the king's offensive strategy in the early part of the civil war was that he tried to pursue two conflicting aims at the same time, a direct, massive frontal attack on London and the conquest of Parliament's supporting areas in the outlying parts of the country.[128] However, insofar as the south of England is concerned, this conflict in aims is largely illusory. In the first place a direct frontal attack on London was only seen as a practical proposition in retrospect.[129] Such a move had failed in November 1642 through lack of numbers and was rejected for similar reasons in August 1643.[130] Secondly, centralisation and decentralisation seem to have been complementary rather than conflicting strategies, but with the former having priority. Detachments from the Thames valley area were used extensively to assist the provincial commands in the winters of 1642/43 and 1643/44 (and also in 1644/45) when active campaigning by the king's field-army had ceased because of the weather, but for the rest of the time his military advisers were preoccupied with concentrating their forces against the main Parliamentary field-army. Moreover the aspirations of provincial commanders were subordinated to those of the main army. At first glance there seems to have been a number of important exceptions to this, but they cannot really be substantiated. The western project of April/May 1643 was concerned essentially with bringing Hopton's army into the Thames valley area, not with opening up an attack on London via the south-coast counties. The siege of Gloucester *was* aimed at clearing the Severn valley of Parliamentary troops, but it was also both a means of keeping the main field-army occupied whilst it was recruited and a bait for luring the earl of Essex's army out of the London area. Similarly Prince Maurice's return into the west of England in August was only a temporary measure. On the surface it appears to be a concession to the strategy favoured by the western officers and gentry,[131] but when Maurice returned he was bound to bring with him a much larger army than that with which he had set out. But the pursuit of a policy of concentration of forces, and in particular the switch from a policy of decentralisation to one of concentration, was heavily dependent on the provincial commanders obeying the orders they received from the king's council of war. In the first year of fighting all went well. The marquis of Hertford ferried his infantry across the Bristol Channel and joined the main field-army in time for the battle of Edgehill; in April 1643 Rupert and Maurice returned from the West Midlands in time to take part in the attempted relief of Reading; and in June and July the Cornish contingent in the western army obeyed the royal command to pursue Waller rather than setting siege to Exeter. In 1644, however, Prince Maurice, following the example set by the marquis of Newcastle in the northern theatre of the war in the previous summer, disobeyed the king's orders, and as a result forced the main field-army onto the defensive, and altered the whole course of the 1644 campaign in the south. Charles did nothing to discipline his nephew, and this set in motion a disfunction in the Royalist command structure which lasted till the end of the war: the council of war took decisions on the assumption that provincial commanders would promptly obey orders, whilst the provincial commanders, knowing that they would not be disciplined simply for disobeying orders, acted on their own initiative in the belief that they were better informed than the council of war. This led inevitably to disaster in June 1645 when the king faced the New Model Army at Naseby with only half of his cavalry, a predicament which was the direct result of the decision of the Prince of Wales's council in the west of England to put regional interests before those of the central command.[132]

Notes

[1] eg. J.S. Morrill, *The Revolt of the Provinces* (1976); D.H. Pennington and I. Roots, *The Committee at Stafford* (Manchester, 1957); C. Holmes, *The Eastern Association in the English Civil War* (1974); I. Roy, 'The English Civil War and English Society' *Military History Yearbook* 1, ed. B. Bond and I. Roy (1975), pp.35-42.

[2] J. Adair, *Roundhead General : A Military Biography of Sir William Waller* (1969); V.F. Snow, *Essex the Rebel* (1970).

[3] P. Young, *Edgehill* (Kineton, 1967); J. Adair, *Cheriton* (Kineton, 1973); A. Woolrych, *Battles of the English Civil War* (1961); H.C.B. Rogers, *Battles and Generals of the Civil War* (1968). P. Young and R. Holmes, *The English Civil War* (1974) gives the most authoritative account of the battles.

[4] S.R. Gardiner, *History of the Great Civil War* 4 vols. (1893ff); R. Ashton, *The English Civil War* (1978).

[5] Gardiner, *Great Civil War* vol. 2, pp.113, 182; Woolrych, *Battles*, p.93; Young and Holmes, *Civil War*, p.228; Rogers, *Battles and Generals*, p.196; C.V. Wedgwood, *The King's War* (1958), p.405; M. Bence-Jones, *The Cavaliers* (1975), p.74.

[6] C. Russell, *Crisis of Parliaments* (Oxford, 1971), p. 352.

[7] *Letters of Queen Henrietta Maria*, ed. E. Green (1857), p.166; Wedgwood, *King's War*, p.177.

[8] M.D.G. Wanklyn, 'The King's Armies in the West of England 1642-46' (unpub. MA thesis, Manchester Univ. 1966), p.96.

[9] D.M. Loades, *Politics and the Nation 1450-1660* (1974) and I. Roots, *The Great Rebellion* (1966) contain a number of errors, and Loades uses the trident strategy of 1643 as evidence of the king's strategic ability (op.cit., p.424). G.E. Aylmer, *The Struggle for the Constitution* (1963) contains a thoughtful assessment of the war marred by the section on the role of the navy.

[10] J.P. Kenyon, *Stuart England* (1978), pp.149-51, 363.

[11] C.H. Firth, 'Clarendon's History of the Great Rebellion', *English Historical Review* xix (1904), pp.473-75.

[12] See Wanklyn, thesis, ch. 5-10 for detailed criticism of Clarendon's account of the 1645 campaign in the west of England.

[13] Edward, Earl of Clarendon, *The History of the Rebellion and Civil Wars in England*, ed. W.D. Macray (Oxford, 1887), v. 440.

[14] Ralph, Lord Hopton, *Bellum Civile*, ed. C.E.H. Chadwyck-Healey, (Somerset Record Society, 1902), pp.1-2; C(ommons) J(ournals), II, p.711; T(homason) T(racts) E.109.24.

[15] P.Zagorin, *The Court and the Country* (1969), pp.93-4; Clarendon, *Rebellion*, iv.924-26; F.T.R. Edgar, *Sir Ralph Hopton, The King's Man in the West* (Oxford, 1968), pp.17-24.

[16] C(alendar) of S(tate) P(apers) D(omestic) 1641-43, p.389; Calendar of Clarendon State Papers (Oxford, 1869ff.), ii, p.146.

[17] C.S.P.D. 1641-43, p.366; Clarendon, *Rebellion*, v.441; Adair, *Waller*, p.45.

[18] Hopton, *Bellum Civile*, pp.10-17; C.S.P.D. 1641-43, pp.389, 390; Clarendon, *Rebellion*, vi.33.

[19] Hopton, *Bellum Civile*, pp.18-19; Sir John Hinton, *Memoirs* (1679), p.8.

[20] Merc(urius) Aul(icus) p.12.

[21] Hopton, *Bellum Civile*, pp.17-24.

[22] D. Underdown, *Somerset in the Civil War and Interregnum* (Newton Abbot, 1973), p.37; Adair, *Waller*, p.58.

[23] Clarendon, *Rebellion*, vi. 155; Merc. Aul., pp.12, 66, 148-49, 207; J. Bamfield, *Apologie* (The Hague, 1675), p.5.

[24] Merc. Aul., p.112; B. Whitelock, *Memorials of the English Affairs* (1732), p.68;

Clarendon, *Rebellion*, vi.235-36, vii.53; *The Vindication of Richard Atkyns*, ed. P. Young, (1967), p.8.

[25] A. Fletcher, *The County Community in Peace and War : Sussex 1600-1660* (1975), pp.259-61; A. Everitt, *The Community of Kent and the Great Rebellion* (Leicester, 1966) p.187; B(ritish) L(ibrary) Add(itional) Manuscripts 27402, f.89.

[26] The cavalry regiments of the earl of Crawford and lord Grandison, and the dragoon regiment of Edward Grey (Young, *Edgehill*, pp.211, 236; G.N. Godwin, *The Civil War in Hampshire* (1904), pp.38, 42, 44). See also C.S.P.D. 1644, pp.2-3.

[27] The king certainly had advance knowledge of the rising in West Sussex and was apparently the instigator of the Winchester coup (BL Add. Ms 27402, f.89; Fletcher, *Sussex*, p.259).

[28] In 1638 London received the bulk of its imported grain from Kent and Sussex (F.J. Fisher, 'The Development of the London Food Market 1540-1640' *Essays in Economic History*, ed. E.M. Carus-Wilson Vol. 1 1954, p.138) and the cutting-off of the coal trade with Newcastle, which was in Royalist hands, must have made the capital precariously dependent on wood from the Weald (R. Howell, *Newcastle-upon-Tyne and the Puritan Revolution* (Oxford, 1967), p.154. Also the ironworks of the Weald supplied ordnance and other materials of war. The main gunpowder mills seem to have been near Guildford in Surrey (C.S.P.D. 1644, p.93; ibid, 1644-45, pp.607-08).

[29] Young and Holmes, *Civil War*, pp.118-19; Adair, *Waller*, pp.51-2.

[30] Green, *Letters of Henrietta Maria*, pp.174, 180, 203; Merc. Aul, p.208; E.B.G. Warburton, *Memoirs of Prince Rupert and the Cavaliers*, Vol. 2 (1849), pp.165-66. Warburton is unreliable as a secondary source, but he reproduced much of Rupert's correspondence. All the references to Warburton in this article relate to primary source material.

[31] Ibid., pp.155-65; Bodl(eian) Lib(rary) Tanner MS, 62, f.76; Merc. Aul. p.208.

[32] Green, *Letters*, pp.197-98; Wiltshire County Record Office, 413/444 (Quotations in typescript from a missing part of Prince Rupert's 'Diary').

[33] Merc. Aul, pp.224, 232; Sir Samuel Luke, *Journals*, ed. I.G. Phillips (Oxfordshire Record Society, Vol. 42, 1961) p.69; Warburton, *Memoirs* Vol. 2, pp.191-94.

[34] Ibid, Vol. 2, pp.190, 195; E.A.B. Barnard, 'Some Original Documents concerning Worcestershire and the Great Rebellion', *Worcestershire Archaeological Society*, Vol. 5 (1927-28), pp.84-87; Merc. Aul, pp.240, 261; Hopton, *Bellum Civile*, p.45; Green, *Letters of Henrietta Maria*, p.215.

[35] Edgar, *Hopton*, p.89; Wedgwood, *King's War*, p.215; Adair, *Waller*, p.70; Warburton, *Memoirs* Vol. 2, pp.189-90; Hopton, *Bellum Civile*, p.45; P(ublic) R(ecord) O(ffice) WO 55.459 f.144; Merc. Aul. p.262.

[36] W.H. Black, *Docquets of Letters Patent* (1837), pp.27-28. Hertford signed a commission for Edward Seymour to raise a regiment of foot on 18 April (Historical Manuscripts Commission, Duke of Somerset MS., p.65).

[37] A.R. Bayley, *The Great Civil War in Dorset* (Taunton, 1910), pp.65-7; Bodl. Lib., Clarendon MS. 22, f.35; T.T.E.100.17; T.T.E.105.8; Hist. Mss. Comm. Portland MSS.Vol. 1, p.706.

[38] Bamfield, *Apologie*, p.5.

[39] Merc. Aul., pp.248-49, 256, 261.

[40] C(alendar) of S(tate) P(apers) V(enetian) 1642-43, p.283.

[41] Wedgwood, *King's War*, p.215; Young and Holmes, *Civil War*, p.125; I. Roy, 'Royalist Ordnance Papers', *Oxfordshire Record Society*, Vol.43 (1964), p.226.

[42] Barnard, *Worcs. Arch. Soc.*, Vol. 5, pp.86-7.

[43] B.L. Harleian MS. 6852, ff.68-9; Merc. Aul., p.261; 'The Papers of Henry Townshend', ed. J. Willis-Bund, *Worcestershire Historical Society* (1915-19), pp.139-50; T.T.E.110. 12, 17.

[44] Clarendon, *Rebellion*, vii.94; Merc. Aul. p.263.

[45] Clarendon, *Rebellion*, vii.94; Young and Holmes, *Civil War*, pp.120-22.

[46] Clarendon, *Rebellion*, Vol. 3, p.67n; Warburton, *Memoirs* Vol. 2, pp.188-90.

[47] T.T.E.110. 12, 17.

[48] Warburton, *Memoirs* Vol. 2, p.195.

[49] Luke, *Journals*, pp.73-76; Warburton, *Memoirs* Vol. 2, pp.194, 196.

[50] Merc. Aul. pp.240, 242; Hist. Mss. Comm. Portland MSS Vol. 1, pp.710-11. He was possibly at Bristol, but Adair is surely mistaken in his view that Earle could have ridden from Dorchester to Gloucester in a single day (Adair, *Waller*, p.70).

[51] Bodl. Lib., Clarendon MS. 22, f.43.

[52] Ibid, f.87.

[53] Adair, *Waller*, pp.51-53, 62, 68.

[54] Prince Maurice did not arrive in England till mid August 1642. Carnarvon had received his commission by 10 July (Old Parliamentary History, Vol. 11 (1751-62), p.280; Wilts. C.R.O. 413/444, Rupert's 'Diary', ff.2-6).

[55] Luke, *Journals*, p.81.

[56] Bodl. Lib., Clarendon MS. 22, f.43; T.T.E.110. 10; Warburton, *Memoirs* Vol. 2, p.195n; Hist. Mss. Comm. Portland MSS. Vol. 1, pp.709-10.

[57] Ibid, pp.112, 710-11.

[58] J. Willis-Bund, *The Civil War in Worcestershire* (Birmingham, 1905), pp.9306; Hopton, *Bellum Civile*, pp.45-6.

[59] Ibid, p.50; 'The Trevelyan Papers' (*Camden Society*, 1st series, Vol. 105, 1872, pp.235-38); Underdown, *Somerset*, pp.51-54.

[60] Sir Bevil Grenville to Colonel Edward Seymour, 19 June 1643 (Warburton, *Memoirs* Vol. 2, p.232).

[61] Young and Holmes, *Civil War*, pp.125-41; Adair, *Waller* pp.70-97.

[62] Hopton, *Bellum Civile*, pp.58-62; Merc. Aul., pp.420-21, 429-30.

[63] Rogers, *Battles and Generals*, p.96; Edgar, *Hopton*, p.131.

[64] Warburton, *Memoirs* Vol. 2, p.268; Clarendon *Rebellion*, vii. 155, 191. The earl of Carnarvon was at Dorchester by 2 August. (Ibid, vol. 2, p.157; Merc. Aul., p.420).

[65] Clarendon, *Rebellion*, vii. 154-55; Merc. Aul., p.427.

[66] Wilts. C.R.O. 413/444, Rupert's 'Diary', ff.23-4; Clarendon, *Rebellion*, vii. 157-58, 177.

[67] Gardiner, *Great Civil War* Vol. 1, pp.63, 67.

[68] e.g. C. Thomas-Stanford, *Sussex in the Great Civil War and Interregnum* (1910), p.71.

[69] I. Roots, *The Great Rebellion* (1966), pp.75-6; J.E.C. Hill, *The Century of Revolution* (1961), p.112; Loades, *Politics and the Nation 1450-1660* (1974), p.424; Young and Holmes, *Civil War*, p.98; Woolrych, *Civil War*, p.44; R.E. Sherwood, *Civil Strife in the Midlands 1642-1651* (Chichester, 1974), p.58.

[70] Kenyon, *Stuart England*, p.149.

[71] e.g. Edgar, *Hopton*, p.138. The concept was first proposed by A.H. Burne in *Battlefields of England* (1950).

[72] M. Ashley, *The English Civil War* (1975), p.75. R.N. Dore, *The Civil War in Cheshire* (Chester, 1966), p.23. See also M.D.G. Wanklyn, 'The Campaigns in Sussex and Hampshire in the Winter of 1643' (unpub. B.A. thesis, Manchester Univ. 1963, pp.3-5).

[73] The classic case of the successful use of a strategy of interior lines against a numerically superior enemy is Frederick the Great's defence of Prussia in the Seven Years War.

[74] Dore, *Cheshire*, p.23.

[75] Gardiner, *Great Civil War* (1886 ed), p.78, citing J. Rushworth, *Historical Collections*, pt.III, Vol. II (1692), p.70. The reference is missing from the 1893 edition, though the text is very similar.

[76] Ashley, *Civil War*, p.79.

[77] T.T.E. 110.8.

[78] T.T.E. 110.24.

[79] Whitelocke, *Memorials*, p.70; Clarendon, *Rebellion*, vii 59; Ashton, *Civil War*, pp.209-10.

[80] C.S.P.V. 1642-43, p.231.

[81] Green, *Letters of Henrietta Maria*, pp.205, 211, 219, 225; See also Lord Cromwell's letter of February 1643 (Bodl. Lib., Calendar of Carte MSS Vol. 11, f.66).

[82] Clarendon, *Rebellion*, vii. 100, 105, 110; ibid, Vol 3, p.66n.

[83] Luke, *Journals*, p.88; Merc. Aul. p.427.

[84] Clarendon, *Rebellion*, vii 177; Wilts. CRO. 413/444, Rupert's 'Diary', ff.23-4; Green, *Letters of Henrietta Maria*, p.225. See also Sir Phillip Warwick, *Memorials of the Reign of Charles I* (1703), pp.267-71, though there is some uncertainty about the actual date of Warwick's mission to York.

[85] Clarendon, *Rebellion*, Vol. 3, p.66n. This passage refers to new successes in the west, but there were none between the battle of Braddock Down in January and the battle of Stratton in May. It also mentions the 'visible distraction at London', the sort of phrase used later to describe disputes in August between the earl of Essex and the 'war party' at Westminster and in the City. Possibly the episode took place immediately after the capture of Bristol when the king had recalled Hertford to Oxford (Warburton, *Memoirs*, Vol. 2, p.268).

[86] Black, Docquets, pp.53-6. The six colonels were Sir Nicholas Crispe, Sir Edward Bishop, Sir Edward Ford, Sir Edward Dering, Richard Spencer and Thomas Covert.

[87] Bodl. Lib., Tanner MS. 62, f.107b.

[88] Hist. Mss. Comm. Portland MS. Vol. 1, p.126.

[89] B.L. Harleian MS. 6852, f.122.

[90] A. Everitt, *Kent*, pp.190-99.

[91] Warburton, *Memoirs* Vol. 2, pp.225, 243, 245, 273; Young and Holmes, *Civil War*, pp.126-37.

[92] Hist. Mss. Comm. Portland MSS. Vol. 1, p.130; Adair, *Waller*, p.52.

[93] Ibid, 7th Report, p.445; L.J. VI, p.232.

[94] Warwick, *Memoirs*, pp.260-61; Young, *Atkyns*, p.28; Wedgwood, *King's War*, p.253; R. Bulstrode, *Memoirs and Reflections* (1721), pp.94-95; M. Ashley, *Rupert of the Rhine* (1976), p.56.

[95] Young and Holmes, *Civil War*, pp.82-3.

[96] Wilts. C.R.O. 413/444, Rupert's 'Diary', f.23; Hopton, *Bellum Civile*, pp.60-61.

[97] Ibid; Warburton, *Memoirs*, Vol. 2, pp.286-87.

[98] Ibid.

[99] Warwick, *Memoirs*, pp.260-61; M. Coate, *Cornwall in the Great Civil War and Interregnum* (Truro, 1963), p.98.

[100] Clarendon, *Rebellion*, vii. 152.

[101] Bodl. Lib. Wood Pamphlets 378.1 pp.76-80; Merc. Aul., p.988; Reading Corporation Archives PY vi/38.

[102] Hopton, *Bellum Civile*, pp.60-62; Bodl. Lib., Dugdale MS.19, f.33.

[103] Bamfield, *Apologie*, p.7; Clarendon, *Rebellion*, vii. 296-98; Warburton, *Memoirs* Vol. 2, pp.307-08.

[104] Clarendon, *Rebellion*, vii. 238-39.

[105] This recovery in morale is shown by the way in which the Poole garrison repulsed the earl of Crawford's attack in September (Bayley, *Dorset*, pp.115-17).

[106] Adair, *Waller*, pp.105-13.

[107] Ibid, pp.122-30; Hopton, *Bellum Civile*, pp.67-74; Bamfield, *Apologie*, pp.7-10.

[108] Ibid, p.11; T.T.E. 78.22; Hopton, *Bellum Civile*, pp.70, 71-77; C.S.P.V. 1643-44, p.66.

[109] Sir Samuel Luke, *Letterbook 1644-45* (Bedfordshire Record Society, Vol. 42, 1963), p.629, 633, 635.

[111] C.S.P.D. 1644, pp.49, 57, 75.

[112] J. Adair, *The Battle of Cheriton* (Kineton, 1973), p.113; C.S.P.D. 1644, pp.30, 54, 57, 64, 69.

[113] C.S.P.D. 1644, p.75; Hopton, *Bellum Civile*, pp.77-81; B.L. Add. MSS. 33596, f.204.

[114] Clarendon, *Rebellion*, vii.17; Sir Edward Walker, *Historical Discourses upon Several Occasions* (1705), p.7; Adair, *Cheriton*, pp.148-49; Young and Holmes, *Civil War*, p.171; Rogers, *Battles and Generals*, p.124.

[115] The Royalists lost between 400 and 600 men, mostly cavalry, as opposed to nearly 2000 at Alton and Arundel (Hist. Mss. Comm. Portland MSS. Vol 3, p.109; Adair, *Cheriton*, p.195; Warburton *Memoirs* Vol 2, p.404; T.T.E. 39.24; Bamfield, *Apologie*, p.12).

[116] Wanklyn, BA. thesis, pp.70-73.

[117] C.S.P.D. 1644, pp.134-35, 151.

[118] Adair, *Waller*, p.151; Young and Holmes, *Civil War*, pp.182, 205; L.J. VI, p.505.

[119] Clarendon, *Rebellion*, viii.17.

[120] C.S.P.D. 1644, pp.131-32. According to the Kingdom's Weekly Intelligencer, Waller, Essex and Manchester would have had 28,000 men under their command (T.T.E. 42.28).

[121] Bodl. Lib. Clarendon MS. 23, f.187; E.A. Andriette, *Devon and Exeter in the Civil War* (Newton Abbot, 1971), p.100. The forces of the Oxford army and Hopton's corps combined would have numbered about 12,000 men (Walker, *Discourses*, p.8-12).

[122] Walker, *Discourses*, pp.8, 12.

[123] Bayley, *Dorset*, p.130; Luke, *Journals*, p.130.

[124] Hist. Mss. Comm. Duke of Ormonde MSS, new series, Vol 1, p.75; Merc. Aul., p.934.

[125] Clarendon, *Rebellion*, viii.21; Warburton, *Memoirs* Vol. 2, p.406.

[126] Walker, *Discourses*, pp.27, 41-2.

[127] B.L. Harleian MS. 6988, f.107 (Sir Edward Nicholas to Maurice 28 May 1644). Appended to the letter is a note in the king's handwriting to the effect that this was not an ordinary despatch from a secretary, 'but a particular direction from me upon mature deliberation'.

[128] Aylmer, *Struggle for the Constitution*, p.123.

[129] Clarendon, *Rebellion*, vii.239; Wilts. CRO. 444/413, Prince Rupert's Diary, ff.23-6.

[130] Ibid; Young and Holmes, *Civil War*, p.82.

[131] Merc. Aul., p.427; Clarendon, *Rebellion*, vii.152.

[132] Wanklyn, MA. thesis, pp.214-18.

The Distribution of Wealth in the Vale of Berkeley, Gloucestershire, 1660 – 1700

J.P.P. HORN

Gregory King considered that 'to be well apprized of the true state, and condition of a nation' one needed two fundamental pieces of information: the number of its people, and its wealth. These, 'of all others, and at all times, [were] the most useful and necessary.'[1] During recent years the study of population in past societies has become one of the most important developments in historical research. Historical demography has firmly established itself as a discipline related to, but nevertheless quite distinct from the mainstream of social and economic history.[2] In contrast, the second of King's 'two main articles,' wealth, has received comparatively little attention. Where it has been studied at all it has usually taken the form of general analyses for the country as a whole over long periods of time, or descriptions of particular social groups.[3] It certainly has not produced in this country anything like the canon of work currently available for population history.[4]

The cause of this backwardness can be partly attributed to King himself. His 'Scheme of the Income and Expense of the Several Famillies of England,' produced in 1696, has for years provided historians with a convenient short-cut to describing wealth and social structure throughout the nation.[5] G.S. Holmes has found it used in at least a dozen text books, from G.N. Clark's *The Wealth of England*, published in 1946, to J.D. Chamber's *Population, Economy and Society in Pre-Industrial England*, published in 1972.[6] And yet the statistical basis of King's table in Holmes's opinion 'is patently far more the product of strained deduction, of mathematical juggling, or even plain guesswork, than of firmly-grounded information.'[7] In his view, it 'has been responsible for much complacency and confusion about the pre-industrial social structure . . .'[8]

Rather than attempting a general account of the distribution of wealth in England, which considering the present state of knowledge would inevitably be full of errors, it is here suggested that local studies in aggregate may provide more satisfactory results.[9] Just as demographers have relied upon data from hundreds of parish registers to construct a broad outline of population change in England during the past four centuries, so historians studying wealth must base general conclusions on analyses of as many different parts of the country as possible.

The aim of this article is to describe the distribution of wealth in one part of Gloucestershire, the Vale of Berkeley, between 1660 and 1700. Probate inventories are the main source supplemented by wills, administrations, hearth tax returns, Overseers of the Poor accounts, parish registers, and manorial records. Part one discusses the problems involved in using inventories to measure wealth. Part two attempts to ascertain the representativeness of inventoried decedents compared to all decedents. Part three provides the results of an analysis of the distribution of wealth in the Vale of Berkeley, and part four considers the relationship between real estate and personal wealth.

I

There are a number of problems involved in using probate inventories to measure wealth distribution which fall into two broad categories: the omission of goods and the accuracy of the appraiser's valuations.[10] According to Henry Swinburne, 'the things that are to be put into the Inventory, are all the goods and chattels and rights which were the Testator's, or did belong, or were due unto him at the time of his death . . .'[11] These usually included clothes, household furniture, crockery, cutlery, kitchen implements, plate, money, tools, raw materials, crops, livestock, stored produce, credits, and investments.[12]

Conversely, certain items, by law or custom, were not entered. From the historian's point of view, the most serious of these is real estate. Since inventories are lists of a decedent's movable property, freehold land and long-term leases (which were accorded similar status to freehold) do not appear in them.[13] Things that were an integral part of a freehold were also considered the property of the heir rather than the testator and were not appraised, for example: grass, trees, fish, doves in a dovecot; and in the dwelling house, window panes, wainscot, and fixed furniture. Strictly speaking, debts owed by a decedent should not have been listed because technically they were other men's property, although in practice they frequently appear. Finally, although by law a wife's possessions, *bona paraphenalia*, belonged to her husband and hence should have been valued in his inventory, it was customary to except her 'convenient apparell, agreeable to her degree.'[14]

Another drawback is the unofficial omission of goods. Perishable foods such as butter, eggs, and milk are rarely mentioned.[15] Householdstuff, livestock, and money already bequeathed may not be included in an inventory; or an inventory may have been only partially completed before going through probate. The season of the year when the inventory was taken will also affect its contents. At various times crops, livestock, dairy products, or manufactured articles may be sold and will not appear in an inventory. In so far as the distribution of wealth is concerned, this should not represent a serious problem since the goods sold off should be replaced in another form, as money, debts receivable, or investments. If one is measuring the incidence of certain items such as crops, however, these seasonal fluctuations must be taken into account.

Whether or not goods were accurately appraised is of some consequence when using inventories to study wealth. Despite the official requirement that appraisers make 'true and perfect' valuations, it is clear they did not always do so.[16] Prices assigned to livestock, for example, should reflect their market value, but in practice they can vary a great deal and often cannot be attributed to differences in the age or quality of the stock. In a study of Cumbrian inventories, 1660–1750, J.D. Marshall found that the valuations placed on cattle and sheep were sometimes considerably lower than market prices[17] On the other hand, C. Howell and J.S. Moore commenting on Leicestershire and Gloucestershire inventories respectively have found that crop and livestock prices reflect the market price.[18] Evidence from the Vale of Berkeley confirms their view.[19] The important point is that where possible prices given in inventories should be compared to external evidence such as farm accounts, diaries, or prices in local markets. It cannot be taken for granted that inventory valuations are reliable.

The valuation of secondhand furniture and clothing must necessarily have been rather arbitrary. Different men might have appraised the same items at different prices. Is there any way of checking the consistency of valuations of household goods? One method is to compare two different appraisals of the same estate which follow each other within a few years. For example, Edward

Fig. 1:   The Vale of Berkeley, Gloucestershire.

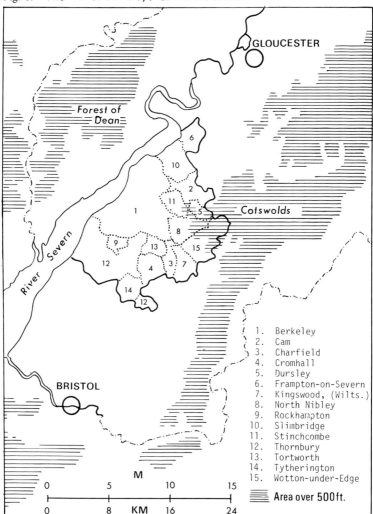

1. Berkeley
2. Cam
3. Charfield
4. Cromhall
5. Dursley
6. Frampton-on-Severn
7. Kingswood, (Wilts.)
8. North Nibley
9. Rockhampton
10. Slimbridge
11. Stinchcombe
12. Thornbury
13. Tortworth
14. Tytherington
15. Wotton-under-Edge

Area over 500 ft.

Huntley of Berkeley, died in 1686 and his widow, Mary, a year later. The household goods of his estate were valued at £47.05, while those in the inventory of Mary, £45.49.[20] John Clutterbuck, also from Berkeley, died in 1681 and had his householdstuff valued at £38.69. The same goods were valued in the inventory of his widow, Sarah, three years later, at £38.93.[21] It may not be always possible to compare all household goods as in the two examples above, but individual items might appear in both inventories and can be checked against each other. In sum, while it is likely that now and again goods were incorrectly appraised it appears that the majority of inventories provide fairly reliable valuations of their contents. As Moore says, 'Without assuming that appraisers were infallibly accurate, we may nevertheless conclude that they were reasonably honest and conscientious, and that their work is worthy of serious consideration.'[22]

II

Situated between the river Severn in the west and the Cotswolds in the east, the Vale of Berkeley extends for about fifteen miles between Gloucester and Bristol (see figure 1). It displayed a mixed economy in the seventeenth century, with dairying on the fertile clay lowlands, sheep and corn husbandry on the Cotswolds escarpment, and cloth production centred on Wotton-under-Edge, Dursley, and Cam. The population of the fifteen parishes here studied was approximately twelve thousand in 1650 and remained steady until the end of the century when it rose slightly.[23]

Seven hundred and seventy-three inventories have survived for the period 1660–1700, including those from the Prerogative Court of Canterbury, and combined with a further 210 inventory valuations found on wills, in Will Act Books, on letters and accounts of administration, and in Consistory Court Journals provide a grand total of 983 estates.[24] The first question, and most crucial, is how representative is the inventoried population compared to the population as a whole? What proportion of decedents are represented by inventories?

One method of assessing inventory coverage is to compare the number of adult males who died in the region each year to the number of those leaving inventories.[25] Ideally, this should be accomplished by linking each inventory to the decedent's entry in the burial register, but this may only be possible where the area being studied is comparatively small. For the Vale, nominal linkage would have been too time-consuming and therefore it was necessary to use ratios, that is, simply counting all the adult male decedents and comparing the annual totals to the number of extant inventories. Nominal linkage was undertaken for Berkeley, the largest parish in the region, and produced a coverage of 34.3 percent between 1678 and 1699. In other words, 34 out of every 100 males who died in that period left an inventory. This figure is very close to that achieved by ratios (approximately 32 percent) suggesting that although not as accurate as nominal linkage, ratios are nevertheless fairly reliable.[26]

Using burial registers to compute the annual number of adult male dead raises a number of problems.[27] One must be sure that registers are reasonably comprehensive and do not badly under-report deaths because of inefficient record-keeping, civil disturbances, or nonconformity. In the Vale, nonconformity was gaining strength in the market towns of Dursley, Wotton-under-Edge, and Thornbury after 1660.[28] Cloth-producing areas such as Cam and Stinchcombe also attracted large numbers of dissenters, especially Quakers.[29] For the most part, however, the registers seem reliable up to 1700, and where possible have been checked alongside records of nonconformist burial grounds.[30] Even if the registers are complete there are bound to be errors in identifying adult males or because some decedents were not buried in their home parishes.[31] Yet no claim is being made that this method will give absolutely precise results, rather it seeks to provide an indication or rough estimate of inventory coverage.

Between 1678 and 1699 coverage throughout the Vale ranged from a low of 17 percent to a high of 40 percent with an average of about 30 percent. This is the best coverage the region provides for the pre-industrial period.[32] How does it compare to other areas? J.D. Marshall found that in Hawkshead, Cumbria, 32 percent of adult males are represented by inventories between 1660 and 1700.[33] Much higher rates have been found in colonial Maryland and Massachusetts. In the latter, Daniel Scott Smith estimated that 42 percent of decedents from Hingham left inventories between 1726 and 1786,[34] while in Maryland coverage was well over 60 percent during the second half of the seventeenth century;[35] the highest rate likely to be found anywhere in the English-speaking world in the early-modern period. Although this is pure speculation, I would expect coverage in most English communities to be around 20 percent.[36] Towns, with large numbers of poor and where the ecclesiastical machinery was possibly less successful in ensuring that decedents' estates were inventoried for probate, are likely to have even lower rates. Rural parishes which were centres of nonconformity, or which attracted many poor people, or were in dioceses where the church courts were especially inefficient might also have low coverage.

Assuming that three men in ten from the Vale of Berkeley went through probate, who were those who did not? One group grossly under-represented by inventories is the poor. Only 69 men and women worth less than £10 in personalty left inventories, comprising just 7 percent of the total sample. How can this be explained? Possibly fees exacted by the church courts for proving a will or administration dissuaded some from going through the process.[37] These fees, however, were not particularly onerous, except for the destitute. Richard Burn's comment of the mid-eighteenth century could equally well apply to the end of the seventeenth century: 'it is agreed on all hands, that the fees . . . are become much too small, by the great alteration in the value of money and the prices of things.'[38] More probable is the common sense view that the poor were unlikely to make wills because they had little to bequeath. Verbal arrangements made before death may have settled what property there was on the next of kin, and since the value of the goods was so low there would have been little risk of embezzlement.[39]

One of the main difficulties in trying to establish why some people went through probate and others did not is that there is very little information on the procedure immediately after a person's death. If a person died intestate the local church courts were empowered to appoint an administrator, usually the widow or next of kin. In theory, apparitors in each rural deanery were to cite any executor or administrator to prove a will or undertake an administration provided two weeks had elapsed since the person's death.[39] In the Vale there is little evidence of people being presented for failing in this duty.[40] Perhaps the courts turned a blind eye as far as the poor were concerned because there was small recompense for them in the form of fees. They may have encouraged the making of wills but could not, or did not wish to enforce it. Indeed, this may have been their attitude towards most people because fully 70 percent of decedents failed to go through probate.

Considering the poor formed a large proportion of those from the Vale who did not leave inventories, it is important to ascertain the extent of poverty in the area. One of the best sources for this purpose is the hearth tax, especially the return of 1664.[41]

Householders who did not contribute to the parish poor rate or who had less than twenty shillings income per year from land or £10 in goods were officially exempt from the tax and listed as non-chargeables. In 1664 non-chargeables accounted for nearly 50 percent of all householders in eleven of the fifteen parishes.[42] The figure for 1672 is 36 percent but these returns are less reliable.[43] Using these levels as upper and lower bounds, between a third and a half of the Vale's entire population was deemed as poor in the 1660s and 1670s.

Was this level maintained for the remainder of the century? Evidence from Overseer of the Poor accounts for five parishes suggests that it was.[44] Annual disbursements to the poor in Thornbury, Slimbridge and Stinchcombe rose gradually after 1672, while in Berkeley and Kingswood there was a sharp increase during the 1690s. Although the data are fragmentary, it is clear that the level of poverty did not decline in the last two decades of the century, and may have even increased.

It may be objected that hearth tax returns with half their population listed as non-chargeable are somewhat suspicious. But there are good reasons for believing these levels to be fairly accurate. According to the militia muster of 1608, 40 percent of the able-bodied men in the Vale were engaged in the textile industry (see table 1).[45] During the second half of the seventeenth century, as the industry's fortunes fluctuated many workers became temporarily or permanently unemployed.[46] John Barnsdale, minister of Cam, lamented in 1666, that 'the generality of the poore and meane people of our Parish (wch are many) [who] have . . . their dependence uppon the trade of cloathing . . . are now almost wholly out of imployment . . .'[47] Eleven years later, John Smyth commented on the Kingswood district, 'It formerly depended much upon clotheing, but is now decayed with the trade . . .'[48] The Gloucestershire justices of the peace wrote to the Privy Council in 1691 informing them of the starving condition of unemployed workmen 'as their faces (to our griefs) do manifest.'[49] Comparing the Vale to other areas, in Kent the proportion of exemptions was between 26 and 38 percent during the 1660s, and in Leicestershire and Devon, approximately a third in the early 1670s. For the nation as a whole, Gregory King estimated that 55 percent of the population was excused or insolvent when the poll tax was collected in 1691.[50]

Establishing the extent of poverty is an important part of this method because it goes a long way to explaining why inventory coverage is relatively low or high. In the Vale those parishes with low coverage tended to have high proportions of non-chargeables. Dursley, Stinchcombe, and Wotton-under-Edge, for example, have low coverage at well under 25 percent, but they all have large numbers of poor. On the other hand, Charfield and Rockhampton were comparatively free of poverty and both have high coverage. Thus there is a strong correlation between inventory coverage and levels of poverty.

Allowing that between a third and a half of the Vale's adult population was too poor to be likely to leave inventories (none of those described as non-chargeables went through probate), this suggests that the proportion of wealth holders (decedents above the poor) who left inventories was between 45 and 60 percent. Quite clearly, a substantial number of wealth holders also failed to go through probate. Yet if the wealth holders who left inventories can be shown to be a representative cross-section of all those people above the poor who should have left them, then the inventoried population can be used as a sample of the whole group. The wealth of those who made inventories can be construed as representative of those above the poor who did not.

One method of assessing the representativeness of inventoried wealth holders is to compare their occupational structure to that of a group of males also skewed in favour of the upper ranks of society.[51] The occupations of prospective bridegrooms seeking marriage licences from The Diocesan Chancellor provides one such source.[52] Brian Frith states that 'the practice of marriage by licence was not limited to any particular social class,' but it is apparent that poorer groups, such as labourers and manual textile workers, are very much under-represented.[53] Table 2 shows the similarity in occupational structure between persons leaving inventories and those seeking marriage licences. Half of inventoried decedents were described as yeomen and husbandmen compared to 45.7 percent of the bridegrooms, while 23.8 percent of the former were involved in the textile industry compared to 29.2 percent of the latter. The discrepancy between the two groups in category I, 'Gentry and Professions,' can be partly explained by the tendency of bridegrooms to call themselves gentlemen whereas their less charitable neighbours described them as yeomen in their inventories.[54]

The above figures are in contrast to those for all social and economic groups. The 1608 muster shows that only 25.9 percent of men in the Vale were engaged in agriculture as opposed to 41.9 percent in the textile industry (see table 1). Nor was this a matter of

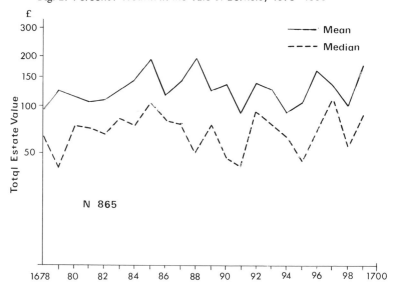

Fig. 2: Personal Wealth in the Vale of Berkeley 1678–1699

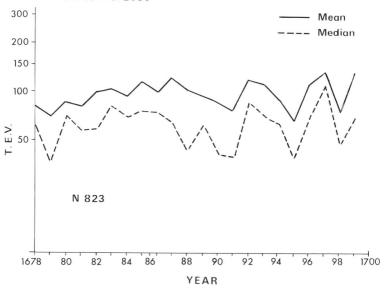

Fig. 3: Personal Wealth in the Vale of Berkeley 1678–1699, Trimmed of Estates over £500

changing occupational structure during the course of the seventeenth century. The occupations of males given in a sample of parish registers at the end of the century are remarkably similar to those of 1608.[55] These results not only confirm that inventoried wealthholders are a representative cross-section of all wealthholders, but also illustrate that the majority of poor who failed to go through probate were the lower paid workers in the textile industry — besides other unskilled men such as labourers, weavers, clothworkers, drawers, and scriblers —

III

Two methods of analysis were adopted for measuring the distribution of wealth in the Vale of Berkeley: first, an annual series of means and medians; and second, a percentage distribution.[56]

It was possible to compute means and medians for a twenty-two-year period between 1678 and 1699. As one would expect, there was a good deal of secular fluctuation — more wealthy people dying in one year than another — but there was no clear trend of increasing or decreasing wealth (see figures 2 and 3). Similarly, the median remained steady and except between 1686 and 1690 followed the mean closely, suggesting that the distribution of wealth of those above the poor was constant over this period.[57]

Although it is impossible to say with any certainty, it appears that wealth rose considerably between 1620 and 1680 (see figure 4). Forty-one inventories or valuations have survived for the period 1618–1621, and 152 between 1645 and 1649. Annual mean wealth ranged from £20 to £60 in the earlier period; £50 to £99 during the 1640s; and £100 to £200 after 1678. Inflation was partly responsible for this increase. During the first three decades of the seventeenth century the price of consumables varied between 400 and 600, according to the index compiled by Phelps Brown and Hopkins (base 100, 1451–1475), but rose steeply to over 800 by 1650.[58] Prices then declined only to rise sharply again after 1655. Yet whereas there was a long term fall in prices after 1662, generally ranging from 550 to 700, wealth described in inventories continued to increase. It should be stressed that these conclusions are tentative because it was not possible to ascertain inventory coverage for the 1640s, while for the earlier period coverage was low.[59] However, it is unlikely that differences in the sorts of people going through probate account for the whole of the disparity between wealth levels in the 1620s and 1680s. Among inventoried decedents, therefore,

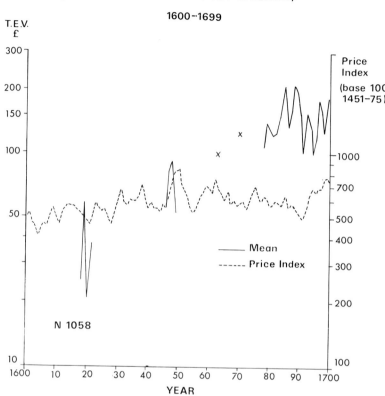

Fig. 4: Personal Wealth in the Vale of Berkeley
1600–1699

there seems to have been a major increase in personal wealth as the century progressed.[60]

The most serious drawback of using means and medians to represent the distribution of wealth is that, at best, they include only half the total population. While wealth distribution remained constant after 1678 among inventoried decedents, poverty may well have been increasing among those persons too poor to go through probate. Secondly, means do not provide an indication of the relative proportions of the population who enjoyed certain levels of wealth. For this reason a percentage distribution analysis was undertaken.

Inventoried decedents were divided into five categories:

1) £10   Very poor. Includes paupers, labourers, and widows.

2) £10–£49   Poor to Lower-Middling. Includes poor textile workers such as tailors, weavers, and clothworkers.

3) £50–£99   Lower-Middling. Includes artisans, food and drink suppliers, and husbandmen.

4) £100–£249   Middling-Rich. Includes yeomen, butchers, and bakers.

5) £250 plus   Rich. Includes mercers, clothiers, gentry, and clergy.

Cut-off points were determined by the mean wealth of the different occupational groups (see appendix). The results are given in table 3. Seven percent of estates were worth less than £10; nearly a third were between £10 and £49; slightly over a fifth were between £50 and £99; a similar proportion were between £100 and £249; and finally, 15 percent were worth over £250. There were changes in the proportions over the forty-year period studied, 1660 to 1699, but no trend towards greater or lesser wealth in one group than another.

These figures represent the personal wealth of the top 50 or 60 percent of decedents who were wealth holders. How would the inclusion of the poor alter these results? Taking the number of poor to have been between 33 and 50 percent of the total population and placing them in a £0 to £49 category,[61] the following proportions are obtained (see table 4): 60 to 70 percent of the entire adult population had less than £50; 11 to 15 percent had between £50 and £99; 12 to 16 percent had between £100 and £249; and 7.5 to 10 percent had over £250. Thus the overwhelming impression is that the vast majority of people in the Vale were poor. Approximately, two thirds had less than £50, and probably many of these had a good deal less. In contrast, the number of middling and rich persons was much smaller, comprising about a quarter and 10 percent of the population respectively.

Admittedly, these results are fairly crude. It is assumed that the proportion of poor was stable between a third and a half for the whole period 1660–1699, whereas in the 1690s it may have increased. Persons described in the hearth tax returns as non--chargeable are assumed to have had less than £50, but it is impossible to determine their precise level of wealth. Neither does the above distribution take account of the variations from parish to parish which were probably considerable. Nevertheless, it does serve to illustrate one of the salient features of seventeenth-century society: wide-spread and deep-rooted poverty. Such 'was the price of industrial innocence in pre-industrial England.'[62]

The distribution of wealth in the Vale of Berkeley between 1660 and 1700 was extremely inequitable, but whether it was more or less so than other areas remains to be seen. Marshall's figures for Cumbria, 1661–1690, show that between 81 and 86 percent of his sample had less than £100; and these results do not include the poor who failed to leave inventories.[63] 'Cumbrian living standards,' Marshall comments, '. . . were evidently bare, not to say primitive. There is no doubt at all, allowing for whatever omissions appraisers of peasant property may have made, that Cumbrians did not have as many and varied goods as peasants in Midland and Southern counties.'[64] Inventories for mid-Essex and the Frampton Cotterell area in Gloucestershire display a greater similarity to those of the Vale of Berkeley. Sixty-three percent of the mid-Essex sample, and 58 percent of the Frampton Cotterell inventories were valued at less than £100 compared to 61 percent for the Vale.[65] Again, these figures do not include the poor, and there is no indication of whether inventory coverage was good or bad. The Vale certainly had greater numbers of poor than the Frampton Cotterell district where only 11 percent of householders were non-chargeable in 1672.[66] It is quite likely, therefore, that although the Vale was fortunate in its natural resources — fertile soils and good pasturage for dairying, and the swift-flowing streams of the Cotswolds providing water-power for the clothing industry — these very resources attracted a relatively large proportion of poor people.[67] Thus the Vale's mixed economy supported not only a small group of middling to wealthy farmers, clothiers, shopkeepers, and artisans, but also a large body of poor textile workers and labourers.

IV

Perhaps the most intractable problem involved in using inventories to study wealth is that they contain little information on real estate. The inclusion of landed property might substantially alter the percentage distribution given above.

At an early stage in this research it became apparent that it would be impossible to trace the exact amount of land owned by each individual. The pattern of landholding in the Vale was complex. No less than twenty-eight manors criss-crossed the fifteen parishes here studied, owned at any one time by seventeen lords.[68] Rentals and surveys from sixteen manors have survived but only eleven proved of use in this analysis.[69] Nor was manorial tenure the overwhelmingly dominant form of landholding in the area, freehold was also important.[70] Examining hundreds or thousands of deeds would have been immensely time-consuming, with no guarantee of tracing all inventoried decedents. There is also a strong likelihood that land attributed to an individual from manorial records or deeds might be relevant to one stage in his life but bear no relation to the property he owned in old age or at death. Where a sample is small it might be feasible to trace landholding over an individual's lifetime, but where samples approach a thousand persons other methods must be found.

The basic question is this: Would the inclusion of landed property invalidate the results obtained from estimating the distribution of wealth from personal estates? Is there a correlation between personal and real wealth?

The principal sources used in this investigation were rentals and surveys from ten Berekeley manors, land transfer records from the Berkeley Court Baron, and wills.[71] Wherever possible landed property was linked to the sample of inventoried decedents to ascertain whether real estate increased in proportion to personal wealth. If acreages were not given it was nevertheless noted that an individual owned unspecified amounts of copyhold or freehold land. In this way it was possible to determine whether some wealth groups were more likely than others to have land mentioned in wills and rentals.

First, some general comments about landholding on the Berkeley manors. Over four hundred persons residing in five parishes rented property from George Lord Berkeley in 1667.[72] Of these, 31 percent rented a house, cottage, shop, or less than 4 acres; 27 percent had between 5 and 19 acres; 20 percent had between 20 and 49 acres; 14 percent had between 50 and 99 acres; and just 4 percent had 100 acres or more. Thus three-fifths of tenants had less than 20 acres and four-fifths less than 50 acres (see table 5). No figures are available for the 1660s but according to a rental of 1634 which lists individuals paying chief rent, only about a third of freeholders owned in excess of twenty acres, while 13 percent had over fifty acres.[73] These figures suggest that whether freeholder or copyholder the amount of land owned by each individual was usually small.

Tenants made up just over 30 percent of all householders living on the Berkeley manors, while freeholders comprised less than 20 percent.[74] Even assuming that there was no overlap between these two groups it is clear that at least one-half of the population was landless. Little is known about these people but many of them probably rented dwellings or land on short term leases from large freeholders in the area or were sub-tenants of copyholders. In sum, approximately half the population had no land at all, and the majority who did had less than twenty acres. The distribution of real estate, like personal wealth, was very unequal.[75]

Data from the Berkeley manors indicate that there is a correlation between personal and landed wealth. No evidence on land was forthcoming for nearly half the decedents worth less than £10, and of the remaining half the vast majority owned either a single tenement or less than ten acres. The proportion of decedents owning in excess of twenty acres and, or, several tenements steadily increased in relation to personal wealth: from 12.6 percent of decedents in the £10 to £49 category to 52.5 percent in the £250 plus category (see table 6). Only three decedents in the £50 to £99 group owned over fifty acres compared to nine in the £100 to £249 category and twenty-five in the £250 plus category. Seven of the eight persons who owned over one hundred acres were worth more than £250. As an individual's personal wealth increased so did the likelihood that land would be mentioned in one source or another. It was impossible to trace any land for 20 percent of persons worth over £250 compared to double that proportion for decedents in lower wealth groups.

So much for the Berkeley manors; what of the other ten parishes in the Vale? Manorial records were of no use for these parishes and wills proved of limited value.[76] Of 448 decedents, 28.6 per cent were intestate, and over 30 percent of those who did make wills did not mention any land whatsoever. Conclusions based on this sample must therefore be tentative. Where property was itemized it most frequently took the form of dwelling houses. Wills mentioning one dwelling usually belonged to persons worth less than £50, while decedents leaving more than one property generally had over £100. There was a strong correlation between wealth and the probability that a will would mention land. Under 10 percent of estates worth less than £50 had wills giving details of land compared to 20 percent for the £50 to £99 group, 28 percent for the £100 to £249 group, and 43 percent for the £250 plus group.

A study of chattel leases valued in inventories confirmed that the rich were more likely to own land than the poor (see table 7). The great majority of leases found in the estates of the poor and lower-middling groups were valued at under £20 and most commonly refer to a house, tenement, or garden. By comparison, 43 percent of the middling estates (those worth between £100 to £249) and 73 percent of the rich had leases worth over £50. Half the chattel leases mentioned in the inventories of rich persons were valued at over £100.[77]

The most important conclusion of this investigation is that real wealth and personal wealth do seem related. Common sense suggests that this should be the case. Big yeomen required more land for their livestock and crops than their smaller neighbours, while rich clothiers, mercers, and gentlemen were likely to have more capital to spare for investing in real estate than less wealthy men. Of course, this does not mean that personal wealth can be used as a surrogate for total wealth, but what it does indicate is that the distribution of wealth estimated from inventories is reliable. The relative proportions of poor, middling, and rich are reasonably accurate. If real estate were added the range of wealth would increase and the differentials become larger, but it would not alter greatly the proportions of the component groups. Thus inventories can provide a means of stratifying society into wealth groups and also suggest minima for the differentials between those groups.

Conclusion

The aim of this essay has been to outline a method for measuring the distribution of wealth in local society by using probate records in conjunction with a variety of other sources. It is recognized that not all areas of England are as fortunate as Gloucestershire in having a seventeenth-century occupational census, but where there are good series of inventories, wills, reliable parish registers, and extant hearth tax returns this method should be possible. Considering the time and energy expended what are its advantages? Estimating inventory coverage provides a degree of control over the data. Two samples of inventories, from different periods or areas, may produce very different wealth distributions, but this might simply be the result of more, or less, rich decedents being represented in one sample than the other. An area with few poor people going through probate may seemingly have a high level of wealth, whereas a neighbouring area with more poor leaving inventories may appear less prosperous. The results obtained from an analysis of the distribution of wealth are obviously dependent on the sorts of people leaving inventories. Therefore it is important to check how representative they are of the whole population and whether the proportion of rich and poor changes over time.

The principal advantage of using inventories to study wealth distribution, however, is that they contain a mass of information which can be of value in other related analyses. 'Where else,' concludes Francis Steer, 'could we get such evidence for the development of, and changes in, household furniture, the improvement of living conditions, the incidence of particular trades, the names and values of a multitude of objects and goods which reflect the day-to-day needs of all types of society?'[78] Moreover, used with caution, inventories provide historians with an unparalleled opportunity to compare these aspects of everyday life across time and space.[79]

As G.S. Holmes points out, 'The social structure of pre-industrial England was a thing of infinite subtlety. It deserves to be studied intensively . . . and in its own right.'[80] Much the same can be said of the distribution of wealth. Local studies, such as this of the Vale of Berkeley, may provide the key to a greater awareness of the relationship between wealth and social structure, and to a better understanding of wealth distribution throughout seventeenth-century England as a whole.

Table 1

Occupations of Militiamen compared to those of Male Decedents leaving Probate Records, Vale of Berkeley, 1608 – 99

Occupational Category	Militiamen, 1608[a]		Decedents Leaving Probate Records, 1660–99[b]	
	N	%	N	%
I. Gentry and Professions	45	2.2	58	8.9
II. Agriculture	529	25.9	328	50.5
III. Food and Drink Trades	95	4.7	36	5.5
IV. Textile Industry	856	41.9	155	23.8
V. Building/Woodwork Trades	103	5.0	30	4.6
VI. Metalwork	44	2.2	14	2.2
VII. Leather Trades	105	5.1	16	2.5
VIII. Semi-skilled and Unskilled Labour	254	12.4	9	1.4
IX. Miscellaneous	10	0.5	4	0.6
Total	2041	99.9	650	100.0

Sources: a)   John Smyth, *Men and Armour for Gloucestershire in 1608,* (London, 1902). John W. Wyatt, unpublished research.

b)   Gloucestershire Record Office, Probate Inventories, 1660–99; Consistory Court Journal, 1668–1676; Will Act Book, 1678–1681; Wills, 1660–99; Register of Administrations, 1677–1683; Register of Wills and Administrations, 1683–1704; Accounts of Administration, 1684–99.

Public Record Office, P.C.C. Inventories, PROB 4 and 5.

Table 2

Occupations of Male Decedents leaving Probate Records compared to those of Prospective Bridegrooms seeking Marriage Licences, Vale of Berkeley, 1660 – 1699

Occupational Category	Decedents leaving [a] Probate Records, 1660–99		Prospective [b] Bridegrooms, 1661–84	
	N	%	N	%
I. Gentry and Professions	58	8.9	54	13.0
II. Agriculture	328	50.5	189	45.7
III. Food and Drink Trades	36	5.5	16	3.9
IV. Textile Industry	155	23.8	121	29.2
V. Building and Woodwork Trades	30	4.6	9	2.2
VI. Metalwork Trades	14	2.2	7	1.7
VII. Leather Trades	16	2.5	18	4.3
VIII. Semi- and Unskilled Labour	9	1.4	–	–
IX. Miscellaneous	4	0.5	–	–
Total	650	100.0	414	100.0

Sources: a) See Table 1, source (b).

b) Brian Frith, ed., *Gloucestershire Marriage Allegations, 1637–1700*, 2 vols., (Records Section of the Bristol and Gloucestershire Archaeological Society, 2 and 9).

Table 3

Unadjusted Percentage Distribution of Personal Wealth, Vale of Berkeley, 1660 – 99

Decade	£<£9.99 %	£10–£49.99 %	£50–£99.99 %	£100–£249.99 %	£250 plus %
1660–9	5.0	32.5	23.8	22.5	16.3
1670–9	9.2	34.8	24.1	20.6	11.3
1680–9	4.8	30.3	23.6	24.7	16.6
1690–9	9.9	32.6	18.8	24.7	14.1
1660–99	7.0	31.8	22.2	23.9	15.1
N 983					

Source: See Table 1, source (b).

Table 4

Wealth Distribution Adjusted to Include the Poor

Assumption A: 50% Poor (1664 Hearth Tax indicates that 50% of households were non-chargeable)

£<£50	£50–£99	£100–£249	£250 plus
69.4%	11.1%	12.0%	7.5%

Assumption B: 33.3% Poor (1672 Hearth Tax)

£<£50	£50–£99	£100–£249	£250 plus
59.2%	14.8%	15.9%	10.0%

Source: See Table 1, source (b).
        P.R.O., E179/247/16; E179/247/13; E179/247/14.

Table 5

Distribution of Rented Land on the Berkeley Manors, 1667

Holding (Acres)	N	%	Cumulative %
House/Cottage/Shop or less than 4 acres	126	30.7	30.7
4 – 9	54	13.1	43.8
10 – 19	57	13.9	57.7
20 – 49	82	20.0	77.7
50 – 99	56	13.6	91.3
100 – 199	13	3.2	94.5
200 – 499	2	0.5	95.0
500 plus	1	0.2	95.2
Others	2	0.5	95.7
Unknown	18	4.4	100.1
Total	411	100.1	

Source: 'Rentals of Different Manors, 1667,' Berkeley MSS, Unbound books, 50, Berkeley Castle.

Table 6 **Landownership and Personal Wealth, Berkeley Manors, 1660-1699**

Wealth Group	No Land	<19 Acres	20-49 Acres	50-99 Acres	100+ Acres	Tene'ts, Houses, Etc.	Land (no acreage)
<£ 10	47.2	38.9	2.8	—	—	8.3	2.8
10-49	48.0	30.3	4.0	2.9	—	5.7	9.1
50-99	46.8	15.3	6.3	2.7	—	11.7	17.1
100-249	31.2	13.9	11.5	6.6	0.8	9.8	26.2
250 plus	20.7	—	15.9	22.0	8.5	6.1	26.8
N 526							

Note: All figures percentages.

Sources:
Probate records, see Table 1, source (b). 'Rentals of Different Manors, 1667,'

Berkeley MSS, Unbound books, 50, Berkeley Castle; Berkeley Manor Court Books, 1656-1661, 1666-1671, 1676-1682, 1680-1688, 1688-1693, 1694-1702, General Series Nos. 50, 52, 55, 56, 57, 60, Berkeley Castle; 'Manor of Hill *als* Hull in County of Gloucester, [1650], G.R.O., D 908; 'An Estimate of E[dward] F[ust] his Estate in the County of Gloucester, taken June 1660,' G.R.O., D 908; 'Rental for the Manor of Hill for the year 1674,' G.R.O, D 908; 'The halfe yeares Rentall of the old Rents of the mannor of Worteley, 10 April 1678,' G.R.O., D 1086, M15.

Table 7 **Personal Wealth and Chattel Leases, Vale of Berkeley, 1660-1699**

Wealth Group £	Value of Chattel Leases				
	£<19	£20-49	£50-99	£100-200	£200 plus
<10	70.8	20.8	4.2	4.2	—
10-49	53.8	30.8	9.6	5.8	—
50-99	26.7	20.0	23.3	26.7	3.3
100-249	29.5	27.3	13.6	15.9	13.6
250 plus	9.8	17.1	22.0	29.3	22.0
N 191					

Note: All figures percentages.

Source: Probate inventories, 1660-1699, G.R.O.; Public Record Office, P.C.C. Inventories, PROB 4 and 5.

Appendix

Mean and Median Personal Wealth of Males by Occupation or Status, Vale of Berkeley, 1660-1699

Occupation or Status	Mean £	Median £	N
Mercers	563.01	440.60	12
Clothiers	369.57	213.95	35
Clergy	327.42	210.56	10
Tanners	307.19	348.50	7
Gentry	280.80	163.00	39
Butchers	219.03	126.41	7
Yeomen	172.23	137.80	223
Bakers	128.26	137.54	7
Blacksmiths	93.07	92.09	14
Husbandmen	86.29	58.78	49
Innholders/Victuallers	72.02	73.98	18
Carpenters	70.43	46.28	12
Shoemakers/Cordwainers	54.34	44.29	6
Clothworkers/Drawers	50.51	38.18	21
Tailors	49.63	24.31	10
Weavers	46.86	40.08	58

N 528

Sources: See Table 1, source (b).

Notes

I would like to thank Dr J.D. Marshall for his help and advice in preparing this article.

[1] Gregory King, 'Natural and Political Observations and Conclusions upon the State and Condition of England, 1696,' in *An Estimate of the Comparative Strength of Great Britain . . .*, ed. George Chalmers (London, 1804), Appendix, p.31.

[2] See, for example, Michel Fleury and Louis Henry, *Des registres paroissiaux a l'histoire de la population: manuel de dépouillement et d'exploitation de l'état civil ancien* (Paris, 1956); *idem, Nouveau manuel de dépouillement et d'exploitation de l'état civil ancien* (Paris, 1965); Pierre Goubert, 'Registres paroissiaux et demographie dans la France du XVIe siècle,' *Annales de Demographie Historique*, (1965), pp. 43-48; *idem*, 'Recent Theories and Research in French Population Between 1500 and 1700,' in *Population in History, Essays in Historical Demography*, ed. D.V. Glass and D.E.C. Eversley, (London, 1965), pp. 457-473. Thomas H. Hollingsworth, *Historical Demography* (Cambridge, 1969), pp. 160-166. For a description of the methods employed by the Cambridge Group for the History of Population and Social Structure, see *An Introduction to English Historical Demography: From the Sixteenth to the Nineteenth Century*, ed. E.A. Wrigley, (London, 1966).
(London, 1966).

[3] E.J. Buckatzsch, 'The Geographical Distribution of Wealth in England, 1086-1843. An Experimental Study of Certain Tax Assessments,' *Economic History Review*, (hereafter *EcHR*), 2nd ser., III (1950), pp. 180-202; R.S. Schofield, 'The Geographical Distribution of Wealth in England, 1334-1649,' *EcHR*, 2nd ser., XVIII (1965), pp. 483-510; J.P. Cooper, 'The Social Distribution of Land and Men in England, 1436-1700,' *EcHR*, 2nd ser., XX (1967), pp. 419-440; Richard Grassby, 'The Personal Wealth of the Business Community in Seventeenth-Century England,' *EcHR*, 2nd ser., XXIII (1970), pp. 220-234; Mildred Campbell, *The English Yeoman under Elizabeth and the Early Stuarts*, (London, 1967. Orig. publ. 1942), pp. 217-220; A. Simpson, *The Wealth of the Gentry, 1540-1660*, (East Anglian Studies, 1961); M.E. Finch, *The Wealth of Five Northamptonshire Families* (Northants Record Society, XIX, 1956). Useful local studies of wealth distribution include Margaret Spufford, 'The Significance of the Cambridgeshire Hearth Tax,' *Proceedings of the Cambridge Antiquarian Society*, LV (1962), pp. 53-64; R. Machin, 'Social Structure from Tudor Lay Subsidies and Probate Inventories. A Case Study: Richmondshire (Yorkshire),' *Local Population Studies*, No. 12 (Spring, 1974), pp. 9-24; W.G. Hoskins, *Industry, Trade and People in Exeter, 1688-1800* (University College of the South-West of England, Monograph No. 6, 1935), pp. 111-122; J.D. Marshall, 'Social Structure and Wealth in Pre-Industrial England.' (Paper presented to the British Association for the Advancement of Science, Sept, 1977).

[4] This situation is in contrast to the numerous articles on wealth distribution undertaken by scholars of colonial American society, for example: Alice Hanson Jones, 'Wealth Estimates for the American Middle Colonies, 1774,' *Economic Development and Cultural Change*, XVIII, no.4, pt.2 (July, 1970), pp. 1-172; *idem*, 'Wealth Estimates for the New England Colonies about 1770,' *Journal of Economic History*, XXXII (1972), pp. 98-127; Gloria L. Main, 'Personal Wealth in Colonial America: Explorations in the Use of Probate Records from Maryland and Massachusetts, 1650-1720,' (Ph.D. diss., Columbia University, 1972); *idem*, 'Probate Records as a Source for Early American History,' *William and Mary Quarterly*, 3d ser., XXXIII (1975), pp. 89-99; Russell R. Menard, P.M.G. Harris, and Lois Green Carr, 'Opportunity and Inequality: The Distribution of Wealth on the Lower Western Shore of Maryland, 1638-1705,' *Maryland Historical Magazine*, LXIX, (1974), pp. 169-184; T.L. Anderson, 'Wealth Estimates for the New England Colonies, 1650-1709,' *Explorations in Economic History*, XII (1975), pp. 151-176.

[5] Gregory King, *op.cit.*

[6] G.S. Holmes, 'Gregory King and the Social Structure of Pre-Industrial England,' *Transactions of the Royal Historical Society*, 5th ser., XXVII (1977), p. 41*n*.

[7] *Ibid.*, p. 63.

[8] *Ibid.*, p. 41.

[9] *Ibid.*, p. 65*n*.

[10] For considerations of the problems of using inventories, see Marshall, *op. cit.*, pp. 2-3; Grassby, *op.cit.*, p. 220. John S. Moore, ed., *The Goods and Chattels of Our Forefathers; Frampton Cotterell and District Probate Inventories, 1539-1804* (Chichester, 1976), pp. 2-4.

[11] Henry Swinburne *A Treatise of Testaments and Last Wills* (1677, Orig. publ. 1590), p. 345.

[12] *Ibid.*, pp. 345, 349.

[13] *Ibid.*, pp. 345-346. David Hey states that leases held for less than 100 years were considered chattels and were therefore to be entered in an inventory, *An English Rural Community: Myddle under the Tudors and Stuarts* (Leicester, 1974), p. 73.

[14] Swinburne, *op.cit.*, p. 346.

[15] None of these items appeared in a sample of over 800 inventories from the Vale of Berkeley, 1587-1700.

[16] Swinburne, *op.cit.*, p. 349.

[17] Marshall, *op.cit.*, pp. 10, 52, 53.

[18] Cicely A.H. Howell, 'The Economic and Social Condition of the Peasantry in South East Leicestershire, A.D. 1300-1700,' (unpubl. D. Phil. diss., Oxford University, 1974), pp. 179-180; John S. Moore, private correspondence with the author.

[19] Data on the price of crops and livestock in the Vale of Berkeley were obtained from the following: 'The Farm Accounts of Nathaniel Clutterbuck of Eastington', [Gloucestershire, c. 1650-1673], 'Gloucestershire Record Office, (hereafter G.R.O.), D149/F13; 'John Thurston's Accounts. [1705-1706],' G.R.O., D866/E3; 'Accounts of Coz. John Harding, [1680],' G.R.O., D149/A4; Nathaniel Thurston's Account Book, 1680,' G.R.O., D866/E1.

[20] G.R.O., Inventories, 1686/115 and 1687/14.

[21] G.R.O., Inventories, 1682/2 and 1684/122.

[22] Moore, *op.cit.*, p.4.

[23] Population figures for the 17th century were derived from the following: 1603, Gloucester diocese parishes, number of communicants: British Library, Harleian MS. 594, ff. 224-255; 1650, all parishes, number of families: C.R. Elrington, 'The Survey of Church Livings in Gloucestershire, 1650,' *Transactions of the Bristol and Gloucestershire Archaeological Society*, (hereafter *B.G.A.S.*), LXXXIII (1964), pp. 93, 95, 96, 97; 1664, Hearth tax, all parishes, numbers of households: P.R.O., E179/247/16; 1672, Hearth tax, all parishes, numbers of households: P.R.O., E179/247/13, E179/247/14; 1676, Compton Census, Gloucester diocese parishes, number of communicants and dissenters: William Salt Library, Stafford MS. 33.

[24] G.R.O.: Inventories, 1660-1699; Consistory Court Journal, 1668-1676; Will Act Book, 1678-1681; Wills, 1660-1699; Register of Administrations, 1677-1683; Register of Wills and Administrations, 1683-1704; Accounts of Administrations, 1684-1699; P.R.O., Prerogative Court of Canterbury Inventories, PROB 4 and 5.

[25] Marshall, *op.cit.*, pp. 37-39. An alternative method using model life tables is discussed in Carole Shammas, 'The Determinants of Personal Wealth in Seventeenth-Century England and America,' *Journal of Economic History*, XXXVII (1977), pp. 675-689.

[26] A survey of extant parish registers is given in *Guide to Parish Records of the City of Bristol and the County of Gloucester*, ed. Irvine Gray and Elizabeth Ralph, (Records Section of the Bristol and Gloucestershire Archaeological Society, vol. 5, 1963).

[27] Hollingsworth, *op.cit.*, pp. 139-145, 187-195; Thomas H. Hollingsworth, 'The Importance of the Quality of the Data in Historical Demography,' *Daedalus*, (Spring, 1968), pp. 415-432; John T. Krause, 'The Changing Adequacy of English Registration, 1690-1837,' in Glass and Eversley, *op.cit.*, pp. 379-393.

[28] G.R.O., D2052.

[29] *Ibid.*

[30] *Ibid.*

[31] The problem of decedents being buried outside of their home parishes was mitigated by studying a fifteen-parish region. If a decedent was from another parish it was usually recorded in the burial register. On the basis of this information it appears that only a small fraction of the dead were buried outside of their native parishes.

[32] Coverage before 1678 is poor. Only 55 inventories have survived for the period 1587-1650, and none between 1651 and 1659. After 1660 coverage improves but is not consistently high until after 1677. This peak lasts for abut 20 years before declining after 1697.

[33] Marshall, *op.cit.*, p. 38.

[34] Daniel Scott Smith, 'Underregistration and Bias in Probate Records: An Analysis of Data from Eighteenth-Century Hingham, Massachusetts,' *William and Mary Quarterly*, 3d ser., XXXII (1975), p. 104.

[35] See Menard, Harris, and Carr, *op.cit.*, pp. 174-176; Russell R. Menard, 'The

Comprehensiveness of Probate Inventories in St. Mary's County, Maryland, 1658 to 1777: A Preliminary Report,' (MS., Hall of Records, Annapolis, Maryland, 1976); Main, 'Personal Wealth in Colonial America,' pp. 28-37.

    [36] This estimate is based on conversations with John S. Moore and J.D. Marshall, and the research of Carole Shammas, *op.cit.* I should like to stress that this opinion is entirely my own and refers to limited periods of high coverage only.

    [37] According to the Statute 21 H.8.c.5.ff.2-7, persons leaving less than £5 worth of personal goods were exempt from fees except 6d for the scribe. Persons worth between £5 and £40 paid 3s 6d, and persons worth over £40 paid 5s. These provisions were revised by Archbishop Stratford as follows: persons worth less than 30s paid 6d; persons worth between 30s and £5 paid 1s; between £5 and £20, 3s; between £20 and £60, 5s; between £60 and £100, 10s; between £100 and £150, 20s; and for every £50 above this limit, 10s more. See Richard Burn, *Ecclesiastical Law*, II, (London, 1763), pp. 625-626, 642.

    [38] *Ibid.*, p. 628.

    [39] Ronald A. Marchant, *The Church Under Law: Justice, Administration, and Discipline in the Diocese of York, 1560-1640* (Cambridge, 1969), pp. 31-32.

    [40] This statement is based on an examination of causes brought before the consistory court of the diocese of Gloucester, 1639-1683. I am obliged to Dr. Andrew Foster for his help and advice concerning this material. G.R.O., GDR volumes 205, 211, 219, 221, 232.

    [41] P.R.O., E179/247/16.

    [42] There were no returns for Frampton-on-Severn, Kingswood, Thornbury, and Tytherington.

    [43] P.R.O., E179/247/13, E179/247/14.

    [44] Berkeley Borough and Alkington, 1683-1713, Berkeley MSS., 173, Berkeley Castle; Kingswood, 1674-1698, G.R.O., P193, OV 2/1; Slimbridge, 1635-1693, G.R.O., P298a, OV 2/1, 2/2; Stinchcombe, 1667-1700, G.R.O., P312, OV 2/1; Thornbury, 1655-1690, G.R.O., D688/1, P330, OV 2/1.

    [45] John Smyth, *Men and Armour for Gloucestershire in 1608* (London, 1902); John W. Wyatt, unpublished research. I would like to thank Mr. Wyatt for generously allowing me to use his data.

    [46] J. de L. Mann, *The Cloth Industry in the West of England from 1640-1880* (Oxford, 1971); R. Perry, 'The Gloucestershire Woollen Industry, 1100-1690,' *B.G.A.S.*, LXVI (1945), pp. 49-137; Jennifer Tann, *Gloucestershire Woollen Mills* (Newton Abbot, 1967); Peter J. Bowden, *The Wool Trade in Tudor and Stuart England* (London, 1962).

    [47] 'A Booke of actes, rates, and monuments of the parish of Cam in the County of Gloucestershire . . . [c.1625-1730],' Berkeley MSS., General Series, 95, p. 50.

    [48] Cited by Tann, *op.cit.*, p. 38.

    [49] *Ibid.*

    [50] L.A. Clarkson, *The Pre-Industrial Economy in England, 1500-1750* (London, 1971), pp. 233-234.

    [51] It is recognized that there may be differences between the occupational structure of living males and that represented by decedents. However, these differences should not invalidate the general conclusions presented here.

    [52] Brian Frith, *Gloucestershire Marriage Allegations, 1637-1700* (Records Section of the B.G.A.S., vols. 2 and 9, 1954, 1970).

    [53] *Ibid.*, p. xviii; Appendix C, pp. 213-214.

    [54] It is not uncommon for persons to describe themselves differently in their will compared to their neighbours' opinion of them in their inventory. For the purposes of this study, the description of occupation or status in the inventory was given precedence over that in the will.

    [55] See burial registers of Berkeley, 1696-1706; Cromhall, 1697-1705; Dursley, 1680-1699; and Wotton-under-Edge, 1688-1707.

    [56] Chattel leases were not included in the totals in order to remove land entirely

from the calculations. Personal wealth is therefore defined in this study as all movables except leases. This procedure raises problems about the interpretation of the wealth of those estates where only inventory valuations survive. It is obviously impossible to ascertain whether they include chattel leases or not. However, the great majority of inventories (75%) do not show any evidence of leases and it is likely that a similar proportion applies to inventory valuations. Almost all the valuations refer to the period 1677-1683 and do not influence the results after 1684. Considering their value in supplementing the inventory sample it was decided not to leave them out.

[57] The relationship between the mean and median provides a crude indication of whether wealth was becoming more, or less, equally distributed. See, for example, Menard, Harris, and Carr, *op.cit.*, pp. 171-174. It was considered unadvisable to attempt to adjust the data to the age structure of the living population for the following reasons: 1) the inventory sample is representative of only about half the total number of adult decedents from the region and is biased towards the wealthier members of society; 2) the age structure of both the living and the dead is unknown; 3) age-specific mortality rates are unknown. An analysis of the relationship between age and wealth will be reserved for a subsequent study.

[58] E.H. Phelps Brown and Seila V. Hopkins, 'Seven Centuries of the Prices of Consumables, Compared with Builders' Wage Rates,' *Economica*, XXIII (1956), Appendix B.

[59] During the 1640s burial registers are generally less reliable because of the disruption caused by the Civil Wars, while for the 1618-1621 period only 41 estates have survived for a 4-year period. Assuming that the population was not significantly higher in the 1680s than in 1618-1621, an average of 10 inventories per year is well below the 30 to 40 average for the later period.

[60] For similar conclusions, see Hey, *op.cit.*, p. 55; Marshall, *op. cit.*, p. 35.

[61] The official requirement was that persons with less than £10 in personal goods should be exempted from the hearth tax but it is possible that persons described as non-chargeable had more than this or had acquired more by the time they died. Although £50 is an arbitrary limit, it is considered unlikely that the poor who failed to go through probate had more than this.

[62] Clarkson, *op.cit.*, p. 238.

[63] Marshall, *op.cit.*, p. 13.

[64] *Ibid.*, p. 12.

[65] *Ibid.*, p. 13.

[66] Moore, *op.cit.*, pp. 24-25.

[67] For the attraction of forest-pasture regions, see Thirsk, ed., *Agrarian History of England and Wales*, p. 80; P.A. Slack, 'Vagrants and Vagrancy in England, 1598-1664,' *EcHR*, 2nd ser., XXVII (1974), pp. 374-376.

[68] See John Smyth, *op.cit.*, *passim*, and Robert Atkyns, *The Ancient and Present State of Gloucestershire* (London, 1712), *passim*.

[69] Ten manors located in the parishes of Berkeley, Cam, North Nibley, Slimbridge, and Wotton-under-Edge were owned by the Lords Berkeley, and the manor of Hill, in Berkeley, was owned by Edward Fust: 'Rentals of Different Manors, 1667,' Berkeley MSS., Unbound books, 50; 'Manor of Hill *als* Hull in County of Gloucester, [1650],' G.R.O., D908; 'Rental for the Manor of Hill for the year 1674,' G.R.O., D908. Other rentals are extant for Frampton-on-Severn, Dursley, Kingswood, Thornbury, and Wotton-under-Edge but do not give acreages or only refer to one or two years.

[70] Atkyns, *op.cit.*

[71] 'Rentals of Different Manors, 1667,' Berkeley MSS., Unbound books, 50; Berkeley Manor Court Books, 1656-1661, 1666-1671, 1676-1682, 1680-1688, 1688-1693, 1694-1702, General Series, 50, 52, 55-57, 60, Berkeley Castle; G.R.O., Wills, 1660-1699. I would like to thank the Trustees of the Berkeley Estate for allowing me to use the records held in the muniment room of Berkeley Castle.

[72] 'Rentals of Different Manors, 1667'.

[73] 'A booke of rentalls of all the Lord Berkeleys lands, [1634], MS., Gloucestershire Collection, 16066, Gloucester City Library.

[74] Atkyns, *op.cit.*

[75] *Ibid.*, p. 22.

[76] In particular, wills were disappointingly silent on acreages of land bequeathed and on the total amount of land owned by the testator.

[77] G.R.O., Inventories, 1660-1699; P.R.O., P.C.C. Inventories, PROB 4 and 5.

[78] Francis W. Steer, 'Probate Inventories,' *Short Guides to Records*, no. 3 (The Historical Association, n.d.), p. 290.

[79] See Main, 'Personal Wealth in Colonial America;' Shammas, *op.cit.*

[80] Holmes, *op.cit.*, p. 65.

Two 1820 steam vessels entering Margate Harbour.   (Margate Public Library).

Water communications to Margate and Gravesend as coastal resorts before 1840

J. WHYMAN

Whilst the emergence of popular seaside resorts is attributed invariably to railways, the resorts of Margate, Gravesend, Herne Bay, Broadstairs, Ramsgate, Deal, and Dover assumed varying significance as pre-railway Kentish watering-places, and railways only contributed to but did not induce the popularization of Margate and Gravesend. This is a distinction which belongs to water communications, specifically to steamboats in the case of Gravesend, and to hoys, sailing packets, and steamboats in the case of Margate; but whereas bathing in salt water had its origins in Gravesend late in the eighteenth century,[1] a somewhat different and earlier time scale must be applied to Margate.[2]

The 1847 holiday season was the first to benefit Margate by way of an influx of railway visitors travelling on the first railway link between London and Thanet, namely the South Eastern Railway which, having been extended from Ashford, was opened to Margate on 1 December 1846. Although that event was a milestone in Margate's history,[3] Margate was by then more than a century old as a sea-bathing resort. Indeed, it was a Margate carpenter, named Thomas Barber, who had launched the town on to a new career as a watering place when he first advertised a sea water bath with 'convenient Lodgings to be Lett', in *The Kentish Post and Canterbury News Letter* of 17 July 1736.

Margate's pre-railway 'popularization' can be indicated in several ways. Water communications were vital to its early rise to maturity as an English seaside resort. The lower fares which prevailed on hoys and steamboats, compared with those on coaches, introduced a cross section of visitors, so that Margate soon became an exception to the general rule that Hanoverian watering places were almost exclusively the resorts of the upper classes. Margate did not benefit from royal patronage which contributed so enormously to the expansion of Brighton or Weymouth.[4] The prosperity of Margate and Brighton resulted from contrasting causes (hoys and royalty) and was observed by *The Times* of 1 September 1804.

> Margate, August 30 . . . has not been so full of visitors for eight years past . . . Every *hoy* or, according to the modern term, every *packet* is literally *loaded*. The smallest of these vessels brought down 120 persons yesterday morning . . . [But] there are not here, at present, many persons of high rank and fashion.
> Brighton, Thursday, August 30 . . . is at present unusually full of company; and the presence of his ROYAL HIGHNESS has its obvious influence on the vivacities of the place.

Margate was also the first seaside resort to become 'popular' in the widest interpretation of that word, and especially as applied to amenities and recreations, a fact acknowledged by historians and historical geographers, including Professor Gilbert.[5] Gravesend with an even closer proximity to a teeming London, being fed with visitors from the natural highway of the Thames, was 'popular' from the outset. To *The Maidstone Journal and Kentish Advertiser* of 31 May 1825, this town was 'universally known as the goal of every young cockney's Sunday excursion', where 'excellent accommodations for bathing of every kind have been provided'.

Two distinct phases can be identified in the development of water communications and the expansion of Margate and Gravesend before 1840. Prior to 1815, hoys or sailing packets played a decisive role in Margate's early rise to maturity as an English seaside resort. During 1814, however, Sir Marc Brunel introduced to Margate harbour the first steam packet, *The Thames*, powered only by one 16 h.p. engine[6] and this event introduced the steamboat era, which reached its zenith during the 1830's. Margate between 1815 and 1840 enjoyed increasing renown as a well developed and popular steamboat resort. Despite a long history of water communication between Gravesend and London, the economic and social significance of which did not escape the notice of Daniel Defoe and other contemporaries of the eighteenth century,[7] Gravesend rose suddenly to fame as a popular Thamesside resort following the introduction of steamboats in 1815. Their impact was so immediate that a 'flood-time came. Steamboat companies were formed . . . Piers were proposed [and] erected . . . Baths were erected. Pleasure gardens were founded and developed.'[8]

Travelling by hoys or sailing packets and their impact on the growth and character of Margate before 1815.

Margate's development as a seaside resort is portrayed from the middle of the eighteenth century in guidebooks, directories, topographical works, newspapers, and journals, several of which attributed Margate's success to hoys and sailing packets. Two references suffice to illustrate this point. Intending visitors were informed in 1797 that

> during the season, eight Packets sail to and from *London* alternately, and frequently make the passage in ten or twelve hours. They not only bring a great part of the company, but [also] such necessaries, for their accommodation, as cannot be supplied by *Margate* . . . These vessels are fitted up with a degree of elegance and convenience, that at once shows the emulative spirit of their owners, who are men of respectability; and to whose persevering exertions *Margate* must be thought not a little indebted for its present prosperity.[9]

Five years later it was suggested that 'it is perhaps owing . . . to the very superior accommodation which they afford, as well as to the civility and attention of the masters and seamen who navigate them, that Margate stands so highly distinguished in the list of watering places'.[10]

Historians argue that railway communications have determined the fortunes of most English seaside resorts,[11] yet a journey to Margate presented no great obstacles, because hoys and, later, steamboats operated regular, frequent and cheap services from and to London. Margate's eighteenth-century prosperity was founded on communications by hoy or sailing packet, exploiting the almost exclusive advantage of a direct and low-cost water-communication link with London, using the Thames as a natural waterway.

The significance of hoys was apparent to John Lyons when he compiled Margate's first guidebook in 1763.

> As *Margate* is only a large village, you cannot expect that it should be so regularly supplied with shops, as a market-town; not but that there are several good ones, and many very reputable Tradesmen. This deficiency is, in a great measure, supplied by the numerous articles to be found in most of them, and by their ready and quick communication with *London* by the Hoys. Was it not for the assistance of these vessels, it would be almost impossible for *Margate*, and the country round it, to furnish entertainment for the vast numbers of people who resort to it. They are sloops of eighty or a hundred tons burden. There are four of them, two of which sail in alternate weeks . . . They usually leave *Margate* on *Friday* or *Saturday*, and London on *Wednesday* or *Thursday*. Passengers, of whom there are often sixty or seventy, pay only 2*s* 6*d* and the freight of baggage

is inconsiderable. They sometimes make the passage in eight hours, and at others in two or three days, just as winds and tides happen to be for, or against, them . . . The passage is cheap, and in fine weather extremely pleasant and agreeable . . . The Masters are very careful, decent men . . . They transact incredible business.[12]

Although by then Benjamin Beale had perfected the famous Margate bathing machine, Margate was still an infant resort, having as yet to embark on a sustained building boom which produced fashionable squares and permanent assembly rooms from 1769 onwards, circulating libraries from 1766 onwards, a permanent Theatre Royal in 1787, a charter for holding a twice weekly market in 1777, and the first of several Improvement Acts from 1787 onwards.

Hoys, as single-masted cargo sailing vessels, usually carrying corn into London and returning to Thanet with shop goods,[13] had developed the habit of conveying 'passengers and luggage along the sea coast'[14] prior to the onset of sea bathing. They can be traced back to the 1630s.[15] Passengers and their luggage triumphed ultimately over corn and other cargo and purely passenger-conveying sailing packets or yachts emerged which were considered somewhat superior to the old hoy. Greater respectability was bestowed on hoys by renaming them 'packets' as the watchful eye of *The Times* noted on 1 September 1804.

Table 1, derived from details found in contemporary guidebooks, directories, and newspapers, summarizes the number of hoys, packets, or yachts and the trend of fares on the London to Margate run between 1763 and 1815.

TABLE 1: *Vessels employed and the fares charged on the London to Margate sea route, 1763_1815*

Year	Hoys	Packets or yachts	Fares
1763	4		2s 6d
1770	5		2s 6d
1780	5	1	2s 6d
1789	6		4s
1792	6		10s 6d, 6s, 4s
1796	3	8	10s 6d, 7s, 5s

Year	Hoys	Packets or yachts	Best Cabin	Fore Cabin
1802		9	7s	5s
1807	3	9	7s	5s
1809	2	9	9s	7s
1811	3	11	9s	7s
1812	7	7s	5s	
1815	7–13	7s	5s	

There was an impressive increase in the number of vessels operating between 1763 and 1811. During the Napoleonic Wars between 1811 and 1815 some of the packets were switched from passenger carrying to troop carrying, but from advertisements placed in *The Times* it is clear that at least seven packets continued to ply regularly with passengers between London and Margate during the summer months of 1812 to 1815. The minimum single fare ranged from 2s 6d to 7s falling back to 5s in 1812 and 1815 — double that of 1763. A single fare obtained between 1763 and 1789, with complete stability until after 1780. The 1790s produced differential fares which were associated with greater comfort. Guidebooks of that decade emphasized how the packets were 'fitted up in an elegant and commodious manner, and furnished with good beds',[16] which were a real amenity whenever the hoys were becalmed or delayed by contrary winds or storms and as a result extended the sea voyage to and from London beyond a single day. By the 1800s some of the packets boasted 'a state-room or after-cabin, which 'could] be engaged by a select party for five or six guineas,[17] and three packets operating in 1815 had private state cabins, which could be hired separately.[18] Children in arms were conveyed at half fare in 1812.[19] In 1780, baggage was carried at under 6d per cwt,[20] and at later dates 'proportionably cheap'.[21]

Compared with the twice weekly sailings noted by John Lyond in 1763, a 1796 directory published a much improved pattern of sailings (see Table 2) which were daily during the season, with the added observation that 'the expense for each passenger is very moderate'.[22]

TABLE 2: *A list of yachts sailing between Margate and London during the season (1796)*

Name of Vessel	Sails	Returns	Fares	Master
Robert and Jane	Sunday	Thursday	5s 7s After Cabin 10s 6d	Capt. Kidd
Royal Charlotte	Monday	Friday	5s 7s	Capt. James Laming
Britannia	Friday	Wednesday	5s, 7d	Capt. Finch
Diligence	Saturday	Wednesday	5s, 7d	Capt. Sandwell
Duke of York	Tuesday	Saturday	5s, 7s	Capt. Kennard
New Rose in June	Wednesday	Sunday	5s, 7s, After Cabin 10s 6d	Capt. Palmer
Princess of Wales	Wednesday	Sunday	5s, 7d, After Cabin 10s 6d	Capt. Hillier
British Queen	Thursday	Monday	5s, 7s	Capt. R. Laming

'The Old Margate Hoy', as immortalized in 1823 by Charles Lamb,[23] was a popular target for caricature and literary and poetic licence. George Saville Carey offered the following advice to travellers in 1799: 'should you be disposed to go by water to Margate, you will often be under the necessity of arming yourself with a great deal of patience, and a good store of victuals; you must shut your eyes from seeing indecent scenes, your ears from indecent conversation, and your nose from indelicate smells'.[24] Both the arrival and departure of a hoy attracted great crowds, known as 'hoy fair', when Margate pier frequently accommodated 'upwards of a thousand persons of *all* distinctions, indiscriminately blended together'.[25]

Passengers frequently had to contend with long delays or were buffeted by storms. In 1832 Captain Kennett Beacham Martin who, prior to being an employee of the General Steam Navigation Company, had commanded a sailing packet for six years, praised the captains for their 'good pilotage and nautical skill' but noted that the elements were fickle and that a voyage 'begun in pleasurable anticipations too often terminated in delay and disappointment: on those occasions the passengers' provisions became exhausted, and ill humour seated itself beside the empty hamper'.[26] On one occasion (19 August 1781) a hoy arrived at Margate at one o'clock 'with very great difficulty', due to high winds and rough seas, so that 100 passengers, predominantly females, found themselves 'in a very dangerous and pitiable situation'.[27] Five years later a Margate hoy bound for London 'with near 100 persons on board' collided with a collier 'and very narrowly escaped going to the bottom'.[28] During 1797, one hoy bound for Margate took twenty-seven hours to complete its voyage, the passengers being driven below deck by rain which 'made them as comfortable as the people in the black hole [of] Calcutta'.[29] When *The Grand Falconer* was 'dismasted off the Reculvers' early on Sunday morning, 16 September 1810, its passengers were landed at Herne Bay and proceeded to Margate 'some on foot, and others in carts and other carriages'.[30]

In 1763, John Lyons had declined to recommend the hoy 'too strongly to Ladies of great delicacy',[31] yet, some years later, on her first visit ever to the seaside Catherine Hutton travelled down to Margate 'in nine hours and forty minutes [but] went back in thirty-six hours'. She recalled how 'for four hours after we got upon the sea I was miserably ill and in strong hysterics'.[32] Her travelling companion, Mrs André, 'was so disgusted with the hoy that she returned to town in the diligence'.[33] For one correspondent of 1800 the return passage was 'too fine to be expeditious', yet 'my female friends, . . . mild and fine as it was, were very sick indeed'.[34]

Despite such disadvantages a hoy journey to Margate did not necessarily occupy more time and was much cheaper than travelling by road. In 1771, the landward journey of 72 miles from London to Margate was accomplished in thirteen or fourteen hours at total fares of 16*s* to 19*s*.[35] During the 1790s the single coach journey cost between 21*s* and 26*s*.[36] or four or five times the minimum hoy fare of 5*s*. When Joseph Farington, R.A., the topographical artist and diarist, returned from Broadstairs to London he left Margate by coach at 5 a.m. on 27 August 1804, and arrived fourteen hours later in London at 7 p.m. prior to which he spent the night of the 26th in a Margate hotel.[37] Although coaches ran more reliably to scheduled timetables, which was one advantage they had over the erratic times of the hoys, the latter did offer passengers opportunities to stretch their legs and it still took eleven hours to accomplish the coach journey as late as 1815.[38]

It is not easy to calculate the total traffic which was handled by the Margate hoys and yet they seem to have carried more passengers than the coaches. Individual coaches accommodated up to six passengers inside,[39] with others riding on the outside. Even allowing for the 'great complaints' which were levied during August 1802 at the Brighton coaches for being 'loaded with passengers, not less than eight or ten persons being frequently stowed on the outside',[40] each individual coach carried relatively few passengers. The position could be very different on the individual hoy. A guidebook of 1797 proudly announced that the hoys 'sometimes bring above a *hundred* passengers at a time',[41] and this figure is supported by newspaper reports[42] it being noted by *The Times* on 16 September 1797 that 'so great is the rage for watering places, that the Margate packet had, the week before last, 152 passengers on board'. The maximum number of passengers who could be carried at any one time had risen considerably from the 60–70 mentioned by John Lyons in 1763.[43] On 24 August 1800, *The Observer* revealed that 'seven hoys last week conveyed to Margate 1,342 persons'.

In 1792 it was calculated that 'vessels bring and carry during the Bathing Season to and from London 18,000 passengers'.[44] This estimate is supported by figures which were presented in 1850 to the *Select Committee on Ramsgate and Margate Harbours* and which are shown in Table 3.

TABLE 3: *Passengers travelling to and from Margate on sailing packets.*[45]

April to April	No. of Passengers
1812–13	17,000
1813–14	20,506
1814–15	21,577

The volume of traffic handled by the hoys, coupled with their lower fares as compared with coaches, had important social consequences for Margate. Hoys were instrumental in bringing to Margate, perhaps more than to any other resort, a widening cross-section of society during a century which was so noted for elegance and high living. Cheap water communications facilitated the development of Margate as a middle and lower-class resort. In 1778 it was specifically stated of Margate that 'the middle and inferior classes may have recourse to the benefits of this place by the cheapness of a sea voyage; as hoys and yachts are continually passing between this place and *London* for the conveyance of goods and passengers at a very cheap rate'.[46] In 1789 it was further noted that 'the chief of the company which come by the hoys are, as you may naturally suppose, of the inferior cast; very few persons in genteel life come by water, without they are recommended by their physicians so to do, to experience the sea-sickness, which is thought to be very beneficial in some complaints'.[47] It became distinctly unfashionable to be seen travelling to Margate in a hoy, *The Times* being no less explicit on 10 September 1803 when it observed that 'at Margate the distinctive title of Fashionables is given without reserve to all the visitors of that agreeable watering place, who do not arrive there by the Hoy'.

Newspaper reports show that hoys lowered the social tone of Margate. According to *The Morning Post and Fashionable World* of 17 August 1795 'several caricaturists are now at Margate, [and] the exhibitions of the *City Ladies* ascending from the Hoys . . . present daily the most *whimsical* exhibitions'. *The Times* of 5 August 1799 noted how 'Margate is already beginning to be crowded, as usual, with all sorts, and for all purposes', added to which 'some tradesmen have gone down to get, and others to get rid of their money'.[48]

Wealthy families who avoided the hoy, nevertheless, took advantage of the cheaper water communications to transport their domestic servants. John Baker's diary records how on 12 September 1777 'the Hoy came in about 12 and in it the maid (Sally Matthews) Mrs Woodington hired in London'.[49] Domestic servants certainly accounted for a proportion of the summer passengers by hoy, as George Keate observed during the 1770s.

> There are always merry folks aboard. . . A crowd affords variety. . .It consisted of a few gentlemen, who, like myself, enjoyed a passage by sea; - some decent shopkeepers, and their wives, who had been washing off the summer dust of LONDON, - and the remainder chiefly composed of the servants of families, that had left MARGATE, who were all extremely communicative, and appeared to have spent their time in that happy idleness, which such an excursion from home usually gives them.[50]

Subsequently from the mid-1790s onwards domestic servants and shopkeepers were joined by patients travelling to and from the Margate or General Sea Bathing Infirmary which, being intended for poor people suffering from scrofula or tuberculosis, opened its doors at Westbrook on the outskirts of Margate during 1796 as 'the country's first hospital for tuberculosis'.[51] Its foundation five years previously in 1791 owed much to the famous eighteenth-century Quaker physician, Dr John Coakley Lettsom (1744–1815), who firmly believed that fresh air, sea water, sunlight, and regular habits were essential to the treatment of many diseases, especially those of the chest, and all tubercular troubles.[52] In promoting the institution he argued on 2 July 1791 that

> among the numerous places of resort on the Sea-coast none appeared to him, as well as to several others to whom he had intimated his design, so proper as Margate or its vicinity, the extreme salubrity of that part of the coast, and the ready and cheap conveyance thither giving that Place a decided preference to all others.[53]

Hoys fixed the location of a 'General Sea Bathing Infirmary' at Margate, as was made clear in 1801 in 'Hints for Establishing a Sea-Bathing Infirmary at Margate for the Poor of London', for 'by the Thames, a cheap conveyance to sea water is commanded, and hence Margate, or its vicinity, seems peculiarly adapted for this salutary purpose'.[54] By January 1816, within twenty years of its opening, it had treated 3756 patients.[55]

Margate was fairly unique in attracting shopkeeping holiday makers from the 1770s onwards. Some London shopkeepers set themselves up in business during the summer months but George Keate observed others who travelled to Margate purely for recreation and pleasure: 'the decent tradesman slips from town for his half-crown, and strolls up and down the Parade as much at his ease as he treads his own shop, [while] his wife, who perhaps never eloped so far from the metropolis before, stares with wonder at the many new objects which surround her'.[56]

Hoys stimulated the holiday trades of Margate, as *The Times* was quick to report during September 1804.

> We are now gathering in a most plenteous harvest. Ship and coach loads of cocknies are arriving every day, so that we are fuller than we have been all this season, which is one of the fullest we have ever known. Our lodging houses can with difficulty muster an extra bed for a new visitor; and all the provisions in our market are bought up early in the morning. .
>
> Our bathing machines are all in a state of constant requisition, and. . . our Doctors find the number of their patients considerably on the increase.[57]

Popular entertainments of the 1800s were pier promenading, a camera obscura and donkeys,[58] it being 'the fashion. . . especially at *Margate* for the Company to amuse themselves by riding on Asses'.[59]

Early-nineteenth century Margate suffered no want of popular amusements and during September 1810 was 'crowded with company, and indeed may be considered as London in miniature, being in many circumstances an epitome of that vast metropolis'.[60] It seems logical, therefore, to apply the label 'London-by-the-Sea' to Margate at an earlier date than it is applied to Brighton.

Travelling on steamboats and their impact on the growth and character of Margate and Gravesend, 1815–40.

Any analysis of pre-railway transport developments in Kent attaches little importance to the two canals which were constructed within the county.[61] Of considerable significance, however, were steamboat developments down the Thames to Gravesend and beyond to Herne Bay, Margate, and Ramsgate. The introduction of steamboats to Kent was as far reaching as the subsequent construction of railways. Compared with road, river, and harbour improvements, and canal and railway developments, the effects of steamboats were predominantly social rather than economic, being confined almost wholly to passenger transport, involving a substantial and expanding excursion element.

The introduction of steamboats to Gravesend and to Margate coincided with the end of the Napoleonic Wars. 1815 was the significant year when the *Marjory* became the first passenger steamer to work regularly on the Thames, running between London and Gravesend on alternate days;[62] when 'several gentlemen of London formed themselves into a company for establishing steam vessels between the metropolis and Margate';[63] and when steamboats began plying regularly from London to Margate, including the *Thames*[64] which *The Times* of 8 July 1815 described as a 'rapid, capacious and splendid vessel', having 'the peculiar advantage of proceeding either by sails or steam, separated or united, by which means the public have the pleasing certainty of never being detained on the water after dark, much less one or two nights, which has frequently occurred with the old packets'.[65] During September 1815, *The Gentleman's Magazine* reported on how 'a *Margate* hoy of large dimensions, propelled by steam, goes constantly to and from London to Margate, [and] from its novelty, and the certainty of its arrival within a given time (about twelve hours), it is much thronged with passengers'.[66]

A mixed reception was bestowed on the first steamboats. One early admirer of steamboats was (Sir) Rowland Hill, who was staying in Margate during the summer of 1815. He recollected how on 3 July,

> we went to see the steamboat come in from London. It is worked by means of two wheels, resembling water-wheels, one of which is placed on each side of the vessel, and about a-half sunk in the water. It comes from London and returns three times in each week. It generally performs the voyage in about twelve hours. In the best cabin there is a handsome library, draught-boards, etc. It is surprising to see how most people are prejudiced against this packet. Some say that it cannot sail against the wind if it is high; but when it entered the harbour the wind and tide were both against it, and the former rather rough, yet I saw it stem both. There was a great crowd, and much enthusiasm, though carpers predicted failure, and sneered at 'smoke-jacks'.[67]

Technologically, steamboats were not particularly successful in their early days — they employed auxiliary sail, their machinery failed frequently, and their working expenses were heavy.[68] The *Marjory* plying to Gravesend was sometimes laid up for repair over several days before being withdrawn from service at the end of her first season.[69] The opening years of Thames steamboat navigation witnessed engine and boiler explosions. The year 1817 saw a *Select Committee Appointed to Consider of the Means of Preventing the Mischief of Explosion From Happening on Board Steamboats*,[70] and witnessed the devastating news contained in a notice posted up at Lloyds on 3 July, announcing that 'The *Regent* steam packet, bound to Margate, was burnt to the water's edge, yesterday afternoon, off Whitstable [with] crew and passengers saved'.[71]

Any competition between steamboats and sailing packets was short lived. The former's technical superiority improved with each passing season such as to warrant the following observation as early as 1819.

> The benefits arising from the noble intervention of *Steam Vessels* and no-where more sensibly felt than in the Isle of *Thanet*. . .The *Sailing Hoys* have been known to be 72 hours in going from *London* to *Margate*. . .A *Steam Vessel* might actually make *nine* voyages, while the *Sailing Packets* are making *one*! Such is the great improvement that has lately been introduced into the mode of conveyance between *London* and *Margate*.[72]

Some among the sailing packets reverted to being trading vessels, plying to London, or to other British and Flemish ports.[73]

As the safety and technical performance of steamboats improved so they were more favourably received. Lord Broughton travelled down to Margate on 28 July 1820 on 'the *London Engineer* steam yacht. . . 270 people on board — a magnificent spectacle alto-gether', but 'a few years ago I recollect laughing at the notion of applying steam to these purposes'. Three days later he returned on the *Eclipse* steam yacht which departed at 8 a.m.

> We arrived by this extraordinary mode of making progress at Tower Stairs, quarter to four in the afternoon, passing by all sailing boats as if they were at anchor. . . Six hours and a half — 88 miles by water; passage money, 15s; music, 1s; sailors, 1s. Eighty passengers pay the expenses. All above — profit.[74]

Samuel Taylor Coleridge was equally impressed when he recalled on 10 October 1825 'how impossible it would have been fifteen or even ten years ago for me to have travelled and voyaged. . . 120 miles with fire and water blending their souls for my propulsion'.[75]

From 1820 onwards, steam navigation proved immensely success-ful and there is no shortage of official statistics and contemporary comment to prove the point. Figures presented to the 1850 *Select Committee on Ramsgate and Margate Harbours* revealed an impres-sive but fluctuating growth of passenger traffic on steamboats be-tween London and Margate during the sixteen years following the end of the Napoleonic Wars.

Between 1820-21 and 1829–30 the total number of passengers carried between London and Margate exceeded half a million at 532,249, compared to 191,849 between 1812–13 and 1819–20. The increase in the average number carried per annum from 23,981 to 53,225 as between these two periods[77] represented an increase of about 125 per cent. It is hardly surprising that the original steward of the *Thames* and *Eclipse* steam vessels argued in 1828 that 'the inhabitants of Margate ought to eulogize the name of *Watt*, as the

TABLE 4:*Passengers conveyed by water to and from Margate, 1815/16-1830/1.*[76]

April to April	No. of Passengers
1815–16	21,931
1816–17	16,519
1817–18	21,462
1818–19	33,196
1819–20	39.658
1820–1	43,947
1821–22	38,712
1822–3	41,971
1823–4	41,952
1824–5	53,657
1825–6	58,527
1826–7	59,997
1827–8	72,798
1828–9	71,937
1829–30	48,751
1830–1	98,128

founder of their good fortune; and *Steam Vessels*, as the harbingers of their prosperity'.[78]

Four years previously *The Times* had reported that 'the introduction of steamboats has given the whole coast of Kent . . . a prodigious lift'[79] and if anything the expansion of traffic to and from Gravesend was even more impressive. By 1831 about 120,000 passengers travelled annually from London to Gravesend, in boats 'now admirably managed and admirably conducted', the numbers formerly being 'nothing like what they are now'.[80] Single vessels were proceeding to Gravesend with 500 passengers on board.[81]

Individual steamboats of the 1820s carried many more passengers than the sailing packets which had preceded them. They achieved greater speeds, developed a reputation for their comfort and regularity, and represented altogether a much more pleasant and convenient way of travelling than by stage coach. By the early 1820s the average time taken to complete a journey between London and Margate had been reduced from nine hours or over to seven hours and under.[82] *The Maidstone Journal and Kentish Advertiser* of 31 May 1825 reported a voyage from Margate in six and a half hours at 14 m.p.h.; 'sojourners to this asylum of health and pleasure may well call this *flying* by steam'. By 1830 'a JOURNEY to Margate, which thirty years ago might have occupied a whole week only in going and returning, may now be performed in a sunny afternoon; and before the week is elapsed, the whole of Margate may have been explored, and the traveller safe back to his own London residence'.[83] The quickest passage ever by 1831 was achieved by the

Royal Adelaide in five hours seventeen minutes from Margate to London,[84] by which time the London/Gravesend journey had been cut from four or five hours to three.[85]

Although 'previous to steam navigation, there was a great number of parties in the course of the summer who went out in boats to Gravesend', hiring 'two, four,six, or eight watermen to row them', which now (1836) 'is all done away with',[86] it is hardly surprising that it was steamboats, not railways, which pioneeered day excursions further afield. Reductions in journey time permitted day excursions to Margate before the end of the 1820s. *The Maidstone Journal and Kentish Advertiser* of 26 August 1828 reported how Captain Grant had run the *Columbine* 'from London to Margate and back in the day', having on board an 'unprecedented freight of 660 merry souls', even though the turn round at Margate allowed only for taking on 'a fresh supply of provisions and exchanging a few "how do you do's" with the gay inhabitants of this corner of England'.

The comfort and luxury of a Margate steamboat, of 100 h.p. and 'equipped to the taste of the present times', costing already £20,000 by 1825,[87] as against £5000 to £10,000 in 1817,[88] were emphasized in 1831.

> [Travellers] will, doubtless, be astonished at the accommodations which they will find on board; the cabins being fitted up in the most elegant manner, and with every possible attention to comfort. The company are provided with draughts, chess boards, etc., and an excellent band of music. . . It would be an act of injustice towards the stewards were we not to notice their great activity and civility, and the excellence of the refreshments provided. The dinner, which consists of joints, boiled and roasted, of the very best quality, all vegetables that are in season, and pastry, wines, dessert, etc., is served up in a style both pleasing and surprising, when the limited size of the kitchen is considered.[89]

As if to labour the point *The Morning Herald* of 11 July 1827 noted how the Duke of Devonshire had travelled to and from Margate by steamboat, dining at the *table d'hôte,* causing 'his own fruit to be produced at the dessert' and permitting 'his servants to wait upon the company at table'.

The number of steamboats on the Margate run doubled from five in 1820[90] to ten by 1827;[91] six of the ten belonging to the Old (or Regular) Margate Company and four to the General Steam Navigation Company.[92] Varying from 80 to 160 h.p. they offered 'accelerated locomotion', plying 'with almost the precision of clockwork'; landing on Saturdays 'in the height of the season. . . from 800 to 1000 persons at Margate'.[93] During the 1828 season one or more boats left London for Margate every morning at nine o'clock

With Compliments

Alan Sutton

Alan Sutton Publishing Limited
17a Brunswick Road
Gloucester GL1 1HG

Telephone (0452) 419575

TABLE 5: *The number of passengers landing and embarking annually at Gravesend Town and Terrace Piers and Margate Pier, 1830/1–1841/2.*[96]

Year[a]	Gravesend			Margate
	Town	Terrace	Total	
1830–1	291,681		291,681	98,128
1831–2	187,687		187,687	85,399
1832–3	290,420		290,420	86,852
1833–4	292,169		292,169	76,456
1834–5	570,452	68,882	639,334	70,330
1835–6	550,267	153,192	703,459	108,625
1836–7	362,285	262,768	625,053	77,907
1837–8	342,622	291,120	633,742	82,704
1838–9	359,008	328,928	687,936	80,211
1839–40	468,186	344,668	812,854	87,850
1840–1	589,194	454,505	1,043,699	88,338
1841–2	570,059	571,226	1,141,285	96,777

Note (a) For Gravesend, July: for Margate, April to April

and their 'regularity, speed and certainty, . . . joined to the social pleasures of the passage,. . . justly entitle [their] proprietors to the unprecedented patronage they enjoy'.[94]

Captain Martin, having experience both of hoys and steamboats, approved of steam navigation as he saw it in 1832. During the previous twelve years he had never been obliged.

> to anchor upon the passage, or put back to port in consequence of any fault, accident, or defect in the steam machinery. . .During a period of six years in sailing packets my return of passengers conveyed amounted to 3,107. . . With these I witnessed many unpleasant casualties, from the breaking of spars, and coming in contact with other vessels. . . In twelve years. . . in the command of different steam vessels I have had under my care 128,047 passengers, not one of whom received the slightest personal injury. If a sailing packet. . . conveyed 800 passengers in a month, it was thought an extraordinary affair; yet, during the last four weeks [June/July 1832], our returns in the City of London steam packet give 5,356 persons.[95]

If the 1820s were notable for steamboat successes, the 1830s and 1840s produced the heyday of steamboat traffic prior to the introduction of railways. There was a substantial augmentation of traffic during those decades which surpassed anything previously witnessed.

The annual traffic to and from Gravesend more than tripled in a decade. By the early 1830s the number of passengers landing and embarking at the Town Pier had reached almost 300,000 annually. Ten years later the Gravesend boats were handling in excess of a million passengers annually at the Town and Terrace Piers. The number of passengers arriving at and departing from Margate totalled 2,219,364 over the thirty-five years between 1812–13 and 1846–7, giving an annual average of 63,410 passengers. That average was exceeded in every year during the 1830s. Margate's steamboat traffic more than quadrupled between 1817 and 1835. A record total was reached in 1835–6 at 108,625. There were annual fluctuations in the number carried but against a total traffic of 532,249 passengers between 1820–1 and 1829–30, 854,462 were conveyed between 1830–1 and 1839–40. The average numbers carried per annum during the 1830s were 60 per cent up on the 1820s at 85,446, compared to 53,225. Yet another peak figure was attained in 1842–3 at 102,647. Margate's steamboat traffic reached a maximum of 640,804 passengers between 1840–1 and 1846–7, which as an annual average of 91,541 represented a further 7 per cent rise compared with the 1830s.[97]

An 1836 parliamentary committee heard some interesting evidence concerning the steamboat traffic then passing up and down the Thames. On a summer's day 130 steam vessels were alleged to pass through the Pool of London, with some Gravesend boats achieving four passages daily.[98] A witness, with a proprietary interest in Margate steamboats, recalled having 'come up from Gravesend with upwards of 1100 people and we have come with upwards of 900 from Margate — that was last Whit Monday, it was an excursion to Margate and back'.[99] A director of one of the Gravesend companies claimed to have landed 3000 passengers in about 45 minutes, and

TABLE 6: *Passengers by Steam Packets between London and*

Gravesend	)		670,452
	)	From Returns	
Herne Bay	)		30,102
	)	of Pier Dues	
Margate	)		107,188
Ramsgate estimated at			50,000
Sheerness, Southend, The		)	
		)	
Nore, Dublin,		)	
		)	200,000
Falmouth, Northern and		)	
Foreign Ports		)	
Annual Amount of Traffic			1,057,742
viz: 10% to Margate	)		
	)		
5% to Ramsgate	)	18% to the Kent coast	
	)		
3% to Herne Bay	)		
BUT over 60% to Gravesend			

'we might land from one boat 1000 people'.[100]

Submitted also as evidence was a table showing the 'Present Amount of Traffic by Water'.[101]

Twelve different companies operated steamboats below London Bridge between 1829 and 1846.[102] Competition was keen between rival companies; larger, more powerful vessels were constructed and journey times were reduced still further. Six different companies competed for the Margate passenger traffic in 1836 and 1841.[103] The fastest passage ever between Margate and London by 1846 was four and three-quarter hours.[104] An advertised Sunday afternoon steam packet trip from London to Gravesend in 1835 left at two and arrived at about four, 'allowing parties to remain on shore an hour or two, returning by the late Packets.'[105] During the same month it was reported that 'Gravesend is filling fast, and the various steamers have little cause for complaint . . . The *Diamond* [has come] to the Pier in 1 hr 45 mins . . . This is by far the greatest feat ever performed by any Steamer on the River'.[106]

Competition between steamboat companies resulted in lower fares. Initially fares were relatively high at 3*s* to 4*s* in the best cabin and 2*s* in the fore cabin on the London to Gravesend run in 1815–16,[107] while the lowest Margate fare was 12*s* compared with an 1815 hoy fare of 5*s*. Fares declined during the 1820s, so that on the Margate run single fares between 1824 and 1829 were 20 per cent lower than in 1819–20, at 12*s* in the best or saloon cabin and 10*s* in the fore cabin, as against 15*s* and 12*s*.[108] The decline continued until averages of 7*s* and 6*s* were reached from 1835 onwards,[109] and to much lower levels whenever competition between the steamboat companies was intense. The 1830s were notable for extreme fluctuations in fares, as anticipated by a report in *The Maidstone Journal and Kentish Advertiser*, as early as 7 October 1828, to the effect that 'so great is the competition between the rival companies, who run vessels between London and Margate, that the conveyance to Margate on Monday morning was gratis, the passengers having nothing to pay but the pier dues'.

The years 1835-36 witnessed very low fares from London to Margate. Potential travellers were invited by the Commercial Steam Packet Company to 'Observe!!!' that Mondays, Wednesdays and Fridays were the 'Cheap Days from Margate to London', during July 1835, at 4*s* in the saloon, 3*s* in the fore cabin, and 2*s* for a child under twelve.[110] On 27 June 1835 *The Dover Telegraph and Cinque Ports General Advertiser* had reported that some steamboats were charging only 2*s* per person from London to Margate, from which

MARGATE PACKET.

The Royal Charlotte,

BURTHEN 90 TONS,

(An entire new Veffel, with many very extenfive additional Conveniences)

JAMES LAMING, *Owner,*

ROBERT PALMER, *Master,*

SAILS FROM

DICE QUAY, *Billingsgate, London,* every FRIDAY, and from *Margate* to *London* every MONDAY,

During the Seafon.

After Cabin, 7s.—*Fore Cabin,* 5s. *each Passenger.* *Children in Arms, Half-Price.*

This Veffel takes in Goods at the ufual Freight—All and every the Dangers and Accidents of the Seas, and of Naviga- tion of whatfoever Nature or Kind, or howfoever occafioned, exeepted.

J. Laming may be fpoken with on Board; at the Gun Tavern, Billingsgate; at No. 8, Finch Lane, Cornhill; or at his Houfe, Duke Street, Margate.

*** No Money, Plate, Watches, or Jewels will be accounted for, unlefs delivered to the Mafter, and paid for accordingly.

To prevent Miftakes, the Friends of J. LAMING are requefted to infert the Words *ROYAL CHARLOTTE* on their Directions.

Warren, Printer, Margate.

An advertisement for a Margate packet in 1803.   (Margate Public Library) the proprietors had to pay 15*d* pier duty for each individual. Receiving only 9*d* from each passenger was the equivalent of only one penny for every ten miles of the ninety mile journey. Effectively this was one tenth of the one penny per mile which found its way into the coffers of the parliamentary trains after 1844.[111] On 24 May 1836 *The Times* advertised the General Steam Navigation Company's regular summer fares at 5*s* and 4*s*, 'exclusive of Pier Dues at Margate', but 'on those days the unjustifiable opposition is continued. . . the fares will be 2*s* and 1*s* 6*d*.' 'Ruinous'[112] opposition of this sort arose from interlopers intervening to undercut the normal fares. A minimum fare of 1*s* 6*d* was a shilling less than the prevailing hoy fare between 1763 and 1780.

Similar trends were apparent on the Gravesend run, with *The Kentish Observer* of 28 August 1834 noting that 'travelling was never cheaper than at present', since 'one may travel in any of the steamers on any day, except Sunday, for 1*s* to Gravesend', while during July 1845 it was possible for the Star packets to offer 'Fresh Air and Cheap Excursions for the million' to Gravesend and back for only 9*d*.[113] Nine years previously fares to Gravesend had been as low as 6*d*[114] and a steamboat proprietor was asked: 'What is the present [1836] fare from London to Margate?' –'The present fare is a very reduced one: they are conveyed under prime cost; they are taken to the Isle of Thanet and Margate at 3*s*, 4*s*, and 5*s* and to Ramsgate for 1*s* 6*d* . . .'[115] Another steamboat proprietor actually confessed to 'hardly know[ing] what the [Margate] fares are now – I believe you may go almost for nothing', whereas before the 'great competition' of 1835-36 'the fares were 7*s* and 9*s*'[116]

Steamboats pioneered daily, Sunday, and weekend excursions to Gravesend, Sheerness, Herne Bay and Thanet, as well as daily commuting between Gravesend and London. Businessmen took their families down to Gravesend to stay and then commuted to and from London on the steamboats, it being argued in 1831 that they were 'of great importance to. . . mercantile men, who require to be in London early in a morning to fulfil their duties; to them. . . speed is necessary'.[117] During 1835 the Gravesend and Milton Steam Packet Company advertised its first vessel as leaving Gravesend pier at 6.30 a.m. on weekdays, so as to arrive in London around 8.30 a.m.,[118] there being 'many. . . persons who live at Gravesend or take lodgings for the summer months'.[119] A letter from a passenger to *The Gravesend and Milton Journal* of 25 April 1835 confirmed that 'the *Diamond*. . . left the Pier, at Gravesend, on Wednesday morning. . . at 6.30 and arrived at London Bridge at 8.17, thus performing the passage in 1 hr 47 mins, a distance of 32 miles'.

Weekend commuting to Margate allowed fathers and sons who lacked guaranteed holidays to join their families for weekends on the coast. Steamboats facilitated this sort of family arrangement by means of a late Saturday arrival, known as 'The Hats' Boat' or 'The Husbands' Boat', whereby

> the male part of the visitors generally go up and down to London for their business, leaving their families on the coast. . . The good men wind up their week's business on the Saturday afternoon, and then embark to rejoin their wives and children. All circumstances favourable, the husbands' boat ought to arrive at 9, or 9.30 in the evening, and the wives expect its arrival at that time.[120]

As an encouragement to family and periodic travel the Margate Regular Steam Packets – *Eclipse, Venus, Albion, Dart, Magnet,* and *Hero* – advertised during July 1827 'Family Passage tickets, in parcels containing six or twelve, price 4 gns per dozen', and 'Personal Season Tickets 3 gns each, offering great advantage to the purchaser as these vessels now make 26 passages a week'.[121] When railways appeared on the scene they competed with the steamboats in offering special Saturday to Monday tickets to the seaside.[122]

Regarding day excursions, numerous advertisements can be found in *The Times* from the 1820s onwards. On 1 July 1825, the Gravesend steamboats, *Sons of Commerce, Swiftsure,* and *Favourite* (see Pl.2), were advertised as leaving at eight and returning at four, for 3*s* in the saloon cabin and 2*s* in the fore cabin, and on Sundays 3*s*.[123] Two years later Gravesend day excursion fares were promoted at 1*s* 6*d* and 1*s* respectively, rising to 2*s* on Sundays.[124] On 25 June 1829 Londoners could go on the 'Third annual, extraordinary and interesting marine excursion – the *Hero* Steam Packet, Capt. Large, to Margate and back, 13–14 hours. This packet has engines of 100 h.p. by Messrs, Watt & Co. . . A military band on board. Leaves Tower Stairs 7.30 a.m. Tickets 10*s* each. Refreshments.'[125]

Day excursions at low fares permitted working class travel, a fact which did not pass unnoticed in the press, with some contemporaries adopting an unsympathetic view of the working classes enjoying an outing. Respectable passengers complained of too much drinking on board, having 'their morals shocked at the low orders of passengers'.[126] It was felt in 1834 that recklessly low fares tempted 'loose characters' who annoyed 'respectable passengers. . . by their intrusion'.[127] Moreover, steamboats provided rich pickings for pickpockets. *The Maidstone Journal and Kentish Advertiser* of 16 September 1828 noted that on one Margate steamer they had committed robberies to the value of £300. It was alleged on one occasion that company agents failed to rectify 'the presence of three notorious thieves', thereby allowing '320 passengers to be subjected to robbery'.[128]

Another complaint levied against day excursions concerned the overcrowding of individual vessels, as *The Times* of 23 May 1839 lamented.

> The manner in which the steamers are crammed with passengers during the holy days is highly dangerous. It was really frightful to see the steamboats pass up and down the Pool during Monday and Tuesday, crowded as they were with human beings. . . The little boats carried 300, 400, and 500 persons, and the larger ones. . . to Gravesend, Herne Bay and Margate frequently took down and brought up 500, 1,000, and 1,500 passengers. Collisions were nearlyu occurring several times between the rival steamers. . . in coming in and going away from the landing places; and it is fearful to contemplate the dreadful sacrifice of human life which must have been the result if a collision had taken place.

Excursions involved Sunday travelling which found hostile mention in an 1832 *Select Committee on the Observance of the Sabbath Day*. Having explained how six or seven steamboats, and at least 1500 passengers, arrived on Sundays, from the beginning of June until the latter part of August, Lieut. John Petley when asked if the arrival of such numbers disturbed the tranquillity of Gravesend on the Sabbath day, answered, 'Most exceedingly. . . The town resembles more a fair than a Sabbath-day. . . They land. . . when persons are coming from places of worship, and are highly calculated to do injury to young persons, to remove the impressions that they have received from religious instruction'. He agreed, however, that excursionists brought business into the town, 'principally to the public houses,. . . to the letters of vehicles. . . and donkeys'.[129]

The Secretary to the New Gravesend Company having explained how his company ran up to three vessels on a Sunday morning, which generally took 2½ hours to arrive, each with 250–300 passengers on board, argued that profits accrued both to the company and to trading interests within Gravesend, since 'we have generally on the Sunday that class of people that cannot go during the week', such as 'artisans and mechanics, and persons in business'. Although Sundays attracted 'some shopkeepers and tradesmen', the lower classes predominated as 'a very considerable majority', and 'the better class go down in the week time'. Generally the passengers behaved themselves despite 'much drinking of spirits — I do not find anything like indecorum on board. . . [and] at Gravesend. . .

you generally find them spreading their little cloths, and taking their refreshment on the grass. . . I have never seen anything like a tumult or anything like disorder.'[130]

A third witness admitted to having travelled on a Sunday boat which ran to Margate, where he had observed 'ladies and gentlemen sitting in the cabin with their books, and religious books', with 'as much attention paid to religion there as elsewhere', but this was a regular sailing, 'for persons that cannot get away from their business at any other time', there being 'no more harm in a boat going to Margate on [a] Sunday, with these sort of persons, than a person riding in his carriage to church'.[131]

Sunday travelling flourished beyond 1832. On one Sunday alone during August 1834, 6070 passengers boarded nine steamers,[132] while two years later steamboats were landing over 8000 people at Gravesend on a Sunday.[133] There must be some implications in these and other figures which have been quoted for that famous historical debate on early-nineteenth century working-class standards of living.

Living standards apart, the vast expansion of steamboat traffic to and from Gravesend profoundly affected the growth, popularity and economy of that town. Life ceased to be dominated by servicing commercial shipping passing up and down the river, and instead by 1831 'the resort of persons by steam conveyance forms the chief source of the subsistence of the inhabitants'.[134] Eleven years later it was observed of 'the most frequented town on the River Thames' that

> the thousands of visitors who here keep holiday during six or eight months of the year have insured resources to the inhabitants more to be depended on than the fluctuations of trade. New houses, new streets, hotels, reading rooms, public baths, and pleasure gardens have all appeared in succession since the introduction of steam on the river.[135]

Such building developments and improvements are commonly associated with railways as *The Times* noted at the end of August 1860 when reporting on the 'Results of Excursion Trains'.[136]

Within twenty years, between 1821 and 1841, the number of houses within the jurisdiction of the Corporation of Gravesend (which included the adjoining parish of Milton) more than doubled[137] and yet, with one million passengers annually in the early 1840s 'accommodation was quite at a premium' and it was no uncommon occurrence to pay 10s for the privilege of spending a night in an armchair.[138] Steamboat companies, piers, new accommodation, and amusements changed the character of Gravesend, which 'has a bustling air, and seems to be. . . half sea-port, half watering-place', for 'go where you may, you are sure to find shrimps to sell and "lodgings to let"'[139]

Although Margate's character and popularity had been moulded before 1815, steamboats brought added prosperity to the resort. *The Times* of 28 September 1824 noted how Margate was 'unpopular with the fasionable world, but continues more or less the summer retreat of the "London citizens", being visited almost entirely by 'the inhabitants of eastern London during the early part of the season'. *The Morning Herald* of 11 July 1827 confessed that Margate was 'the least fashionable' and yet 'the most frequented watering place in England'. Fifteen years later, Margate flourished as 'a favourite watering place for the inhabitants of London', abounding 'with all the resources for health, pleasure and amusement which distinguish well-frequented towns of this class',[140] there being perhaps 'no town in the southern parts of England which, in proportion to its rank and station, is more popularly known, by name at least, than Margate'.[141]

In 1845; which was the year before the South Eastern Railway linked Margate to London, Mrs Elizabeth Stone invited her readers to look at Margate sands.

> They appear one indiscriminate moving mass of cabs, cars, carts and carriages; horses, ponies, dogs, donkeys and boys; men, women, children and nurses; and, the least and the biggest – babies and bathing machines. Imagine. . . all proper associations and accompaniments: little boys with spades; nurses with babies; mammas with sewing, etc.[142]

She also noted how

> thirty years ago Margate and Ramsgate were crowded in the season by whose who now would not be seen out at Brighton, and perhaps will not continue to go there long. It requires marvellous courage now to confess any interest in places so utterly discarded by fashion as are Margate and Ramsgate. They are still crowded, but by decidedly unfashionable people.[143]

While railways had yet to make an impact on these two Thanet resorts, Brighton had welcomed the arrival of its first London train on 21 September 1841, occupying thereafter 'the place which Margate had once held in the affections of earlier generations of cockneys',[144] and so could indeed be called 'the lungs of the great capital'.[145]

Notes

[1] It was on 18 May 1796 that forty-nine residents joined in a subscription of five guineas each in order to found a bathing establishment, whereupon 'they purchased a machine at Margate to begin with', which was first used on 27 June 1796, R.P. Cruden, *The History of the Town of Gravesend in the County of Kent* (1843), p. 449; also F.A. Mansfield, *History of Gravesend in the County of Kent* (1922), p. 30, or *The Kentish Notebook*, ed. G.D. Howell, vol. II (1894), p. 90. Several improvements came to Gravesend during the second half of the eighteenth century, and among them 'proper machines have lately been established here, with every requisite accommodation for sea bathing', E. Hasted, *The History and Topographical Survey of the County of Kent*, vol. III (2nd edn., Canterbury, 1797), p. 320.

[2] J. Whyman, 'A Hanoverian Watering Place: Margate before the Railway', in *Perspectives in English Urban History*, ed. A. Everitt (1973), pp. 138–60.

[3] Such as to warrant mention and an illustration in *The Illustrated London News*, 5 Dec. 1846, no. 240, vol. IX (July–Dec. 1846), p. 368.

[4] E.W. Gilbert, *Brighton: Old Ocean's Bauble* (1954), pp. 11–17.

[5] *Ibid.*, pp. 18–20.

[6] A.M. Kay, 'Growth of Settlement in Margate and Its Region' (unpub. Dip. Geog. thesis, London Univ. 1951), p. 86.

[7] Daniel Defoe reported rather incredibly of Gravesend that 'it is the town where the great ferry (as they call it) is kept up between London and East-Kent, it is hardly credible what numbers of people pass here every tide, as well by night as by day, between this town and London: Almost all the people of East-Kent, when they go for London, go no farther by land than this town; and then for six-pence in the tilt-boat, or one shilling in a small boat or wherry, are carry'd to London by water', *A Tour Through the Whole Island of Great Britain*, vol. I (Everyman's Library, rev. edn. 1962), p. 101. In 1796, it was noted that 'the fare from Gravesend to London is now 9*d* each passenger', and 'coaches are provided to convey passengers to Rochester, Chatham, etc. at 1*s* 6*d* each, so that a person may be conveyed from London to Chatham, upward of 30m. for 2*s* 3*d* which is one of the cheapest instances of travelling in the kingdom', G.M. Woodward, *The Eccentric Excursion* (1796), pp. 43–4.

[8] A.J. Philip, *A History of Gravesend and Its Surroundings* (1954), p. 174.

[9] 'By an Inhabitant', *The Margate Guide, A Descriptive Poem with Elucidatory Notes* (Margate, 1797), p. 75.

[10] *The New Margate, Ramsgate and Broadstairs Guide* (2nd edn., Margate, 1802), p. 50.

[11] The most recent support for this view is presented in J. Anderson and E. Swinglehurst, *The Victorian and Edwardian Seaside* (1978), p. 18.

[12] J. Lyons, *A Description of the Isle of Thanet and particularly of the Town of Margate (1763), pp. 14-15.*

[13] Throughout the eighteenth century the Isle of Thanet was famous as a commercial corn producer for the London market; on the importance of hoys in this connection see J.H. Andrews, 'The Thanet Seaports, 1650–1750', *Archaeologia Cantiana*, LXVI (1953), pp. 37–44, or in *Essays in Kentish History*, ed. M. Roake and J. Whyman (1973), pp. 119–26, as well as D. Baker, 'The Marketing of Corn in the First Half of the Eighteenth Century: North-East Kent', *The Agricultural History Review*, XVIII (2) (1970), pp. 126–50.

[14] R. de Kerchove, *International Maritime Dictionary* (2nd edn., 1961), p. 382.

[15] Lyons, *Isle of Thanet*, p. 15, or *The Gentleman's Magazine*, LXXII (1802), p.

176, while W. Jerrold, *Highways and Byways in Kent* (1907), p. 110, refers to John Taylor, 'the water poet', who relates that in 1637 'a Hoy from Rochester, Margate in Kent, or Feversham and Maidstone' sailed to London.

[16] *The Kentish Traveller's Companion (5th edn., Canterbury, 1799), p. 265.*

[17] *The New Margate, Ramsgate and Broadstairs Guide* (5th edn., Margate, 1809), p. 53.

[18] *The Times*, 12 July 1815.

[19] *Ibid.*, 16 July 1812 and 22 July 1812.

[20] *The Margate Guide* (1780), p. 19.

[21] *The New Margate, Ramsgate and Broadstairs Guide* (1809), p. 53.

[22] *A Short Description of the Isle of Thanet; being chiefly Intended as a Directory for the Company Resorting to Margate, Ramsgate and Broadstairs (Margate, 1796), pp. 23, 97-8.*

[23] 'Margate. . . was our first sea-side experiment, and many circumstances combined to make it the most agreeable holyday of my life. We had neither of us seen the sea. . . [but] can I forget thee, thou old Margate Hoy, with they weather-beaten sun-burnt captain, and his rough accommodations?', Charles Lamb, *The Last Essays of Elia* [1833], ed. E. Blunden (Oxford, 1929), p. 34.

[24] G.S. Carey, *The Balnea: or, An Impartial Description of All the Popular Watering Places in England* (1799), pp. 34–5.

[25] *The New Margate, Ramsgate and Broadstairs Guide* (6th edn., Margate, 1816), p. 56.

[26] Captain K.B. Martin, *Oral Traditions of the Cinque Ports and Their Localities* (1832), p. 28.

[27] *M(orning) H(erald) and D(aily) A(dvertiser)*, 22 Aug. 1781; also *M(orning) C(hronicle and) L(ondon) A(dvertiser)*, 23 Aug. 1781.

[28] *G(eneral) A(dvertiser)*, 22 Aug. 1786. Shortly after this episode the *M.C.L.A.* 9 Sept. 1786 reported over 1000 colliers crowding into the Pool of London, making it impossible 'for any vessel of greater burthen than 30 tons to reach higher than the beginning of Wapping'.

[29] *The Times*, 16 Sept. 1797.

[30] *The Morning Chronicle*, 19 Sept. 1810.

[31] Lyons, *Isle of Thanet*, p. 15.

[32] *Reminiscences of a Gentlewoman of the Last Century: Letters of Catherine Hutton*, ed. C. Hutton Beale (Birmingham, 1891), pp. 24–5.

[33] *Ibid.*, p. 25.

[34] K(ent) R(ecord) O(ffice), Cobb MSS.

[35] *Gentleman's Magazine*, XLI (1771), p. 167.

[36] *Universal British Directory of Trade, Commerce and Manufacture* (1796) and *A Short Description of the Isle of Thanet*, pp. 95–8.

[37] *The Farington Diary*, ed. J. Greig, vol. II (1923), pp. 278–9.

[38] *The Times*, 11 July 1815.

[39] As per footnote 36 above.

[40] *The Times*, 18 Aug. 1802.

[41] *The Margate and Ramsgate Guide in Letters to a Friend* (1797), p. 15.

[42] For instance, *M.H.D.A.*, 22 Aug. 1781; *M.C.L.A.*, 23 Aug. 1781; *G.A.*, 22 Aug. 1786; *Morning Post and Gazetteer*, 28 Aug. 1799; *The Times*, 1 Sept. 1804.

[43] Lyons, *Isle of Thanet*, p. 15.

[44] *The Kentish Companion for the Year of Our Lord, 1792* (Canterbury, 1792), p. 160.

[45] *Report from the Select Committee on Ramsgate and Margate Harbours; Together with the Proceedings of the Committee [and] Minutes of Evidence*, P.P. [660] (1850), p. 169.

[46] Defoe, *A Tour* (8th edn., 1778), p. 139.

[47] *Margate and Ramsgate Guide in a Letter* (1789), p. 12.

[48] Quoted also in J. Ashton, *Old Times: A Picture of Social Life at the End of the*

Eighteenth Century (1885), p. 65.

[49] *The Diary of John Baker*, ed., P.C. Yorke (1931), pp. 417–18.

[50] G. Keate, *Sketches from Nature, Taken and Coloured, in a Journey to Margate* (5th edn., 1802), pp. 245–7.

[51] C. Dainton, *The Story of England's Hospitals* (1961), p. 93.

[52] *Ibid.*, p. 93; also A. Raistrick, *Quakers in Science and Industry* (1950), p. 311.

[53] K.R.O., *The Original Minutes of the Margate Infirmary, 1791–3*, 2 July 1791.

[54] J.C. Lettsom, *Hints Designed to Promote Benificence, Temperance and Medical Science*, vol. III (1801), pp. 236–7.

[55] *Gentleman's Magazine*, LXXXVI (1816), p. 17.

[56] Keate, *Sketches from Nature*, p. 66.

[57] *The Times*, 13 Sept. 1804.

[58] J. Whyman, 'The Uniqueness of Margate as a Seaside Resort (Part VI)', *East Kent Critic*, 170 (June 1977), p. 3.

[59] *The Thanet Itinerary or Steam Yacht Companion* (1819), p. 42.

[60] *Morning Chronicle*, 8 Sept. 1810.

[61] Mentioned, for instance, in F.W. Jessup, *Kent History Illustrated* (2nd edn., Maidstone, 1973), pp. 50–1 as The Royal Military Canal and the Thames and Medway Canal.

[62] F Burtt, *Steamers of the Thames and Medway* (1949), p. 8. This seventy-ton, sixty-three-foot vessel, built of wood in 1814 at Dumbarton was propelled by a 14 h.p. engine.

[63] R.B. Watts, *A Topographical Description of the Coast between London, Margate and Dover. . . With an Account of the First Application of Steam. . . in Propelling Vessels* (1828), p. 9.

[64] Burtt, *Steamers*, p. 10.

[65] Quoted also in R.A. Fletcher, *Steamships: The Story of their Development to the Present Day* (1910), p. 66.

[66] *Gentleman's Magazine*, LXXXV (1815), p. 272.

[67] Sir Rowland Hill and G.B. Hill, *The Life of Sir Rowland Hill and the History of Penny Postage*, vol. I (1880), pp. 134, 135–6.

[68] Burtt, *Steamers*, p. 8. Apart from costing initially anything between £5000 and £10,000, Mr George Dodd pointed out in 1817 that their 'furniture and decorations alone form an expensive item; they are also very expensive to maintain, especially on the Thames, by reason of the great cost of coal', in evidence 21 May 1817 before *The Select Committee Appointed to Consider of the Means of Preventing the Mischief of Explosion From Happening on Board Steamboats*, P.P. [422] (1817), p. 37.

[69] Burtt, *Steamers*, p. 8.

[70] P.P. [422] (1817).

[71] *The Times*, 4 July 1817; reported also at some length in *The Maidstone Journal and Kentish Advertiser*, 8 July 1817, the *Regent*, 'with a crew of ten men, and about forty passengers', having cost '£11,000 to construct'.

[72] *Steam Yacht Companion*, p. 25.

[73] *Ibid.*, (2nd edn., 1822), p. 26.

[74] *Recollections of a Long Life by Lord Broughton*, ed. Lady Dorchester, vol. II (1909), pp. 133-4.

[75] *Letters of Samuel Taylor Coleridge*, ed. E.H. Coleridge, vol. II (1895), p. 743.

[76] *S.C. on Ramsgate and Margate Harbours*, P.P. 1850, p. 169.

[77] Whyman, *Perspectives in English Urban History*, p. 153.

[78] Watts, *Topographical Description*, p. 10.

[79] *The Times*, 28 Sept. 1824.

[80] Mr. R.P. Cruden in evidence 23 Sept. 1831 before *The Select Committee on Steam Navigation*, P.P. [335] (1831), pp. 80–1, QQ.1437, 1446.

[81] Mr C. Beer in evidence 29 Sept. 1831 before *ibid.*, p. 121, Q.2193.

[82] Seven hours being quoted by Thomas Cromwell, *Excursions in the County of Kent* (1822), p. 113.

[83] G.A. Cooke, *A Topographical and Statistical Description of the County of Kent* (1830), p. i.

[84] *Kentish Gazette*, 1 April 1831.

[85] Mr Cruden before *S.C. on Steam Navigation*, P.P. 1831, p. 81, Q.Q.1447–8.

[86] Mr J. Banyon, Clerk to the Waterman's Company, in evidence 25 July 1836 before *The Select Committee Appointed to Inquire into the State of the Port of London*, P.P. [557] (1836), pp. 258–9.

[87] W. Bain, 'Remarks on the Progress of Steam Navigation', *Blackwood's Edinburgh Magazine*, XVIII (November 1825), p. 544.

[88] Mr Dodd before *S.C. Appointed to Consider of the Means of Preventing. . . Explosion*, P.P. 1817, p.37.

[89] G.W. Bonner, *The Picturesque Pocket Companion to Margate, Ramsgate, Broadstairs and the Parts Adjacent* (2nd edn., 1831), pp. 6–7.

[90] W.C. Oulton, *Picture of Margate and Its Vicinity* (1820), p. 113, viz: the *Engineer, Eclipse, Favourite, Victory* and *Majestic*.

[91] *A Week at Margate* (5th edn., 1827), p. 4, viz: *Eclipse, Venus, Albion, Columbine, Dart, Harlequin, City of London, Hero, Royal Sovereign*, and *Magnet*; also *The Morning Herald*, 11 July 1827.

[92] *The Morning Herald*, 11 July 1827; Watts, *Topographical Description*, p. 13.

[93] *The Morning Herald*, 11 July 1827.

[94] Watts, *Topographical Description*, p. 13.

[95] Martin, *Oran Traditions*, pp. 27, 29–30.

[96] For Gravesend, Cruden, *Gravesend*, p. 537, his town pier figures for 1833–4 and 1834–5 being confirmed by Mr W.A. Coombe, town clerk of Gravesend, in evidence 28 March 1836 before *The House of Commons Committee on the London and Blackwall Commercial Railway Bill*, House of Lords Record Office, Committee Office Evidence, vol. XV (1836); for Margate, *S.C. on Ramsgate and Margate Harbours*, P.P. 1850, p. 169.

[97] *S.C. on Ramsgate and Margate Harbours*, P.P. 1850, p. 169; also Whyman, *Perspectives in English Urban History*, pp. 138–9, 153–4.

[98] Mr Taylor, a Thames pilot, and Mr J. Ferguson, manager of the Gravesend Diamond Steam Packet Company, in evidence 23 and 24 March 1836 before the *Commons Committee on the London and Blackwall Commercial Railway Bill*.

[99] Mr G.W. Clifton in evidence 26 March 1836 before *ibid.*

[100] Mr G.C. Redman in evidence 14 May 1836 before *ibid.*, vol. XVII.

[101] Submitted to *ibid.*, 30 March 1836.

[102] Burtt, *Steamers*, pp. 29–59, including the General Steam Navigation Company, the Milton and Gravesend Steam Packet Company, the Margate and London Steam Packet Company, the Star Steam Packet Company, the Gravesend Steam Packet Company, the London and Herne Bay Steam Packet Company and the Diamond Steam Packet Company.

[103] Whyman, *Perspectives in English Urban History*, p. 153.

[104] *The Times*, 27 May 1846.

[105] *Gravesend and Milton Journal*, 30 May 1835.

[106] *Ibid.*, 16 May 1835.

[107] Burtt, *Steamers*, pp. 9–10.

[108] Calculated from advertisements appearing in *The Times*.

[109] *Ibid.*, and *S.C. on Ramsgate and Margate Harbours*, P.P. 1850, p. 169.

[110] *The Dover Telegraph and Cinque Ports General Advertiser*, 4 July 1835.

[111] It was stipulated by The Regulation of Railways Act, 1844, better known as the Cheap Trains Act, that all railways had to run at least one train daily charging a minimum fare of 1*d* per mile third class.

[112] Mr J. Knill in evidence 30 March 1836 before the *Commons Committee on the London and Blackwall Commercial Railway Bill*.

[113] The Times, 1 July 1845.

[114] Capt. J. Fisher in evidence 25 March 1836 before the *Commons Committee on*

the London and Blackwall Commercial Railway Bill.
    [115] Mr J.L. Jones in evidence 25 March 1836 before *ibid.*
    [116] Mr Clifton in evidence 26 March 1836 before *ibid.*
    [117] Mr Cruden before *S.C. on Steam Navigation*, P.P. 1831, pp. 81, 83, Q.Q.1447, 1486.
    [118] *Gravesend and Milton Journal*, 25 April 1835.
    [119] Mr White in evidence 14 April 1836 before the *Commons Committee on the London and Blackwall Commercial Railway Bill.*
    [120] 'The Isle of Thanet', *The Land We Live In* (c. 1840s), pp. 147, 152: also J. Whyman, 'Visitors to Margate in the 1841 Census Returns', *Local Population Studies*, 8 (Spring 1972), p. 24.
    [121] *The Times*, 9 July 1827.
    [122] For instance: ' "Saturday to Monday at the Seaside", cheap trains by the South Eastern Railway every Saturday afternoon from London Bridge to Margate at 2.30 p.m. and 5.30 p.m. returning on Sunday evening, or Monday morning. Fare there and back 8s 6d, 3rd class; 12s 6d, 2nd class; and 17s 6d, 1st class', *City Press*, 12 May 1860.
    [123] *The Times*, 1 July 1825.
    [124] *Ibid.*, 3 July 1827, 4 July 1827.
    [125] *Ibid*, 24 June 1829.
    [126] *Gravesend and Milton Journal*, 30 Aug. 1834.
    [127] *Ibid.*, 13 Sept. 1834.
    [128] *The Times*, 28 Aug. 1835.
    [129] In evidence 28 July 1832 before *The Select Committee on the Observance of the Sabbath Day*, P.P. [697] (1832). p. 252, Q.Q.3892–3, 3895, 3898.
    [130] Mr L. Gilson in evidence 25 July 1832 before *ibid.*, pp. 205–7, Q.Q.3270, 3272, 3275, 3283, 3286–8, 3290, 3316.
    [131] Mr S. Knight in evidence 25 July 1832 before *ibid.*, p. 208, Q.Q.3355, 3357, 3359.
    [132] *Kentish Observer*, 21 Aug. 1834.
    [133] Mr Clifton in evidence 26 March 1836 before the *Commons Committee on the London and Blackwall Commercial Railway Bill.*
    [134] Mr Cruden before *S.C. on Steam Navigation*, P.P. 1831, p. 80, Q.1437.
    [135] W.H. Bartlett, J.D. Harding and T. Creswick, *The Ports, Harbours, Watering Places and Picturesque Scenery of Great Britain*, vol. I (c. 1842).
    [136] 'The revolutions in places are as strange as those affecting their inhabitants and the most secluded spots have been the first to change. . . The place is inundated by excursionists, who crowd its lodgings and consume its stores, till new markets are op⸻d, and new hotels rise. . . Marine Terraces, Sea Villas, "Prospect Lodges", "Bellevues", hotels, baths libraries, and churches soon accumulate', *The Times*, 30 Aug. 1860.
    [137] Cruden, *Gravesend*, pp. 533–4, viz: number of houses in:

Year	Gravesend	Milton	Total
1821	646	462	1108
1841	939	1354	2293

    [138] *Invicta Magazine*, vol. II, (2), (December 1911), p. 94.
    [139] *The Pictorial Guide to Gravesend and Its Rural Vicinity: A Holiday Handbook* (1845), p. 8.
    [140] *The Journey Book of England: Kent* (1842), p. 127.
    [141] *Saturday Magazine*, XXI (1842), p. 645.
    [142] Mrs E. Stone, *Chronicles of Fashion*, vol. II (1845), pp. 299–300.
    [143] *Ibid.*, p. 298.
    [144] Gilbert, *Brighton*,pp. 139–42, 152.
    [145] *Ibid.*, p. 152, quoting from *The New Monthly Magazine*, LXI (1841), p. 171.

Agriculture and Land Use in Cornwall Circa 1840*

R. J. P. KAIN AND H. M. E. HOLT

Introduction

In August 1836 Parliament passed the Tithe Commutation Act which put an end to more than a century of dispute over the payment of tithe to the Church and lay tithe owners. The multiplicity of local tithing customs and practices was swept away and replaced by an annual rent charge which was to vary according to the price of wheat, barley and oats. The Tithe Commission was constituted and its commissioners and agents made enquiries concerning the extent of titheable land in every parish.[1]

Some tithe remained to be commuted in about three-quarters of the parishes and townships of England and Wales. If tithe owners and tithe payers could not agree the rent charge, then the Act empowered the commissioners to impose an award. Once the total rent charge had been ascertained, land owners were required to have the titheable lands surveyed so that it could be apportioned according to the actual state of cultivation. This apportionment was recorded for all time on a map and in a schedule. Together these constitute a 'parish tithe survey'.[2] In addition, all correspondence and minutes of evidence taken at parish meetings were kept together in a tithe file. Where a voluntary agreement, rather than a compulsory award, for the amount of rent charge was made, an assistant tithe commissioner was required to visit the tithe district

* Research for this paper was financed by a grant from the Social Science Research Council which is gratefully acknowledged. We would also like to thank Mr Rodney Fry and Dr John Buckett of the University of Exeter for their assistance with base maps and computer mapping respectively. Rosemary Robertson of the Institute of Cornish Studies kindly commented on an earlier version of the article.

and to write a report advising whether or not the agreement was fair and ought to be confirmed. To help them judge these agreements and organise their reports, assistant tithe commissioners were provided with printed 'questionnaire' forms on which to describe the output and methods of farming they encountered. The completed questionnaires are retained in the tithe files and contain much local information on the nature of farming made by these skilled and practised observers. The tithe files were 'discovered' in the 1960s and the form of the printed reports and their value as a source for agricultural historians and historical geographers have been described by Elwyn Cox and Brian Dittmer.[3] Very briefly, two types of forms were employed. In the principally arable farming counties of the country, it was expected that rent charge would be checked by calculating the value of a tenth of the gross produce of the crops, usually obtained by multiplying acreage by yield. Grassland in these areas was valued according to its yield of hay and the agistment value of its pasture. In mainly pastoral, livestock-rearing counties, an alternative questionnaire form was used which put less emphasis on the arable but more on the value of animal products. An estimate of the number of various sorts of stock kept in the parish was required. This latter type of form was used in Cornwall.

In February 1978, the Social Science Research Council commenced funding a project based at the University of Exeter to index the contents of all 14,800 tithe files, to transcribe all the agricultural statistics from the 6,728 reports on agreements, and to map these data by computer for all counties where the density and quality of data coverage merits cartographic treatment.

This paper on Cornish agriculture and land use *circa* 1840 forms part of this national project and this fact has conditioned its content and methods. These may be summarised as follows:

1. For reasons of space, only a selection of the maps it is possible to construct from the tithe files has been included.

2. To facilitate comparisons of maps *between* counties, for this national project, the interval scales for classing data are the same for each county. This inevitably means that they are sub-optimal for indicating the finer regional variations *within* a county.

3. The text is based almost entirely on comments made by assistant tithe commissioners and others preserved in the tithe files. There are some references to major secondary commentaries such as W.F. Karkeek's *Prize Essay*, 'On the Farming of Cornwall' but it has not been our intention to augment these with detail from estate records and other primary archival material.

4.   Besides being based on the analysis of a single source, this study is cross-sectional in character and is, therefore, more descriptive than explanatory in nature. The tithe survey was, though, compiled at a particularly critical juncture in the history of British agriculture.[4]

The analysis is concerned with Cornish agriculture as represented by those parishes where the titheable acreage exceeded 90% of the area. Large areas of eastern-central Cornwall are thus omitted, together with Bodmin Moor, where tithe data are partial and potentially unrepresentative (see below).

The tithe files of Cornwall

No parishes in Cornwall were entirely tithe free, although some contained tithe free estates or categories of land which were exempt from tithes. The files of parishes where tithes were commuted by award usually contain the minutes of award meetings and a schedule of the land use of titheable land. Some files also contained a copy of the draft award. Crop acreages are not usually given in these, although for a few parishes there are more detailed accounts of land use and crops. For the parish of St. Eval, for example, an estimate of the titheable produce of the parish includes the acreages and yields of wheat, barley and oats; for Michaelstow there is a schedule indicating the crops grown in each field and for St. Gorran a valuation of the small tithes.[5] The files for parishes which were commuted by agreement usually contain the report to the Tithe Commissioners in London by an assistant tithe commissioner, and often lists of questions sent to the tithe owners and the land owners by the assistant commissioner to elicit information for his report, and, in about half the files, a copy of the draft agreement. For most parishes only one report was completed; some do have more as at Endellion which was divided into four prebends for commutation purposes with a report on each.[6] A subject index of the contents of the whole body of 212 Cornwall tithe files has been compiled and is included here as an appendix. For those parishes with printed reports on agreements, the agricultural data were also transcribed to form the source for compiling the computer maps of land use and farming *circa* 1840 which are presented below.

In Cornwall, three main factors influenced the reliability and accuracy of these data. These are the precise format of a report, the assistant commissioner who compiled it, and the source from which data included in the report was obtained.

In the first year of working after the Act, printed questionnaire forms were not used to help standardise the reports. The land use and crop data in these few, early manuscript reports are not consistent with those given for other parishes on the later printed reports and so we have not entered these data into our analysis. Although, the printed forms were uniform, some assistant commissioners were much more explicit in their answers than others. For example, at Mawnan, William Glasson gave the precise extent of individual crops grown on the arable, *viz.* '46.3.0 in potatoes and turnips on average, 187.0.0 in wheat, 236.0.0 in barley, 47.0.0 in oats'.[7] However, at Madron which was visited by James Jerwood, it is not possible to ascertain the crop acreages because he did not specify areas sown but noted two alternative rotations, *viz.* 'wheat (1), barley or oats (2), seeds (3,4,5) or wheat (1), green crop (2), barley (3), seeds (4,5)'.[8] Table 1 lists the assistant commissioners who worked in Cornwall and the chronology of their reporting.

The assistant tithe commissioners usually provided some indication of the accuracy of the acreages, yields and livestock numbers in their reports. Very often, land use data were obtained by estimation. Some assistant commissioners like Charles Pym stated specifically that they viewed the parish to make their estimates but William Glasson who compiled a large proportion of the Cornwall reports appears to have accepted both land use data provided by land owners and accounts of tithe payments in past years by incumbents with little attempt to verify their authenticity. Some categories of information were also more difficult to elucidate than others. Ascertaining the correct numbers of the different types of livestock was a frequently encountered problem as was enumerating the precise acreages of common and waste. An indication of some 'rough and ready' estimation can be instanced by the common practice of rounding figures to the nearest ten.

Transcribing the data and calculating indices for mapping

The draft articles of agreement preserved in the files of some parishes provide one source of land use acreages. It is not at all unusual to find that these (which are the same as those recorded in the preamble to the parish tithe apportionments preserved in the County Record Office) are in disagreement with those stated on the printed report questionnaire. These differences are not necessarily a result of errors but rather because different definitions of arable and pasture land were employed in the two documents. In the reports on agreements in the tithe files, assistant commissioners were asked to estimate the acreage of arable defined as the 'land actually ploughed in the present or last season, whether sown with corn, planted with roots or fallow, but excluding seeds.' In the articles of agreement in the tithe apportionments on the other hand, arable was any land that had been ploughed in the previous seven years. The arable acreages which enter into our analysis are those of the printed reports and do not, therefore, include seeds acreage. This procedure has been adopted because in Cornwall, as in other counties of western England and Wales, seeds usually lay for three years and quite often for upwards of ten or more years before being ploughed up. After the first year when they were mown for hay, they were pastured until deterioration eventually necessitated ploughing. In some parishes the assistant tithe commissioners enumerated different types of pasture separately and so defined the role of seeds clearly. For example, at Mawgan in Pyder, William Glasson listed, '615 seeds, 400 meadow, 1950 very bad rough pasture, 1213 in pasture after the seeds until broken up again for tillage'.[9] We have taken our pasture acreages from the printed reports and so seeds are included in our pasture classification.

Orchards were neither very extensive in Cornwall nor particularly valuable. In the assistant commissioners' reports they were frequently included in the total pasture acreage, probably because they were valued as much for pasture as for the tithe of fruit they produced. Although the specific acreage of orchards was not requested on the printed questionnaire form, it was usually possible to deduce this from either manuscript notes which accompanied the printed questionnaire, from a description of his valuation noted by the assistant commissioner at the end of his printed report form, or in the draft articles of agreement. Orchards for these places could be coded separately from pasture. Similarly, market gardens were usually included in the arable acreage on the questionnaire but separately elsewhere in the file. Their acreage could thus be deducted from the arable before coding.

The acreage of timber woodland was not required for the printed report because only coppice and underwood were titheable. Woodland of more than twenty years' growth was exempt from tithe in Cornwall. The extent of commonland was particularly difficult for the assistant commissioners to ascertain. Firstly, they had to decide whether to enumerate the Cornish 'crofts' (see below) as arable, pasture or common. These were often valued at only a few shillings or so an acre and their acreage set out under 'common' in the printed report. An instance of this difficulty is provided by William Glasson's report on Luxulian. He enumerated 594.1.0 acres of common and then under this stated, 'of crofts and moors called in schedule arable but which never has been broken up — 846.0.0'. Later, when assessing the value of pasture he wrote, 'of crofts and moors what is called Pasture in schedule — 10 shillings per acre'.[10] Crofts, moors and down have all been entered as 'common' in our analysis.

In summary, obtaining land use figures from the 'pastoral' type printed reports as used by assistant tithe commissioners in Cornwall is not the simple matter of copying and coding acreages as it is with reports used in counties of the arable east. Similar problems arise with obtaining the acreage of crops. In the Cornish tithe files the actual acreages of crops are rarely stated in answer to the question on the extent of arable land. Generally only the total arable acreage and the course of crops are noted, the latter being that which the assistant commissioner, from his observations and enquiries, considered to prevail in the parish. It is, however, possible to derive estimates of the acreage of individual crops by dividing the arable acreage by the number of courses less the number of seeds courses included in the rotation. In fact, this is exactly the same method that assistant commissioners employed themselves to obtain crop acreages in eastern counties. For a number of reasons it is not possible to derive the acreages of all crops in all parishes in this way. First, more than one rotation might be stated; secondly, the courses in a rotation may not be numbered; and thirdly, two crops might have been grown in one course. For example, at Marham Church, William Glasson recorded a rotation of 'wheat, barley or oats — part potatoes and a small quantity of turnips'.[11] With such an imprecise description of the rotation it is clearly not possible to derive crop acreages. For many Cornish parishes it is nevertheless possible to calculate the acreage of seeds grown as in most reports two acreages of 'arable' were enumerated: the first in answer to question one of the printed report does not include the acreages of seeds, while a second, defined as 'arable including seeds' is usually set out in a land use valuation at the end of the report. Where the latter is missing, the acreage of arable including seeds can usually be found in a manuscript note accompanying the printed report or in the articles of agreement. The acreage of seeds is then derived by subtracting the 'arable' acreage not including seeds from the 'arable' that included seeds.

Only parishes for which tithe data cover 90 per cent or more of total area have been entered into our analysis. Experience from previous studies has shown that when coverage levels are as high as this then the data should be truly representative of a whole parish.[12] It is usually possible to determine the extent of coverage of a parish from internal evidence in the tithe files. For example, a statement of the total parish acreage to compare with the titheable acreage, a schedule of exempt estates, or an indication that one specific land use was exempt and not enumerated can be used to decide whether to accept or reject the data in a particular parish report. Sometimes there is no such helpful information in the file and recourse has to be made to external evidence, notably areas of parishes stated in the 1851 census of population.[13]

All the data were transcribed in the Public Record Office directly on to printed coding forms and then punched on IBM cards, edited and corrected. A base map indicating those parishes with acceptable data was compiled from the Index to the Tithe Survey edition of the Old Series Ordnance Survey one-inch maps (Figure 2). Boundaries were then electronically digitised from this and a series of maps of land use, crops and livestock produced using a modified version of the GIMMS 3 computer mapping routine.[14] Some examples of these maps illustrate the following sections and the data are summarised in Tables 2 and 3.

The physical environment of Cornish agriculture

Some elements of the physical structure of Cornwall are summarised on Figure 3; these are discussed in more detail in a number of accessible surveys of the region.[15] Broadly speaking, the rocks underlying a large proportion of the Cornish peninsula are igneous and they greatly affect both the relief and the soils of the county. The high granite moorlands of Bodmin, Hensbarrow, Carnmenellis and the Lands' End Peninsula, besides being exposed to the weather, are also ill-drained. Around the granite intrusions are areas of metamorphic rocks and between these are zones of sedimentary strata. Mid and east Cornwall is a dissected plateau country varying in altitude from 200 to upwards of 800 feet, while its soils range from light or medium loams to heavy clays. In the north east, north of a line from Camelford to Launceston, there are outcrops of Carboniferous culm measures with soils grading from stony loams to heavy clays. The western coastlands are broadly similar to mid and east Cornwall. There is also a small extent of alluvial land in the county as around Penzance. Cornwall's maritime climate lacks extremes of temperature; rainfall is experienced all the year round, the maximum usually occurring in winter. Strong winds, particularly from the north west, could damage crops and this was a factor which assistant tithe commissioners did take into account when making their valuations. At Moorwinstow ·'adjoining the North Channel and open to the blast from it, corn is very often lost, very healthy for sheep'; at Minster the north west wind in winter 'which here is from November to May so cuts up the herbage and very much deteriorates its value'.[16]

Land use in Cornwall circa 1840

Two previous studies of Cornish agriculture which have used tithe survey evidence, those of T.R.B. Dicks and N. Hilton both stress that in 1840 there was a considerable arable acreage in this county.[17] In the Lands' End Peninsula, Hilton considered that the maximum extent of arable farming was reached in the 1840s. He was aware, though, that the arable acreages recorded in his source, the tithe apportionments, did include rotation grasses so that the extent of arable could not be used as an indicator of the efficiency of husbandry. Dr Dicks, on the other hand, appears to make no allowance for the inclusion of infrequently ploughed land in the arable category and thus the picture of arable farming that he draws is somewhat misleading. Figure 4 is a map of arable excluding rotation grasses compiled from evidence recorded by assistant tithe commissioners in their reports on tithe agreements. It shows that in only one parish, St Minver, was the annual acreage of land under crops greater than 40 per cent of total land area. W.F. Karkeek in his *Prize Essay,* 'On the Farming of Cornwall', reported that in this district of slate and sandstone rocks there was much very valuable soil and that the usual course of cropping was 'to break two years old pasture for wheat, barley and seeds, and occasionally 4 and 5 per cent of potatoes preceeding the wheat'.[18] For all other Cornish parishes with extant data in the tithe files, less than 40 per cent of their area was occupied by arable; for many the figure was less than 20 per cent. Parishes on the Hartland Plateau and Bodmin Moor had particularly low proportions of arable to pasture.

Associated with these low arable acreages were exceptionally long rotations; the four-course rotation typical of eastern counties was found in only a very few Cornish parishes. The traditional Devon and Cornwall system of paring and burning old grassland and then manuring it with sea-sand, lime, seaweed or pilchards, depending on availability, and then growing several crops of corn, the last being undersown with grass seed, was still being followed by many farmers.[19] Rotations of five to eight years were the most frequently recorded, the variation in length being just a matter of how many years a piece of land was allowed to lie in seeds. Karkeek noted that a new rotation was being adopted in some parts of Cornwall '*viz.* wheat, turnips or other green crop, followed by barley or oats and laid down to pasture for two or three years'.[20] In his opinion, the Norfolk system was only successful on farms of substantial capital, a fact which he thought would limit its general adoption throughout Cornwall.[21]

Crops on the arable

The acreages of particular crops, the proportions of the arable that they occupied and their yields *circa* 1840 are summarised in Table 3. In most parishes for which precise figures are stated, wheat occupied about a third of the arable *circa* 1840 (Figure 5). Statements in the tithe file reports suggest that when ley pastures were broken up, they were generally sown with wheat the first year and then the next year with barley or oats with which some grass seeds were sown. Where the convertible system was being followed, wheat averaged less than a third. This was the case at Anthony in the East where approximately one quarter of the arable was in wheat, about the same in turnips and about a third in barley.[22] At Pelynt, the figures for grain crops were much the same 'but here only a sixth was in turnips and some oats were also grown'.[23] The wheat yields quoted in the tithe files do not vary greatly over the county. They were low compared with eastern parts of England, rarely as high as 24 bushels per acre while yields of 16 bushels per acre or less were recorded in a majority of parishes (Figure 6).

Barley usually followed wheat under the old Cornish system, and a root crop where the convertible system of husbandry was practised. However, the tithe files record that in many parishes both barley and oats were being grown in the second season that land was under the plough and the assistant commissioners frequently neglected to quote separate acreage figures. For this reason maps of barley and oats are not presented. The tithe files do indicate, however, that barley was grown in all but one of the parishes for which tithe file crop data are extant. In some of the south-eastern parishes like Anthony where no oats were grown, barley occupied more than a third of the arable acreage. Barley yields varied from 16 bushels per acre to 40 bushels per acre; yields of more than 32 bushels were not uncommon particularly in the west of the county (Figure 7). Relative to the rest of England, barley yielded better in Cornwall than did wheat. Rham also noted this fact, remarking that the naked barley, pillez, was much grown in the western part of the county for the purpose of fattening pigs and poultry and for making into gruel for fattening calves. He says 'it is highly productive and well worthy of being introduced into other parts of the country'.[24]

In only three parishes for which data are extant was more than one third sown with oats. These were the three inland parishes of St Stephen in Branwell, Gwennap and Trewenn all situated on the granite uplands. In fact at St Stephen, little other grain was grown. Elsewhere, the percentage of arable in oats rarely exceeded more than one fifth and in the productive south-east they were very little grown. Although it is not possible to ascertain precise acreages of oats for a useful number of parishes, the tithe files do record the yield of oats for almost all of the parishes where their cultivation was noted. As Figure 8 shows, yields were highest in the west of the county where in several parishes the figure exceeded 40 bushels an acre. In some poor, eastern parishes, yields as low as 16 bushels an acre were recorded.

The cultivation of pulse crops, peas and beans, is rarely noted in the tithe files and Karkeek confirms that they were a rarity in Cornwall. 'The bean' he says, 'has been tried by Mr Enys of Enys, but with only partial success'. 'I have obtained' he says, 'in most instances a full crop of stalks and flowers, varying from 4 to 5 feet high, but on the whole the yield was below the general average of the kingdom'.[25]

From evidence in the tithe files, turnips and potatoes were quite widely grown. However, in their reports the assistant commissioners frequently classed them together as one course in the rotation so again no maps are presented of the data for the few parishes for which separate information is available. Yields of these crops which generated mainly small tithes were also not given in consistent form; William Glasson, for example noted yields of turnips in tons per acre rather than the more common £ per acre.

Potato growing was especially important in the parishes of the south-west of the peninsula around Penzance. The tithe files again do not record the acreages of potatoes in any consistent fashion but Table 4, which presents the acreages available for nine parishes, indicates the importance of the Penzance district as an area which supplied the London market with early potatoes. In Penzance parish itself, a dispute in 1840 over the amount of tithe payable on potatoes led assistant commissioner George Louis to summon evidence from a wide range of farmers. This evidence, recorded at length in the tithe file, supports his summary statement that '2 crops in one year are produced either of potatoes, or one crop of potatoes and one of turnips: the first crop is estimated at £40 an acre, the second at £10 as regards the worth of the produce. Onions and cabbages are also grown, worth if onions from £40 to £60 – if cabbages, £20 to £30 per acre'.[26] Early potatoes could fetch a really high price, James Jerwood at Gulval quoted £100 per acre.[27] There was also, of course, the corollary that in bad years there could be a total failure; between 1839 and 1845, the potato crop in Cornwall was badly affected by disease.[28]

As might be expected from comments on the nature of rotations in the section above, seed crops formed a large proportion of the pasture acreage in Cornwall. The tithe files are rather silent on precisely which artificial grasses were grown but from a number of comments it appears that a large proportion was clover as at St Minver where Charles Pym in 1838 noted that 'from the nature of the soil in a large portion of the parish the green crop, chiefly clover, is of little value after the first year and is much affected by a dry season'.[29] Karkeek included both sainfoin and lucerne in his list of crops rarely grown in Cornwall but said that rape had been introduced with some success as a preparation for wheat.[30] The pattern of yields of mown hay from seeds is indicated in Figure 9. In the north-east, a number of parishes obtained yields of less than 20 cwts but the average was 22 cwts per acre, quite respectable by national standards. Yields by weight were, of course, difficult for assistant commissioners to check; they were well aware of the great difference in the weight of hay from artificials when freshly mown or after stacking. At Ludgvan, William Glasson noted, 'of hay when green in the field 2 ton per acre or one ton seven hundred when dry and fit to cut out of the stack'.[31]

Manures and fertilisers applied to the arable were a matter of interest to the assistant tithe commissioners as the extent of manuring and marling could affect the quantity of titheable produce. In coastal parishes sand, seaweed and fish were usually fairly easily obtained and were applied in quite liberal quantities to land newly brought into tillage from grass.[32] Inland, it was more difficult to procure manures. At Week St Mary, for example, it is reported that 'sand is procured with difficulty on account of the hills and bad roads and lime is very expensive, rarely if ever used'.[33] Similarly, at St Columb Major, William Glasson noted that the parish lay 'a long distance from lime kilns the nearest being 12 miles – also a distance of 5 miles from sand so that this parish is not well situated as for many others for procuring manure'.[34] Generally, lime was reported to be more easily available along the south coast than in north coast parishes.[35] Karkeek also recorded some of the first instances of bone dust being used in Cornwall as a preparation for the turnip crop.[36]

Grassland

Figure 10 indicates the distribution of grassland in Cornwall *circa* 1840 according to the criteria of definition noted in the *introduction* above. This illustrates the fact that when the acreage of long ley pastures is added to that of 'permanent' grass, then Cornwall can properly be characterised a 'grassland county' and a corrective provided to the somewhat misleading evidence in tithe apportionments.[37] In the 1840s in Cornwall, there was no great extent of natural meadow, a deficiency that was made up largely by the practice of laying down the arable with artificial grasses. Hay was then cut from both meadows and ley pastures.

In many parishes, more than 60 per cent of total acreage was down to grass in any one year *circa* 1840. One group of parishes in this category is in the extreme north-east of the county on the Hartland Plateau and around the fringes of Bodmin Moor. In this area the soil is mainly a heavy clay and although the larger, progressive farmers tried not to leave their seeds down for more than three years, Karkeek reported that many of the smaller farmers on the moors took three corn crops in succession and then left the land free from tillage for many years to recover.[38] A second area of extensive grassland lay to the north-east of Truro including parishes such as Probus, St Erme and Newlyn. Very few parishes in Cornwall had grassland percentages falling within the 20–40 per cent band, a common level for southern and eastern England. Some places which had low grassland figures had correspondingly high percentages of common as at St Just in Penwith and Gwennap.[39] No Cornish parish for which data is extant in tithe files had less than 20 per cent pasture.

If Figure 10 is compared with Figure 11 which is a map of meadow yield, it can be seen that high yields of mown grass do not correspond with parishes with a high proportion of grassland but rather with the reverse. Parishes on the Hartland Plateau had more than 80 per cent of land under grass but mowing yields of less than 25 cwt per acre. The highest yields occurred in the extreme south-west of the county. In St Just in Penwith, Gulval, St Erth and Breage, yields were more than 30 cwt an acre which ranked among the best in the country at this time. In the eastern parts of the county, yields are generally lower at around 20–25 cwt per acre while in a few places in north-east Cornwall they dipped below 20 cwt. These few parishes apart, the evidence of the tithe files suggests that Cornish farmers obtained some of the best meadow yields in the country.

Very many parishes in Cornwall also possessed large areas of rough grazing, known locally as 'crofts'. This land of very low titheable value, though sometimes quite valuable for the summer pasture of stock, was often enumerated under the heading reserved for common in the tithe file reports.

Livestock

As noted in the introduction, the tithe files of the principally pastoral counties contain evidence on the number of stock pastured on the parish grasslands. Cornwall is no exception to this rule so that for most parishes where tithe was commuted by agreement, assistant commissioners estimated the numbers of cows, bullocks, horses and sheep kept in the parish. Unfortunately the tithe files are silent on pig rearing, although it is known that pigs were kept in substantial numbers in many parishes in the west of the county. In Gwennap, for example, William Glasson chanced to remark in his report that about 4,000 pigs were kept.[40]

Assistant commissioners who were primarily concerned with the produce of the grass were more concerned with numbers of animals rather than breeds which they rarely mention by name. This highlights a serious deficiency in tithe survey evidence. Tithe was a tax and although the surveys and papers produced in the course of its commutation do assist in reconstructing some aspects of farming, they are concerned in a systematic way with only those aspects of direct concern to the calculation and apportionment of rent charge. In Cornwall, for example, the first forty years of the nineteenth century had witnessed the introduction of many improved breeds of cattle and sheep but on this improvement assistant commissioners were silent, needing only to count heads to assess grassland rent charge.

Figure 12 plots the number of cows per 100 acres of pasture and shows that stocking densities varied little over the county. In east Cornwall there was no parish for which data is available with more than 10 cows per 100 acres, in the west densities were a little higher ranging into the 30s per 100 acres. The number of bullocks per acre of pasture varied much more than the stocking ratio of cows (Figure 13). The lowest densities of bullocks were to be found in the eastern part of the county. Densities were generally higher in the west but there were marked variations from parish to parish. The highest density was recorded for Madron which includes the town of Penzance. The distribution of sheep shown on Figure 14 is in marked contrast to that of cattle. With the exception of the Hartland Plateau area, the densities of sheep were greater in the east than the west. The stocking density of horses did not vary much; horses were as much dependent on grains like oats for feed as they were on pastures. In the east of the county no parish had more than 10 horses per 100 acres but in the west in a few parishes the density did rise to between 10 and 30 per 100 acres.

Unfarmed land

The extent of *woodland* in Cornwall *circa* 1840 was not consider-able; no parish for which tithe file data is extant had woods occupy-ing more than 20 per cent of total parish area, although it must be reiterated that the woodland category was probably one of the least accurately estimated or surveyed by assistant commissioners because mature timber was exempt from tithe, only underwood and young plantations were titheable. Nevertheless, the general picture which the tithe files provide of the distribution of woodland probably holds true, *viz.* an absence of woodland in extreme south-western parishes and with less than 10 per cent in a majority of others. Some coppice yields are available for a few parishes and from this limited data it seems that this was most prized around the Fal estuary where values were usually greater than 15/- per acre per annum, whilst elsewhere it fell below this figure. There is also evidence that the demand for coppice for metal smelting was on the decline.[41] Commons, many of them very poor, were also extensive in Cornwall (Figure 15). They were important for summer grazing of cattle while the crofts, as noted above, were occasionally fenced for a couple of years and ploughed for one or two corn crops.

Postscript

In this article we have presented in summary fashion some of the tithe file evidence which bears on the nature of land use and farming in Cornwall *circa*1840. The pattern that tithe surveys describe is the end result of a multitude of decisions by farmers and land owners; tithe maps and apportionments are largely silent on the mechanisms of agricultural organisation and the processes producing change around mid-century. We hope that this short article has illustrated some of the areas in which evidence from the Cornwall tithe files can illuminate matters on which the maps and apportionments are either unhelpful or in fact downright misleading. There is also much more material as yet untouched in the tithe files of this county which we have indexed by subject in the appendix.

[1] E.J. Evans, *The Contentious Tithe: The Tithe Problem and English Agriculture,* 1750-1850 (1976); E.J. Evans, *Tithes and the Tithe Commutation Act 1836* (1978); R.J.P. Kain, 'Tithe as an index of pre-industrial agricultural production', *The Agricultural History Review,* 27 (1979), pp. 73-81.

[2] H.C. Prince, 'The tithe surveys of the mid-nineteenth century', *The Agricultural History Review,* 7 (1959), pp. 14–26; R.J.P. Kain, 'The tithe commutation surveys', *Archaeologia Cantiana,* 89 (1974), pp. 101–8.

[3] E.A. Cox and B.R. Dittmer, 'The tithe files of the mid-nineteenth century', *The Agricultural History Review,* 13 (1965), pp. 1–16.

[4] R.J.P. Kain, 'Compiling an atlas of agriculture in England and Wales from the tithe surveys', *The Geographical Journal,* 145 (1979), pp. 225–241.

[5] Public Record Office. Inland Revenue, I.R. 18/388, 477, 401.

[6] P.R.O. I.R. 18/383.

[7] P.R.O. I.R. 18/462.

[8] P.R.O. I.R. 18/451.

[9] P.R.O. I.R. 18/461.

[10] P.R.O. I.R. 18/448.

[11] P.R.O. I.R. 18/454.

[12] A.D.M. Phillips, 'A study of farming practices and soil types in Staffordshire around 1840', *North Staffordshire Journal of Field Studies,* 13 (1973), pp. 27–52; 'Agricultural land use, soils and the Nottinghamshire tithe surveys *circa* 1840', *East Midland Geographer,* 6 (1976), pp. 284–301; R.J.P. Kain, *The Land of Kent in the Middle of the Nineteenth century,* unpublished University of London Ph.D thesis (1973).

[13] Parish acreages in the 1851 census were derived from the tithe surveys.

[14] T.C. Waugh, *GIMMS Reference Manual*, Inter-University/Research Council Series, Report No. 30 (1977).

[15] Reference might be made, for example, to A.H. Shorter, W.L.D. Ravenhill and K.J. Gregory, *Southwest England* (1969).

[16] P.R.O. I.R. 18/466, 478.

[17] T.R.B. Dicks, *The South-Western Peninsulas of England and Wales: Studies in Agricultural Geography, 1550–1900*, unpublished University of Wales Ph.D. thesis (1964); N. Hilton, 'The Land's End peninsula: the influence of history on agriculture', *The Geographical Journal*, 119 (1953), pp. 57–72.

[18] W.F. Karkeek, 'On the farming of Cornwall', *Journal of the Royal Agricultural Society of England*, 6 (1945), p. 413.

[19] W.L. Rham, *The Dictionary of the Farm* (1845), p. 154.

[20] Karkeek, *J.R.A.S.E.*, 6 (1845), p. 433.

[21] *Ibid.*, p. 437.

[22] P.R.O. I.R. 18/341.

[23] P.R.O. I.R. 18/486.

[24] Rham, *Dictionary* (1845), p. 154.

[25] Karkeek, *J.R.A.S.E.*, 6 (1845), p. 432.

[26] P.R.O. I.R. 18/488.

[27] P.R.O. I.R. 18/403.

[28] Sir C. Lemon, 'On a disease in potatoes', *J.R.A.S.E.*, 4 (1843), pp. 431–5; J. Couch, 'Further remarks on the potato disease', *Report of the Royal Cornwall Polytechnic Society*, 16 (1848), pp. 1–2; 'Further enquiries into the nature and effects of the prevailing disease in potatoes', *Report R.C.P.S.*, 15 (1847), pp. 1–11; J.S. Enys, 'Remarks on double cropping as a means of lessening the risk of growing potatoes', Report R.C.P.S., 14 (1846), pp. 15–17.

[29] P.R.O. I.R. 18/479.

[30] Karkeek, *J.R.A.S.E., 6 (1945), p. 432.*

[31] P.R.O. I.R. 18/447; see also the land agent Henry Badcock's comments on harvesting seeds in *Practical observations on the Husbandry of the District* (1849), pp. 23-4.

[32] P.R.O. I.R. 18/381.

[33] P.R.O. I.R. 18/542.

[34] P.R.O. I.R. 18/367.   [35] P.R.O. I.R. 18/381.

[36] Karkeek, *J.R.A.S.E.*, 6 (1945), p. 403.

[37] Dicks, *The South-Western Peninsulas* (1964).

[38] Karkeek, *J.R.A.S.E.*, 6 (1845), p. 414.

[39] P.R.O. I.R. 18/405, 418.

[40] P.R.O. I.R. 18/405; Rham, *Dictionary* (1845), p. 154.

[41] P.R.O. I.R. 18/362.

Table 1

Authors and dates of reports on agreements for tithe commutation in Cornwall

Assistant Commissioner	Total	1837	1838	1839	1840	1841	1842	1843	1844	1845
James Jerwood	61			1	24	19	9	4	3	1
William Glasson	44		11	24	9					
Charles Pym	6	2	4							
Fred. Leigh	2				2					
George Louis	2		1					1		
William Richards	1			1						
TOTALS	116	2	16	26	35	19	9	5	3	1

Source: P.R.O. I.R. 18/337–548

Table 2

Land use in Cornwall c. 1840

land use	sample size	acreage enumerated	% acreage enumerated	acreage for whole county (sample x 3.0727)
Arable	74	65,877	24.4	202,420
Grass	74	152,228	55.5	467,751
Wood	74	9,113	3.2	28,002
Common	74	54,939	15.0	168,811
Orchards	73	1,928	0.8	5,924
Gardens	73	228	0.1	701
TOTALS		284,313	99	872,207

'Sample size' in Tables 2 and 3 is the number of parishes with extant data for particular land uses and crops. These sample data have been used to obtain estimates for the whole county by aggregation using variable multipliers based on the relationship between area covered by sample and total area of Cornwall. In the case of land use in Table 2, for example, this multiplier is calculated as 3.0727. As can be seen from Figure 3, parishes with extant tithe data are not uniformly distributed over the county; Bodmin Moor and east-central Cornwall are under-represented. Nevertheless, it is contended that the sample data provide a better basis for estimation of production quantities for Cornwall than can be obtained from other, even more fragmentary, mid-nineteenth century sources.

Table 3

Crop acreages, yields and gross produce in Cornwall c. 1840

Crop	Sample size	Mean % arable *	Mean yield	County acreage	Gross produce in millions of bushels
Wheat	47	31.75	17.9 bus	64,268	1.15
Barley	24	30.73	28.2 bus	62,204	1.75
Oats	25	9.86	31.0 bus	19,959	0.62
Pulses	74	0	–	–	–
Turnips	58	0.62	3.0 £s	1,255	–

* The remainder of the arable was sown with a variety of fallow crops, green crops and potatoes none of which was enumerated sufficiently consistently to be incorporated in the Table.

Table 4

Potato cultivation in Cornwall circa 1840

parish	date of report	potato acreage	titheable acreage
Gwennap	1838	73	5291
St Johns	1840	30	658
Lanlivery	1840	100	6492
Launcells	1840	140	5385
St Mewan	1838	12	2240
Pelynt	1840	100	417
St Stephens in Branwell	1838	121	7980
St Stephens by Saltash	1841	200	4993
St Veep	1839	30	2274

List of Figures

1. Printed report on a tithe commutation agreement, Parish of Lanteglos-by-Fowey. Reproduced by permission of the Public Record Office, London. These printed reports were usually accompanied by hand-written covering notes containing further information.
2. Some elements of the physical environment of agriculture in Cornwall.
3. Boundaries of tithe districts with extant data. Compiled by Rodney Fry from the Tithe Index Edition of the Old Series Ordnance Survey one-inch maps. A key to the tithe district numbers is provided in the index.
4. Arable excluding seeds as a percentage of titheable area *circa* 1840.
5. Wheat as a percentage of arable *circa* 1840.
6. Yield of wheat in bushels per acre *circa* 1840.
7. Yields of barley in bushels per acre *circa* 1840.
8. Yield of oats in bushels per acre *circa* 1840.
9. Yield of clover and seeds in cwts per acre *circa* 1840.
10. Grassland including seeds as a percentage of titheable area *circa* 1840.
11. Yield of meadow in cwts. per acre *circa* 1840.
12. Cows per 100 acres of pasture *circa* 1840.
13. Bullocks per 100 acres of pasture *circa* 1840.
14. Sheep per 100 acres of pasture *circa* 1840.
15. Common as a percentage of titheable area *circa* 1840.

Fig 1.

31 JULY 1839

Parish of *Lanteglos by Fowey*   County of *Cornwall*

QUESTIONS.	ANSWERS
1.—How many Acres of Arable Land (including under that description the Land actually ploughed in the present or last season, whether sown with corn, planted with roots or fallow, but excluding seeds)?	*900 Acres in Corn 250 in roots 1150*
2.—What is the course of Crops?	*Wheat Barley or Oats & then wop Turnips or Potatos or Barley then Seeds*
3.—What is the nature of the Soil?	*thin light gravelly soil on this or Clay Slate*
4.—What is the Sub-soil?	*Clay Slate & occasionly Quartz.*
5.—What description of Timber grown in the Hedge-rows, or otherwise; Oak, Elm, Ash or Beech?	*a few Elm*
6.—What is the fair average rentable Value per acre of the Arable Land?	*25/. per acre*
7.—What is the number of Acres of Pasture, including seeds?	*420 of Seeds 250 of Meadow & Pasture 830 Pasture after Seed until broke up again for tillage 20 orchard 1520*

(2)

QUESTIONS.	ANSWERS.
8.—What is the nature of the Soil ?	*as at N° 3*
9.—What is the Sub-soil ?	*same as N° 4*
10.—What description of Timber ?	*small Oak Elm & in Plantations*
11.—What is the number of Acres of Common? *or Cliff ground that cannot be converted into tillage .*	*100 Acres*
12.—Stock :	
Number of Cows?	*60*
Ditto - Bullocks?	*320*
Ditto - Horses? *Helts*	*102*
Ditto - Sheep? *& Lambs*	*1700*
13.—What is the fair average rentable Value of the Pasture ?	*30/ plane for eed Cwt 25/ for D° for D° Eat off 15/ for the Pasture after Seed 40/ for the Meadow & Pasture £3 — for the orchard*
14.—Ditto, of the Common ?	*2/6 p acre*
15.—Average Composition on the seven years previous to Christmas 1835 -	*£. s. d. Enclosure £2.15 Glebe } 528. 0 .0*
Add average amount of Rates, if paid by the Occupiers or Landowners for the Tithe-owner - - - -	*paid by the owners £528. 0. 0*

(3)

VALUATION.

	£.	s.	d.

1150 Arable One-fifth of the Arable, at *25* per Acre — *287.10.0*
420 Seeds — 315 ~ *30/ & there ~ 105~ 20 / & 8/8* — *72.3.9*
830 —— One-eighth of the Pasture, at *15/* per Acre - *77.16.3*
250 Meadow & Pasture . . ~ *46/ & & &* - *62.10.0*
100 —— One-eighth of the Common, *so (24/ & 2/6* per Acre - *1.11.3*
20 — *orchard* . . . ~*£3- & 8 & &* - *7.10.0*
2770 Total

	Total - - -	£ *509.1.3*	
315 Great Tithes above 1.15 Glebe			
225 Vicarial above Total Rent-charge, exclusive of Glebe - -	*540.0.0*	
540. £1. Glebe			
	Difference - - - £ *30.18.9*	

Remarks, stating the peculiar circumstances of the Parish, which may affect the value of the Tithe. *No particular circumstance Except roads very bad & very rolly Upon the Great Tithes having been yearly valued & led to the Farmer & taken in kind, and the small Tithes Leased to Yeoman of the Parish, in the Vicars life they have taken as near the full value as possible. W. Clapton*

Lanteglos by Fowey 8 July 1829

Fig 2.

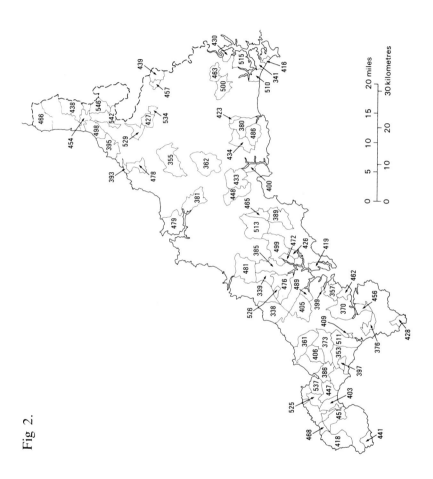

Fig 3.

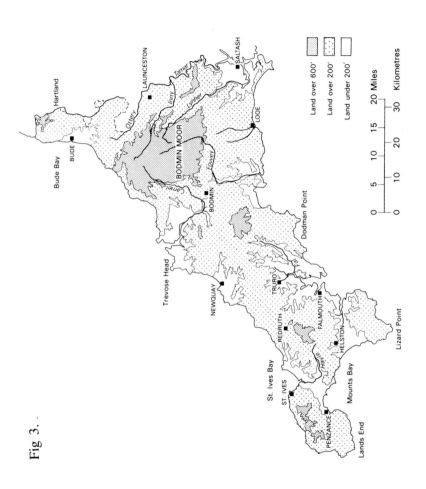

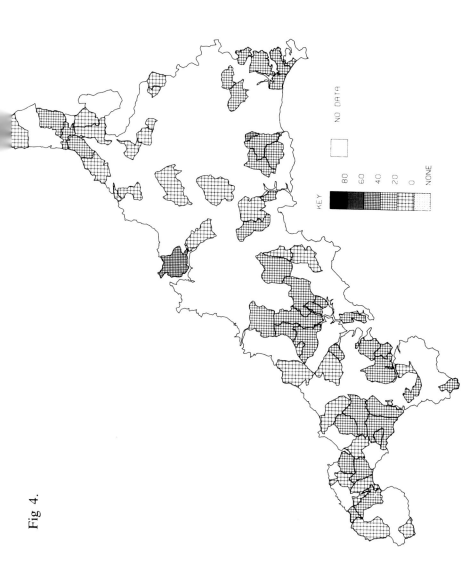

Fig 4.

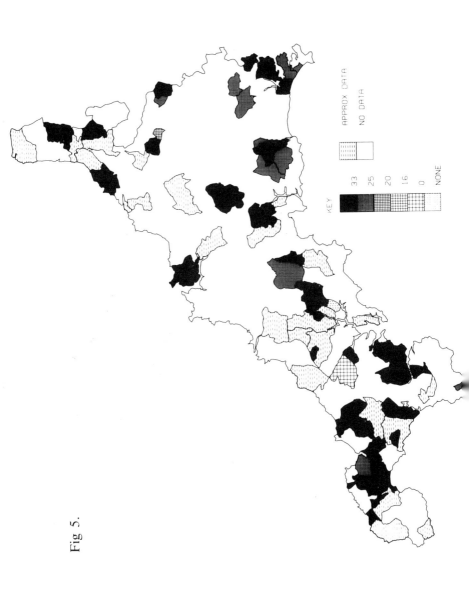

Fig 5.

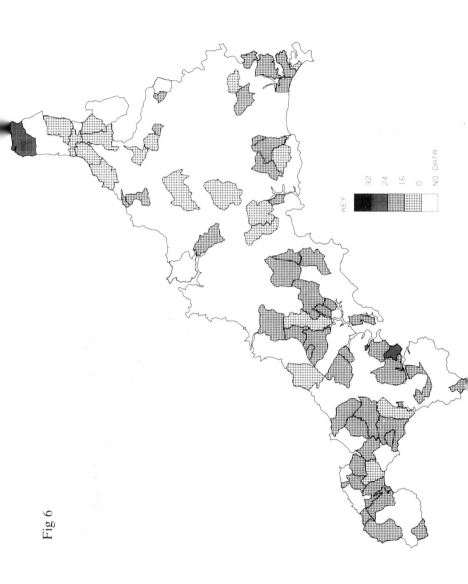

Fig 6

KEY
32
24
16
0
NO DATA

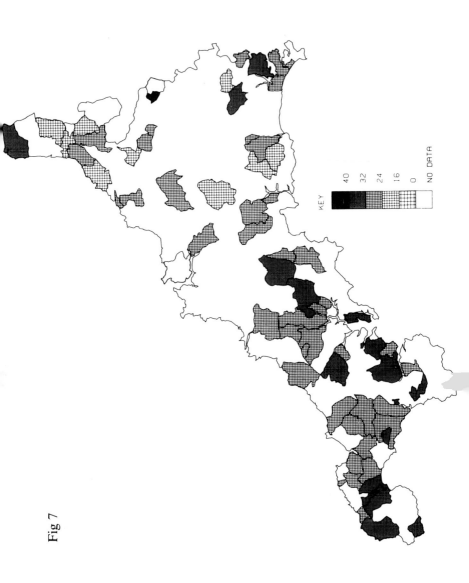

Fig 7

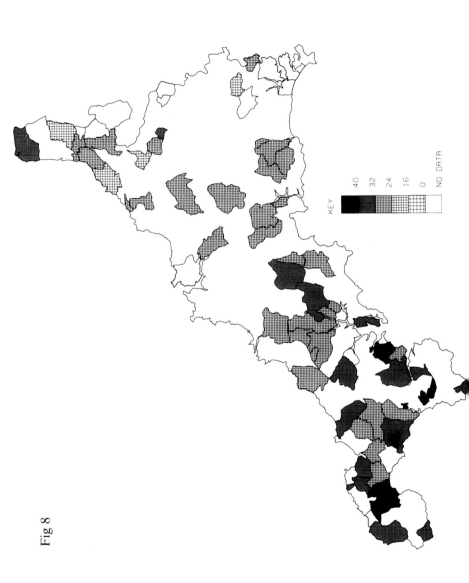

Fig 8

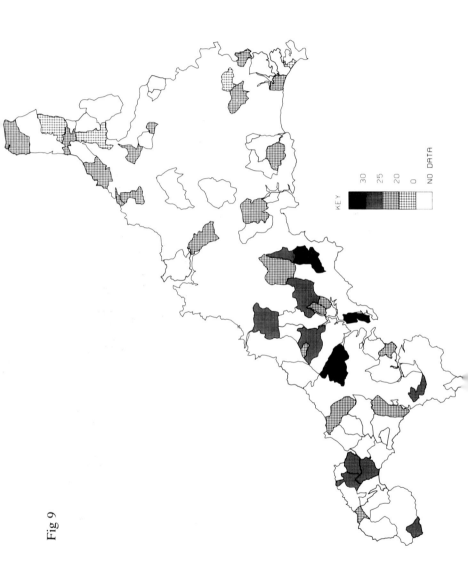

Fig 9

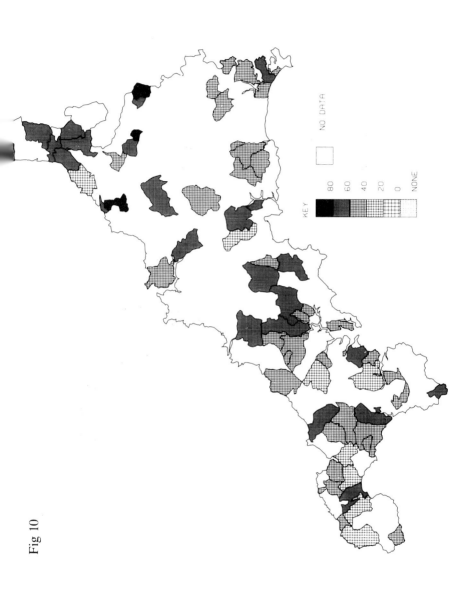

Fig 10

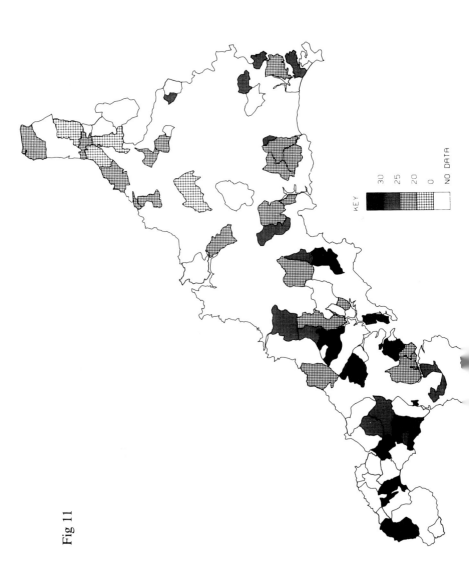

Fig 11

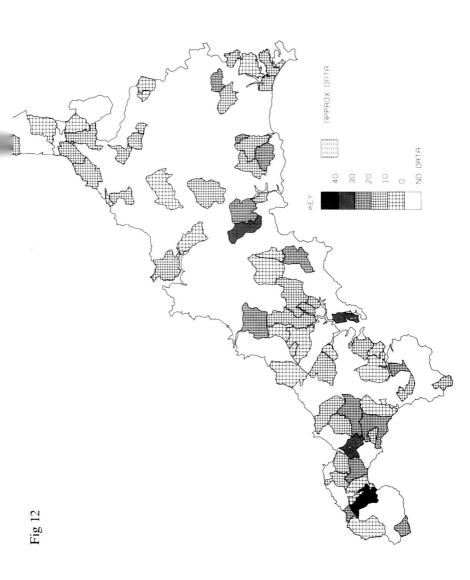

Fig 12

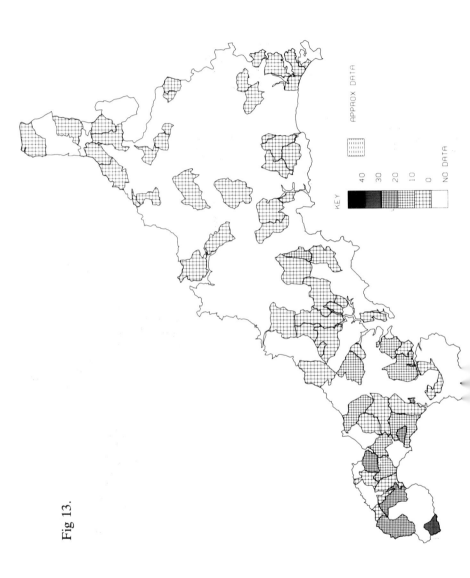

Fig 13.

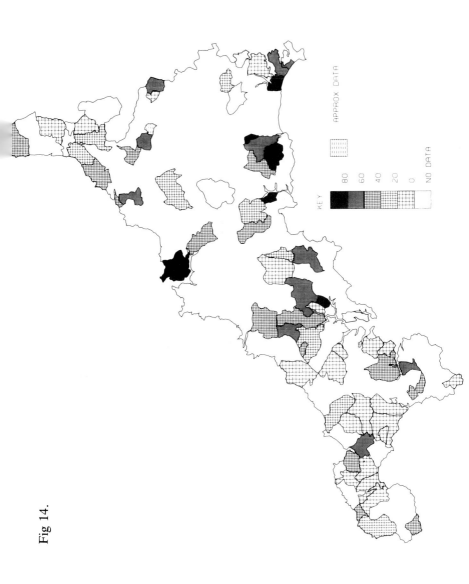

Fig 14.

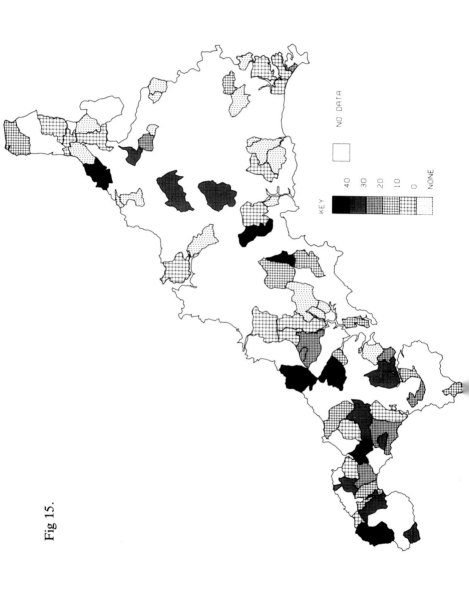

Fig 15.

Appendix

Cornwall

P.R.O. Reference Numbers and Tithe District Names

337 Advent	370 Constantine
338 St Agnes	371 Crantock
339 St Allen	372 Creed
340 Alternun	373 Crowan
341 Anthony in the East	374 Cubert
342 St Anthony in Meneage	375 Cuby
343 St Anthony in Roseland	376 Cury
344 St Austell	377 Davidstone
345 St Blazey	378 St Dennis
346 Blisland	379 St Dominick
347 Boconnoc	380 Duloe
348 Bodmin	381 Egloshayle
349 Botus Fleming	382 Egloskerry
350 Boyton	383 Endellion
351 Braddock	384 St Enoder
352 Bradridge	385 St Erme
353 Breage	386 St Erth
354 St Breock	387 St Ervan
355 St Breward	388 St Eval
356 Bridgerule West	389 St Ewe
357 Budock	390 Falmouth
358 St Buryan	391 Feock
359 Callington	392 Filley
360 Calstock	393 Forrabury
361 Camborne	394 Fowey
362 Cardynham	395 St Gennys
363 St Cleather	396 St Germans
364 St Cleer	397 Germoe
365 St Clements	398 Gerrans
366 Colan	399 St Gluvias
367 St Columb Major	400 Golant
368 Cornelly	401 St Gorran
369 St Columb Minor	402 Grade

403 Gulval
404 Gunwalloe
405 Gwennap
406 Gwinear
407 Gwithian
408 Helland
409 Helston
410 St Hilary
411 Illogan
412 St Issey
413 St Ive
414 St Ives
415 Jacobstow
416 St Johns
417 St Juliot
418 St Just in Penwith
419 St Just in Roseland
420 Kea
421 St Keverne
422 St Kew
423 St Keyne
424 Kilkhampton
425 Ladock
426 Lamorran
427 Laneast
428 Landewednack
429 Landrake with St Erney
430 Landulph
431 Lanhydrock
432 Lanivet
433 Lanlivery
434 Lanreath
435 Lansallos
436 Lanteglos by Camelford
437 Lanteglos by Fowey
438 Launcells
439 Lawhitton
440 Lesnewth
441 St Levan
442 Lewannick
443 Lezant
444 Linkinhorne

445 Liskeard
446 Lostwithiel
447 Ludgvan
448 Luxulian
449 Mabe
450 St Mabyn
451 Madron
452 Manaccan
453 Marazion
454 Marham Church
455 St Martin or St Keyne
456 St Martin in Meneage
457 St Mary Magdalene
458 St Mary Scilly Isles
459 St Mary Truro
460 Mawgan in Meneage
461 Mawgan in Pyder
462 Mawnan
463 St Mellion
464 Menheniot
465 St Mewan
466 Moorwinstow
467 Morvah
468 Morval
469 Mullion
470 Mylor
471 St Merryn
472 Merther
473 Mevagissy
474 St Michael Carhayes
475 St Michael Penkivel
476 Kenwyn
477 Michaelstow
478 Minster
479 St Minver
480 St Neot
481 Newlyn
482 North-Hill
483 Otterham
484 Padstow
485 Paul
486 Pelynt

487 Penryn
488 Penzance
489 Perranarworthal
490 Perranuthnoe
491 Perranzabucoe
492 Petherwin South
493 Petherick Little
494 Phillack
495 Pillaton
496 Pinnock St
497 Poughill
498 Poundstock
499 Probus
500 Quethiock
501 Rame
502 Redruth
503 Roche
504 Ruan Lanihorne
505 Ruan Major
506 Ruan Minor
507 Sancreed
508 Scilly Isles
509 Sennen
510 Sheviock
511 Sithney
512 South-Hill
513 St Stephens in Branwell
514 St Stephens in Launceston
515 St Stephens by Saltash
516 Stithians
517 Stoke Climsland
518 Stratton
519 Talland
520 Tamerton North
521 St Teath
522 Temple
523 St Thomas the Apostle
524 Tintagel
525 Towednack
526 Tregavethan
527 Tregony Borough
528 Tregony St James

529 Treneglos
530 Tremayne
531 Tresmeer
532 Trevalga
533 Trewarlet
534 Trewenn
535 St Tudy
536 Tywardreth
537 Uny Lelant
538 Veep St
539 Veryan
540 Warbstow
541 Warleggan
542 Week St Mary
543 Wendron
544 Wenn St
545 Winnow St
546 Whitstone
547 Withiel
548 Zennor

Subject Index to Cornwall Tithe Files

Numbers are Public Record Office Class I.R.18 References

Tithes

History of Tithe Payment: 378 458 492 517

Exemptions from Tithe: 352 362 396 401 427 433 470 523

Tithe in kind: 341 351 355 371 395 400 437 448 450 462 474 479
513 538 540

Compositions: 337 348 349 354 359 372 375 378 379 384 387 388
390 391 392 394 396 398 401 402 408 412 415 417 421 422 424
425 435 440 443 445 449 464 467 469 470 471 473 474 477 482
484 485 488 492 493 495 496 497 501 504 507 512 516 519 520
521 522 524 527 528 532 533 535 539 540 544 548

Moduses: 337 347 350 356 366 379 387 396 402 408 422 441 471
477 493 495 509 517 520 521 524

Glebe: 340 347 354 359 360 363 365 372 375 384 387 391 392
396 398 401 402 404 408 410 415 417 422 425 429 432 436 443
445 450 464 468 470 473 480 483 493 495 496 497 504 506 507
512 516 519 522 524 527 528 532 535 539 544 548

Rural Landscapes

General Topographic Descriptions

Local: 364 389 400 448 466 541

Regional: 347 377 389 395 400 455 505

Settlements

Village Morphology: 351 447 536

Farm Houses and Buildings: 468

Fields

Open Fields: 448 462 537

Woodland

Hedgerow Timber: 339 341 342 345 355 357 358 361 362 364 367
368 369 370 373 376 377 380 381 382 383 385 389 395 399 400
405 406 407 409 411 413 416 420 423 426 430 431 433 434 437
438 439 442 444 446 448 452 454 455 456 457 460 461 462 463
465 466 468 472 475 476 481 487 489 491 494 498 499 500 502
505 510 511 513 514 515 525 526 531 536 538 541 542 543 545
546 547

Coppice: 351 362 368 370 380 399 413 419 422 423 430 431 444
463 468 476 478 486 489 492 499 500 510 515 547

Plantations; 347 351 361 370 385 407 411 423 427 437 448 451

Woodland Management: 347

Poor Woodland: 472   478   489   498   511   526

Uncultivated Land

Commons: 378   405

Furze, Gorse and Heathlands: 358   479

Moorland: 355

Agriculture

Factors Influencing Agriculture
A. Environment

Climatic Hazards: 395   461   466   478   529

Land Required Drainage: 373   389   416   542

Productive Soil: 345   367   371   376   381   403   515   538

Poor Soil: 343   367   381   395   478   491   505

Heavy (Clay) Soil: 338   339   341   342   357   361   364   368   369   373   376
380   385   389   395   397   399   406   411   413   416   419   420   427   428   430
434   438   439   442   452   456   457   460   463   465   468   472   476   479   481
486   490   491   498   500   502   505   510   513   514   515   518   525   526   530
541   545

Loamy (Turnip) Soil: 361   362   371   382   389   405   416   431   442   446   461
466   510   513   514   545

Light Soil: 347   371   376   393   395   399   400   406   407   423   426   428   433
437   444   448   451   455   456   457   460   461   472   475   478   531   536   538
541

Several Varieties of Soil: 362   364   368   369   373   545

Sand or Gravel: 341   405   494   515   518

Peat: 355   405   411   431   442   502   503   513   525   546

B. Transport and Marketing

Good Local Roads: 407   448   462

Poor Local Roads: 351   364   377   383   389   395   400   423   437   531   537
542

Turnpike and Main Roads: 377   537   545

Water Carriage: 343   364   426   475   515   545

Canals: 364

Railways: 448   541   545

Markets Accessible: 403   447   515

Markets Inaccessible: 351   395   400   466   531
Provincial Markets: 347   488   537
London Market: 403

C. Management

Landowners and their Estates: 357 362 441 461

Farm Size: 347 468 513 537

Leases: 373 380 411 451

Common Grazing: 380

Lammas and other Common Rights: 503 513

Rents: 403 419 451

Agricultural Change and Improvement

Lime: 364 367 381 455 461 475 513 531 542 545

Seasand: 364 367 381 385 455 461 475 513 531 541 542 545

Seaweed: 367

Arable Farming
A. Rotations

General Comments: 343 371 376 381 382 383 385 400 405 407 409
426 437 441 444 447 448 454 455 461 462 465 466 475 478 492
505 509 513 529 531 536 538 541 542 545

Irregular Rotation: 371

3-Course Rotation: 358 364 367 518 534

4-Course Rotation: 377 389 393 395 403 457 472 518 530

5-Course Rotation: 338 341 342 347 351 353 357 361 368 369 370
373 380 386 397 399 406 411 416 418 419 420 423 428 430 433
438 439 451 452 456 460 468 476 479 481 486 489 490 491 492
494 498 499 500 503 510 511 514 515 525 526 543 547

6-Course Rotation: 338 339 362 413 416 427 431 433 434 463 487
498 502

7-Course Rotation: 442 453 537

More than 10-Course Rotation: 453

B. Discussion of Corn Crops

Corn Yields: 389

C. Forage Crops Cultivated

Clover: 351 361 367 479

D. Roots and Fallows Noted

Turnips: 455 461 492

Potatoes: 341 345 364 376 381 383 385 393 395 400 401 403 405
409 416 423 426 433 437 438 444 446 447 448 451 454 455 461
462 465 466 478 486 488 492 505 513 515 531 536 537 538 541
542 545

E. Quality of Arable Farming
High Farming: 451   476
Low Farming: 416

Livestock Farming
A. Grassland
Good Quality Pastures: 409
Irrigation and Water Meadows: 377   444
Marsh Grassland: 363

B. Livestock
Cattle Breeding: 444
Cattle Fattening: 441
Dairying   441
Sheep Breeding: 347   448   541
Horses: 378
Pigs: 489   395   405   407   448   462
Poultry   389   395   405   407   462
Hay: 358   389
Butter: 389

Fruit, Vegetables and Industrial Crops
Fruits: 360
Cabbages: 409   488
Onions: 488
Reeds and Oziers: 421

'An Undoubted Jewel': a case study of five Sussex country houses, 1880-1914

P. BLACKWELL

'The efforts of social man, directed from immemorial time toward the stability of things, have culminated in Worsted Skeynes. Beyond commercial competition — for the estate no longer paid for living on it — beyond the power of expansion, set with tradition and sentiment, it was an undoubted jewel, past need of warranty'.[1]

So wrote John Galsworthy of his fictional *Country House* in 1907. Throughout the novel, Worsted Skeynes and its stolid, unimaginative inhabitants are assailed by malignant forces from a new, less structured and moralled, more urban and commercial society. Nevertheless, the old values and way of life emerge, in the end, deeply scarred but intact; a symbol of all Galsworthy despised, yet could never totally reject.[2] Like many novelists Galsworthy offered sympathetic insights into the fabric of his world which an historian can ill afford to ignore.

Studies of political, economic and legal changes have led most historians to see the late Victorian and Edwardian eras as the 'Indian Summer' of the English landed élite; a period of gradual but inexorable decline in social position and power, leading to almost complete collapse by the outbreak of war.

Even contemporaries, perhaps dazzled by the dramatic changes occurring around them, lamented the passing of 'traditional' English rural society. T.H.S. Escott felt that the 'squire à la mode' had replaced his eighteenth century predecessor in most counties; this fashionable gentleman was rarely if ever resident in his country seat, but spend most of his time in London, the centre of a glittering social whirl.[3] C.F.G. Masterman also struck a gloomy note when he wrote that '. . . estates are encumbered or falling into decay', while at the same time, 'in exercise and enjoyment, in parties and pleasure gardens . . . the decay passes almost unnoticed'.[4]

Modern historians have drawn a similar picture. According to G.E. Mingay and F.M.L. Thompson, falling farm rents undermined the position of the country squire, and caused retrenchment or re-investment in non-agricultural concerns. Under these pressures, traditional relationships with the tenantry and local community dis-integrated.[5] The dissipations of London society, Keith Middlemas maintains, were threatening the strength of the gentry family and distracting the squire and his lady from their age-old occupations and responsibilities. Increased reliance on servants for the care of children hastened the decay. Middlemas also suggests that servant-keeping was becoming a form of competitive consumption, rather than a social responsibility marked by traditional patterns of paternalism and deference.[6] Leonore Davidoff has described the decline of close-knit, exclusive upper class society, and the replace-ment of kinship ties as a prerequisite for admission, by a set of elaborate and arbitrary rules.[7]

Most historians point out the effect on the gentry of a series of legislative changes, amongst which were: the Reform Acts of 1867 and 1884; the introduction of county, rural, and parish councils; the House of Lords crisis of 1909; and the Ground Game Act and Agricultural Holdings legislation.[8] Each piece of legislation may be seen as an attempt to chip away at the wall of privilege and deference which had once surrounded the gentry.[9]

The traditional rural life-style was also beleaguered by the influx of the new commercial and industrial wealthy, who bought up the estates of improverished gentry families.[10] F.M.L. Thompson probably sums up the consensus of historical opinion when he concludes his chapter on the 'Indian Summer' of the landed interest:

'The beginning of the break up of large estates may more profit-ably be seen as the natural culmination of the whole trend of the preceding generations. The landed interest had lost its pre-eminence and now land was losing many of its attractions'.[11]

In the light of these views, must we conclude that Galsworthy was simply blinded by his own wishful thinking when he depicted the successful resistance of Worsted Skeynes to outside pressures? Or was he describing a human reaction to change which gives the lie to 'circumstantial' history?

Obviously, the social, political and economic changes of the late nineteenth century were affecting the traditional life-style of the gentry. Yet evidence from the five Sussex country houses examined in this study suggests that the process of decline was almost imper-ceptible in the period 1880-1914: attitudes and habits of life were not changing as rapidly as the objective conditions of landowning.

Many features of the eighteenth century squire's existence persisted well into the twentieth; as many continuities with traditional rural society and the life style of the gentry may be observed in the late Victorian and Edwardian period, as changes.

The basis of this paper is a collection of the household papers of five country houses in Sussex. These records are a largely untapped source for the social historian: they reveal, with startling richness, the inner workings of each household. In addition to wage books, stewards' accounts, inventories, agents' letterbooks and other business-related materials, are the personal letters and appointment diaries of the families themselves. Certain objections to such evidence cannot be denied; analysis requires a certain amount of 'reading between the lines' and educated guesswork. Much of the material is not directly comparable, either in terms of time span or the type of information supplied. The sample is small, and not representative: there are two estates over 10,000 acres in size, and only one under 4000. Sussex itself, out of the mainstream of industrialisation and urbanisation, was not a typical county. To this, one can only make the usual answer in defence of local history: that a small-scale study may be as accurate as a more generalised view, which glosses over regional and individual differences. A study of this sort may expose evidence which does not fit into the prevailing model of drastic change and decline, and may point the way to further exploration.

A short introduction to the families involved in the study may be useful. Henry Wyndham, the second Earl of Leconfield, was born in 1830, married Constance Dalmeny in 1867, and succeeded to his title in 1869. There were six sons and three daughters in the family, born between 1868 and 1888. Lord Leconfield was succeeded by his second son in 1901. Their major residence was Petworth House, although they also maintained a house in London and owned substantial lands in Yorkshire and Cumberland. Charles Henry Gordon-Lennox, the sixth Duke of Richmond, succeeded in 1861 at the age of forty-three. His wife, Frances Harriet Greville, bore him four sons and two daughters between 1845 and 1865. His eldest son, also Charles Henry, succeeded him in 1903. The family divided their time between Goodwood House, a London house, and Gordon Castle, the centre of their extensive Scottish estates. Colonel Edward Frewen, a member of a very old Sussex gentry family, married Anne Mary Bing in 1873, and fathered two sons and one daughter. Brickwall, a Jacobean mansion at Northiam in East Sussex, was the Frewen residence, although economic necessity sometimes forced them to move to smaller houses and let the family home. Bertram, Earl of Ashburnham, married Emily Chaplin in 1888 and succeeded to his extensive property in 1898. When he died in 1919, he was survived only by one daughter, and his brother succeeded to the title, which is now extinct. Bertram was deeply involved in Carlist activities for most of his life and spent little time at his seat, Ashburnham Place. Sir George Croxton Shiffner married Elizabeth Greenall in 1854; they had two sons and four daughters. The family lived at Coombe Place in Hamsey, near Lewes, where George was also the rector. He was succeeded by his eldest son John in 1906.

For the class to which these men belonged, the basis of wealth had traditionally been agricultural. Regardless of how small the holding, land had an almost mystical significance for the gentry family. In the late 1870s farm rents began to fall, and the returns on agricultural investment decreased. Paul Thompson, like many other historians, paints a black picture of agriculture in Britain by the early twentieth century:

> Left to the mercies of the market, unprotected by state subsidies, the Edwardian countryside was economically and socially moribund . . .'.[12]

In some cases, this provided the impetus for landowners to exploit other sources of income, such as stocks, mineral rights and urban ground rents. It has been claimed that land was no longer as lucrative, nor as important an asset as it once had been.

In the five Sussex country houses examined here, however, it appears that sources and levels of income did not change dramatically prior to World War One. Unfortunately income figures are not complete enough to be conclusive. At Petworth, farm rent receipts rose slowly between 1895 and 1900, and the estate agent was able to report in 1896: '. . . audits this year have been very satisfactory; there are few arrears . . .'.[13] The Ashburnham estate did see a decrease in income between 1875 and 1885, although not a serious one, and in any case, the 1875 levels were being approached again by 1899.[14] Fragmentary evidence for Coombe Place suggests steady gains in receipts between 1898 and 1906.[15] At Goodwood House a discernible decline did take place, in spite of the Duke of Richmond's expertise as an agriculturalist. However, this apparent decline may be due to a change in book-keeping practice; it is not clear whether the later figures included the Scottish rents, as the early ones did. In any case the decline was not steady: income was higher, for example, in 1884 than in 1873.[16]

Were new sources of income distracting these landlords from investment in, and concern for, their agricultural holdings? The 1903 will of the Duke of Richmond reveals that the value of his farm rents totalled £232,236 while the mansion, park and garden was valued at £20,500. Compared to this, the £12,777 invested in stocks and bonds represented a very minor source of income.[17] For George Shiffner, the £1,090 realised on his bank stocks in 1891, or the £809 from the sale of consols in 1892, represented a more important, but still relatively insignificant, part of his budget.

It is probable that none of these houses depended for major parts of their income on non-agricultural funds. Indeed, they had little opportunity to diversify their local holdings, as Sussex was outside the mainstream of large-scale industrial and urban development. In any case, the capital necessary for investment was rarely available on estates where property was still securely tied up in settlements, jointures and mortgages.

In the area of household expenditure, the surviving records show even more clearly a continuation, as opposed to retrenchment, of the comfortable gentry life-style. In spite of the increasing cost of servant-keeping, the size of these households did not decrease. The grand style is represented by Goodwood, where there were twenty-five servants employed in 1875, including such non-functional, status-enhancing domestics as a groom-of-the-chamber and three footmen. This staff was maintained throughout the period, and only decreased substantially in 1917, after the introduction of conscription and the ready availability of lucrative war work. By 1920, the staff numbered twenty-one.[18]

At Petworth there were thirty-two servants in 1879, and still thirty-one in 1891. After the death of Lord Leconfield, the staff was reduced to twenty-three; by 1902, however, the household had returned to the customary size.[19]

At Ashburnham in 1878 an estate agent suggested a substantial reduction in staff as a money-saving measure. The suggestion was not taken up, however; sixteen to eighteen servants were always kept, although the family was rarely in residence.[20]

Household and estate records also seem to suggest that landlords continued to invest in improvements: for example, Petworth was completely painted and redecorated and a new plumbing system was installed in 1906, and a complete electrical system was added in 1909.[21] The amounts spent on Ashburnham Place varied from £290 to £1,354 between 1875 and 1900. Repairs to the estate property cost £891 in 1875, £2,315 in 1900.[22]

At Goodwood, expenditure on the house increased dramatically between 1875 and 1902. Amounts spent on the gardens were staggering: £1,720 in 1873, £2,032 in 1908. Even Coombe Place, whose owners had a much smaller disposable income, had new plumbing and electrical systems by 1906.[24] The Frewens paid regularly into a Land Improvement Company and they apparently took their responsibilities to the estate very seriously. In the midst of serious financial embarrassments, the agent wrote to Colonel Frewen to recommend the installation of a new drainage system:

'It is the only thing to be done, but I am really sorry for you as 600 or 700 pounds a year added to the burden of the estate just now is a serious thing'.[25]

If the ample lifestyle of England's landed classes was being cramped by lower incomes and higher prices, expenditure on sport is one area where cutbacks might be expected.

Game preservation continued to be a large item at Ashburnham, where costs varied between £700 and £903 per annum in the period 1880 to 1899; the 1899 figure was considerably higher than that of 1880.[26] At Goodwood game expenditure reached a high of £1,452 in 1913.[27] But racing was, as it still is, Goodwood's chief sport, and one of the most costly; the Dukes of Richmond in this period maintained the Goodwood racecourse out of their own pockets.[28]

At least as costly was the Leconfields' maintenance of a private pack of hounds, one of the last in England. In 1888 the Earl employed six kennelmen and sixteen gamekeepers and assistants, a huntsman, and two whippers-in.[29] According to Trollope, the cost of such an extensive establishment was in excess of £2,500 a year.[30] Reginald Leconfield, one of the Earl's younger sons was a famous sportsman: he owned twelve hunters and hunted seventy days a year. He paid 10,000 guineas for a share in a race horse which once won the Gold Cup at Ascot. A big game enthusiast, he made trips to South Africa and the American Rockies in search of quarry.[31]

It has also been suggested that gentry families in financial straits cut back on their traditional charitable donations. At the two houses for which figures are available, Ashburnham and Goodwood, more was being spent on charity in 1900 than in 1873, and in the case of Goodwood, more in 1908 than in 1900.[32]

Expenditures on food and drink also remained high in this period, in spite of rising food costs. At Goodwood in December 1888, an amazing 2769 pounds of meat were consumed; in April 1898, the figure was 3055. Large-scale entertainments were a tradition which seemed unaffected by restraint. In January 1891, 152 guests were received at a ball; at a similar event in 1908, there were 197 guests. It was customary to have sixty house guests for Goodwood race week.[33] At Petworth, cellar records attest to a similar unstinting hospitality. For example, in January 1889, 92 bottles of claret, 5 of port, 6 of sherry, 11 of whisky and 42 of other wines, were consumed. At a ball in 1908, the guests downed 62 bottles of gin, 8 of peach brandy, and 89 of claret.[34] The Ashburnhams also enjoyed entertaining. In 1909 the earl held a ball for 500 in London, at which champagne, whisky, cognac, claret and moselle cups helped to wash down a cold buffet of salmon, sole, lobster, pigeon, liver, tongue, chicken, ham, desserts, fruit, sorbet and raspberry ice-cream.[35]

It would appear that, in spite of falling incomes in some cases, many gentry households were maintaining the generous and comfortable life-style of their eighteenth century counterparts. The keeping of such meticulous accounts as those on which these figures are based seems in itself, however, to suggest an increasing awareness of expenditure. Household and personal account books record items such as postage stamps and rail and cab fares, trivial amounts in terms of overall expenses. However, this careful book-keeping was not a nineteenth century development. It reminds us of Mingay's characterisation of the eighteenth century landowner: '. . . fond of entertaining and not averse to some show and extravagance, and yet still careful to watch expenditure and keep minutely detailed accounts'.[36] But figures alone cannot reveal the changes in lifestyle and attitude which a beleaguered class might be expected to exhibit. Was the traditional gentry household breaking down internally? Were master and mistress becoming distanced from their families and servants: were the traditional ties disintegrating?

The Leconfield family letters seem to reflect a closely-knit, affectionate family. Lady Leconfield wrote almost daily to her children's nurse when she was away from Petworth, and received detailed accounts of their health and activities. As they grew older, the children themselves began to correspond with their mother, and continued to do so while at school and long after. Lady Leconfield's letters were apparently eagerly awaited in the nursery. Nurse wrote in 1884: '. . . Mr. Hughie has been very busy printing a letter to your ladyship yesterday and today . . . he and Maggie received their letters tonight before going to bed, which were a great delight'.[37] This family affection does not seem to have diminished as the children grew older. When the eldest son, George, gave his maiden speech in Parliament, his mother wrote that it had been read by the whole family 'with great joy and delight', and added that '. . . we are all looking forward to seeing you tomorrow, the house never seems the same when you are not in it'.[38] On another occasion, when Lady Leconfield was in Ireland and nursing her son Reginald, who had been injured in a hunting accident, her daughter Maggie wrote: 'Of course, I need not say how dreadfully we miss you here, all the more now the boys are coming home'.[39] Lord Leconfield also displayed a genuine and immediate interest in his children, not conforming to the archetype of the remote and severe Victorian *paterfamilias*. A letter written to his wife in 1899 is full of domestic detail: 'Bumps has returned (from school) looking very well and with a good report. Edward's is of course a very disappointing one . . . Maggie has immensely improved in her playing'.[40]

The Frewen letter reveal a similar pattern of family relations in a smaller gentry household. Anne Frewen reported every detail of her infant son's activities to her husband when he was away from home. The Frewen sons wrote cheerful and affectionate letters to their mother from school and long after they had grown up and taken up their careers.[41]

Lady Beckwith's memoir of family life at Goodwood is also very different from the conventional picture of the Edwardian noble family; caught up in high society and meeting only at the parties of mutual friends.

'Considering our own early influences, first and foremost I must place my father, for he was not only the kindest and wisest of counsellors, but also the most devoted father . . . And I think I can say no family was more united, and none loved each other with such mutual affection'.[42]

Another traditional aspect of family relations in these gentry households was the importance of the extended family. The Wyndhams paid frequent visits to relatives throughout Britain, and often went to 'Unce Archie' in Edinburgh. Maggie's round of visits to country houses always included those of her many relations. She wrote from London in 1912 that: 'I spent Thursday afternoon looking up relations, but all are away, even Aunt Constance'.[43]

But family ties went beyond mere socializing. Edward Frewen's cousin was one of his trustees during a period of financial crisis at Brickwall, and took a great interest in the estate, doing all in his power to prevent the decline of the family fortunes. Edward himself provided one of his needy cousins with a benefice, and loaned a needy one £400 to set up a medical practice.[44]

Even the grand Ashburnham household maintained close kinship ties. A guest book kept between 1879 and 1882 reveals that more than half of the visitors were members of the immediate or extended family.[45] At Goodwood it was said that '. . . everywhere there were relations, near and distant'.

The children of these Sussex gentry families seem to have conformed to a traditional pattern in their later careers. Of the nineteen males examined: nine attended an old public school, five Oxford, one Cambridge, and four military colleges. Eight served as Guards officers, while three entered other armed services, one became a cleric, and one a member of the Royal household.[46]

The gentry household consisted not only of the family members, however, but also of a large and complex network of servants. It has been suggested that the pressures of modern society were putting an unbearable strain on the ties which had once bound family and non-family members of the gentry household together: masters and mistresses were becoming distanced from the day-to-day operations, and in consequence, the reciprocal bonds of paternalism and deference were breaking down.

The evidence of Lady Elizabeth Shiffner's personal account books suggest that she had not relinquished her share of the housekeeping duties: she was responsible for the sale of home farm produce and for paying the female servants. She kept a notebook with recipes for mayonnaise, home remedies, furniture and metal polish, and even 'lotion for horses' legs'. She also performed such everyday tasks as the taking of an inventory of the linen and china at Coombe Place. The management, hiring and firing of servants were often mentioned in her diaries.[47] The diaries also reflect a beneficent paternalism toward servants. A New Year's Eve servants' dance was a regular event at Coombe Place, and Christmas treats included trips to the theatre in Brighton and gifts.[48]

The ladies of Petworth also took a lively interest in the running of he household. Maggie's letters to her mother discuss such matters as choosing carpet for the servants' hall (she had '. . . found a large rug made up of some bits of cheerful red brussels carpet for 18s.'), the purchase of fruit and flour for Christmas cakes, accommodation for the maids of house guests, and other domestic problems.[49] The letters also reflect a close partnership between mistress and house-keeper, especially in the management of other servants: 'Mrs. Forty (the housekeeper) wishes to ask you if we ought not to be looking for another still-room maid, as Amy will soon be leaving'.[50]

The involvement of the master in the everyday life of a gentry household was also important, in spite of T.H.S. Escott's claim that '. . . the claims of society have acquired precedence over the duties of home'.[51] Lord Leconfield spent a day in London in 1899 interviewing a valet and having 'a stormy interview with the fishmonger' about the quality of the supplies sent to Petworth. Maggie reported that he had suggested the use of a particular household soap which he believed would be cheaper than the usual brand. His main role, though was in the hiring of male servants, over which he took infinite pains.[52] Evidence from other households studied also suggests that the master was active in domestic matters. The meticulous account books kept by stewards and housekeepers were obviously intended for his scrutiny. Relations with servants in the traditional gentry household had gone far beyond a mutual interest in domestic management. An emotional interdependence, paternalism on one side, deference on the other, bound together the members of the household. Such antiquated notions seem to have survived the factory age in some Sussex country houses.

Paternalism was double-edged; servants, like children, were both cared for, and firmly admonished. Maggie, the Leconfields' youngest daughter, wrote with concern about the butler, whose temper '. . . is just awful now; last night he blew up the footman quite out loud in the dining room. I cannot think what is wrong'. She also observed that the housekeeper was 'always thinking of her own position and taking offence at nothing'; Maggie thought that a servants' dance 'might hearten her up'. On the other hand, when a housemaid took to wearing costume jewellery, the housekeeper was told to 'give her a good talking', and the maid was eventually dismissed.[53]

Lady Beckwith remembered that relations between the Duke of Richmond and his staff '. . . could not be said to have been anything but ideal'.[54] At Goodwood, as at Petworth and the smaller houses, Christmas treats were customary. A servants' ball was usually the high point of the season; in 1908, 197 guests attended such a ball at Goodwood. Even at Coombe Place, sixty guests were present at a servants' dance held in 1888.[55] Lady Elizabeth noted in her personal accounts such items as '2s.6d. — servants to theatre', while her husband recorded 'presents to housemaids — 2 pounds'.[56]

Lady Beckwith also assures her reader that the servants at Goodwood 'enjoyed the stateliness of the regime'. But here our reliable information ends. We have very few servant diaries or accounts to balance the view from the top. Length of service has been suggested as one objective measure of loyalty amongst servants. Lower servants tended to change jobs frequently in the households in this study. However, those who attained higher rank, and became more closely involved in the lives of their employers, often had remarkable service records. The butler at Goodwood in 1927 had first been hired in 1893, and the housesteward had also served the family for over twenty-five years. Mrs. Forty was the housekeeper at Petworth for more than fifteen years, and Mrs. Sumpter, the children's nurse, lived on in the household until her death.[57] An incident at Petworth in 1898 suggests that true devotion to a master was still to be found. Shortly after one of Lord Leconfield's sons was involved in a near-fatal hunting accident, his youngest son entered a steeple chase, causing his father great anxiety. Pattinson, the house steward, took it upon himself to cable his master as soon as the race was over, that his son was unhurt.[58]

Traditionally, landowners and their tenants and villagers had been linked together by a commonality of interests and mutual respect. Evidence from the five Sussex houses of this study suggests that this relationship, too, had changed little by the early twentieth century. When the Frewens, in dire financial straits, were forced to let Brickwall, a correspondent wrote to Colonel Frewen from Northiam that: '. . . nothing can be expected to go right here until you come back again'. 'A Frewen in propera persona', he asserted, 'seems only natural'.[59] The choice of the word 'natural' unconsciously alludes to an almost organic tie between a landowner and his land. Even when fox-hunting was under severe attack elsewhere for the damage it caused to crops, Colonel Frewen's tenants seemed to consider it his natural prerogative to hunt over their land. One of his farmers wrote in 1881 that he was '. . . highly gratified at the good run you had' on his land, and piously hoped that he would continue to 'find a share of good foxes'.[60]

In return, we find evidence that Edward Frewen was a concerned and understanding landlord. His agent obviously expected a sympathetic response when he wrote that one of the tenants '. . . has no means of paying anything at present . . . I think he told me that he had eight children at home'. On another occasion, a long-standing tenant wrote to report that '. . . our grandson Anthony is getting on very well' in his new job, and to express his gratitude for 'the influence you used to get him appointed'.[61]

The final mark of respect for Edward Frewen was the message his tenants addressed to his wife on his death in 1919:

> The Colonel was a kind and sympathetic landlord and worthily upheld all the best traditions of a long and renowned ancestry . . .[62]

However conventional the sentiments may seem, their expression is part of a long tradition of deference and loyalty.

This relationship between squire and tenantry is reflected in the records of other households, but never more forcefully than in a speech delivered by the Duke of Richmond in 1884:

> I look upon myself and the tenantry as members of one large, vast, and I am happy to be able to add, united family . . . It is my duty — and I endeavour to carry it out — to look after the interests myself personally, individually, of the humblest crofter on this estate as well as the wealthiest tenant.[63]

Traditionally, the landlord had looked after the interests of his tenants in bad times, as well as in good. The squire had always been the chief source and organiser of charity in his locality.

Among the charitable acitivities supported at Goodwood were: the provision of an estate nurse, annuities, pensions and coal allowances for retired labourers and servants, several cricket clubs and agricultural societies, church and clerical organisations, and local schools in fifteen villages. Charity also took more personal forms: for example, 600 quarts of soup were doled out to the poor from the Goodwood kitchens every month in winter.[64] The Petworth Park Friendly Society organised annual fêtes held in the gardens, and Lord Leconfield himself participated in all the planning. He also personally scrutinised applicants for admission to an almshouse he maintained at Tillington. Pensions, Jubilee treats and special allowances for the needy were part of his magnanimity towards his tenants.[65]

In 1890 the Shiffners were supporting their local Diocesan Association and several other church funds, several hospitals, the Hamsey cricket club, the church choir and the Lewes musical society. In 1887 Sir George mounted a Jubilee celebration in Hamsey which included a dinner for 300 men, a tea party for the women and children, sports, and bonfires at night at Coombe.[66]

F.M.L. Thompson has suggested that '. . . the direct contributions of the great landowners diminished and their role as visible protectors and benefactors of their communities declined' during the late nineteenth century.[67] In fact, evidence of the five Sussex houses in this study suggest that local philanthropy continued to take up an important part of the landlords' time and money. The squire's wife and daughters were also involved in the distribution of charity in the community; this had long been an important link between the landowner and tenantry. Lady Shiffner organised fund-raising for the Home Missions and for the purchase of a church organ. She regularly attended 'ladies' work' meetings, visited the local work-house, and organised the annual Hamsey school feast.[68] Her daughter-in-law continued the practice long after the outbreak of World War One. Although she worked at the Pavilion hospital as a nurse, she felt that Hamsey was 'her special love', and the 'well-being of the church . . . her chief concern'.[69] As Lady Leconfield once wrote:

'. . . though social work was not organised as it is now, there was full scope for individual energy, especially in the country, where parish life was a continual round of activity'.[70]

The philanthropic activities of these country landlords had a different quality from those of their urban middle class counter-parts. They did not seek to 'improve' or control, but simply to re-distribute some of their surplus income to people whose needs they understood. The landlord was still personally involved and knew the recipients of his bounty by name. It was this sort of charitable activity which had been seen as a traditional link between the two rural classes.

The landlord's role as political leader of his community, either as representative or patron, had been eroded by the gradual democrat-isation of government at all levels throughout the nineteenth century. Nevertheless, there is evidence to suggest that traditional attitudes towards the gentry's right to rule persisted. Certainly Edward Frewen's aunt believed that her nephew was the most natural representative for the county. When he turned down the nomination in 1880, she reminded him of the '. . . horrid nuisance it will be if some vile Liberal gets in. Your father's son should rather sell every horse and hound than allow such a thing to happen'.[71] Frewen, in spite of his reluctance to run as a candidate, was an important Conservative organiser in his locality, as were George Shiffner and Lord Leconfield in theirs.

Often, however, the squire's influence depended simply upon the expectation that once his wishes were known, they would be respected by tenants and employees. Lord Leconfield's agent, dis-covering that a tenant had openly supported a Liberal candidate sternly advised that '. . . it would be better he should consult your lordship before taking any active part in any of these election questions'.[72]

There is considerable evidence to suggest that the landowners of Sussex were still deeply involved in the making and administration of laws in their region. Between 1880 and 1914, nine men owned the five estates examined in this study. Between them, they held fifteen commissions of the peace and five deputy-lieutenancies. Three served as Members of Parliament, one as Lord-Lieutenant of Sussex and Chairman of the West Sussex County Council, one as Vice-Chairman and Alderman of the Council, and one as High Sheriff. In addition, four served as officers in the local Volunteers or Yeomanry and three as Guardians of the local Poor Law Board.

The established links between the gentry and the established church also seem to have survived the strains of modern society. Colonel Frewen took a personal interest in the affairs of his parish, to the extent of ensuring that a prospective curate at Northiam was '. . . fond of cricket and not stuck-up like some of his fraternity'.[73] Sir George Shiffner, as rector of Hamsey and rural dean of Lewes, combined the two institutions in his own person. He was very active in local and diocesan affairs and in the Hamsey Temperance League.[74] All of the men supported numerous church organisations and charities financially.

Nor did Sussex landowners appear to have relinquished their roles as leading agriculturalists. The memoranda of the Earl of Ashburnham's estate agent reveal that he consulted his employer on the minutiae of estate management-labourers' wages, the price of hops, railway rights-of-way, and individual applications for rent reduction.[75] George Shiffner's diaries show him buying livestock, consulting with his agent over water supply and vacant farms, carrying the hay, and treating a cow with 'milk fever'.[76] Even the grand seventh Duke of Richmond was well-known for his interest in agriculture; he was particularly enthusiastic about livestock breeding, and was considered an authority on the subject.[77] Sussex landowners had not yet become mere *rentiers*. Their tenants could feel that they shared many of the same concerns and interests.

Traditionally, county social life had been on a small scale, involving visiting neighbours and playing country sports, within an intimate circle of long-time friends and family members. T.H.S. Escott noticed at the end of the nineteenth century, that the exclusivity and parochialism of country society was breaking down; the aristocracy were seen to '. . . flit from mansion to mansion during the country house season . . . existence for the fashionable and wealthy is thus one unending whirl of excitement'.[78]

In these five Sussex families attitudes towards socializing and leisure pursuits seem to fit a traditional model. Fox-hunting remained the single most important gentlemanly activity. As a boy,

Edward Frewen felt that its importance lay in '. . . making you nice and tired so that you feel as if you had done something'.[79] Horse-racing also continued to be popular; at Goodwood, of course, it was particularly important. The family always returned from London in time for race week and entertained many house guests. The seventh Duke was also an avid hunter; he revived the Goodwood hunt and served as its master until 1894.[80]

George Shiffner's diaries reveal that country sports were also important to the lesser gentry. In his diary for May 1885, there are nine references to hunting or shooting, in December 1887 seven, in March 1890 eleven, in January 1897 four. The summer months were dominated by cricket, but tennis, stoolball and croquet were also popular.[81]

Most social events in these country households retained their simple, local nature. Maggie Leconfield, for example, described a typical week of activities to her mother in a letter dated 1893. Her sister and brother had attended a charity concert in Pulborough, a picnic and fishing expedition was planned, a neighbour was enter-tained to tea, friends visited to play golf, and so many visitors came during an afternoon at-home that '. . . it was difficult to keep them all going at the same time'.[82] Anne Frewen's social life also involved many local visits. On one day in 1876 she drove to Rye to 'leave cards' at one house, and visit four others, before returning home to find that neighbours had called at Brickwall while she was away.[83]

Lady Elizabeth Shiffner's diaries also reveal that country social events were modest and localised. During a typical week in August 1895: she and her husband visited friends in Lewes, while their children attended a cricket match in Brighton; a ladies' cricket team played and took tea at Coombe; her daughters attended the Glynde tournament; her husband and daughters attended a garden party at a nearby house; and a second cricket match was held at Coombe.[84]

The wealthier families spent less time at their country seats. The Duke of Richmond's family spent the season in London, returned to Goodwood for race week, spent August, September and October in Scotland, and then returned to Goodwood for the winter. Entertaining was also on a larger scale. This was also true of the Leconfields and the Asburnhams. But seasonal movements and extravagant hospitality had always been a part of the aristocratic life-style. In the face of the new industrial wealth, social exclusive-ness did not break down; even Escott admitted that Petworth and Goodwood remained two of the most selective houses in the country.[85]

It is always dangerous to write the history of attitudes and life-styles on the basis of circumstantial evidence. There is no doubt that the social, economic and political position of the English gentry was deteriorating during the late nineteenth and early twentieth centuries. In retrospect, it is easy to see the period as an 'Indian Summer' before the long winter that began in November 1914. Without the benefit of this hindsight, however, some evidence suggests that many country families continued to live and think much as they always had.

The small sample of households examined here can no more than point the way to further investigation; the rich source of nineteenth century household records and accounts lies untouched in many county record offices. This study had suggested that, amongst the gentry of Sussex, continuities with the past may have been as significant as change, decline and forcible modernisation. Agricultural incomes showed no dramatic declines; lavish expenditure on houses, gardens, hospitality, large staffs, and sports continued up to, and after, World War One. Within the families, there is evidence of strong affective bonds and loyalties, rather than of disintegration and decay. Both masters and mistresses continued to play their accustomed roles as household managers and leaders of the local community. Their relationships with domestics, tenants and other dependants were marked by the expected attitudes of paternalism and reciprocating deference.

Of course, it is impossible to ignore the signposts of change and decline. Perhaps what we see in the late nineteenth century gentry is not a class submerged, but one successfully adapting its most resilient values to modern society.

Notes

[1] John Galsworthy, *The Country House* (1907, 1926) p.129.

[2] Samuel Hynes, *The Edwardian Turn of Mind* (Princeton 1968) pp.72-75.

[3] T.H.S. Escott, *England. Its People, Polity and Pursuits* (1890) p. 105.

[4] C.F.G. Masterman, *The Condition of England* pp. 157-159.

[5] G.E. Mingay, *The Gentry* (1976) pp.176-190.

[6] Keith Middlemas, *Pursuit of Pleasure* (1977), *passim*.

[7] L. Davidoff, *The Best Circles* (1973), *passim*.

[8] D. Roberts, 'The Paterfamilias of the Victorian Governing Classes' in *The Victorian Family*, ed. A.S. Wohl (1978) *passim*.

[9] C.D. Orwin, E.H. Whetham, *A History of British Agriculture 1846-1914* (1964) pp.42-46.

[10] Mingay, *The Gentry*, pp.173-180.

[11] F.M.L. Thompson, *English Landed Society in the Nineteenth Century* (1963) p.25.

[12] Paul Thompson, *The Edwardians: The Remaking of British Society* (1971) p.38.

[13] W(est) S(ussex) R(ecord) O(ffice) *Petworth House Mss.*, no. 2884, 1895-1900.

[14] E(ast) S(ussex) R(ecord) O(ffice) *Ashburnham Place Mss.*, no. 1755-1760, 1880-1910.

[15] E.S.R.O. *Shiffner Mss.*, no. 259, 1888-1896.

[16] W.S.R.O. *Goodwood House Mss.*, no. 764, 1873-1913.

[17] *Ibid.*, no. 952, 190.

[18] W.S.R.O., *Goodwood House Mss.*, no. 1096-1098, 1869-1920.

[19] W.S.R.O., *Petworth House Mss.*, no. 5111, 1879-1911.

[20] E.S.R.O., *Ashburnham Place Mss.*, no. 2668, 1878.

[21] W.S.R.O., *Petworth House Mss.*, no. 2885, 1906; no. 5207, 1909.

[22] E.S.R.O., *Ashburnham Place Mss.*, no. 1775-1760.

[23] W.S.R.O., *Goodwood House Mss.*, nos. 5270-5289, 1871-1913.

[24] E.S.R.O., *Shiffner Mss.*, no.3254, 1906.

[25] E.S.R.O., *Shiffner Mss.*, no. 4185, 1880.

[26] E.S.R.O., *Ashburnham Place Mss.*, nos. 1755-1760, 1880-1913.

[27] W.S.R.O., *Goodwood House Mss.*, nos. 5270-5289, 1883-1913.

[28] Victoria History of the Counties of England, *A History of Sussex*, vol. II (1907) p.454.

[29] W.S.R.O., *Petworth House Mss.*, nos. 2317-2319, 1888.

[30] A. Trollope, *British Sports and Pastimes* p.87.

[31] W.S.R.O., *Petworth House Mss.*, no. 5293.

[32] E.S.R.O., *Ashburnham Place Mss.*, nos. 1755-1760, *Goodwood House Mss.*, nos. 5270-5289.

[33] W.S.R.O., *Goodwood House Mss.*, 1104-1105.

[34] W.S.R.O., *Petworth House Mss.*, no. 2643.

[35] E.S.R.O., *Ashburnham Place Mss.*, nos. 978-987.

[36] Mingay, p.116.

[37] W.R.S.O., *Petworth House Mss.*, nos. 1624-1626, 1884.

[38] *Ibid.*, no. 1627, December 6, 1894.

[39] *Ibid.*, no. 1658, December 1899.

[40] *Ibid.*

[41] E.S.R.O., *Frewen Mss.*, nos. 4182-4183, 187-188, 1873-1897.

[42] Lady Muriel Beckwith, *When I remember* (1936) p.36.

[43] W.S.R.O., *Petworth House Mss.*, no. 1648, 1912.

[44] E.S.R.O., *Frewen Mss.*, no. 4186, 1884.

[45] E.S.R.O., *Ashburnham Place Mss.*, no. 2786, 1879-1882.

[46] The information in this paragraph was derived from several sources including: W.T. Pike, *Sussex in the 20th Century* (Brighton: W.T. Pike and Co., 1910) *Burke's Landed Gentry* (1965) *Burke's Peerage and Baronetage* (1975).

[47] E.S.R.O., *Shiffner Mss.*, 1529-1534, 1547, 1548, 1355, 869-872.

[48] E.S.R.O., *Shiffner Mss.*, no. 1529, 3466, January 1890.

[49] W.S.R.O., *Petworth House Mss.*, nos. 1641, Nov. 1905, 1648, Dec. 1898, 1647, 1911.

[50] *Ibid.*, no. 1655, 1899.

[51] Escott, p.308.

[52] W.S.R.O., *Petworth House Mss.*, no. 1655, 1899.

[53] *Ibid.*, nos. 1655, 1898, 1638, 1907.

[54] W.S.R.O., *Goodwood House Mss.*, no. 1105.

[55] E.S.R.O., *Shiffner Mss.*, nos. 865, 867, January 1888, 1889.

[56] *Ibid.*, nos. 1529, 3466.

[57] W.S.R.O., *Goodwood House Mss.*, nos. 1096-1098 and C. Leconfield, *Random Papers*, (published privately at Petworth House).

[58] W.S.R.O., *Petworth House Mss.*, no. 1655, 1899.

[59] E.S.R.O., *Frewen Mss.*, nos. 4206, 1885, 4198, 1895.

[60] *Ibid.*, no. 4197, 1881.

[61] *Ibid.*, nos. 4207, 4210, 1895-98.

[62] *Ibid.*, no. 4198, 1919.
[63] W.S.R.O., *Goodwood House Mss.*, no. 764, October 1884.
[64] Thompson, p.209.
[65] W.S.R.O., *Goodwood House Mss.*, nos. 5270-5289, nos. 1104-5.
[66] W.S.R.O., *Petworth House Mss.*, no. 2885, 1906-08.
[67] E.S.R.O., *Shiffner Mss.*, nos. 3557, 3462, June 1887.
[68] *Ibid.*, nos. 836-879.
[69] From a local newspaper clipping, owned by Mrs. Elizabeth Fooks, Horsted Keynes, Sussex.
[70] Leconfield, p.75.
[71] E.S.R.O., *Frewen Mss.*, no. 4186, March 1880.
[72] W.S.R.O., *Petworth House Mss.*, no. 2885, 1902.
[73] E.S.R.O., *Frewen Mss.*, no. 4199.
[74] W.S.R.O., *Petworth House*, no. 1661, 1918.
[75] E.S.R.O., *Ashburnham Place Mss.*, nos. 2419-2422, 1886-88.
[76] E.S.R.O., *Shiffner Mss.*, nos. 3462-3471, 1887-1896.
[77] 'Nomad', 'The late Duke of Richmond and Gordon . . .', in *The Sussex County Magazine* (1928), p.120.
[78] Escott, p.305.
[79] W.S.R.O., *Petworth House Mss.*, no. 1634, November 1899.
[80] 'Nomad', pp.118-119.
[81] E.S.R.O., *Shiffner Mss.*, nos. 486-489.
[82] W.S.R.O., *Petworth House Mss.*, no. 1655, April 1898.
[83] E.S.R.O., *Frewen Mss.*, no. 4183, 1876.
[84] E.S.R.O., *Shiffner Mss.*, no. 877.
[85] T.H.S. Escott, *Society in the Country House* (1907) p.39.

Inter-War Housing Policy: A Study of Brighton

P. DICKENS AND P. GILBERT

1. Some wider issues

Before describing the circumstances of our particular area it should be stressed that the intention is to contribute to a set of more general discussions and debates concerning the origins and social effects of early British housing policy.

In 1872–3 Engels wrote his famous tracts collectively entitled *The Housing Question*.[1] He suggested that the problem of substandard housing was endemic to capitalist society and attempts at reform within a free market economy were doomed to failure — moving slums around rather than eradicating them. Until recently Engels' radical position has remained relatively unexplored, but in recent years there has been a resurgence of interest in the 'political economy' of housing. A number of authors (not unsympathetic to Engels' outlook but not necessarily sharing his gloom regarding prospects for reform) have continued to explore the nature of housing in late capitalist society, extending their analyses to a range of contemporary issues – including the intervention of the government.[2]

As the analyses have become expanded an increasing number of contentious issues have arisen. For example, a somewhat over-polarised debate has emerged in which some authors would claim that early state intervention should be interpreted primarily as an economic necessity (capitalist interests thereby ensuring a supply of relatively productive and docile labour) while other authors would give prominence to the role of political struggle (state housing being a response to working class discontent).[3] Such debates can, in our view, become over-simplified and abstract: it would seem highly unlikely that any one cause can be convincingly advanced for such a major social change as the introduction of a national housing programme. Economic necessity does not preclude political pressure and we would wish to remain alive to these and other historical causes.

But, while somewhat arid, such discussions do reveal the paucity of historical information on which to develop arguments and theory. On the basis of the Glasgow experience, for example, it might be surmised that during the First World War Red Clydeside was reproduced all over the country, with troops dispatched to quell rent-strikers throughout the land and the Cabinet in permanent session suppressing landlords' profits and hurrying through new housing legislation. So the empirical question remains: to what extent was working class pressure over housing vocalised throughout the country and, where it existed, what effects did it have?

Again, in referring to 'the state' and 'state housing policies' it might be suggested that legislation passed in Parliament would have a dramatic effect on house-building throughout Great Britain. Yet legislation passed by central government was (and remains) mainly 'enabling' in nature: the scale of local authority house-building in a particular area being highly dependent on a number of factors, including the local balance of class forces. So our study is intended as somewhat more than an isolated piece of local history. We are outlining some of the local pressures which contributed to the creation of a welfare state and, in discussing the activities of one authority, we are examining how this welfare state in turn affected one community.

As regards the relationships between central and local government two further issues have influenced our empirical analyses. The first concerns the distributive effects of policy, the question being: who came to live in the local authority housing? Earlier studies have suggested that the better off amongst the working class actually benefitted.[4] If this is again the case, the question then is: should such an effect be interpreted as resulting from punitive local authority allocation policies — and associated notions of the 'deserving poor'? Alternatively, is the explanation primarily economic: high interest rates and rent levels ensuring that the new housing came to be occupied by those who least needed it? The second issue associated with central-local government relations is concerned with the separation between social consumption policies (housing, schools and so forth) being primarily associated with the *local* level while intervention over production and employment is mainly conducted by *central* government agencies. Light can be thrown on the reasons for these divisions (which it is now, of course, easy to accept as natural) by examining some of the early instances of intervention. Again, the explanation can be seen as primarily economic (central government defending national economic interests against international competition) or political (central government insulating key decisions over industrial investment from working class influence[5]). Again, we would hesitate before offering a monocausal explanation although — as stated later in this paper — we remain sceptical regarding conspiracy theories of history.

Finally, we have tried to assess what bad housing conditions and attempts to improve them meant to those living in and associated with such conditions. In discussing such general concepts as 'the capitalist economy' or 'the state' we are in danger of ignoring individuals' perceptions or dismissing as 'ideological' the beliefs which rationalise (or reject) social injustice.

Our main aim has been to map a terrain for investigation. The questions we are asking cannot be answered mechanically, proved or disproved since the evidence we have amassed and our interpretation of it must be largely subjective. This study — like, presumably, most forms of historical analysis — finds itself delicately balanced on a knife-edge of empirical 'facts' and value-laden assertions.

2. Inter War Housing: A Summary of National Policies

The Addison Act of 1919 — in which the Government undertook to reimburse local authorities all losses incurred above the product of a penny rate — was the first real commitment by central government to housing provision.[6] The introduction of this legislation can only be adequately explained by reference to a number of political and economic pressures around the time of the First World War and the early 1920s. Official reports[7] gave weight to the widely held view that housing problems were one of the main reasons for working class discontent. And industrial unrest not only raised the spectre of 'international bolshevism' but, during the War years, threatened to hold up armaments-production and associated large- profits by industrial capital. The Addison Act must also be seen in the context of another social change — the decline of the private rented sector. Pre-war health legislation and the introduction of rent restrictions in 1915 hastened the already declining numbers of houses being built for rent.[8]

But the Addison Act, although important as the first major piece of housing legislation, was introduced in a period of high interest rates — leading to high building costs, high rents and the eventual

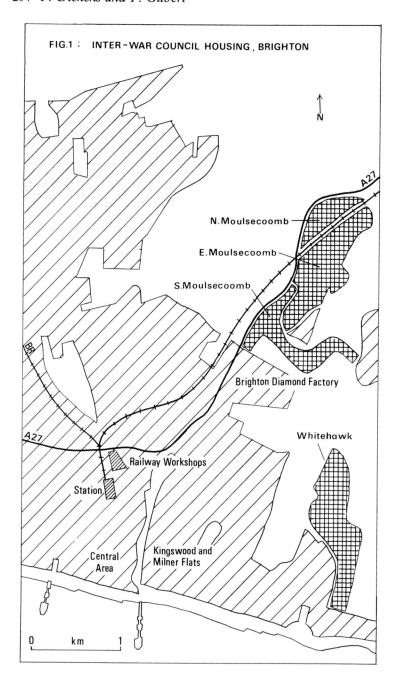

FIG.1 : INTER-WAR COUNCIL HOUSING , BRIGHTON

N

A27

N.Moulsecoomb

E.Moulsecoomb

S.Moulsecoomb

BR

Brighton Diamond Factory

A27

Whitehawk

Railway Workshops

Station

Central
Area

Kingswood and
Milner Flats

0   km   1

collapse of the scheme. By the time the Chamberlain Act had come into force in 1923 the postwar Coalition Government had fallen and the Conservatives were giving private enterprise its head. With the advent of the first Labour Government (and John Wheatley's Act of 1924) the emphasis was put back on municipal housing with a £9 flat-rate subsidy, controlled rents, and harnessing of the building industry.[9]

Legislation associated with the late 1920s and 1930s is again directly linked to the changing fortunes of the labour movement combined with major economic upheaval. The failure of the 1926 General Strike and a surge of unemployment meant a period of relative labour submission. And pressure from the City to cut public expenditure, and from the building societies to use the funds which had been loaded on to them after the Stock Market crash, induced successive governments to pull back from the provision of general needs housing and to give its backing to slum clearance. This latter led to a decline in the status of council housing and to new conflicts between tenants in the public sector.[10]

It is important to re-stress the relative autonomy of local authorities in interpreting all these housing acts. While the Ministry of Health exercised fairly rigid control over space-standards and costs, local authorities had ·(and indeed still have) considerable freedom over rent-levels. Local authorities could also introduce schemes which catered for particular sections of the working class. In 1937, for example, the Brighton Medical Officer of Health reported that:

> "The danger of building a large number of small houses is that the casual worker for whom there is a relatively limited amount of work available in Brighton, will be encouraged to migrate here. It should therefore be the policy of this non-industrial town to erect commodious, healthy houses and not to adopt minimal standards."[11]

The form in which legislation was actually implemented was thus highly dependent on *local* class-structures, labour markets and political pressures. It is to these that we now turn.

3.   A Ragged Garment with a Golden Fringe

Brighton has always been a town of extremes, at least since the nature of its existence changed from being a fishing village called Brighthelmstone to a thriving town with a considerable stake in the holiday-making business. An anonymous contributor to the *New Monthly Magazine* described the Brighton of 1841 as a place of two distinct classes, 'those who make the town an hotel, and those who live by providing for their entertainment'.[12] This division was reflected in housing classes: on the one hand there was the sea-front with its three-mile range of palatial houses, attractive shops and fine hotels. While behind the facade, up the side of Brighton's hills, were the back streets of dingy slums in which housing conditions were as bad as those of many northern cities.

There were two factors that made Brighton's slums worse than most other cities. Firstly, many of these houses had been built with inferior bricks and mortar made of sea-sand,[13] and they were thus so damp that they were covered with lichens. The second reason is that the hilly terrain caused most houses to be built with basements, and these, with no damp courses, gave rise to much hardship to the occupants — as late as 1967 we find the chairman of the Housing Committee speaking of those 'poor devils living in wet, smelly old basements'.[14] Dr. William Kebbell, physician to the Brighton dispensary in the mid 19th century, called attention to the numbers of deaths caused by consumption, 217 per annum, and to the fact that this being one-fifth of the total deaths, was

"a larger proportion than that which obtains in Liverpool for the same complaint, and which is the most unhealthy town in the country."[15]

Edward Cresy, a Commissioner to the Board of Health, in his report on Brighton of 1849, commented on the extent of overcrowding there, sometimes as many as 17 persons sleeping at one time in a small room, some rooms being without window, fireplace or ventilation.[16] No wonder then that Kebbell castigated the municipal authorities in his contention that 'the streets and districts of the poor' are 'a disgrace to any civilized people.' When Dr. Taffe, Brighton's first Medical Officer of Health, came to the town in 1874, he supported Dr. Kebbell's observation that the worst slums in Brighton were those around Edward Street. In his report on the housing survey of East Brighton he recommended that unhealthy areas such as Carlton Hill and Hereford Street should be cleared; as Dr. Forbes, then Medical Officer of Health, remarked in his *Annual Report* of 1939, 'only now, 60 years later, are we completing the work he argued for'.

When we come to the early 20th century, eye-witness accounts suggest that conditions have changed little. Jack Langley, writing about his childhood, says:

"In those days, because people had nothing, nothing at all — you never knew when your next door neighbour was going to commit suicide. People would be unable to pay their rent, which would only be five shillings for a house, and that shared with two or three families, living in slum conditions, not dirty, but crowded because there was not enough money . . . The burden of life was intolerable."[17]

Both Langley and Albert Paul[18] recall that it was necessary for them to queue at the corporation soup kitchens to supplement a meagre family diet.

Increased awareness of conditions of the gap between the haves and the have-nots added to the growth of working class organisation, creating a climate of discontent both before the First World War and afterwards. In 1908 a demonstration by unemployed workers on the arrival of King Edward VII in Brighton aptly illustrated the sensitivity of tourist and property interests to unrest in the town; the *Brighton Herald* stating baldly that:

"The man who will militate against the success of the visit is an enemy of the town."[19]

Eleven years and a world war later, the King's successor delivered his own verdict to representatives of the local authorities:

"If a healthy race is to be reared it can be reared only in healthy houses . . . If unrest is to be converted into contentment, the provision of good houses might prove one of the most potent agents in that conversion."[20]

At the Brighton level we are faced with similar concerns, though perhaps in different proportions. One goad to the Corporation to commence public building was the classic concern over sanitary conditions, especially as they affected the tourist industry.[21] Another was that in 1921 Brighton was, with the exception of West Ham, the most densely populated county borough in England and Wales,[22] and the grim reality behind the palatial facade must have been beginning to appear. Besides the problems of population pressure and bad housing, Brighton contained, and still does, significantly high seasonal unemployment, low wages and high rents. This fact, combined with the demands of returning soldiers, and the strike of locomotive workshop employees and railway workers in January 1918, put pressure on the Brighton Corporation. In January 1919 7,000 soldiers awaiting demobilisation marched on Brighton Town Hall.[23] Attacks on the police by servicemen were becoming commonplace and, at a large public demonstration, the Brighton Trades Council called on the Town Council 'to find work for the returned fighters in place of doles'.[24] In March 1921 Mr. Martin of the Brighton Board of Guardians was quoted as saying that there was a large number of empty houses in Brighton, because owners preferred to sell rather than rent. The case of a blind ex-soldier who could not get lodgings caused an uproar, and there was a meeting at the Level to protest against this 'deplorable situation of a man who has fought and suffered for his country'. The man and his family squatted in an empty house.[25] This reluctance to let obviously worsened an already grave housing situation. A speech by the Mayor of Brighton, February 1919, mirrored both local and the government's anxiety over industrial unrest:

> "The Mayor said the strikes throughout the country were very critical, especially those in Clyde and Glasgow. The unrest and almost bolshevism was caused by the disgusting situation of the houses in the working class localities. The masters of labour had made large fortunes; the worker's wage was small. There were far more serious strikes in the air; national strikes for one; railway workers and miners among others: . . . Brighton was to be likened to a ragged garment with a golden fringe. It certainly had a beautiful fringe. But the garment! The Town Council had been trying during the past year to build a considerable number of houses on the Moulsecoomb Estate, 94 acres of which were to be purchased compulsorily. These were to be houses in the real sense of the word.'[26]

4. Local Implementation of Central Government Legislation: A Brighton Case Study

The fact that several energetic members of Brighton Council, notably Alderman Carden and Councillors Southall and Colbourne, were convinced of the need to provide houses for the working classes on a lavish scale did not mean that there was no opposition to the scheme, some of it from surprising quarters. That the *Brighton Gazette* should oppose the central government's housing policy is not surprising, since the paper was the voice of Brighton ratepayers and property interests,[27] and oppose it did from both practical and class interest points of view. On the 1919 Addison Housing Bill, it wrote that while it was 'a nice mandate' it might be more realistic if the Government provided cheap materials and an increase in skilled building operatives.[28] Bowley,[29] writing of the period, places much of the blame for the failure of Addison's scheme on the failure of the Government to control the prices of building materials, and reassure the trades unions over long-term building plans; a failure that was rectified by Wheatley in his 1924 Act.[30] A less detached view by the *Gazette* appeared in the editorials of the 2nd and 16th April 1919. The view put forward was that considering the cost of working class housing would have to be met by middle class tenants. These, it was argued:

> 'are just now confronted with increased rentals and increased taxes, concurrent with the refusal of landlords to do any repairs, the advantage enjoyed by the corporation tenants is worth having. It is to be hoped they appreciate the position.'[31]

The editorial of the 16th April quoted an M.P. who pictured the future working man:

> 'basking in his Roman bath, with floated chess boards and scented pools — of course in a subsidised establishment, with perhaps a national kitchen, manicure department, and cigar divan included.'

The Middle Class Union (a national organisation — later to become the National Union of Citizens) represented — along with the Anti-Waste League — the formal opposition to the local authority building programme. The Brighton Middle Class Union expanded rapidly: by the end of 1919 it had twelve members on the Council, with Councillor Mellor (an auctioneer and estate agent) as its founder member. And while the Union's avowed concerns were with the general good (each member, it promised in 1919, 'will protest against extravagance and waste of public money') its altruistic aim of protecting the public purse coincided neatly with the interests of the property lobby and the extension of socialism. The Secretary of the Union, Councillor Burgoyne, had considerable property interests and was Chairman of the Trade Protection Society. Other members included Councillor Keay, J.P. (Chairman of the Sussex Mutual Permanent Investment Building Society) and Councillor Mansfield (for forty years closely connected with the Brighton and Sussex Building Society and on two occasions its Director). The Middle Class Union, though not eventually able to prevent the construction of council houses (the combined pressures of central government ministries, local government representatives and local working-class organisations such as the Trades Unions Council and the Trades Council proved irresistible) was at least able to ensure that high, or 'economic' rents were charged for the new houses, an issue to which we will return shortly. We may note in passing here that, while central (and to a large extent local) government preoccupation in the imediate postwar years was with the provision of additional housing, one voice at least was continually crying out for slum-clearance — although this policy was not to be implemented until the 1930s. This voice (in the Brighton case) was that of the Medical Officer of Health, Duncan Forbes:

from 1919 onwards his reports indicate a distinct unhappiness with the almost total lack of official concern with the slum-clearance issue. His 1919 *Health Committee Report* (required for the 1919 Addison Act) gave an estimated need of over 3,000 houses in the Brighton area, describing in graphic detail housing conditions in Brighton's 'unhealthy areas'. The Bedford Street area, for example, had a death rate of 20.2 per 1000 (compared with 15.78 for Brighton as a whole) and a mortality rate for children under a year old of 153 per 1000 (compared with 91 for Brighton). The street's death rate for pulmonary tubercle, a good indicator (as Forbes pointed out) of housing conditions, was in 1919 a third higher than for Brighton generally.

The other pro-housing pressure group operating in Brighton was the Church. The most outspoken of the clergy was the Rev. Rhodda Williams. During a debate on 'the perils of profit' in 1920 he stated,

> 'The very lack of houses is an indictment of the private profit system. The criterion on which the nation operates is not does the nation want houses; but will it pay certain individuals to build houses? And because private individuals who ordinarily build houses do not see how they can make a profit, the nation goes without houses.'[32]

The debate in the Council Chamber over the principle and scale of local authority housebuilding in Brighton was astringent.[33] For a start, while the President of the Local Government Board in the House of Commons had spoken of £5–600 per house being the national figure, the Borough Surveyor was talking in terms of £900, at which there were cries of 'too much'. The Labour group complained that it could provide well-to-do people with 'a nice little cottage' and 'solve the servant problem for them', but with 'a rental of 12/6d. per week it would not meet the requirements of manual workers.' They asked for diversity of design and different rentals. Those who represented the ratepayers felt that 'ratepayers will probably be asked soon for more than a penny rate (A voice: 'They will')'. One speaker said that the proposals could easily fall between two stools. She had visited good corporation dwellings built a few years ago and 'she had never seen such squalor and misery as she had seen in some of them'. The tenants could not afford the rents and had crowded them with lodgers.

> 'If the Council build houses now to let at 12/6d. per week, either the people for whom they are intended will not get them, or they will overcrowd them and we shall have all the miseries of slumdom over again'.

Alderman Burberry, a local landlord, said he knew for a fact that working men would not afford 12/6d. 'At the present time I have 8-roomed houses let at 8/- per week and I have had to call once or twice for the rent (laughter).'

The will of the Mayor, Alderman Herbert Carden, prevailed, however: Brighton was to have houses, and houses of style and substance:

'When members say houses are not wanted in Brighton I do not know where they live. My life is made a burden and a worry by discharged soldiers and other people constantly coming to me and saying they have nowhere to go because they cannot get a house or a flat . . . If we do not start we will cause grave concern in the labour world, as it will be thought that we are playing with the question.'[34]

Similar apprehensions to those of the dissenting Councillors, however, had been voiced by a Labour Party activist who later obtained a house at Moulsecoomb, A.F. Gaaston, and by an ex-soldier, in letters to the *Brighton Herald*.[35] Both letters were concerned that the new local authority houses would only be afforded by the 'exempted parasites', not the returned heroes, and while Gaaston suggested concrete houses as a cheap alternative, the ex-soldier puts forward his priorities:

'Give them a bit of ground with security of tenure, on which to grow their own fruit and vegetables and keep a few chickens, and it would be home to them with whatever kind of house you care to stick upon it, provided it is water-tight and sanitary'.

and again,

'If it is wished to insure against it (i.e. Bolshevism), be willing to pay a reasonable premium.'

When built the garden suburb at Moulsecoomb was in one sense a great success. Musgrave describes it as

'among the most imaginatively laid-out housing schemes in the country, ranking almost equal with the famous garden cities of Letchworth and Welwyn',

far superior to the areas of private development at Patcham, Ovingdean, Rottingdean and Woodingdean.[36] A description of the estate is held up as an example in the Ministry of Health's official publication *Housing*,[37] and town planners came from all over the world to see it, one planner describing it as 'Utopia At Moulsecoomb'.[38]

In many respects, however, the doubts of many were upheld. The houses did not cost £900 each, but trapped in rising costs, they were an incredible £1,120 each, and that without counting the cost of the land, roads, sewers, etc. A glance at the relevant housing statistics will show the enormous expense of these houses compared with subsequent inter-war local authority houses.[39] In the 1919 debate, 12/6d. had seemed too high a rent for the working classes generally, but the rents at Moulsecoomb in 1922 were between 26/- and 32/6d. depending on the type and size of the house.[40] These houses, partly through rent levels, and partly through the selection process, were not available to the ex-service working men for whom they were designed. Marion Fitzgerald,[41] speaks of most heads of families falling into the artisan category, and this is substantially true. A detailed study of the *Parish Baptismal Register*[42] from 1922–1944 shows a large number of artisans in various trades, such as jewellers employed by the nearby Oppenheimer works.

This group of workers (many of which were disabled soldiers) become incidentally the subject of intensive *central* (as well as local) government concern and, eventually indeed, Cabinet decision-making. The issue was raised in Cabinet[43] by the Minister of Labour Sir Montague Barlow on 19th March 1923 as 'a most serious and urgent question'. After outlining the depressed state of the local diamond industry since the War Sir Montague wrote:

'Great pressure has been put upon me by the ex-Service men and the British Legion, and also by the Labour Party, who are very anxious that the factory should be maintained. I have also received representations from the Brighton Town Council on the same lines. It will be something like a tragedy if the 250 ex-Servicemen, largely disabled, who have been earning a decent living at the factory, are now turned into the streets.'

Thus for the Cabinet this relatively small but (at a local level) serious unemployment problem became of pressing 'central' concern. As Barlow wrote at the end of his memorandum:

'Our only hope of absorbing the vast mass of unemployed which we are now carrying is the development of existing and, so far as possible, of new industries. If the Brighton Diamond Factory is closed, not only will the 250 mainly disabled men lose their livelihood, but we are deliberately sacrificing the prospects of establishing an entirely new industry in the country.'

The Cabinet,[44] after deliberation as regards the commercial viability of the factory, agreed that a special bill be passed to inject £150,000 capital into the industry, despite the fact (mentioned by Barlow) that the Bank of England had been advised by a rival South African consortium that the Brighton diamond business was doomed to commercial failure. In the event, this interesting early attempt at State-support of an ailing industry to stave off unemployment and militancy did indeed fail: by late October the Dutch managers had left, the organisation had been broken up and the Bill for 'The National Diamond Factory' was abandoned. But, despite its failure, this early form of nationalisation shows how sensitive central government could be to an area which still contained a large number of potentially (and actually) unemployed ex-Servicemen.

Another group which was well-represented at a local level but with which central government was, as is well-known, extremely concerned throughout the country during the 1920s, was the railmen. The strike by this group provided, as we have seen, one of the main spurs for the local government housing provision in the Brighton area. The case of the railmen is interesting: a large number of them also came to live on the new Moulsecoomb housing estate: an example of how a powerful section of the working class can become further fragmented and perhaps politically incorporated. Among the railmen were two future Labour Councillors, W. Whiting and C.G. Manton, the latter becoming Chairman of the Moulsecoomb Housing Committee and giving his name to Manton Road. The white-collar workers ranged from a foreman at the Post Office, through an estate agent and numerous civil servants, to a company director and a political secretary who worked at Downing Street. Among this class were two thorns in the side of the Housing Committee, F.S. Kilner, a merchant's clerk who became secretary to the vocal Moulsecoomb Ratepayer's Association, and H.E. Banks, secretary to an insurance company who took on the secretaryship of a 1930s' phenomenon, the Moulsecoomb Tenants Defence League.

Not only did the houses in the garden suburb not go to the class that they were built for, but some of them went to people from outside Brighton. On 30th November 1921, the Housing Committee accepted applications for houses on the estate from persons living outside Brighton and as late as 1936 Councillor Simcock, opposing a rate increase for council tenants, asserted that the Council had 'to advertise throughout the countryside to get tenants for South Moulsecoomb.'[45] In the same debate Councillor Manton stated that the 'houses at South Moulsecoomb were the highest rented municipal houses in England'. One result of the high rents was a constant battle for reductions and a stream of tenants away from the estate.[46]

In addition to house-building rates, rent-levels were another important area in which local authorities, as we have mentioned, were relatively autonomous in relation to central government. As Bowley has stressed, central government largely opted out of decisions in this field during the interwar years: local government was urged to maintain both 'low' and 'economic' rents — final determination of rent-levels being left to the local authorities themselves. High interest-rates combined, in Brighton at least, with the strength of the Middle Class Union ensured that rents were 'economic' — being particularly high in the period of high building-costs after the War. But it should be stressed that until 1936, local government was under pressure from the Ministry of Health to maintain relatively high rents: a Circular from the Ministry issued in October 1919,[47] for example, made it clear that there was no intention by central Government to subsidise rents on a permanent basis.

But, by the mid 1930s, substantial changes in housing finance were introduced at central government level which, although still leaving much discretion to local authorities (over, for example, the extent of rate subsidy), allowed inequities in rent-levels to be evened out. In 1935 the local authority Housing Revenue Account became statutory and authorities were allowed to introduce 'pooled' historic cost systems whereby rents on low-cost or older houses could 'subsidise' rents of tenants in other council properties. And the Housing Act of 1936 also had potentially important implications for rent policy. This Act allowed the establishment at local level of 'Standard Rents' which permitted the benefits of declining building-costs to be spread over all council properties. By the late 1930s this legislation allowed local authorities such as Brighton to overcome the rent anomalies referred to earlier and thus reduce the possibilities of tensions between council tenants.

In all, 478 3-bed parlour type houses and 78 4-bed parlour type houses were built at South Moulsecoomb with some more added under the 1924 Housing Act. The houses were 'well and solidly built',[48] the layout was generally considered pleasing, and the gardens, with ample space for vegetable growing and chicken runs, were everything the ex-soldier asked for. Some tenants in the Avenue kept pigs for some time, pigs being a valuable part of the family economy; vociferous complaints from other tenants soon put a stop to this, however;[49] although, perhaps surprisingly, family income was allowed to be supplemented by lodgers.[50]

For those who could afford to stay there, however, South Moulsecoomb was a relative paradise. One of the first tenants were

Mr. and Mrs. Imms. He was a disabled serviceman from Ringmer who had married his wife, who had been in service, and moved to Brighton when he joined the railway police. Their lodgings in central Brighton consisted of two furnished rooms, a shared kitchen, a shared outside WC and no bathroom, for which they paid 15/- per week. When they felt like a bath, they went to the public baths. In 1922 they obtained the tenancy of 79, The Avenue, a three-bedroomed parlour-type house, with kitchen, bathroom, sitting room, WC and a large garden. 'All that', said Mrs. Imms, 'and not much to put in it.' The rent was 22/- per week, a large amount for a family only bringing in £2 18s 6d. There were disadvantages in living at Moulsecoomb; the loneliness in the new community when the husbands went off for their work (often 12 hour shifts); the lack of community facilities; and the distance from the shops. But the community associations were formed and a church and hall were built. Thus many Moulscoombers seem to have felt part of a community: 'We were all very proud of it,' said Mrs. Imms.[51]

In 1929 a garden fete was held at Moulsecoomb Place and the *Brighton Herald* spoke of a thriving outpost of Brighton, with 'a younger sister garden suburb of almost equal promise at North Moulsecoomb.' The Rev. W.H. Carpenter, welcoming the Mayor, proclaimed Moulsecoomb to be Brighton's 'youngest child. The youngest child is often the dearest child, and I trust that Moulsecoomb will always be very dear to the heart of Brighton.'

North Moulsecoomb was built between 1926 and 1930,[52] under the 1924 Wheatley Act which provided generous subsidies for the Local Authorities[53] (£9 per house for 40 years) and did not impose upon them an obligation to prove that private enterprise could not build the houses. The subsidies, added to the fall in the cost of building materials and Wheatley's arrangements with the unions, enabled these 3 bedroomed parlour houses to be built for about £550 each as opposed to £1,120 in South Moulsecoomb. The fact that in the 1970s some of the walls of houses in North Mousecoomb began to bulge because the original wall ties were not galvanised has tended to cause people to think that North Moulsecoomb was badly planned and poorly built. Indeed, North Moulsecoomb was planned on such generous lines as South Moulsecoomb, but several factors in its inception contributed to later difficulties — some of which have a bearing on the other two estates. Firstly, the houses at North Moulsecoomb were planned to cost on average £100 per house more than they eventually did, but the Ministry of Health would not sanction the scheme, as, though it recognised the particular difficulties appertaining to building materials and operatives in Brighton, £650 per house was 'considerably in excess of the average tender price which is now being received by local authorities generally.[54] Secondly, the general local authority practice of accepting the lowest tender, a practice followed by Brighton, resulted in builders' taking short cuts to avoid extensive losses, or going broke so that another builder had to finish the job. The Housing Committee's *Minutes* are a veritable elephants' graveyard register of defunct building firms. The panel of architects reported to the Housing Committee[55] that damp in houses on the Queens Park Site was caused by the choking of external wall cavities after shortcuts by the contractors. Whether the defective wall ties were a method of getting the costing through the Ministry, or corner-cutting by the contractor, is now a matter for conjecture, but the hardship caused to families in North Moulsecoomb is not. Very few facilities were provided on the estates, and again this is understandable in its context, though it may now appear to have been short-sighted. Firstly, there was a split in informed thinking by the Ministry and the Garden City Association over the priorities in the new estates, the question being whether it was a primary duty to provide balanced estates with houses, open spaces and amenities in proportion, or whether the need for houses was so great that it overrode all other considerations. The Brighton Corporation took the latter view and when the Chichester Diocesan Fund wrote asking permission to buy a site for a hall at North Moulsecoomb to be used for social and religious purposes, it was turned down specifically because of the demand for dwellings.[56] That offers from brewers to build public houses on the new estates were turned down causes little surprise. The J.P.s' attitude to licensed houses is a history in itself; suffice to say that not only local magistrates and councillors felt that drink was the root of the evils in city centres, but many artisans disapproved of drink though they understood social reasons for drunkenness. When Marion Fitzgerald did her survey in 1939, for example, an appreciable number of North Mouslecoomb tenants volunteered the information that they were teetotallers.[57]

Another reason for the lack of facilities was that it was thought that nature had already provided amenities enough. At the Fete in 1929 the Mayor postulated that:

'The conditions under which the people of Moulsecoomb live are well nigh ideal and form a great contrast with the lot of many of those who live on the hillsides of Brighton.'

Brighton was already a high rate paying borough[58] and it may well have been impolitic to provide the new estates with recreational facilities which city centre ratepayers might feel they were paying for, while being denied the advantages afforded to Moulsecoomb. In a Council debate in 1936, Councillor Hay protested that those councillors who represented wards with council houses wanted the council to subsidise these at the expense of other ratepayers:

'The tenants of council houses have wonderful amenities: beautiful schools and recreation grounds, and now the Council have even started building public halls, which the people don't seem to be using much. What about the central town tradesmen, their assessments are up and their trade is down because of the big company shops.'[59]

The Moulsecoombers, though the persistent Mr. Kilner, barraged the Housing Committee for a hall[60] and eventually obtained one in 1934. It was to be used for concerts, dances, socials, lectures and flower shows, and that was its trouble, for it appealed to only one section of the community. As a speaker from the Joseph Rowntree Social Service Trust said to members of Brighton Rotary Club in 1936:[61]

'Community centres have been provided in some instances but it seems to me that they have not been run on quite the right lines. They have excellent secretaries and organisers, but there is too much tendency to run them on the lines of 'uplift' and education, and people, if they do not acutely resent these things, are not attracted by them. Some organisers have complained that while they can always make their Whist Drive or weekly Dance pay, nobody seems to take any interest in their Esperanto classes. That is not all that surprising!'

The lack of facilities on the Moulsecoomb estates, especially in North Moulsecoomb, which even today has only a small hall (St. George's Hall) was a repeated complaint.[62]

We must not impose present perceptions on the past, however. Housing conditions in central Brighton were often very bad and most people were pleased to be on the Moulsecoomb estates, despite the high cost of rent and transport[63] and lack of entertainment. Marion Fitzgerald records that 'most of the people said they liked being on the estate, and only a few would prefer to go back to town.'[64] Mr. Richard Bean, a printer, who lives at Barcombe Road, records in a parish magazine, 'Eventually we settled at Moulsecoomb (North), what a wonderful place.' A look at the *Baptismal Register* indicates that there were both artisans and manual workers, but no white collar workers or professionals as in South Moulsecoomb. The houses were uniformly of the 3-bedroom parlour variety, the Government's still stressing the prime need to cater for families with children.[65]

We come now to East Moulsecoomb, an estate about which many inaccurate statements have been made by people who should know better. Musgrave[66] seems to rank it with South Moulsecoomb and calls it 'one of the finest municipal housing estates in the country'. Petra Grifiths' Shelter reports, *Homes Fit for Heroes*[67], goes to the other extreme and says that it was built for slum clearance. In fact East Moulsecoomb was a polyglot development, with different house sizes and built under different Housing Acts. In fact, while £166,000 was spent on houses under the Slum Clearance (1930) and Consolidated (1936) Acts, including houses specifically to relieve overcrowding as opposed to slum clearance. £128,000 was spent under the 1925 Act, for the provision of houses for the working classes generally, even though there were no subsidies available (these having ended in 1932). The Shelter Report's statement is true to the limited extent that East Moulsecoomb has become identified as a slum clearance estate, but this is due to various complicated factors.

In the late 1920s it was becoming clear that the main twenties' Housing Acts had failed to bring about the desired effect. The houses built had been insufficient in number to meet the demands of the more affluent working-class and so the 'filtering-up' theory had not worked in practice. The rents of the new houses were too high for the poorest households, and, in any case, local authorities selected tenants according to 'respectability', cleanliness and rent-paying capacity.[68] As Bowley writes:

'If the purpose of the Second Experiment (i.e. the 1923, 1924 and 1925 Acts) is defined as the provision of a supply of working class houses at rents within the reach of the majority of families . . . then the experiment must be regarded as a failure.'[69]

The answer for both Conservative and Labour parties[70] was that while Council housing should remain as a permanent institution, it should only have the limited purpose of dealing with those who could not find dwelling in the private sector. In 1933 the Coalition Government, with Hilton Young at the Ministry of Health, decided to abandon the Wheatley subsidy altogether. So while 'the decks were cleared for what was to become the biggest private building boom in British history'[71] the Greenwood subsidies of 1930, tied exclusively to slum clearance, ensured that the sanitary principle associated with the 19th century was alive and well.

Both unfitness for human habitation (1930 Act) and overcrowding

(1935 Act) were strictly defined. In the former case the subsidy increased with the number of persons rehoused and was thus particularly useful in meeting the needs of large and poor families. The overcrowding problem often overlapped with that of unfit habitations, and because the 1930 subsidy was larger there was an incentive (or temptation) for local authorities to adopt the latter.[72] There was a danger in all this, however, and it ws the danger of propaganda. The Government's propaganda was most effective in stimulating local authorities to clear their slums, but it must have also made many townspeople wonder what monsters were going to crawl out of the old terraced houses once they were under the threat of a clearance order.[73] Greenwood, speaking to the Conference of Municipal Corporations in 1930,[74] spoke of 'the horrible thing in our midst'. 'I hope you will do your duty,' he went on, 'because public opinion is ripening and I will do my best to ripen it still further. I believe it is a perfectly practicable proposition to rid the country of slums in ten years.' When Greenwood spoke of the 'horrible thing' he meant slum dwellings, but it is not difficult to imagine that in people's imaginations, horrible habitations and horrible inhabitants were linked. It is obviously a mistake to believe that working class areas are somehow homogeneous. Langley described railwaymen's houses in New England Street, Brighton, in St. Peter's Ward: 'Those streets were highly respectable. They were really well kept houses, rented from the Railway Company.'[75] He wrote of those people who did not face their responsibilities in a world of 'exacting standards of work and behaviour',[76] but got drunk, fought in the 'blood Hole' outside Hove Station and begat large numbers of children who were a burden on the rates.[77] The local politicians also pushed for slum clearance while increasing popular horror for the slums themselves. The *Gazette* held an interview in 1938 with Alderman Miss Margaret Hardy, M.B.E., J.P., Brighton's first woman Mayor. 'Educationalist, social worker and philanthropist', Miss Hardy was a Baptist of strong views:

> I want you to think of all these conditions (i.e. drink, slums, immorality, dishonesty, broken homes) as coming together and, so to speak, jostling one another. Into this repulsive mass a seed is dropped. That seed flourishes and grows and another young delinquent is started and another child criminal begins his career.'[78]

Three other factors increased the distaste of other council tenants for the slum clearance tenants. In the first place, slum clearance tenants were thought to be verminous. The Sanitary Inspector had power to examine all those moving to council properties from slum clearance areas and overcrowded houses, something that had not happened with earlier Council tenants. The Medical Officer of Health's *Report* for 1939 states that 117 families removed from clearance areas were disinfested, and of the 495 overcrowded cases granted council tenancies, 80 houses were found to be verminous. Of council houses inspected after the tenants had vacated them, only 6 were found sufficiently infested to warrant fumigation. The second factor is that some of the new tenants would be tuberculous, T.B. being more prevalent among the lower paid, especially labourers, and in the crowded town centre. T.B., a highly infectious disease, was dealt with in isolation hospitals. In Lewes there were spital cottages, and in Brighton there was an isolation hospital built in 1881[79] which later became a permanent sanatorium, and later still, Bevendean Hospital. When Brighton General Hospital converted a ward for tuberculosis sufferers, special basins and receptacles had to be used and 'suitable drainage arranged',[80] and John Langley recalls:

> 'When I was young, T.B. was rife (poverty again) and we were forbidden to mix. Death was inevitable.'[81]

The tenancies sub-committee recommended that a number of houses should be set aside in one locality for the large number of people with T.B. applying for council houses.[82] The Medical Officer of Health disagreed:

> 'I find that most patients are rather sensitive about being labelled tuberculosis, and if we build a group of houses in one locality specially for pthisis patients we might have difficulty in getting them occupied . . . segregation in one locality should be avoided.'[83]

What happened, however, is that a large group of five bedroomed houses was built at the northern end of Birdham Road and into them went a group of tenants of low social status, from clearance areas, some with T.B. and all with low income and large families.

The third factor in the equation is that under the 1936 Housing Act, which was a consolidating Act, rent rebates were allowable for slum clearance tenants but not for those rehoused through over-crowding. This must have caused considerable puzzlement and anger and Marion Fitzgerald put the divisiveness of the situation clearly when she wrote:

> 'The large poor family may need rent relief much more than one from a clearance area, for people in the slums are not necessarily very poor. The

wife of a skilled man in the building trade said that they paid 12/7d for some months after moving from a clearance area, then unexpectedly got a rebate of 2/6d. There is only one child, aged two in this family. The husband was said to be often out of work, but that, unfortunately, is true of the men in the building trade in North Moulsecoomb who pay 14/4d. rent and have larger families. The mere fact of coming from a clearance area should not constitute a claim for rebate.'[84]

When Fitzgerald visited the estate in 1939 she commented that 'the houses, though built in pairs, have pleasing exteriors, and on the whole the interior planning is good.' The Borough Surveyor reported to the Housing Committee in 1936[85] that:

'The elevations would be given a varied treatment, and in this scheme I have introduced bay windows to some houses and French windows in others, in order to break up the monotony and give features of interest.'

As the Second World War approached and building materials began to become scarce and expensive, the Corporation started to cut back on standards in housebuilding, a practice bitterly attacked by the Medical Officer of Health, Dr. Duncan Forbes, who had been one of the prime movers for a coherent, vigorous, yet sensitive, slum clearance policy. In his *Annual Report of 1938* Forbes expressed criticism of the large numbers of houses built at Whitehawk, away from the centres of industry; of the building of flats rather than houses in the town centre;[86] and of the quantity and quality of the council houses being built at that time. On the latter point, Forbes noted that 'this short-sighted policy has all along had the active support of the Minister of Health' and further:

'Cheeseparing seems unnecessary as these houses will be occupied 100 years hence, and after the expiry of the 40 years loan period will be valuable revenue producing assets. In this matter history is repeating itself, as when Tilestone Street, St. Helen's Road, Dewe Road and May Road were built no bath was installed and it is only now that the Council, at considerable expense, is supplying what is now regarded as essential.'

This question of house standards was a very difficult one for local councils. As Bowley[87] points out, there were increased expectations after the First World War, both external, as voiced by the *Tudor Walters Report* of 1918, and internalised through increased publicity given to housing standards and experiments. In Dr. Forbes' report quoted above, a bath was regarded as essential, whereas in the 1919 Council debate, Councillor Titcomb and Mayor Carden had a row over whether a bath was essential or not — Titcomb claiming they would not be used.[88] The truth is, perhaps, that social reformers pressed for standards that people often could not, or did not want to pay for. When Carden suggested that baths and WCs should be provided by the Council in pre-war council properties the subsequent survey showed that most people did not want a bath if they had to pay an extra 2/- per week rent for it.

Who were the tenants who took up residence at East Moulsecoomb? It is very difficult to say in detail and one can only rely on the scant evidence, and on modern works showing trends in tenancy preference. The *Baptismal Register* indicates that the social class of the tenants in East Moulsecoomb was lower than at North Moulsecoomb. There were engine drivers and electricians, but the majority were skilled, or more often unskilled workers in that notably uncertain trade, building. One tenant was Edward Thomas Phipps[89] of 24 Picton Street, an agricultural worker who suffered from tuberculosis. He was rehoused in a three bedroomed council house at 7 Birdham Road specifically because of his poor circumstances. He had a wife and four children and an earning capacity of about £2; he actually received 33/- from the U.A.B. The standard rent for the house was 13/7d but Phipps received a rebate of 6/8d; he quickly got into arrears and, despite notices to quit, no further payment was forthcoming. There were at least three other persistent non-payers in Birdham Road, the tenant at No. 27 also being a tuberculosis sufferer and refusing to pay 7/6d rent out of a 12/- rent allowance made by the Social Welfare Committee. This must have caused anger among both housing officials and non-rebate tenants alike.[90]

If a few people exploited the new housing opportunity given to them, others expressed dissatisfaction at any attempt to rehouse them. The Medical Officer of Health in his *Report* to the Housing Committee on 20th October 1937, pronounced that not more than a quarter of the tenants of houses in the clearance areas were prepared to move out to the 144 houses being built for them at East Moulsecoomb. The chief reasons were, he felt, monetary, one being the extra cost of transport, the other the likelihood of having to pay an extra 3 or 4s per week in rent (something that was later lessened by the rebates).[91] For less material reasons people were unwilling to move into the flats in the Carlton Hill area, built on the site of former slums. The Medical Officer of Health told the Housing Committee[92] that the Milner Flats were 'extremely noisy and particularly unfitted for the tenants who occupied them.' Later the Kingswood flats and maisonettes were built but despite measures to prevent transmission of noise, only 42 families out of a possible 59 had elected to go there, others absolutely refusing. The flats were disliked because of the common staircase, complaints of noise, and the lack of proper washing facilities. The tenants felt that their children were constantly in trouble, because they could not play without disturbing other tenants. The flats were thought to have a barrack-like elevation and school playground-like surroundings, while other ratepayers in the town were aware that these flats had been erected for former slum dwellers. Finally, the tenants felt that had no opportunity to start to raise themselves from their former level, away from their associates; rather (how much the phraseology of this last reason is the tenant's and how much the Medical Officer of Health's is not certain) they were being herded together with the bad influences one on another, continuing as in the slum.

We are faced, then, in 1939, with South Moulsecoomb and North Moulsecoomb as settled estates, and a mixed influx of new tenants into East Moulsecoomb. But beneath a quiet surface and the acceptance by many of the tenants of the first two Moulscoomb estates as a privileged and élite tenant group in the Borough, there simmered discontent. This was simply and directly put by the Bishop of Chichester in his preamble to Marion Fitzgerald's report on the rents in Moulsecoomb:

> 'Wages are low in Brighton, compared with other towns; and much of the work is casual and seasonal. All the more important to see that the housing conditions are as good and as inexpensive as possible, and that rents are not quite out of proportion to the earnings. The amount of money spent in Brighton for the entertainment of visitors, and for the attraction of holiday makers, is very large. All the more important that there should be no ground for fair criticism as to the living conditions of the working people who compose the vast majority of Brighton residents.'

Marion Fitzgerald's *Report* stated quite simply that rents were so high,[93] and wages so uncertain, especially for those building operatives in North Moulsecoomb who had fair sized families, that drastic economies were being made in basic diet. 'In some cases,' she writes, 'there does not appear to be any visible margin for clothing and recreation.'[94] The men, in fact, who had built the houses, then, like the soldiers before who had fought for them, could not afford to live in them. Fitzgerald points out that the North Moulsecoombers actually needed a three-bedroomed parlour-type house, and that there was little evidence of thriftlessness;[95] the men worked hard at job and gardens;[96] and the women managed as well as possible, but transport, food and fuel cost them more than in central Brighton or in most other parts of the country.[97] Though the South Moulsecoombers generally represented higher income groups, they paid higher rents and often had to supplement the family income by taking in relatives (25% of sample), boarders (10% of sample) or children or mentally handicapped persons (10% of sample).[98] One interesting example is of a woman in North Moulsecoomb who had taken out an endowment policy because she 'wanted her daughter to do better than the others and go into an office'[99] but the difficulty of maintaining the policy and paying the rent of a large enough house to enable the girl to have a spare room for study was crippling. Fitzgerald's summary on North Moulsecoomb is that:

> 'Rents on *this* estate are not exorbitant, but with other essential outgoings leave an insufficient margin for food and clothing in the majority of families. The problem seems to be mainly one of inadequate wages to meet family needs on the modern standards of decent housing, reasonable amenities, and adequate nourishment.'[100]

We have in this paper given particular emphasis to the Moulsecoomb estates, giving less emphasis to other council-house areas in Brighton such as Whitehawk which was started in the late 1920s and which by the mid 1930s, had almost as many housing units as the Moulscoombs. We have at the time of writing little historical information on these other areas; although Whitehawk, as suggested earlier, appears to have been almost entirely occupied by slum-clearance tenants. Unfortunately, no thorough contemporary survey of tenants such as that conducted by Fitzgerald was, to our knowledge, carried out. But a brief survey of contemporary news-papers indicates, as far as rent-levels are concerned, a familiar story. In the late 1930s, for example, the Brighton Town Mission was reporting the following state of affairs on the Whitehawk estate:

> 'Too often the story was one of dire poverty where the woman tried to stretch her money beyond all possible limits.'[101]

We will end our look at Moulsecoomb before the War where we began, in South Moulsecoomb. The date is 24th February 1939, a few months before the *Fitzgerald Report.* The event[102] is a meeting to protest against the increasingly high rents charged by Brighton Corporation. The Vicar, The Rev. Bransby Jones, quoted the Medical Officer of Health for Stockton, as having asserted that on new estates the death rate in some cases had increased from 22% to 33%, while weekly expenditure on food had dropped from 5/2d per head to 4/3d, and with the unemployed man from 3/9d to 2/11d. He advocated the formation of a Tenants' Defence League as in some other boroughs. Mr. H.E. Bankes said that the Borough had betrayed the working man, for the houses were to be for the returned 1914–18 men of the working class and the inclusive rents were not to exceed 15/-. Brighton Corporation had ignored these two ideals. Mrs. Oldfield, a pioneer of the Chelsea Housing Scheme, said that all this was happening while ratepayers' money was lavished on improvements to the Front and entertaining foreign guests. 'Soup kitchens and private charity', she cried, 'might be a salve to the conscience of some, but it was no real alternative to a constructive policy.'

Closing with a vivid detailed description of the misery and want in the parish, caused by the impossible rents, the Vicar urged all to concentrate with steel-like purpose upon one question:

'High rents and no red herrings.'
'Are my statements true as to the poverty.' he asked.
'True' came back the voice of the packed hall.
'Then,' said Mr. Jones, 'we must act together, High rents as a plank and nothing else.'

A copy of the *Fitzgerald Report* was handed to the Housing Committee in November 1939 by H.E. Bankes on behalf of the North, East and South Moulsecoomb Tenants' Defence League. The Housing Committee's succinct answer was that if they could not afford the rents at Moulsecoomb they should seek a transfer to a house they could afford.

While the South Moulsecoombers debated with the Council, their less articulate brethren in North Moulsecoomb queued on the Lewes Road in front of the British Legion Soup Kitchen. These were people who lived in the houses built under the Wheatley Act, they were mainly artisans, men and women who had striven to pay a higher rent so that their children could find a place in the sun in the brave new world that was to be built after the War to end all Wars. Now they were receiving liquid charity just as their fathers had in Hanover Ward in the early part of the century. As a North Moulsecoomber has recounted:

'They were hard times. We stood in great queues along the Lewes Road. All we had to eat in those days was soup and rice and a hunk of bread, doled out at the Soup Kitchen.'[103]

Notes

[1] F. Engel's *The Housing Question* was originally written as three separate news-paper articles. It was published as a single work in 1887; the most common English edition (Progress Publishers, Moscow) being first published in 1954.

[2] Readers wishing to acquaint themselves with this literature may wish to consult the following works. Conference of Socialist Economists Political Economy of Housing Workshop, *Political Economy and the Housing Question* (1975), C.S.E.P.E.H.W., *Housing and Class in Britain* (1976), National Community Development Project *Whatever Happened to Council Housing?* (1976), S. Merrett *State Housing in Britain* (1979).

[3] See P. Dickens 'Social Change, Housing and the State' in M. Harloe (ed.) *Centre for Environmental Studies York Conference 1977. Urban Change and Conflict,* (1978) pp. 336–396, S. Damer 'State, Class and Housing: Glasgow 1885–1919' in J. Melling (ed.) *Housing, Social Policy and the State* (1980) pp. 73–112, D. Byrne, S. Damer 'The State, the Balance of Class Forces and Early Working-Class Housing Legislation' in C.S.E.P.E.H.W. *Housing, Construction and the State* (1980) pp. 63–70. Damer's brief summary of Dickens's argument is regrettably misleading. On the other hand, Byrne and Damer's paper, while making a number of valid theoretical points, does not appear to be based on a thorough knowledge of what actually happened in Glasgow and other towns around 1915.

[4] See, for example, S. Merrett 'Council Rents and British Capitalism' in C.S.E. (1975) pp. 68–91 and F. Gray 'The Management of Local Authority Housing' in C.S.E. (1976) pp. 75–86.

[5] See, for example, J. Dearlove *The Reorganisation of British Local Government* (1979) exp. pp. 239 seq.

[6] This necessarily brief introduction can be supplemented by reading S. Merrett *op. cit.,* esp. Part 1.

[7] In particular *The Report of the Royal Commission on the Housing of the Industrial Population of Scotland* (Cmd. 8731) (1917) and *The Report of the Royal Commission on Industrial Unrest* (Cmd. 8696) (1917).

[8] Much of the recent literature on the decline of the private rented sector gives emphasis to the role of legislation, in particular the Rent Restriction Act of 1915. A valuable paper which corrects this bias (placing emphasis on the economic forces surrounding the production of housing for rent) is P. Kemp *Housing Production and the Decline of the Privately Rented Sector: Some Preliminary Remarks,* University of Sussex Urban and Regional Studies Working Paper 20 (1980).

[9] Wheatley's legislation was highly successful, with 504,500 houses being built under this Act, nearly three times the number built under the Addison Act. See Dickens (1978) *op. cit.,* esp. pp. 365–369.

[10] S. Schiffees 'Council Tenants and Housing Policy in the 1930s: the Contra-dictions of State Intervention' in C.S.E (1976) op. cit.

[11] *Brighton Medical Officer of Health's Report,* 1937.

[12] Quoted in E. Gilbert, *Old Ocean's Bauble* (1954) pp. 186–7.

[13] Gilbert, *op. cit.,* p. 187.

[14] *Evening Argus,* 17 May 1967.

[15] W. Kebbell, *Popular Lectures on the Prevailing Diseases of the Town* (1848) p. 19.

[16] E. Cresy *Report to the General Board of Health on a Preliminary Inquiry into the Sewerage, Drainage and Supply of Water and the Sanitary Conditions of the Inhabitants of the Town of Brighton* (1849).

[17] J. Langley *Always a Layman* (Brighton 1974).

[18] A. Paul, *Poverty-Hardship but Happiness* (Brighton 1974) pp. 18–19.

[19] *Brighton Herald,* 15 February 1908.

[20] See P. Dickens *Class Conflict and the Gift of Housing* (Conference of the International Sociological Association, Messina, 1976).

[21] Dr. Kebbell had remarked in 1848 that he was surprised that the authorities did so little to combat poor sanitary conditions 'considering how much the prosperity of the town depends upon the purity of the atmosphere.' Kebbel *op. cit.*

[22] Gilbert, *op. cit.*, p. 214. C. Musgrave *Life in Brighton*, (1970) M. Fitzgerald *Rents in Moulsecoomb* (Chichester 1939).

[23] *Brighton Gazette*, 8 Feb 1919.

[24] *Brighton Gazette*, 20 Dec 1919, 14 Aug 1920.

[25] Squatting was 'invented' in Brighton during the immediate post-war years by the Vigilante movement; pressurising both local and central government. See P. Dickens 'Squatting and the State', *New Society*, 5 May 1977, Vol. 40, No. 761.

[26] *Sussex Daily News*, 3 February 1919. The General Purposes Committee recommended Brighton Council in October 1918 to make an order under the Housing of the Working Classes Acts 1890–1909 for the compulsory purchase of the Moulsecoomb Estate. *G.P.C.M.* 1 October 1918.

[27] *The Brighton Gazette (and Hove Post)* was also *The Auction, Estate and Property Advertiser.* On 16 April 1919 it bemoaned the fact that the State arrangement left 'no room for the play of ingenious and attractive bargaining'.

[28] *Brighton Gazette*, 26 March 1919.

[29] M. Bowley, *op. cit.*

[30] P. Dickens (1978) *op. cit.*, p. 15.

[31] There were in fact very few corporation houses in Brighton at this time.

[32] *Brighton Herald*, 17 January 1920.

[33] *Brighton Gazette*, 19 April 1919.

[34] These Council statements have been transferred from newspaper accounts into direct speech.

[35] *Brighton Herald*, 26 April 1918. The ex-soldier wrote that it ws difficult to get a job even at £2.10.0d. per week. Men had come back to ruined businesses and unemployment. See views of soldier demanding demob in the *Brighton Gazette* 8 January 1919.
For similar concerns expressed in Bristol see K. Bassett *Public Housing in Bristol 1918–39* (University of Bristol 1976) p. 9. The nearest that many ex-servicemen got to the homes for heroes was painting them in Brighton Corporation's relief schemes (H.C.M. 9 May 1924).

[36] Musgrave, *op. cit.*, p. 389.

[37] Ministry of Health Housing Department, *Housing 1919–20*, 22 November 1920, p. 151.

[38] *Evening Argus*, 23 September 1975.

[39] The fact that the Local Authority was to build obviously raised the price of land, especially as Brighton had had an option on the land since October 1918 (G.P.C.M. 1 October 1918). Moulsecoomb was said to be the best site, but whether any corruption was involved is a matter for further research. The laying out of the open space in the centre of the estate alone cost £3,800 (H.C.M. 17 July 1922). Expenditure exceeded the loan sanction by £16,158 (H.C.M. 9 January 1924). See also: R.G. Baxter, D.J. Howe: 'Municipal Activities in Brighton during the past twelve years' *Proc. Inst. Mun. and Co. Engineers*, Vol. LXIII (1936–7) 31–76.

[40] Housing Committee Minutes (H.C.M.) 15 June 1921.

[41] M. Fitzgerald *op. cit.*

[42] St. Andrews Church of England Church, Moulsecoomb *Baptismal Register*. A comparison with Fitzgerald pp. 7–8 and 33 indicates a decline in middle-class occupation of Moulsecoomb by 1939, due no doubt to the double accent on slum clearance and owner occupation in the Thirties. that
Bassett believes that a comparable 'de-skilling' of the population on council estates took place in Bristol (see Basset *op. cit.*, p. 12). A good example of the reported disillusionment in the working class districts of central Brighton at the class of tenant

selected for Moulsecoomb can be found in the *Brighton Gazette* 23 March 1921.

[43] PRO CAB 24/159.

[44] PRO CAB 23/45.

[45] *Brighton Gazette*, 28 March 1936.

[46] 'The Town Clerk reported that there was an amount of £ 7 15 6d due from the last tenant of No. 48 Colbourne Avenue and recommended that the amount be written off as irrecoverable as it had not been possible to obtain any information as to his present residence.' *H.C.M.* 9 May 1924.

[47] e.g. *H.C.M.* 11 January 1922. The Corporation supported a request by the Moulsecoomb Ratepayers' Association for a rent reduction, and the Ministry of Health allowed exclusive rents to be reduced by 4/-. The Association immediately asked for a further reduction, but the Corporation deemed it unwise to approach the Ministry again 'in view of the loss incurred in connection with the houses.' *H.C.M.* 14 June 1922.
It is worth saying here that the Moulsecoomb tenants at this time saw themselves very much as ratepayers, as, of course, they were. The proportion of rates to rent was about one quarter of the inclusive rent.
The Moulsecoomb Tenants' Association made deputations to the Housing Committee almost every year from 1923 onwards in an attempt to reduce rents (*Sussex Daily News* 28 March 1930). The charging of economic rents also led to difficulties between tenants. When costs fell Council houses elsewhere in Brighton of similar standards to those at Moulsecoomb were let at much lower rents. In 1930 Moulsecoomb tenants were protesting that houses in Bevendean were being let at only 14/-. *H.C.M.* October 1919.

[48] M. Fitzgerald *op. cit.*

[49] *H.C.M.* 11 June 1924.

[50] *cf.* Fitzgerald *op. cit.*, p. 33.

[51] *Interview* with Mrs. Imms 10 March 1977. In 1930 the Imms moved to another three bedroomed house in The Avenue (the Bevendean end) which had been built under the Wheatley Act and was let at 15/- per week.
The Moulsecoomb Ratepayer's Association requested that in view of the contemplated building of 72 houses on the Bevendean Estate to be let at 14/6d to 15/-, 72 tenants from Moulsecoomb should have first call for transfer on completion. The request was refused *H.C.M.* 5 December 1929.

[52] There was pressure for more houses to be built in Brighton for the working classes throughout the early twenties. The Housing Committee *Minutes* record letters from the National Union of Railwaymen Women's Guild and the Brighton and District Tenants Defence Association; and a meeting on the Level demanding more houses. *H.C.M.* 9 May 1923, 10 October 1923, 6 September 1923.
The Brighton, Hove and District Joint Town Planning Advising Committee Preliminary Report (1928) states that 'a serious shortage undoubtedly still exists in many parts of the Region, especially in small dwellings of low rent.'

[53] 'The most generous in the level of subsidy than any since.' S. Clarke and N. Ginsburg 'The Political Economy of Housing' in C.S.E. Political Economy of Housing Workshop *Political Economy and the Housing Question* (1975).

[54] Letter from the Minister of Health to the Housing Committee 7 September 1929.

[55] *H.C.M.* 5 May 1925.

[56] *H.C.M.* 23 July 1926. Cf. Address to Brighton Rotary Club by Mr. Wilson of the Rowntree Social Services Trust: 'the estates were built very rapidly with the idea of providing as many houses as possible': *Brighton Gazette* 28 May 1936. See also Bowley *op. cit.*, p. 196. Oppenheimer wanted to build a maternity and children's hospital at Moulsecoomb but was told that no land was available. *H.C.M.* 7 July 1920.

[57] Fitzgerald, *op. cit.*, pp. 21–2

[58] Gilbert, op. cit., pp. 174 and 227.

[59] *Brighton Gazette* 28 March 1936

[60] e.g. *H.C.M.* 13 February 1924.

[61] *Brighton Gazette* 28 March 1936. It is true that Moulsecoomb had recreation grounds, but there has always been a fierce battle over access. In January 1921 Councillor Wilkinson of the Education Committee told the *Brighton Gazette* that they were looking for a groundsman for Moulsecoomb, for 'the object was to keep people off the playing field'(!): *Brighton Gazette* 26 January 1921.

[62] The lack of shops and other facilities was recognised by several reports in the late Thirties. See Fitzgerald *op. cit.*, pp. 9 and 17. The 1937 Development Plan showed Moulsecoomb as having 3.95 shops and 0.20 pubs per percentage of the total number of properties, compared to 6.0 and 1.08 for Queens Park and 20.36 and 2.38 for St. Peter's Ward; it is concluded that the outlying wards 'may not have a sufficiency of shopping accommodation to meet their local needs'. *County Borough of Brighton, Town Planning Central Area Report and Development Plan* (June 1937).

[63] Fitzgerald, *op. cit.*, p. 17.

[64] *Ibid.*, p. 21.

[65] The Mayor told the Council that the Government had told them that they must build three-bedroomed houses before two-bedroomed flats, because of the needs of families. *Brighton Gazette* 9 April 1919.

[66] Musgrave, *op. cit.*, p. 444.

[67] Petra Griffiths, *Homes Fit for Heroes*, Shelter, June 1975, p. 11.

[58] A good example of this occurs in the Housing Committee *Minutes* of 1932. In late February the Housing Committee is discussing the Whitehawk slum clearance scheme and wanting a 'full statement of the evidence of need which the proposal is based' (*H.C.M.* 17 February 1932). In early March it was reported that the following applications for 1925 Act houses in Whitehawk had been turned down or deferred: four were rejected because the head of the household earned insufficient wages; one was deferred because of an adverse Health Department Report; and another was deferred because of dirty bedding (*H.C.M.* 9 March 1932 and 13 April 1932).

[69] Bowley, *op. cit.*, p. 132.

[70] S. Schifferes, *op. cit.*

[71] N. Branson and M. Heinmann, *Britain in the Thirties* (1971), quoted in N.C.D.P. *Whatever Happened to Council Housing?* (1976) p. 15.

[72] Bowley, *op. cit.*, p. 151.

[73] Sean Damer, writing about 19th Century slum clearance in Glasgow says: 'Needless to say, there was a strong belief that the slum dwellers were there because of 'their own fault'; they wre 'incorrigible', 'inefficient', 'indifferent', 'criminal', 'depraved' . . . Whoever they were they were undesirable and had to be kept under strict control.' S. Damer, *Property Relation and Class Relations in Victorian Glasgow*, University of Glasgow (July 1976) p. 20.

[74] Reported in *H.C.M.* 19 November 1930.

[75] J. Langley, *op. cit.*,

[76] *Cf.* Paul *op. cit.*, p. 6.

[77] Langley, *op. cit.*, p. 8.

[78] *Brighton Gazette*, 19 March 1938.

[79] *Annual Report of the Medical Officer of Health* (1938).

[80] *H.H.C.M.* 13 July 1944.

[81] Langley, *op. cit.* It was not necessarily fatal, but it had to be detected early and convalescence was slow.

[82] *H.C.M.* 16 June 1937.

[83] Ibid. The Medical Officer of Health disliked concentrations and their effects. In his *Annual Report* for 1936 he stated his disagreement with the building of such a large estate at Whitehawk, and did not agree with a block of five-bedroomed houses at East Moulsecoomb. (*H.C.M.* 9 September 1937).

[84] Fitzgerald *op. cit.*, p. 26. cf. Schifferes *op. cit. passim*.

[85] *H.C.M.* 12 February 1936. The cost and design stated, however, indicates a great decline in standards since the 1920s. Dr. Forbes, M.O.H., told the Brighton Rotary Club that because of economies the Ministry was recommending the erection

of housing below the standard which it had laid down itself in 1924. (*Brighton Gazette*, 4 March 1933).

⁸⁶ According to Dr. Forbes, the Ministry of Health would not sanction a loan for houses as distinguished from flats on high-priced land in the centre of town. If Forbes is correct as to this being Central Government policy then there is a need to look closer on the influences on Central Government at this time. There are indications, however, that there were local interests at work. The *1937 Development Plan* advised that 'land which is more suitable for business purposes should not be misused by devotion to housing purposes' (p. 58). In March 1938 there was an argument between Councillors Dutton Briant (a member of a leading firm of estate agents) and Sir Herbert Carden; the former accused the Council of buying property at less than market value, ostensibly for rehousing the working classes, and then using the land for other purposes (*Brighton Gazette* 26 March 1938). Obviously this whole area deserves further study. The outcome was that only the Milner and Kingswood flats were built by the Council in the 1930s and persons from clearance areas were given a choice of these or East Moulsecoomb. The valuable city centre sites were too valuable for rehousing the likes of those who lived there previously. (Cf *H.C.M.* 5 October 1938 and 15 February 1939).

⁸⁷ Bowley, *op. cit.*

⁸⁸ *Brighton Gazette,* 19 April 1919.

⁸⁹ *H.C.M.* 2 November 1939. This man is probably the example given by Fitzgerald on p. 26.

⁹⁰ The East Moulsecoomb Tenants Defence League protested against the rebates for slum clearance tenants on behalf of tenants living in Hodshrove Road who were non-slum clearance tenants (*H.C.M.* 19 January 1938). The houses built for general purposes were let at an economic rent (*H.C.M.* 12 February 1936) at least before standard rents were brought in.

⁹¹ Rents of clearance tenants at East Moulsecoomb were reduced by 25% in late 1937. *H.C.M.* 17 November 1937.
The Medical Officer of Health told the Housing Committee in 1938 that of the 39 families rehoused to date on the East Moulsecoomb estate, the average income was £ 2 4s 1½d, and in 33 cases there was an average increase of rent of 4s 0½d (without taking the rebate into account). In the other 6 cases there was a decrease in rent varying from 1d to 3s 1d. but the increased cost of the journey to work has to be borne in mind, i.e. 2/- from East Moulsecoomb to Brighton if the journey was after 8 a.m. *H.C.M.* 5 January 1938.

⁹² *H.C.M.* 15 February 1939.

⁹³ Fitzgerald pointed out that the only county boroughs with more rents in the highest category (i.e. above 12/–) than Brighton were Croydon and Newcastle (Fitzgerald *op. cit.* p. 32). And as Bowley remarks 'up to the outbreak of the present War it was generally considered that a gross rent of 10/– including rates was the *maximum* (her emphasis) that the families of ordinary unskilled labourers, or even in many cases of semi-skilled labourers could afford'. (Bowley *op. cit.* p. 96). Bowley (p. 113) remarks that Brighton was a high rent borough, but appears to give no adequate explanation. One reason presumably was the amount of finance committed under the Addison Scheme, see Appendix II.

⁹⁴ Fitzgerald, *op. cit.*, p. 8.

⁹⁵ *Ibid.*, p. 22.

⁹⁶ *Ibid.*, p. 21. The most prolific winners of the Corporation Tenants Gardening Competition in the late thirties and early Forties were Mr. Parris of 15 Ringmer Road and Mr. Barnes of 9 Ringmer Road. *H.C.M.* 22 November 1939 and 16 September 1942.

⁹⁷ Fitzgerald *op. cit.*, p. 15.

⁹⁸ *Ibid.*, p. 33.

⁹⁹ *Ibid.*, pp. 20–21.

[100] *Ibid.*, p. 21. The Borough Accountant acknowledged that the rents for houses at South Moulsecoomb were 'well in advance of the general level of rents for council houses.' *H.C.M.* 13 March 1936.

[101] *Brighton and Hove Gazette*, 26 March 1938.

[102] 'Poverty at Moulsecoomb', *Brighton and Hove Gazette*, 25 February 1939.

[103] Interview held in March 1977.

Reviews

John Lowerson, *A Short History of Sussex*, Dawson Publishing, Folkestone 1980, pp. 214, 8 maps, price £10.00.

An alternative title for this book could have been 'A Social History of Sussex', since Mr Lowerson's aim is to emphasize people rather than buildings or the landscape in contrast to other short histories intended for the general reader. He is rightly critical of the sentimental, nostalgic attitude of much popular writing on Sussex, though paradoxically the cover picture of haymaking suggests just such an approach.

The second half of the book, dealing with the nineteenth and twentieth centuries, is the more valuable, drawing as it does on Mr Lowerson's own research. In this period Sussex came to provide both a playground for Londoners and a favoured place of residence, either for commuting or retirement. In 1901 23,000 inhabitants of the county were *rentiers*, and 27 per cent of the total employed population was in domestic service. The richer immigrants are well characterized by their descriptions in W.T. Pike's congratulatory *Sussex in the Twentieth Century*, but Lowerson also illuminates lower social groups like the teachers or the 'minor dynasties of moderate men' represented by William Pawson, clerk of Seaford UDC. There are good, if brief, sections on leisure. Soccer, surprisingly, was popularized by the Woodard schools, which then, 'shocked by the pro-fessionalization of the game', reverted to Rugby football. Golf was not always popular either: the lord of the manor of East Blatchington opposed its playing on Sundays at Seaford, arguing that 'a man who would play golf on Sunday would not be too particular whether he paid his debts'! On twentieth-century history Mr Lowerson is refreshingly anti-nostalgic; it is salutary to be reminded that Fascist sympathies were fairly strong in the coastal towns in the 1930s, and that the influx of Canadian troops in 1941 led to violent clashes with British soldiers over 'WRNS detachments, attractive but in short supply'. The coastal towns, especially Brighton, are given the chief emphasis during the last 175 years, but it could be argued that their history better characterizes the period than that of the rural hinterland.

The first half of the book is less happy. As the author admits, it is hard to write social history before circa 1500 because of the dearth of material; ordinary people only rarely emerge from the mist, and their absence is not fully compensated by references to festivals or (frequently) to riots. But problems are too often over-simplified: the Saxon hundreds were not groups of parishes (page 42), and open fields were not 'practically unknown' north of the coastal plain (page 39). Often too Mr Lowerson takes refuge in vague generalities; for instance, rural communities 'saw the greatest pattern of change during the middle ages although, with a couple of notable ex-ceptions, this was a very long process indeed but with some sudden shifts of direction'. There are also serious mistakes of detail: more than just the church survives at the 'deserted' village of Coombes (page 71), Old

Shoreham was not totally destroyed by the sea, and the clump at Chanctonbury Ring was planted by Charles Goring, not Sir Bysshe Shelley.

The book is stylishly produced, in a similar format to *Southern History*, but at its price, and without illustrations, is expensive. The maps are not always useful; the upper Arun is omitted from all of them, and the 'new town' of Wardour is misplaced on page 70. The standard of proof-reading is low (e.g. Warninghurst for Warminghurst, or Bowyer for Bowers). The index, moreover, is abysmal — selective for places and non-existent for subjects (the entry for 'Weald' seems to give up in despair), yet solemnly including every once-mentioned book or pamphlet.

Victoria County History of Sussex   T. P. HUDSON

Peter Brandon, *A History of Surrey*, Phillimore, Chichester 1977, pp. 128, 48 plates, 12 maps, price £5.95; Barbara Carpenter Turner, *A History of Hampshire*, 2nd edition, Phillimore, Chichester 1978, pp. 128, 43 plates, 13 maps, price £5.95.

A concise, undemanding text and an abundance of illustrations and sketch-maps are the standard features of the Darwen County History Series to which these two volumes belong. Although of limited value to the specialist historian, the series is admirable for the inquiring amateur and the general reader, and provides the teacher of environmental studies with an attractive and reliable source of information for use with more able pupils.

Dr Brandon, the author of *A History of Surrey*, is a professional geographer with a particular interest in the making of the English landscape, so it is not surprising that the interaction of human and environmental factors is given particular prominence in his book. The remarkable variety of surface within the county and the local differences in economic, social and cultural development might easily have resulted in a fragmented narrative, but Dr Brandon manages to bring coherence and clarity to the story. An important theme is the expansion of London and the relentless encroachment of suburban society on the vulnerable Surrey countryside, with profound effects on the county's traditional way of life. The author is at pains throughout the book to describe the changing living and labouring conditions of ordinary people, but he also has much of interest to say about the great estates and country houses and their owners' passion for re-modelling the landscape. To evidence drawn from original documents and intensive fieldwork he adds at every opportunity the testimony of artists and writers such as J.M.W. Turner, John Evelyn and William Cobbett, who lived in or visited the county. Dr Brandon's individual approach means that some of the familiar themes and landmarks in English history are missing — the Norman Conquest, the Reformation and the Civil War, for example, are passed over without comment — but this well written book with its many illustrations and maps, and Carolyn Lockwood's delightful miniature line-drawings, is nevertheless a notable addition to the series.

Mrs Carpenter Turner's *A History of Hampshire* is the second edition of the popular standard work which was first published in 1963. With the last quarter of the original text completely rewritten and the remainder revised in the light of current scholarship, it is in effect a new book, almost double the size of its predecessor. The story is carried down to 1976 and there is fuller treatment than before of the history of Hampshire education and local government. The publishers have increased the number of illustrations and added drawings by Carolyn Lockwood. Mrs Carpenter Turner has also provided a new appendix in which she lists with appropriate details the principal Hampshire record offices, archive collections, museums and local history societies. This is a praiseworthy idea but inevitably some of the information will be out of date long before the book's next edition. The haphazard way in which the select bibliography has been arranged is a minor blemish on an otherwise attractive and workmanlike publication.

Portsmouth   JOHN WEBB

J.V.S. Megaw and D.D.A. Simpson, *Introduction to British Prehistory*, Leicester University Press 1979, pp. xv +560, 225 plates and figs, 3 tables, price £19.00 (cloth), £7.95 (paper)

Since the early 1970s there have been rumours of a new survey of British Prehistory to emerge from Leicester, rumours that were forgotten or discounted as time passed and other publications appeared. But in the last months of the decade Megaw and Simpson's introduction to *British Prehistory* reached the book shops, and rapidly found its place in libraries and reading lists. This volume covers the period from the second half of the last Ice Age, *c*30,000 BC to the arrival of the Romans in Britain, and its geographical scope includes Ireland. There are six authors in all; J.G. Evans who provides an environmental chapter, M.J. Mountain on the Hunter-Gatherer period, D.D.A. Simpson on the first farmers of the earlier Bronze Age, J.V.S. Megaw on the later Bronze Age and Celtic Art, T. Champion on the Iron Age, with I.B.M. Ralston dealing with the Iron Age of northern Britain. Throughout, the book is amply illustrated with excellent line drawings by Morna MacGregor, and a number of new photographs of familiar sites and objects as well as some which are less well known. The cover claims that this hefty production 'provides a basic introduction to the Prehistory of the British Isles in its European setting'. As such it would be welcome to professional, students and interested amateur alike, so to what extent is the claim justified?

Most surveys of British archaeology of whatever period, have a southern bias. Here there is a determined effort by the authors to deal with northern Britain and Ireland as well as the south, a reflection perhaps of the authors' links with northern universities. Wales is paid little attention, and the coverage is uneven, but still the result is a more complete treatment than in any other recent publication. What is lacking is adequate consideration of the European setting, which could perhaps only have been included at the expense of other information, given the already considerable length of the book. But there are times when reference to Europe, however brief, is vital for an understanding of the British material.

Chapter by chapter, the changing approach reflects partly changes of author and partly the sometimes drastic differences in the nature of the evidence from one period to another, and it is not always clear if the modern or the ancient factor predominates. John Evans provides a concise summary of environmental changes, with due consideration of man's influence and a satisfactory balance of summary and detail. One is reminded not only of very great differences between our present environment and that of Prehistoric man but also of the considerable changes within the Prehistoric period. Next, Mary-Jane Mountain deals with the upper Palaeolithic and Mesolithic in a profusely illustrated chapter that includes some useful maps of ice-sheets, and land-bridges with the content. It would appear from the dates of references that this section was completed in the early days of the volume's compilation, since when there has been a blossoming of Mesolithic studies. However, the absence of subsistence strategies and environmental effects is compensated for by the positive inclusion of Scottish and Irish developments and occasional enjoyable asides to the author's present field of work in Australasia.

Derek Simpson's chapters on the Neolithic and earlier Bronze Age provide the backbone of the book, presenting the evidence that everyone with an interest in British Prehistory is assumed to possess but so often does not. For non-specialists who want background, for students who missed lectures, and for professionals with a temporary lack of memory, Simpson provides both a reasonably detailed account of the relevant archaeological material and summaries of many of the more significant articles. On the whole, traditional models are retained (eg. Beaker and Wessex cultures) and traditional interests indulged, with monuments and artifacts receiving fuller treatment by far than either economy or structure. Stone axe redistribution is treated only cursorily. There are, too, a number of statements which are more positive than the evidence allows. No prehistorian can safely assume anything, not even that 'the privileged element in contemporary society' was buried in longbarrows (p.95), nor that pigs have any connection with pastoralism (p.108). These points apart, there is here a reliable and thorough introduction to the archaeological evidence of the period, very much in keeping with the declared aims of the book.

Vincent Megaw's survey of the later Bronze Age adopts a similar traditional approach and, given the nature of later Bronze Age evidence, his section is understandably dominated by typology. Fortunately the southern and southwestern settlements are included to redress the balance slightly, although the radiocarbon dates from these sites imply that they should rather accompany the preceding Wessex material. But then, the later Bronze Age has never been a period to inspire, and the current redating and reshuffling of evidence do not help matters.

The Iron Age emerges in sharp contrast, both in the variety and the volume of the evidence, and in Tim Champion's treatment of the period. He is the only one of the six authors to attempt an interpretative synthesis and he does so with authority and fluency, first discussing the problems of past frameworks of interpretation and the basis or lack of it for chronology, and then presenting the material with a judicious balance of evidence and interpretation. Economy, settlement, technology and artifacts, burial and ritual all receive due attention as does the vexed question of invasions and insular developments. A firm line is taken on certain matters where there may well be room for further argument, as with the dismissal of climatic deterioration in the early 1st millennium, and the assertion of urbanised society in the later Iron Age of the south and east. In this chapter, more than previously, European material is considered where relevant. The section on art is provided by Megaw, here in his element. Northern Britain is given to another expert, Ian Ralston, whose account is all the more useful for being of a region rich in an Iron Age archaeology but usually neglected in so-called 'British surveys'.

Certainly, the volume provides the basic introduction that it claims and that has been so much needed for studies of British Prehistory, and it does so with the bonus of illustrations that alone would make it worth buying. Undoubtedly it will supersede *British Prehistory* (ed. Renfrew 1974) not only for being more recent but also, by and large, both thorough and readable. But it is not an interpretative survey of the prehistory of Britain. There is no tracing of developments, such as Renfrew might provide and Piggott has given us for Europe (*Ancient Europe*, 1965). This is essentially a text-book, a basis for further work, and as such it will free many a course from the presentation of background material, for a move into more special-ised areas of study and interpretation.

University of Exeter   BRYONY ORME

John Collis *et al.*, *Winchester Excavations, vol. II 1949-1960*, Winchester City Museum 1978, pp. xvii + 286, 8 plates, 119 figs, n.p.

John Collis's new volume in the *Winchester Excavations* series is the successor to Barry Cunliffe's much earlier *Winchester Excavations, vol. I 1949-1960*, published as long ago as 1964, in which some of the same material was examined. It sets out, as Professor Cunliffe's volume started to do, to complete the story of the excavations and the chance discoveries made in Winchester before Martin Biddle 'taught us all to think on a larger and more ambitious scale' (p.xv). However, there is yet more, we are warned, to come, for another volume is promised on the finds either only partially published in this volume or not published here at all, and it will be there — not before — that we shall be rewarded with the long-awaited 'general synthesis of the results'.

Essentially, then, this volume must be seen as another interim report, soon to be outdated and no more than 'preparatory to more sophisticated analysis' (p.3). Yet it has its clear purpose in the mopping-up of hitherto unpublished Winchester excavations which are never likely to be discussed in this form or in comparable detail again, and here the volume is entirely successful. We need worry no more about what was found in the Easton Water-Main Trench (South) in the Western Suburb, nor wonder what was observed in the Southern Electricity Board's foundation trenches at Nuns' Walk, in Saxon Road. Layed out before us, with considerable editorial ingenuity and for the first time in reasonable working order, is a large part of that 'hotch-potch' of information which Mr Frank Cottrell and his talented student assistants so painfully assembled in those faraway pre-Biddle years. And all that we can say is that we are grateful that somebody cared enough about the material to do this.

If we are not, as historians, likely to be quite as grateful as we might have been, this is at least partly the fault of the material itself. Such miscellaneous gatherings as these, too distant in time and ill-recorded when they occurred to be susceptible to systematic analysis as it is now understood, do not lend themselves to easy or interesting reporting. Nor would they, one suspects, have deserved publication in this form in any city less conscious of its heritage than Winchester. Rather too often, a specialist contributor will warn us — 'little can be said about these remains' or 'nothing useful can be said about them', only to proceed to the recording of his little or nothing at some length. And while, of course, assessments of this kind must have their role in every archaeologist's notebook, one might doubt that a place could so readily have been found for them in print if two-thirds of the publication costs of this particular volume had not been met by the Department of the Environment.

More than once, Dr Collis enters the lists against his old associate in the excavations, Professor Cunliffe, most usefully on the material from the Westgate Car Park Excavations and on the dating of the Roman defensive bank there explored. And although this is entirely proper in such a context and is usually very discreet, it reinforces the feeling one quite often gets from this volume that we are being allowed in on a private debate — a publicly funded opportunity for one archaeologist to converse in print with another. Mercifully, jargon is avoided in Dr Collis's own work here. However, he has been less successful in editing it out of the contributions of some of his senior colleagues — why, for example, does Mr Barton insist on calling a fire-cover a '*couvre-feu*' (p.229)? And it is this kind of thing, together with Mr Barton's further obsession with his own Orchard Street (Chichester) parallels, with Calvin Wells's absorbed concern in the historical significance of 'squatting facets' in medieval skeletons, and with Jacqueline Qualmann's little private excursion into pottery fabrics analysis, included with her husband's St Paul's Church site report, that must make the reader ever more resentfully aware of his own outsider status in the little world of the Winchester archaeological fraternity. Why, one must ask, should Ken Barton be comparing his medieval jugs with West Sussex wares (even if he dug those up himself) when there are so many more local parallels to hand? Could it be, as Calvin Wells seems to be suggesting, that a large part of Winchester's early population spent both working and leisure hours squatting on its haunches because unable to afford proper chairs? What is the point of a mini-analysis of the St Paul's pottery, admittedly 'scrappy', when Kathy Barclay's long-digested study of the whole Winchester pottery corpus is so shortly to appear in print?

One of the heavier responsibilities of the compiler of a volume of this kind must be to bring out, whether in his introduction or summarised conclusions, the overall significance of the material he has come to know better than anybody else. Here, though, the promise of more analysis to come has allowed Dr Collis to duck this obligation, even on a matter as important as the economic decline of late-medieval Winchester, to which his material certainly seems to point but which is assumed rather than explained. There is good work in this volume — plenty of it — and the history of Winchester would undoubtedly be thinner were it not for publications of this kind. But Dr Collis must forgive us if our enthusiasm for his material is a little chilled by the prospect of a wait (perhaps another fourteen years?) before he will tell us, at last, what it means.

University of Southampton   COLIN PLATT

David Johnston, *Roman Villas*, Shire Publications, Princes Risborough 1979 pp. 64, 23 plates, 25 figs, price £1.50.

This book represents the latest addition to the splendid series 'Shire Archaeology'. It is designed as an introduction to Roman Villas for the general reader. The author states that he has been 'guided by the kind of questions most frequently asked by adult students in his evening classes'. I am sure that many of these questions will be answered by this slim volume as a considerable amount of information has been packed into what is in effect less than twenty pages of text.

The author starts out by attempting to define a villa, a notoriously difficult task about which few archaeologists are totally agreed. He then goes on to describe the simple cottage-house and then its evolution into the more complex villa. In the chapter on architecture and decoration he discusses such things as bath suites, doors, windows etc but rather surprisingly devotes only two lines to mosaic floors. One would have expected something lengthier and more profound from an acknowledged expert especially as it is probably the first thing that comes to the mind of the general reader when thinking of villas, and a glance at the villa plans illustrated show the majority with mosaics.

Attention has changed in archaeological excavations from concentrating purely on the villa to looking at the ancillary buildings and the wider setting in which it was located. This has helped to achieve a wider understanding of the villa's function. This aspect is well covered in the chapters on 'Aisled barns and other buildings' and 'The Villa estate'. The final chapter on 'The end of the villas' discusses the breakdown of the villa system and the hazy sub-Roman phase with just a hint that it may be possible to see the transformation of the Roman Villa estate into the medieval manor.

As the author points out there is a surprising dearth of books specifically on Roman Villas but the bibliography leads the more enquiring reader on to what is available and hopefully the list of villas to visit takes him out to see the real thing. Each entry is supplemented with opening hours and details of access.

Over half the book is taken up by figures and plates, all sensibly grouped at the back of the book. The figures consist of very clear, uncluttered, villa plans and hypothetical reconstructions. The plates include a very wide range of aerial photographs, views of excavations, small finds, reconstructions etc many of which are refreshingly unfamiliar. One is a previously unpublished photograph of 1895!

It is a fact of history that Roman Villas were concentrated in the south-east of Britain and this is reflected in the book. It is therefore especially relevant to historians in the south as a general introduction to the subject.

Fishbourne Roman Palace   D. J. RUDKIN

David E. Johnston, *An Illustrated History of Roman Roads in Britain*, Spurbooks Ltd., Bourne End 1979, pp. 158, 40 plates, 30 figs, Price £5.00.

Roman roads have long interested a great many people, possibly because despite almost two centuries of agriculture and development many traces of them still survive. The fact that some are now beneath modern trunk roads merely adds a sense of continuity. David Johnston's book is the latest in a line of publications on the subject. This is a line that started in 1903 with Thomas Codrington's *Roman Roads in Britain*, a standard work on the subject and still of use today. A monumental milestone was Ivan D. Margary's *Roman Roads in Britain*, first published in 1955 and now in its third edition. It would be unfair to compare David Johnston's book with either of these as it has been written for a different audience and although he does include topographical detail in the concluding chapters, he is not attempting a detailed overall survey.

As an introduction to Roman roads in Britain this is a very useful book. The author commences with a consideration of roads of the Empire in general so putting the importance of roads into perspective, following this by a resumé of previous published work on the subject.

He then goes on to discuss the pattern of development, first military then civil, following this with a chapter on the original surveying of the lines of the roads. Stane Street is used as an example. However, without previous knowledge of surveying methods it is difficult to comprehend. The fact that Pulborough is seen as a key point in the text but is omitted from the plan doesn't help. What is the evidence that Gumber Corner was used in one of the major survey lines?

The succeeding chapter on the building of the roads gives a comprehensive account of the wide range of construction techniques used in Britain. However, the section on major roads is less comprehensive: what for example has happened to the Fosse Way? Is it seen merely as a one-time military frontier? I also feel that it is a serious omission that none of the maps of the British road network bears the names of the major roads, although they are referred to in the text.

The section on visiting the roads is very helpful if used in conjunction with an Ordnance Survey map. I personally found it of use recently when visiting the impressive if problematical Blackstone Edge roadway. The last but by no means least important chapter is on researching roads, the hows and wherefores of carrying out one's own fieldwork, which hopefully will encourage some of the readers out into the field.

The author clearly knows his Roman roads, as might be expected from a founder member of the 'Viatores'. What is also manifestly clear is that he has been badly served by his publishers. There are numerous mistakes in printing ranging from the inversion of figures and transposition of captions to the apparently deliberate insertion into the bibliography of an irrelevant book by the same publisher for advertising purposes. The laying out of the illustrations and plates in relation to the text is also poor.

The geographical coverage is very wide with possibly a slight southern bias and would certainly be of use to Southern historians. However, I would suggest that if anyone wished to study Roman Roads in depth then they would be better served by Margary's book currently available at less than twice the price of this.

Fishbourne Roman Palace   D. J. RUDKIN

Medieval Settlement, ed. P.H. Sawyer, Edward Arnold, London 1976, pp. x + 357, 40 plates, 95 figs, price £23.50.

This book is the result of a colloquium held at the University of Leeds in 1974 and the scope of the various papers reflects the multidisciplinary nature of this field of study. The book is divided into five parts, each of which has an introduction, and there is a separate paper on the anatomy of settlement at the end, and a general introduction by P.H. Sawyer. Part I which deals with 'Territorial Organization: Resources and Boundaries' has an intro- duction by G.W.S. Barrow. In his paper on multiple estates G.R.J. Jones suggests that the origin of the multiple estate dates back to before the Anglo-Saxon settlement and that this early estate pattern is similar to that which existed at the same time in Wales. However, in the case of Aberffraw, this reviewer would argue that the archaeological evidence for a Roman fort and its subsequent refurbishing by Maelgwn Gwynedd is not at present sufficiently convincing to substantiate the idea of a court on the site from the late Roman period onwards. W. Janssen looks at some major aspects of Frankish and Medieval settlement in the Rhineland in the next paper and this is followed by R. Hill's interesting study of the hundred of King's Somborne in Hampshire and D. Owen's survey of churches and daughter chapels in the Kesteven parishes of south-west Lincolnshire. The last two papers in this section by D. Bonney and T.M. Charles-Edwards look at the role that burial mounds played in demarcating boundaries in Wessex and Ireland, respectively.

Part II is devoted to 'Territorial Organization: Internal Divisions' and is introduced and has a paper on the development of the field by C. Thomas. The two papers on the excavations at Wharram Percy in Yorkshire and Store Valby and Borup in Denmark provide a summary of two pioneering projects in the study of deserted medieval villages from an archaeological viewpoint. The work of J.G. Hurst and M.W. Beresford at Wharram Percy over the last 30 years or so has emphasized the multiperiod nature of a medieval village, with houses being constantly rebuilt, a feature which is not usually visible from the surface evidence or apparent in the documentary record. Equally striking are the results from the total excavation, the first of its kind, of the church. A study of the upstanding structure revealed only six building periods while excavation has doubled this to twelve with many other sub-phases. A. Steensberg's excavations at Store Valby also date back to the period just after the war and work started at Borup in the late 1950s. Once again his results confirm the need for further large scale excavations of medieval village sites. It is also interesting to compare Steensberg's approach which is orientated far more to the agricultural aspects of village studies with that of Hurst who deals in greater detail with house-plans.

Part III entitled 'Economic and Social Change' is introduced by P.D.A. Harvey. R. Fossier in the first paper in this section uses private charters to illustrate the development of territorial overlordship in Picardy. Emphasizing the need for archaeologists to provide comprehensive and well illustrated pottery reports, H.E. Jean le Patourel demonstrates in the next paper the various ways in which pottery can be used as evidence of social and economic change. This is a very useful paper and reminds us that pottery is not just a type artefact to be used by the archaeologist to date a particular layer. On page 170 the example of Sutton Hoo as a case of a site where the collection of metal and wooden vessels suggests that very little pottery was used is perhaps an unfortunate choice bearing in mind the very exceptional nature of the burial. The virtual exclusion of pottery in the boat need not imply that pottery was not used by Raedwald and his followers. The final paper in this section by T.M. Charles-Edwards discusses the distinction between land and moveable wealth in Anglo-Saxon England and deals with land grants by the king to nobles and, in their turn, by the nobles to peasants and the resultant obligations of the recipient.

Part IV, with an introduction by R.E. Glasscock, is entitled 'The Evidence'. In the first paper by S.P.J. Harvey we are reminded that earlier lists of estates, hundreds and hides provided a skeletal framework for the Domesday Book. The second section of her paper is devoted to an analysis of the people who appear in Domesday as the 'bordars'. The next three papers by M. Gelling, V.E. Watts and N. Lund deal with place-names with Gelling emphasizing the need for argument to to be based on detailed distribution maps. The use of pollen analysis is well known to prehistorians and Romanists and D.D. Bartley in his paper on the palaeobotanical evidence shows very effectively how it can be applied to a medieval site, in this case Sandal Castle, to trace the vegetational changes around the castle between 1200 and 1645. The final two papers in this section by W.T.W. Potts and E. Sunderland provide an explanation of the use of blood group studies.

The final part consists of two detailed regional studies. K. Dabrowski looks at the region of Kalisz in Poland and W.J. Ford at the settlement patterns in the central region of the Warwickshire Avon. The last paper in the book by B. Roberts, entitled 'The Anatomy of Settlement', consists of a commentary, accompanied by 24 photographs mainly taken from the air, on aspects of medieval and earlier landscapes which have survived down to the present day. Recent excavations at Trwyn Du on Anglesey have revealed a Maglemosian Mesolithic occupation dating back to the beginning of the seventh century B.C. on the edge of the dune-swept area illustrated in plate 8.

In 1979 Edward Arnold published a revised edition of this book, under the same editorship but with the slightly different title of *English Medieval Settlement*. The length was reduced to 176 pages by the omission of all the Continental and a certain number of the English papers. The introduction was revised and the paper on Wharram Percy brought up to date to take account of a further four seasons of excavation. This new edition is a paperback and costs £6.95.

Ancient Monuments Inspectorate,   RICHARD AVENT
Welsh Office, Cardiff.

The South Saxons, ed. Peter Brandon, Phillimore, Chichester 1978, pp. x + 262, 6 plates, 18 figs, price £8.75.

This volume was produced as part of the celebrations for the 1500th anniversary of the arrival of the first Saxon settlers in Sussex. The fact that Aelle's landing may well have been some twenty years earlier than the date stated in the Anglo-Saxon Chronicle is largely irrelevant. The fact that this work has been published is not. It is a milestone in Dark Age Studies and not solely for Sussex. The most exciting aspect about this volume is that it represents an integrated study utilising the accumulated date of both an archaeological and historical nature by acknowledged experts in both fields. The data have been accumulating for a considerable length of time and now finally here one has a synthesis of it.

The work is split up into ten separate contributions commencing with an introduction by the editor and ending with a thought provoking assessment of the evidence by Professor Cunliffe, with suggestions as to how Saxon studies should proceed from this point. Between these two contributions is a vast cache of information on specific aspects of Saxon settlement in the county including: a study of the intriguing 5th-6th century period of change, or is it of continuity?; the archaeological evidence for settlements; an up dated review of place name evidence; a lengthy consideration of Sussex mints; a study of the Saxon penetration into the Weald; Saxon churches, and the Domesday Record of the county. Several models are postulated in the various contributions, not all brand new but all worthy of repetition, ranging from Martin Welch's suggestion of treaty settlement between the Rivers Ouse and Cuckmere, through David Hill's interpretation of the Burgal Hidage to fit Chichester and Lewes, to John Dogson's belief that the place names suffixed with 'ham' and also possibly 'leah/tun' may represent the earliest place names in the colonisation of the area. But such examples as these are just some of the interpretations and models provided in the book. Professor Cunliffe states in the final paper that the range of evidence and the interim conclusions 'represent all that can reasonably be said, at a certain level, about the subject. They bring us hard up against the limits of reasonable inference'. However, one feels that this corpus of material is likely to act as a stimulus to further developments. Certainly it is a book that should be read by all local historians, historical geographers and archaeologists, whose interests impinge in the slightest way on Saxon settlement, not only in Sussex but more widely. Neither should the general reader be deterred by the scope of this work as it is a happy example of contributors with a combination of both academic and literary skills, producing an eminently readable book.

Fishbourne Roman Palace   D. J. RUDKIN

J.C. Sladden, *Boniface of Devon : Apostle of Germany*, Paternoster Press, Exeter 1980, pp. 254, price £7.50; *The Greatest Englishman : Essays on St Boniface and the Church at Crediton*, ed. Timothy Reuter, Paternoster Press, Exeter 1980, pp. 140, price £6.00; David Keep, *St Boniface and His World*, Paternoster Press, Exeter 1979, pp. 64, 5 maps, price £1.20

These three books were all published in connexion with the centenary of the birth of St Boniface being celebrated in 1980. Each appeals to a different readership and each, on the whole, succeeds in achieving what the authors intended. David Keep's excellently produced booklet with plenty of illustrations provides for the needs of junior and middle school children. It contains chapters on the Life, the World and the Church of St Boniface with a final chapter for tourists on Crediton and Exeter. John Sladden writes a biography for the intelligent general reader. Timothy Reuter of Exeter University presents four scholarly public lectures on Boniface by established academics together with a paper, full of interest, on 'The Church in Crediton from St Boniface to the Reformation' by Nicholas Orme.

It seems a pity that a book entitled *The Greatest Englishman* should contain only 140 pages, of which 37 are devoted to Crediton, whose connexion with Boniface is both slight and late, being claimed as his birthplace only from the fourteenth century. It is indeed a slim volume and lacks sections on 'Boniface and the Papacy' and 'Boniface and the Emperors' which topics need both stressing and clarifying. Dr Reuter's own very interesting paper on 'Saint Boniface and Europe' partially, but only partially, meets this need. Nowhere in this volume is there a concluding synthesis to establish the perfectly arguable claim contained in the title. Professor Barlow writes with insight on the saint's English background, while Professor Holdsworth's interesting and well informed paper deals with Boniface the monk and concludes that he was the most important disciple of St Benedict (also commemorated in a centenary in 1980) until the coming of St Benedict of Anaiane (d. 821). Dr Greenaway on 'Boniface as a Man of Letters' brings his customary expertise to bear, but treats of Boniface mainly as a letter-writer of one of the most important collections to survive from the early Middle Ages, rather than attempting to link the literary achievements of his monasteries with Boniface's own training as a scholarly monk in Wessex. This is one of the many sides of this great man which one would have liked to see developed over this centenary.

To write a biography of Boniface is a daunting task. The near-contemporary Lives have their own conventions and consequent problems of interpretation, while Boniface's correspondence, though extremely valuable, is incomplete. Frequently one is left to speculate on unsolved problems. Fortunately, the Ford Lectures of Wilhelm Levison, *England and the Continent in the Eighth Century* (Oxford 1946) provide an admirable scholarly commentary by one with a lifetime of study of the primary sources behind him, coupled with an erudition which few can match today. Dr Sladden attempts something different and brings other skills to bear. The strong points are his knowledge of theology and his mastery of the complex geography necessary for understanding Boniface's many journeys. In this last respect the maps in the end-papers are most welcome, even though all indication of scale is absent. The book is full of narrative, with consequent advantages and disadvantages. There are no footnotes, but there are discussions of some disputed points in appendices, together with indexes and bibliography. In the latter it is surprising that no reference is made (or in any of these volumes) to the work of the Bollandists in the *Analecta Bollandiana*: the doyen of these experts in hagiography, Maurice Coens, wrote an excellent article-review of 35 pages in 1955, which critically assessed the studies produced in 1954.

There is much to praise in Dr Sladden's work. There is much attention to accuracy and detail. Reservations about it stem from an impression that in two important spheres insight is lacking. These are criticism of the hagiographical sources and the importance of the monastic life in Boniface's formation and achievements. He was not only an evangelist, but also a monk. His separation from much of its ordinary conditions should not obscure the fact that he remained a monk all his life or that he provided opportunities for both men and women to live the monastic life in his new territory. The foundations of Fulda and the other abbeys were integral to Boniface's whole plan. The young Church badly needed these centres of Christian stability and learning in a violent and illiterate society.

Sometimes Dr Sladden's interpretation of events goes considerably beyond the sources. Perhaps the clearest example of this is his belief that Boniface at the end of his life rejected the papal alliance with secular power and the acceptance of that power as its own. He claims that Boniface's departure to Frisia involved 'his turning his back on ecclesiastical and temporal authority as he had understood them. It represented an act of private judgment such as the soundest of 16th century Reformers could have approved, and an assertion of the supremacy of the Gospel' (p.216). In reality the explanation is simpler. Boniface was getting very old (nearly 80 if the normal date of 675 is accepted, as it is by Professor Barlow, Levison, and most other writers). It was time for him to make provision for the future, which he did in every way. For a monk, self-effacement and retirement from the political scene were appropriate now that his work was done. It is anachronistic to bring the 16th century Reformers into the argument or to read into Boniface's life a Lutheran attitude to the papacy. Only by historical penetration into the meaning of contemporary sources can we glimpse the outlook and motivation of this great man who died, as he had lived, in complete loyalty to the papacy. The papacy he knew was neither that of the twelfth, nor of the sixteenth or the twentieth century; the Church generally was not centralised and the day-to-day influence of the papacy was frequently slight. Surely it is part of Boniface's achievement that the papacy, during and after his life, developed into a significant factor both in European politics and in effective government of the Church in the West. Subjective hindsight or adhesion to later confessional differences do nothing to elucidate eighth-century realities.

Here then we have three useful books on Boniface, but none of them is outstanding. One may regret the disproportionate place given to Crediton and the uncritical insistence on 680 as the supposed date of his birth. But each of them in its different way should help Englishmen of today to realise that over a thousand years ago English missionaries and scholars left their native country and made a large contribution to the foundation and unity of Western civilization. In the eighth century, quite as much as in the twentieth, England was an integral part of Europe. In the cause of Anglo-German understanding, in assessing the importance of the monastic Order and of the papacy in the formation of Europe, in finding examples of sheer generosity and loyal affection, there is much to be learnt from the lives of Boniface and his companions.

University of Reading   D. H. FARMER

M. Gelling, *The Early Charters of the Thames Valley*, Studies in Early English History, vii, Leicester University Press 1979, pp. 208, 6 maps, price £14.00

Despite the intensive scholarship of two long generations of fine scholars documents of the Anglo-Saxon period are still among the most treacherous grounds to exploit, even for the suspecting historian. Indeed, Margaret Gelling warns that we cannot expect an entirely secure foundation until the edition currently projected by Professor Peter Sawyer is complete, and that such recent guides as the latter's 'annotated list' of Anglo-Saxon charters and the series of hand-lists of 'Early Charters' promoted by the late Professor H.P.R. Finberg, including her own volume for the Thames Valley, must be regarded as 'interim reports'. Nonetheless, these lists have been of enormous help, especially to the local historian, and this latest contribution is no exception. It deals with the counties of Beds, Berks, Bucks, Herts, Middlesex, Oxfordshire and Surrey. It adds to the format of the earlier volumes a manuscript source for each document to indicate where 'copies were made or preserved'. This is helpful, but might have been even more so if, since we are referred in general to Professor Sawyer's list for details of the MS sources, the corresponding entry number in his list had also been cited in each case. It is, however, no great hardship to track it down through the concordances in both works with the editions by Birch and Kemble nor, for the initiated, to discover tucked away in the list of abbreviations under BM Cott or Add that the MSS most frequently cited are cartularies respectively of Abingdon, Worcester, Winchester Cathedral Priory and Chertsey. The proof reading seems exemplary with very few exceptions. (CUL MS fos 2,33 *for* MS Ff.2.33, p.158; PRO E164/128 *for* 164/28, p.20; Faustinus *for* the Faustina group of Cotton MSS, pp.90, 94, 120, 166, and the mysterious *Wulfustho* — nominative retaining the dative case ?, p.17.) The commentary has much of interest. Michael Read has contributed a detailed reconstruction of boundary perambulations for Chetwode-Hillesden, Linslade, Olney, Monks Risborough, Upper Winchendon and Wotton Underwood, Bucks. There are valuable observations by Dr N.P. Brooks, the new general editor, as on the authenticity of King Cenwulf's *pancarta* for Abingdon (no.18) and King Aethelred's confirmation to Christ Church, Canterbury in the handwriting of the scribe Eadui Basan (no.1057). It is one of the disadvantages of the series that the full value of comments on date or authenticity is difficult to appreciate without an accompanying critical edition of the text (as provided, for instance, by Dr Cyril Hart for the charters of Barking and Thorney). A few Latin texts have been included — Offa's grant at Harmondsworth, Middlesex (no.203); one of an interesting group of Chertsey charters associated with Bishop Eorcenwold (no.311); a note concerning a gift by King Edmund to Nithard his *joculator* (no.338), and another note apparently added by Baldwin (later abbot of Bury St Edmunds) to Edward the Confessor's grant of Taynton to St Denis, the authenticity of which is convincingly upheld. An *excursus* on a group of charters after the manner of Finberg or Hart would have been a welcome bonus, but its lack is more than compensated for by Mrs. Gelling's already published contribution to place-name studies. Of the 354 entries in this volume 134 relate to estates in Berks, and her comprehensive study of the material for her three volumes of *The Place-Names of Berkshire* gives this list a special authority.

University of Southampton   E. O. BLAKE

K.J. Barton, *Medieval Sussex Pottery*, Phillimore, Chichester 1979, pp. xi + 265, 49 plates, 92 figs, price £9.50

Ken Barton is well known in archaeological and museological fields as one of the country's leading experts on medieval pottery and his close knowledge of the Sussex material is demonstrated in this volume. It represents an extensive corpus of the known ceramics of Sussex and environs from the 11th to late 15th Centuries.

It is a liberally illustrated volume, essential for such a subject, with 92 pages of line drawings. It is unfortunate that the majority lack a scale and one is forced to assume that they are all reproduced at a common ¼ linear scale. The line drawings are supplemented by 24 pages of black and white photographs which give a much clearer idea of surface decoration. For material such as this one always regrets that colour reproduction is so prohibitively expensive.

The text is full of useful information, but the author's literary style does not make it easy reading, and certainly no concessions are made for the general reader. It is an academic thesis that appears to have been printed more or less verbatim, a fact that I feel should have been made clear in the publishers' comments on the dust jacket.

The work commences with an introduction which rapidly becomes a detailed discussion of the chronology at Bramber Castle. This is followed by a very useful chapter on medieval pottery types, ranging from the ubiquitous cooking pots and jugs through the more mundane roof tiles to exotic aquamanile. The various types are described and dates suggested for them.

Chapter two considers the different wares commencing with Saxo-Norman Wares, both the Chichester rilled wares and a group of anomalous vessels also from Chichester which would seem to fit best into a Saxo-Norman context.

Probably the most distinctive medieval Sussex product is the West Sussex ware jug. The two variants, Binsted type and Horsham type are fully discussed in the succeeding section, followed by a more specific consideration of anthropomorphic decoration which is to be seen on some West Sussex ware products and nowhere better than on the superb example from Pulborough now in the Victoria & Albert Museum.

The final section on specific wares considers the 'Black and White Painted Wares' or 'White Painted Wares' as they are sometimes now more appropriately called.

The actual groups of material are then described such as the Steyning Pit Group, Michelham Priory Ditch Group etc which allows something to be said about the contemporaneity of wares. Finally the most important groups are considered, those from kilns: Orchard Street, Chichester; Ringer; Binstead; Abbots Wood; Hastings; and Rye.

The content is difficult to fault although I would dispute that there have never been excavations in Lewes or Hastings towns, or is this a reflection of the time lapse between writing and publishing? The validity of some of the charts is also open to doubt. The dates on the two axes of the Bramber Castle stratigraphical sequence of sherds do not appear to correlate and the Saxo-Norman cooking pot rim charts are barely statistically viable and give dubious results. Neither can I believe one had a rim radius of only 1cm.

The main fault lies in the major errors in chapter and section headings which appear totally arbitrary and in some cases give a totally erroneous impression eg West Sussex Wares in a chapter headed 'The Saxo-Norman Wares' or various mixed medieval groups under the chapter heading of 'Black and White painted wares'. This would be utterly confusing to anyone without a prior knowledge of the subject. But as I stated earlier, this is a book for the specialist and one that should be on the bookshelf of anyone involved with medieval pottery in the Sussex area.

Fishbourne Roman Palace   D. J. RUDKIN

Proceedings of the Battle Conference on Anglo-Norman Studies 1978, ed. R.A. Brown, Boydell Press, Ipswich 1979, pp. xii + 247, 48 plates, price £12.00

It is difficult to write a paper which will go down well at a conference and then stand the scrutiny of colleagues when printed largely as spoken. It is also hard to find something completely novel to say about the Norman Conquest; and with so many professionals engaged in the same field and reading each other's works, there is now much uncertainty over who have taken what from whom. Even footnotes can mislead, for if an idea is acknowledged it is sometimes attributed only to the latest vulgarizer of the view. It would be simpler if we were to adopt the late R.R. Darlington's opinion that everything worth saying on the subject had already been said by Sir Frank Stenton. Be that as it may, it should be compulsory for all young historians to read at least Stubbs, Freeman, Maitland, and Vinogradoff, as well as their followers. It would then be more generally known, for example, that the distinction between the general, or full, fyrd and the select fyrd of picked men is fully developed in Vinogradoff's now unfairly neglected *English Society in the Eleventh Century* (1908), pp. 14 ff.

Most of the contributors to this volume overcome these difficulties in their different ways very well indeed. Some restate in attractive form their known views on big themes with revisions and further reflections. Such are H.R. Loyn, 'Domesday Book', and John le Patourel, 'The Norman Conquest,

1066, 1106, 1154?'. George Zarnecki, 'Romanesque sculpture in Normandy and England in the eleventh century', reassesses the artistic achievement of Norman sculptors and their influence on the English scene. It is unfortunate for this subject, however, that so little is known about the Confessor's Westminster Abbey. What evidence is there that it was being built while Robert of Jumièges was in England (*i.e.* before 1052)? If the picture on the Bayeux Tapestry can be taken seriously (*e.g.* no triforium stage), is it so certain that Jumièges was the model? And why is it obvious that Norman masons were employed when the only names we have are Leofsig Duddesson, Godwin Gretsith, and Teinfrith?

Three essays on aspects of warfare are of the highest quality. Marjorie Chibnall, 'Feudal Society in Orderic Vitalis', shares with us some of the knowledge she has acquired in the many years spent in editing and translating that chronicler; Rosalind Hill, 'Crusading warfare: a camp-follower's view 1097-1120', entertains with an examination of the attitude of middle-ranking Crusaders; and David Walker, 'The Norman settlement in Wales', makes available the latest views on the marches. Nicholas Hooper's 'Anglo-Saxon warfare on the eve of the Conquest' must have been a useful prelude to a visit to the site of the battle, which, I notice, is sometimes called 'Senlac' in these pages. David R. Cook, 'The Norman military revolution in England', has some sensible things to say about Norman military tactics but wavers over the post-Conquest use of cavalry in an infantry role. And John Godfrey, 'The defeated Anglo-Saxons take service with the Eastern emperor', does his best with the legendary accounts of the English Varangians. Two papers are even more off the beaten track. Raymonde Foreville, 'Le sacre des rois anglo-normands et angevins et le serment du sacre (XIe-XIIe siècles)', considers the evidence of the literary sources on the vexed question of the English coronation oath, and, incidentally, re-affirms her belief, against the 'hyper-critique' of R.H.C. Davis, that the *Carmen de Hastingae Proelio* was indeed one of William of Poitiers' sources — and not *vice versa*. Ann Williams, 'Some notes and considerations on problems connected with the English royal succession, 860-1066', has some very interesting things to say on the subject up to the eleventh century, but can hardly do justice to the complexities of the period 1035-1066 about which so much has been written by so many.

The remaining essay, 'The authority and interpretation of the Bayeux Tapestry', by N.P. Brooks and developed from unpublished work by the late H.E. Walker of Winchester College, is one of the more original and thought-provoking. The different processes which underlie the finished product and the problem of the restoration the tapestry has received are given proper attention. But it can never be said too often that the inter-preter has two basic and quite different questions to answer: what was the scenarist or designer trying to convey? And was the story he tells true in whole or in part? The thesis that the artist was associated with St Augustine's Canterbury is well argued, but some of the inferences are strained. If Edward's dispatch of Harold to Normandy is to be interpreted in the light of Eadmer's story of the earl's attempt to recover his kinsmen who were held as hostages (see my *Edward the Confessor*, pp. 301 ff.), why is there no recognizable picture of the hostages? And although the artist may have been an English monk and sometimes portrayed English military dress and equipment, he must have seen plenty of Norman gear both in the abbey and round the cathedral, and also passing up and down the Dover road. A good case is made for restoring the 'arrow in the eye' interpretation of the scenes showing Harold's death; and I would add one further consideration: the fatal arrow, *lethalis arundo*, of Baudri of Bourgueil and William of Malmesbury is a collocation from *Aeneid*, IV, 73, which would have been familiar to all these writers and would have led them not to the victim's eye, but to his flank.

This is a collection of papers well worth putting together. A conference which inspires lectures of such quality should have a long history; and we look forward to an annual volume.

Kenton, Exeter   FRANK BARLOW

Frank Barlow, *The English Church 1066-1154*, Longman, London, 1979, pp. xii + 340, 2 figs., 5 maps, price £15.00; J.C. Dickinson, *Ecclesiastical History of England: The Late Middle Ages*, Adam and Charles Black, London, 1979, pp. viii + 487, price £12.50

These two volumes have been long awaited. Professor Barlow promised us a sequel to his study of the late Anglo-Saxon church in 1963. The latest full-scale history of the church in England was planned in the 1950's, and Fr. Dickinson's volume joins those by Margaret Deansly and Owen Chadwick, the last of which was published in 1970; at least two further volumes are promised to bridge the gap between the fifteenth and the nineteenth centuries.

Professor Barlow's is the more scholarly of the two volumes, though he has confined himself to printed sources. However, most of the documents relating to the church in this period have been published already and it is unlikely that anything of great significance has been overlooked. As far as the secondary literature is concerned the coverage has been exhaustive, though his dismissal of the *Liber Landavensis* as 'invention' and 'legend' (p.32) suggests that he has not read Wendy Davies' recent work on this subject. Professor Barlow tries throughout the book, quite rightly, to steer the reader away from the conventional 'stained glass' romanticism of some earlier writers on the church in this period, and his chapters on justice, monasticism and schools are particularly challenging. There is rather less re-interpretation in the earlier, more constitutional, chapters. Occasionally his cynicism goes too far. He is perhaps unnecessarily contemptuous of alleged miracles in connection with the ordeal (p.163), and in several places he seems to be uncomfortable in writing about liturgical and theological matters: there are seven and not eight deadly sins, mass is celebrated not 'performed' (p.132) and, although some may have only been able to *speak* English (p.133), surely all parish priests needed to know enough Latin to be able to use the services in the missal and the breviary? It is a pity that the book has no bibliography, though the reader can construct one from a careful sifting of the footnotes used in conjunction with the long, and unnecessarily complicated, list of 'abbreviated references'.

Fr. Dickinson's volume is much more popular, though not very readable.

There are no footnotes, but the bibliography is reasonably comprehensive. As a general introduction to the main lines of English medieval ecclesiastical history it is a balanced guide, though there is a slight bias towards monasticism. The best, and most original, part of the book is the final section with its chapters on charities, education, architecture and worship. But the quality of the contents is much impaired by the absymal style of writing which rarely rises above the stiltedness of an inexperienced undergraduate's essay. There are far too many quotes from, inadequately referenced, secondary sources and an irritating obsession with making, sometimes rather silly, analogies between medieval and modern events. Style apart, however, the contents are sound enough, though one questions the allegation (p.46) that most English parish churches were founded prior to 1066, and the reason for Irish bishops acting as suffragans in England (p.256) was surely the poverty of Irish bishoprics, which necessitated their holders supplementing their incomes, allied with the smallness of their geographical extent, which meant that long episcopal absences did not necessarily lead to an absence of pastoral care.

The quality of presentation of both volumes is very good and there are only a few misprints in each. Though the price may seem high they are both good value in these days of soaring inflation.

Kent Archives Office   NIGEL YATES

The 1235 Surrey Eyre, vol.1, ed. C.A.F. Meekings and David Crook, Surrey Record Society vol.XXXV, Guildford 1979, pp. xiii + 260, 1 plate, price £12.35

The late Mr C.A.F. Meekings was an archetypal scholar-archivist, whose work lay in the careful elucidation of particular classes of document: how exactly they came into being and for what purpose, their precise relationship with other administrative records and so on. The bulk of his published work consists of editions, with illuminating notes and introductions, of documents in the Public Record Office where he was for many years an Assistant Keeper. At his death in 1977 he left in typescript a full edition of the only surviving plea roll from the Surrey eyre of October 1235, a work which he had substantially completed in 1955-6. This has been prepared for the press by Dr D. Crook, whose task has included bringing references up to date and providing a full translation to accompany the Latin text. It is being published by the Surrey Record Society in two volumes. Text, translation and indexes are still to come in the second, while in this first volume is the introduction with two important appendices: a bibliography of the commonplace eyre and biographical notices of the principal Surrey persons involved in the eyre of 1235.

What we have is a masterpiece in its careful unravelling and analysis of the complex legal and administrative processes that lay behind the formal judicial record. It is the fullest account yet published of the workings of the twelfth- and thirteenth-century eyre, going further than the introductions by Mr Meekings and Dr M.T. Clanchy to the crown and civil pleas respectively of the Wiltshire eyre of 1249 (Wiltshire Record Society, 1960 and 1971). While he takes the Surrey eyre of 1235 as a starting point and constant point of reference, Mr Meekings draws on encyclopaedic knowledge of eyre records in general, both published and unpublished. The result is a work of an importance that extends far beyond the bounds of Surrey: it is essential reading for anyone who wishes to consult eyre records or to master the technicalities of thirteenth-century judicial proceedings. Forms of procedure, types of action, writs and other records of the pleas are elucidated and discussed in great detail. There is also discussion of the value — and the limitations — of the various types of entry on the roll for the local historian; while the very full biographical notes on some 120 justices, county officials, jurors and others connected with the 1235 Surrey eyre, which occupy the last hundred pages of the present volume, are themselves a valuable compendium of genealogical and historical information for Surrey and beyond. We look forward to the second volume with the text of the record and translation. The whole will be a worthy memorial of a distinguished scholar of great integrity and erudition.

University of Durham   P. D. A. HARVEY

Lacock Abbey Charters, ed. Kenneth H. Rogers, Wiltshire Record Society, Vol. XXXIV, 1979, pp. vi + 147, obtainable from M.J. Lansdown, 53 Clarendon Road, Trowbridge, price £7.00 + postage.

Lacock is still a lovely village and it contains the only set of conventual buildings for a medieval nunnery still extant in England. The editor was faced with an Old and a New Cartulary, together with a large number of Ancient Deeds and documents of the Court of Wards; he has brought together all that can be considered as charter material, in all 476 pieces, leaving still unpublished a considerable reserve of non-charter documents. This is, then, a full calendar in English, carefully preserving the original spelling of place-names, the acreages and the witnesses, the whole grouped on a topological basis. There are no foot-notes as to persons or places and there is unfortunately no map for those not familiar with Wiltshire. However, the little volume is full of interest in addition to the records of a house of Augustinian canonesses with their grants and leases. The abbey had been founded in 1230 by Ela, countess of Salisbury; on the death of her husband, William Longespee, she took the religious habit and became its first abbess, endowing the nuns with the manor of Chitterne. It is curious that there should be another Ela, countess of Warwick, appearing in a document together with the foundress Ela. The village church was extremely close to the nuns' church. This proximity and the various attempts to solve the problems of patronage, tithes, burial and vicarages and so on, well illustrate the relations between a medieval nunnery and its close neighbours. As for its religious neighbours, Tewkesbury, Cirencester, Bradenstock and Stanley, with the nuns of Amesbury and Shaftesbury, there is no sign of any tension. Lacock surrendered to the Crown in 1539; the last document in date is of 1533, a characteristic lease for 99 years. Some will be surprised to find here 31 documents for North Shorwell in the Isle of Wight; this manor had not been 'acquired', but was the dowry of the daughter of Amice, countess of Devon, Margaret when she joined the community at Lacock.

These charters form a valuable contribution to the history of the Island. Considering the documents from another viewpoint, it is fascinating how they reflect a district of water-courses and ponds. Today the countryside has still been little disturbed, so that the abundant field-names should be full of meaning. There are frequent references to mill : a fulling-mill, destroyed as it was to the detriment of Lacock; and for good measure a fulling-mill, a gig-mill and a grist-mill all adjacent at Bishopstrow. There is a lease to the nuns by the monks of Stanley of a quarry, with a quarry-man among the witnesses. The rector of 'Obeton' was granted permission to construct a piggery in a wood, though he was not to take this as a precedent. Of these different properties one would have liked to learn their comparative value to the abbey. There are a few slips: Brother David the convert of Stanley should be the *conversus*, the lay-brother; Burton should be Barton manor in Whippingham; de Rivers surely should be de Redvers (*de Redveriis*, not *de Ripariis: Complete Peerage*); Robert and William de Glamorgan should read *de Clamorgan*, of a family still living in the Cotentin peninsula. These in no way affect the value of this handy volume, full of interest, especially perhaps on agrarian matters, and not only to historians of Wiltshire.

Quarr Abbey   DOM FREDERICK HOCKEY
Isle of Wight

The Register of the Common Seal of the Priory of St Swithun, Winchester, 1345-1497, ed. Joan B. Greatrex, Hampshire Record Series II, Hampshire County Council 1978, pp. xl + 312, price £4.50
New Forest Documents, 1244-1334, ed. D.J. Stagg, Same series III, 1979, pp. xii + 330, price £8.00

The new Hampshire Record Series is proving to be far from narrow in its scope, for these two volumes both penetrate, if not exactly into unknown territory, then into lands as yet insufficiently explored. With this edition of the *Register of the Common Seal* we are given the earliest of a long series of registers covering five hundred years, giving us an insight into all the variety of its content. Here we see the monastic officials of St Swithun's in activity, the organization of the monastery by the side of the cathedral and the administration of the manors. The editor gives a helpful and studied introduction, indicating the special features of the volume, with explanations of such terms as *manumissio* and *familiaris*; for good measure there is an appendix listing the obedientaries holding office during the period of this register, twenty-three of them. The large number of leases serve also to illustrate such manorial topics as the maintenance of a water-mill or a weir, hedging, fencing and thatching, the water-supply for Winchester College and farming equipment. It is a register which touches medieval life and economy in almost every aspect.

David Stagg has certainly met a long-felt need for an account of the working of the Forest Law as compared with the Common Law, and for transcripts of such documents in illustration of its application in the best known of English forests. His introduction will be valued by the large majority of us who find difficulty in keeping our notions clear on the subject of the Forest, with its special vocabulary. We are given here exchequer documents such as rentals and accounts, assize and legal records of the Forest Courts and various types of inquest. Such a series of 614 items naturally covers a wide variety of forest matters, as well as netting in a large quantity of personal and place-names for the New Forest area. Human nature always feels a secret sympathy for the man with his greyhound who has succeeded in taking a doe: here we meet also the organized gang and the habitual offenders of venison. It is useful to have at hand all this data concerning the administration of the New Forest and the working of the Forest Eyre, yet how it all started and the very early history of it all still remains obscure. An opportunity is provided by this book for comparisons with the working of the Forest Law in other regions and for enquiries into the enclosure of forest land, with the effect of Forest Law on medieval husbandry; indeed, one could hardly possess a more convenient hand-book to every aspect of the medieval Forest. These two editions are in calendar form, almost entirely in English, with the customary indices and maps, neatly produced.

Quarr Abbey   Dom Frederick Hockey
Isle of Wight

The Church Wardens' Accounts of St Michael's Church Chagford 1480-1600, transcribed by F.M. Osborne, Chagford 1979 pp. v + 269, 4 plates, price £6.00 plus 75p postage + packing from Mrs W. Osborne, Bellawuch, Chagford, Devon, 7Q13 5DB

The fine binding, paper and printing of this book conceal a great disappointment. A brief comparison of the photograph of one of the manuscript pages reproduced in the frontispiece suggests that the text offers a paraphrase of doubtful accuracy rather than a transcript. Although the other three photographed pages suggest greater accuracy, the doubt must remain. This, combined with a lack of introduction, critical apparatus, textual notes and index, renders the book sadly useless, for it has clearly been a labour of love.

Salisbury and Wells Theological College   W. M. Jacob

Charles Phythian-Adams, *Desolation of a city: Coventry and the Urban Crisis of the Late Middle Ages*, Cambridge University Press 1979, pp. xxii + 350, 42 tables, 2 maps, 3 figs., 3 plates, price £16.50

This volume offers a specialised study which reveals developments in a particular locality in satisfying detail while drawing comparisons with events elsewhere. The result is of great value in a wider English setting, and its appearance in *Southern History* is entirely appropriate. The general context of the work is the economic decline which affected many urban centres at the end of the middle ages, and the author frequently draws attention to conditions in many towns and cities, including York, Hull, Lincoln, Norwich, Chester, London, Bristol and Exeter. His theme is Coventry's economy and society in the fifteenth and sixteenth centuries, particularly in the period 1500-1530. The full late medieval documentation for Coventry provides a rich quarry, and one of the book's many merits is its discussion of some crucial sources in a series of appendices. These are aimed especially at exploring the evidence for population and social changes in the 1520s which is crucial to the author's argument. This centres around a period of crisis, 1518-1525, which set the seal on over half a century of decay.

Between 1450 and 1550 the population of Coventry dropped from around 10,000 to around 5000. Its economic decline affected all levels of society and while there was some growth after 1570 the medieval levels of prosperity were never recovered. In the fifteenth century Coventry had dominated the midlands economically, as well as having widespread trade contacts, a mint, wealthy religious houses, and the palace of the bishops of Coventry and Lichfield. The decay of textile manufactures is placed firmly by the author at the root of the decline. There were other contributing elements too, notably a subsistence crisis with high wheat prices and a cholera epidemic in 1479, and financial burdens resulting from involvement in the civil wars between 1449 and 1485. The crisis years of 1518-25 included an influenza epidemic, large contributions to royal taxes, poor harvests and high grain prices. The recent extensive conversion of arable to pasture in Warwickshire aggravated this food problem. The growing decline after 1450 was reflected in losses of rents from vacant properties, difficulties of recruitment to the merchant and craft elites, and a reluctance on the part of the latter to undertake expensive civic office.

The reader is not, however, offered simply an analysis of the chronology and causes of decline. The central, and largest, part of the book (*Anatomy of a city*) is concerned with how Coventry's late medieval society functioned. There is much of great interest here, from the description of the 12 - 14 hour working day, through the analysis of the (essentially nuclear) families, poorer cottages and wealthier households, craft fellowships and religious gilds, to the civic councils and officers. The importance of the craft fellowships, numbering over thirty by 1500, is underlined. Their social and economic functions made them 'the basic reference group in society', much more than an 'industrial organization' (p.117). An important feature of the book is its successful linking of this everyday social pattern with the background progress of economic decline. Despite all the stresses, however, particularly in the 1520s, there was no revolution against Coventry's dominant minority. This underlying theme of stability did not indicate a static society. Certainly progress from the lower end to the very top was extremely unlikely, but there was upward movement from among the journeymen to the masters. Conversely, there was considerable downward movement, since the large numbers of children produced by wealthy families could not all be accommodated in the highest levels of society, particularly at a time of economic difficulty. Finally, we are reminded that it was not only economic change which brought an end to medieval society in Coventry. The impact of the Reformation was also very great, bringing demotion of the city's diocesan status, dissolution of its priory, and eventually abolition of its gilds and the ceremonial which had been a conspicuous part of their existence.

There is a valuable discussion of the physical and human geography of the region, some elements of which were crucial to the events under consideration. Coventry could not receive imports directly by navigable inland waterway, a factor which contributed to the food shortage in the 1520s. There are maps to illustrate not only the region but also the lay-out of the city itself. There is some discussion of the relative disposition of its various activities, the markets, butchers and fishmongers in the old Prior's half, and the wool, textiles and clothing production in the old Earl's half. The city map is based very much on that of John Speed (*circa* 1610) for evidence of late medieval built-up areas. Evidence of rentals in the 1520s reveals the four central wards, as might be expected, having the richer houses. Even so, all wards had some of the poorer houses. There is comment on the social value of the city walls and gates in giving physical definition to the inhabitants' view of their own society. The walls did not, however, mark a rigid boundary, and some wards were partly extra-mural. The declining industries of sixteenth century Coventry included that of its carpenters, with the result that it remained 'a timber framed city of the later middle ages' (p.214) down to the eighteenth century. There is brief mention of some of Coventry's medieval town-houses and cottages. But this is not a book which makes a great deal of use of detailed physical evidence. There is a contrast here with, for example, Colin Platt's *The English Medieval Town* (1976), where incidentally, other details of the cottages in Spon street may be found. Although this reviewer would prefer to have been told more about what late medieval Coventry was like to live in, this is not a major criticism since the obvious value of the book lies in its detailed analysis of unusually full documentary evidence.

This will prove a valuable book to many people: to those interested in midland history, in the history of the medieval town, of the medieval economy, and in the technique of local enquiry. For, as the author states early on, the book 'is very much a product of "the *Leicester* school" of local history'. It can be enjoyed both for its general contribution to an understanding of late medieval urban society, and also for its wealth of fully documented detail. It also ought to stimulate work in other areas. How far, the author asks (pp.49-50), was the decline of Coventry's cloth industry due to competition from the local countryside, and how far from that of other cloth-producing areas in Yorkshire, Lancashire, East Anglia, the Cotswolds and Devon? Elsewhere (pp.283-4) he asks whether the decline of Norwich, Bristol, York, Lincoln, Southampton, Salisbury and Hereford was any less marked than that of Coventry, where the situation is revealed in unusually documented detail in the 1520s. If Mr. Phythian-Adams' book prompts others to examine these problems then it will have done a valuable service to national as well as regional history.

University of Exeter

R. A. HIGHAM

R. Machin, *The Houses of Yetminster*, University of Bristol Department of Extra-Mural Studies, 1978, pp. viii + 244, 50 figs, 14 plates, price £2.95, obtainable from the departmental Librarian.

Yetminster, the village of this very detailed study is situated in North West Dorset and possesses an outstanding number of 16th century and 17th century stone houses of high quality. *The Houses of Yetminster* brings together the knowledge of University of Bristol, West Dorset Tutor R. Machin and an enthusiastic local history group. It is fortunate that in 1973 this class expressed an interest in the buildings of Yetminster. This firm foundation has produced a book of national importance drawing together archaeological and documentary sources. By bringing together these disciplines it has been possible to date buildings accurately and establish the reasons for change in the village relating to farm profits, capital investments and security of tenure. The study analyses the reason for the large number of high quality buildings built, and remaining in Yetminster.

Part 1 The House Types. This demonstrates that plan analysis can reveal a most definite progression, and supplemented by examples from adjacent parishes, provides a typological framework which may prove useful elsewhere. Photographs of buildings and key plans are included at the end of the book along with larger scale plans and a few sections and structural details which help with the study. It is a pity that a simple village plan identifying the buildings is not included. Incidentally, it would be interesting to know what percentage of buildings identified in the study are 'Listed Buildings'.

The analysis of 39 plans of local houses show that they fall into one of 5 basic types which can be sub-divided to show a national development of traditional plan forms. This first part of the book is full of detail but I found it hard going in places possibly because I am not familiar with the local area.

Part 2 Historical Problems. The wealth of buildings relate to the successful meadow farming and the urge to improve the properties. The real incentive to improve the building was that the Yetminster farmer knew that he could build with the secure knowledge that his house would remain in the hands of his family provided he paid the appropriate rents and fines; any fear of reposessing the property by the landlord would have inhibited this investment. It is interesting to note that the lord of the manor was required to give tenants free stone and timber for repairs. Rebuilding took place following good harvests; if a farmer wished to rebuild he would invest his profits in loans of £5 or more. In particularly good years he could recall his loans or borrow money on this security and set about rebuilding. Another conclusion reached is that the majority of dated houses everywhere reflect profitable years in the local economy. For example most late 16th century or early 17th century houses in dairy and fatstock areas like Yetminster were probably built in 1600 ± 8 years or 1627 ± 3 years. This dating fits the cycle of Bowden's index of all agricultural product prices and a sample of dated houses from 17 English counties similarly fits this formula.

This is an important book which has been supported by the University of Bristol. All the illustrations and plans are gathered together at the end of the book making it hard to relate them to the text. Its rather academic and detailed approach may make it less popular with the layman. I suggest that if the opportunity and finance is available then a book in revised simplified format would be extremely popular. The book should have had its illustrations related to the text and included guide lines on how this study group brought together their evidence. This would be extremely useful to the many other local groups throughout the country engaged in this important work.

Hampshire County Council   DEANE CLARK

Guide to the Parish and Non-Parochial Registers of Devon and Cornwall 1537-1837, compiled with an introduction by Hugh Peskett, Devon and Cornwall Record Society, Extra Series Volume II, 1979, pp. lxxvi + 258, 42 maps, price £5.00 from the Assistant Secretary, 7 The Close, Exeter.

Hugh Peskett has produced a description of the registers of baptism, marriage and burial for all denominations and an account of their locations supplemented with information about population, civil and ecclesiastical jurisdictions, and notes on the ecclesiastical status, history of the congregation and denominational aspects of the area covered by the diocese of Exeter from 1538 up to 1837. The basis of classification throughout is the parish.

The introduction dealing with the history of register keeping is excellent, especially the section dealing with the non-Anglican congregations, and how much more extensive is the survival of records of non-conformity than is generally realised? However, although Mr Peskett disclaims that his intention was to provide a genealogist's guide to Devon and Cornwall it is difficult to believe this, otherwise why was there not a section in the introduction on the uses of this material for historical research?

The acount of the Anglican registers, probably because of the enormous compression of material, is not always easy to follow. It would also be helpful to know the number of registers rather than merely the first and last dates of the run — perhaps this could have been included at the expense of some of the information about location of transcripts.

The account of the non-Anglican registers reveals a lot of what is, I suspect, new information about the origins of seventeenth, eighteenth and nineteenth century dissent, and here in particular it is a pity that more information is not given as to the wide range of research material available in these records for religious, social, political and economic historians as well as genealogists.

It is to be hoped that the Devon and Cornwall Record Society will follow up this volume with a further one listing all other parish and church records relating to Devon and Cornwall.

Salisbury and Wells Theological College   W. M. JACOB

Theo Brown, *The Fate of the Dead*, D.S. Brewer for the Folklore Society, Ipswich 1979, pp. x + 118, price £8.00

The sub-title of this work, 'A Study in Folk Eschatology in the West Country after the Reformation' defines more clearly the author's theme; namely that the end of the doctrine of purgatory gave free rein to the development of folk myth to explain the inexplicable. It may, perhaps, be questioned whether there was cause and effect. The Reformed, Protestant Church was not interested in the other world; it was concerned with order, perhaps obsessively so. Yet it is inherently unlikely that folk myth was not equally alive under the Pre-Reformation Church; how else could it be suggested, as it is here, that some of the best-known myths are medieval or earlier in origin?

A common characteristic of many of the myths described is their apparent authentication by the inclusion of historical persons among the essential figures. Historical analysis does not, of course, explode the essence of the story, only obscuring its beginning. Outstanding not only for its popularity but also for the possible breadth of its origins is the Devon song 'Widecombe Fair'. The song, it is suggested, may have less to do with the village of Widecombe-in-the-Moor, and more to do with the local word 'widecote', meaning the sky. The grey mare is related to the many hobby-horse customs and to the Teutonic three-legged horses which are found at least as far afield as Mongolia.

Most of the examples given by the author come from Devon rather than from the West Country in general, though their counterparts could no doubt be found in many parts of this country and beyond. The subject almost insists on a discursive approach which mingles tunnels with bottomless pits, hill-top churches dedicated to St Michael with the skull-and-cross-bones motif. It is also a subject with its own phraseology, such as 'otherworld psychopomp'; its own rules, such as the efficacy of Oxford clergymen in laying ghosts, and the value of deep pools in which to lay them. And only one of these fine stories with which the author entertains is described as 'somewhat apochryphal'!

Victoria County History of Somerset   ROBERT DUNNING

G.R. Quaife, *Wanton Wenches and Wayward Wives*, Croom Helm, London 1979, pp. 282, 5 maps, price £11.50

For anyone who likes sex this book should be enjoyable; for anyone who also likes history it might well be frustrating, a condition no doubt frequently felt by many of those whose intimate lives lie exposed in its pages. The book is concerned with illicit sexual activity in Somerset in the first 60 years of the seventeenth century and is based on an examination of the depositions presented to the Court of Quarter Sessions for Somerset and to the Consistory Court of the Diocese of Bath and Wells. As its title suggests, it illustrates, for the most part, the role of spinsters, wives and widows in pre-marital and extra-marital sexual activities and in many cases the inevitable consequences of their actions — illegitimate births. The approach is mainly anecdotal with numerous examples given of the cases in which women were brought before the courts, more for their potential threat to the established social order and to the local community than for reasons of morality. Such an approach tends however to become repetitive, especially by chapter eight dealing with the consequences of illicit sex, and in which a number of cases encountered in earlier pages are reintroduced leaving the reader with a feeling of *'déjà vu'*.

Although the author rightly states that there is no way in which the extent of illicit sex in early-seventeenth century Somerset can be measured, the book is liberally sprinkled with non-specific quantitative statements. Thus we are told that events occurred 'frequently', 'often', 'in large numbers' or in 'dozens' and that there could be 'countless', 'numerous', or 'hosts of' people' involved or that they could simply be 'counted in hundreds'. The impression is thus given throughout the book that illicit sex in Somerset was widespread in all communities throughout the period. However, we are not told how frequently or how often events occurred, nor do we know how numerous or how many hundreds of people were involved except on rare occasions. Such occasions occur in the analysis of the location of the seduction of spinsters and in measuring the number of bastardy orders. In the former category 314 spinsters were involved (Table 3-1 p.75; the last column of this table has no obvious relevance) over a period of twenty years, in the latter some 400 bastardy cases are mentioned. Neither category, therefore, supports the impressionistic view of widespread illicit sex since in the case of spinsters this represents some fifteen to sixteen cases per year in 480 parishes. Hence less than two-thirds of the parishes had a single case in twenty years. And these 'consenting' spinsters include the under 1 in 10 who were seduced through fear of violence! Furthermore, the bastardy cases seem to have numbered less than one per parish over sixty years. Elsewhere there are frequent references to percentages without any indication of the number of observations from which the percentages were obtained. It is thus in attempting to understand the scale of activity discussed in the book that the historian is likely to feel most frustrated.

However, female historians may tend to disagree with this last comment. They may well consider that this publication, analysing a patriarchal society is loaded against their sex, especially when it refers to the 'subworld of the woman' (p.14). The title as well as the tenor of the book tends to perpetuate the male chauvinistic view of society. It is implied that it was only wives who were wayward and widows and wenches who were wanton and who were collectively responsible for what illicit sexual activity occurred, whereas in reality, of course, it was almost always the male who initiated illicit relationships. Rather than 'Wanton Wenches and Wayward Wives' a more appropriate title perhaps would have been 'Libidinous Lechers and Licentious Libertines'!

Finally the quality of production may not be to the liking of some readers since the book appears with unjustified right-hand margins, presumably in an effort to reduce the cost to the consumer. At a price of £11.50, the effort seems to have been in vain.

Portsmouth Polytechnic   BARRY STAPLETON

Brian Austen, *English Provincial Posts, 1633-1840: A study based on Kent examples*, Phillimore, London and Chichester 1978, pp. vii + 192, price £4.95

Professional historians and other writers have shown an interest in the general history of the British Post Office and the conveyance of mails since the late nineteenth century. The significance of this study rests in the fact that it is the first serious history of the development and operation of pre-railway postal traffic at a provincial level. It is based upon post-graduate research carried out at the University of Kent at Canterbury. Brian Austen argues that Kent provides 'a unique opportunity for such a study', principally because 'no other county contains the complete length of a main post road from London' (p.vii). The first regular postal route not surprisingly operated from London to Calais, via Dover. Following the Restoration the number of offices and routes in Kent expanded appreciably. The Dover Road, by serving the most densely populated and most prosperous part of the county, met the needs of a number of important towns en route, and 'soon after the Restoration enjoyed a six-day service', and 'the only road that could boast an equally good service was that to Colchester, which had the same frequency in the late 1670's' (p.20). The first mail coach to Dover ran on 31 October 1785. Three maps outline the expansion of Kentish post routes for c.1700, 1790 and 1839. By 1840, prior to the impact of railways and a uniform pre-paid penny postage, 'there were few villages in the whole county that were not served by an official post' (p.58).

This study embodies a considerable amount of detail both in its text and in 24 tables and seven appendices. The postal history of Kent is carefully related to major developments in the postal history of the country as a whole. Most of the notable communities of the county are mentioned in the text, and parallels are established with places elsewhere in Southern England. General developments in the history of Kent and transport conditions and improvements are also referred to. Major factors influencing the development and efficiency of postal services are analysed, such as the effects of the Civil War, the impact of the Napoleonic Wars, or the specific consequences arising from population growth, the expansion of towns, the seasonal importance of Tunbridge Wells or the rise of seaside towns, especially Margate, Ramsgate and Broadstairs.

Apart from having a substantial index and detailed references, a select bibliography illustrates the wide range of printed and manuscript sources consulted, including painstaking research in the Post Office Records Office. In presentation this study is not without some faults, including obvious typographical errors on pages 71, 76, 99, 113, or 138. Table III on page 33 contains a miscalculation and where is table VII to which reference is made on page 77? Against these minor criticisms Brian Austen has produced an authoritative and most readable study, which should prove of interest and value to economic and social historians, transport historians, local and Kentish historians, not omitting that 'growing number of persons who find relaxation in the study of the postal history . . . of their locality' (p.viii). Hopefully this study will be applied as a model to other regions of the country.

Today the reliability of postal services remains as a popular topic of conversation. It is surprising how good postal services were in the past. In 1816 'the penny post messenger left Ashford at 9 am., arrived at Wye at 10.45am., and stayed there until 2.45pm.'; from there 'he arrived back in Ashford in sufficient time for the letters to be stamped, taxed and forwarded by post to Maidstone the same day' (p.105).

University of Kent   JOHN WHYMAN

The Somersetshire Quarterly Meeting of the Society of Friends 1668-1699, ed. S.C. Morland, Somerset Record Society vol. 75 (1978), pp. ix + 303, from Mrs. S.W. Rawlins, Newton Surmaville, Yeovil, BA20 2RX, price £7.50 plus 70p postage + packing.

Somerset Quarterly Meeting was part of the organization which George Fox established in 1668 for Quakers throughout the county — regularizing, reinforcing and possibly modifying existing practice (p.5) — and which functioned with unbroken regularity till quite lately. The Quakers have been exemplary in both keeping and preserving records, and in this case the names are known of those present at each meeting since December 1669, as well as the nature of the business transacted.

What sort of number of Friends were involved on these occasions? Analysis reveals the number of those attending the first nine meetings (December 1669 to December 1671) as successively 29, 44, 39, 32, 35, 43, 37, 36 and 52. They were by no means always the same set of people. From the second meeting onwards fresh names always appear, usually as an appreciable proportion of the whole meeting (33, 16, 13, 14, 12, 11, 5 and 12). At the same time, six of the Friends who were present at the first meeting attended all, or all but one, of the eight subsequent meetings, and a seventh, John Anderdon, who often transcribed the minutes, though not at the first meeting, was always present thereafter. These formed the backbone, men of enthusiasm and dedication, who practised the consistency and reliability quickly recognized as Quaker characteristics. Six of the seven were what early Quaker historians termed 'First Receivers of Truth': in the previous decade they had welcomed the first Quaker missionaries to Somerset and in most cases opened their homes for meetings for worship. Three of them died in prison for their Quaker convictions.

Prison, indeed, is central to the documents printed here, is their context in a literal sense. Not only were many Somerset Quakers in prison at any one time, some of them for years — Anderdon, for example, from 1662 till 1672 and from 1675 till his death in 1685. As a rule, the Quarterly Meeting was actually held in prison, in Ilchester, at the Friary, which, since the official prison was full, was used as an overflow. Prison thus 'became in effect the centre of Quaker organisation in Somerset' (p.8).

Among the records is a letter of 1685 to Friends in Ireland returning thanks for £15 received 'towards the necessities of the deep sufferrers, & prisoners for trueths testimony' (p.164). Larger sums were received in each of the next two years. 'That tender Sympathizeinge spirit, which our god hath shed abroad in your hearts' was later repaid with interest: in 1693 Somerset Friends sent no less than £113 'for the service & reliefe of poore sufferinge friends in Ireland', the amount contributed by the several meetings, thirty-three in all, being duly recorded (pp.226-7).

The Quakers' intense sense of fellowship and mutual support is the obverse of the aggressive controversies with others which they were carrying on at the same time, though these do not figure in the minutes. Sociologically, both attitudes powerfully express the effort of a new grouping to find self-identification.[1] At another level, they reflect the preciousness of what, in a rich variety of phrases, Friends referred to as 'truth'. The term connoted both a Christian way of life calling for total obedience and the sense of a divine enabling power to which testimony must be borne. Friends' devotion to 'truth' is what underlies their disciplining their errant members on so many counts and, if necessary, disowning them: for paying tithes, getting married by a 'priest', sexual immorality, drunkenness, gambling 'and other Heathenish Practices'. The purpose of discipline was redemptive, not punitive; but those who were unrepentant at falling back into the ways of the world brought shame on 'the truth' and, in effect, excluded themselves.

In Somerset Friends' peace principles were tested sharply by the Monmouth Rebellion of 1685. Nonconformists generally were caught up in a cause which engaged their sympathies, and the Quarterly Meeting went to considerable lengths 'for the cleareing of trueth' and in testimony against any concerned 'in the late warre, contrary to our Christian profession': 'we still adhere to our antient principle, not to seeke for deliverance by carnall weapons' (p.171).

The editing of this volume is lovingly thorough but limited, and is in some ways eccentric. Mr. Morland seems unaware of the Baptists' 'general meetings' up and down the country, which were both similar and prior to those of the Quakers. Because Wells 'apparently had no Friend', it does not follow that 'the Church there remained supreme' (p.6). Not only had Wells a Baptist congregation, the Somerset Baptists often gathered there.[2] The social and religious issues they discussed and the biblical imagery used in their records compare interestingly with those presented here. The variation and overlap in the locations from which the two lots of representatives came also deserve investigation. Even without this, Mr. Morland's full indices of places and of Friends listed by domicile will delight readers who know Somerset.

Birmingham   GEOFFREY F. NUTTAL

¹ See the perceptive article along these lines, in the context of the twelfth century, by C.W. Bynum in *Journal of Ecclesiastical History*, 31 (January, 1980), pp.1-17.

² See *Association Records of the Particular Baptists of England, Wales and Ireland to 1660*, ed. B.R. White, Baptist Historical Society, 1971-4, especially Part 2 (The West Country and Ireland). Cf. also Thomas Collier, *A Looking-glasse for the Quakers*, 1657, p.16: 'In Wells was the seat of the old Ranters'.

A.F. Scott, *The Early Hanoverian Age 1714-1760: Commentaries of an Era.* Croom Helm, London 1979, pp.175, 30 plates, price £7.95

This book forms part of a series on the social history of Great Britain from 55B.C. to 1837. Lavishly produced with bold type, copious illustrations and a colourful dust cover, it promises much to the reader. Appearances can, however, be deceptive. While the editor has ranged far in assembling his materials, the work would have been better for the the more rigorous application of his editorial energies. Bereft of both introduction and index, the book would appear to be intended for VIth formers, but even here the reviewer has his doubts. No attempt is made to introduce the commentaries, but for a few lines prefacing two or three of them. For some inexplicable reason, however, the section of the work dealing with Law and Crime has nine lines of context for the Mary Blandy poisoning case. While collections of commentaries and extracts serve a very useful purpose, that purpose is soundly undermined if the editing is not performed thoroughly and scrupulously. Random checking of commentaries leads to the inevitable conclusion that this has not happened with this book. The commentary on Stourbridge Fair, for example, contains five errors in a paragraph six and a half lines long. The extract headed 'Turnips for Cattle and Sheep' (p.99), has four errors in fourteen lines. To make matters worse, it would appear that little discerning thought was applied to the layout of the work's various sections. As a result, the book suffers from imbalance. Commentaries on 'Education', for example, occupy twelve pages; those on 'Agriculture' a mere one. The section on industry runs to two pages, while 'Historic Events' runs to nine, half of which concern the Black Hole of Calcutta. Nor has uniformity been applied to the citation and presentation of sources. *The London Tradesmen*, 1747 on p.65 becomes R. Campbell, *The London Tradesmen*, 1747 on p.90. Some entries are just not given a source at all, as happens with two from the last section entitled 'England and the Sea'. Advertisements appear in some cases, without source, while the reader is informed that the first extract in the section entitled 'The Poor' comes from the *Times*, rather reminiscent of Prof. H.P.R. Finberg's anecdote of the source cited as 'Public Record Office'. As a set of commentaries, the work should be used with extreme caution. Its relevance to local and regional historians will be minimal. Many of the extracts are easily available in other sources where the task of selection and editing has been performed very much more carefully. While the illustrations go part of the way towards saving the book, their captions should have been used, in several instances, as first drafts only. On p.51, for example, appears an illustration of an eighteenth century Charity School. The reader is told that it is 'From a contemporary engraving' and then, two lines later, that it is 'From an engraving by J. Allen'. Overall, therefore, the work is a disappointment. Greater care would have produced a better result. That the proof reading was carried out some distance from the text does not help matters. Thus it augurs ill to learn from the first caption (p.13) that George I was our most 'competant' Hanoverian monarch.

Portsmouth Polytechnic   JAMES H. THOMAS

Reactions to Social and Economic Change 1750–1939, ed. Walter Minchinton, University of Exeter Papers in Economic History, 1979, pp117, price £2.00

Since time is by definition dynamic, change is as inevitable as the reactions that follow in its wake. The title *Reactions to Social and Economic Change* is therefore something of a catch-all, but this is not to invalidate the value of the contributions brought together in this twelfth issue in the series. Admittedly they range over a small number of possible topics, which must be almost infinite in number, but with one exception the authors reveal fascinating insights into reaction to change in rural communities, in the Church, in local government and by members of the middle class to mass unemployment. That the fifth essay, a descriptive piece on the population and social structure of Lostwithiel by Pounds, culled largely from enumerators' returns and rate books, does not readily mesh with the overriding theme is recognised by the editor, and one should not cavil at its inclusion given the problems of material availability for a series such as this.

Two of the contributions deal with that most topical of contemporary socio-economic problems, unemployment, yet treat reactions to it from very different standpoints. Vinson charts the complex issues involved in the provision of relief works in Southampton in the inter-war years and demonstrates that the threat, or reality of unemployment in the absence of cohesive labour unity caused vested interests to plough their own furrow. As a consequence well organised groups such as the painters, and the servicemen by virtue of public sympathy, succeeded in achieving more than most. We are reminded that in towns such as Southampton the unemployed were in a minority and the fundamental political debate by the mid-1930's was not the relative merits of public works and maintenance, but rather betweel local rates and national taxes and between saving and spending. The role of voluntary organisations in combatting unemployment is examined by Stead. Since such initiatives were essentially middle class they were resented by socialists and communists on principle and by working men as charity, exacerbated by the moral preaching that permeated voluntaryism. For all its interest to social historians and others this solution to the problem had very little effect when viewed against the background of the mass unemployment of the time; that the protagonists should have thought they could provide a panacea is in retrospect not a little pathetic. The piece purports to concern itself with South Wales, but although some attention is paid to this locality the value of the contribution is such that to quibble at its inaccurate title would be to do it less than justice.

Gladstone's article is also concerned with unemployment in the sense that the poor either have no job or one which is inadequate for their requirements. The author's specific concern centres around the Scottish Poor Law Amendment Act of 1845 which removed poor law administration from the hands of the church and placed it in secular control. It is argued that while the industrialisation of society and intellectual change were important catalysts, more important were the divisions within the church itself. The Church of Scotland might have been capable of managing poor relief, but the tenets of the more powerful Evangelicals were regarded as being unrealistic, thereby strengthening the case for secularisation. Bushway's article also investigates cultural change, but almost for its own sake. He submits that protests against change in rural communities between 1750 and 1850 were closely based on existing customs and channels of communication. Apart from a purely intuitive feeling that it is difficult to imagine reaction to change in any other way, the approach appears to be more appropriate to rural sociology than to economic and social history. Accepting the hypothesis that is being mooted by the author, does this knowledge add to our understanding of the results of the reaction in rural communities? On the other hand the article certainly emphasises the value of interdisciplinary studies, which far from being a bandwagon, represent an important research avenue in the social sciences.

Given the escalating cost of printing, it is not too much to pay £2 for the 117 pages of this thought-provoking publication, which will be of considerable use to local and regional historians alike. It is merely a pity that Pounds' paper fits uneasily into the milieu generated by the others.

Portsmouth Polytechnic   R.C. RILEY

The Ansford Diary of James Woodforde, Volume II 1764-5, ed. R.L. Winstanley, Parson Woodforde Society 1979, pp. 193, from G.H. Bunting, 54 Old Fold View, Barnet, Herts.

A complete transcript of the manuscript of Woodforde's diary for the years 1764–5 which includes his ordination as a priest, is of enormous value. As the editor notes in his introduction: 'this volume contains by far the most detailed and exhaustive account of the outer circumstances governing the life of a young curate in a country parish in the mid eighteenth century that I have ever seen . . . Where Woodforde excels, giving the diary its historical importance and lasting value, is in his recital of the small details of everyday existence, the routine actions which everyone carries out but few in any age have had the patience to put on record.'

Here is a quarry for all who study the eighteenth century. For the social historian there is the account of the social interaction of the clergy, the lesser gentry and the prosperous tradesmen in a country town. For the economic historian, the hints as to patterns of trading, occupations and the patterns of expenditure of a man like Woodforde. For the ecclesiastical historian there is the evidence for the survival of public prayers, on all days for which the Book of Common Prayer provides propers, and on Fridays in Lent, in Castle Cary Church for the pattern of pastoral care and administration of occasional offices as well as the economic and social position of a parson like Woodforde.

This transcript shows how drastic was Beresford's editing (*Diary of a Country Parson*, 5 vols., Oxford 1924–32) and gives a great deal more very useful information. The transcript appears to be excellent but the footnotes are unfortunately a little thin, providing mainly biographical information about incidental characters and not directing readers to sources that would help to set Woodforde in a wider context.

In general the Parson Woodforde Society are to be congratulated on this publication, and it is to be hoped that further volumes of transcripts will appear in due course.

Salisbury and Wells Theological College   W.M. JACOB

Mark Chatfield, *Churches the Victorians Forgot*, Moorland Publishing, Ashbourne, 1979, pp171, 157 plates, price £7.50.

This book has scholarly pretensions to discuss Anglican church architecture and furnishings and their relationship to the Book of Common Prayer. The preface makes reference to two of the standard works in this area, Addleshaw and Etchells'*The Architectural Setting of Anglican Worship* and Whiffen's *Stuart and Georgian Church* and the foreword describes this as 'an important book . . . and indispensable addition to the libraries of all ecclesiologists and a useful work of reference'. Unfortunately it is none of these.

The introduction is mercifully brief being largely devoted to an account of the Reformation which reads like a poor fourth form essay. The account of Anglican worship shows little evidence that Mr Chatfield has read Addleshaw and Etchells, with much understanding and appears to assume that the Church of England ceased to practise Catholic worship between 1549 and 1840.

The substance of the text provides some most attractive photographs of eighteenth century church interiors with a commentary that is usually chatty although occasionally providing substantial architectural comment.

The gazetteer of churches with 'prayer book interiors' appears far from exhaustive. The list of Wiltshire churches in the third edition of Betjeman's *Collins Pocket Guide to English Parish Churches* shows that at least 5 or 6 other very fine seventeenth or eighteenth century interiors could have been included and this seems to be true of most other counties.

It is very sad that such a coffee table book aiming to popularise its subject should have such an inadequate text.

Salisbury and Wells Theological College   W.M. JACOB

J.F.C. Harrison, *The Second Coming: Popular Millenarianism, 1780–1850*.
Routledge and Kegan Paul, London and Henley 1979, pp. xvii + 277, 9 plates,
price £9.95.

This is a splendid book, none the less so for promising a good deal more
than it delivers. It is basically an essay on Southcottianism, suitably introduced, and rounded off with comparative American material about Shakers,
Mormons and Millerites which proves in the end not very illuminating. If
every man is his own nonconformist, Professor Harrison almost concludes
that every man was his own millenarian. Since millenarian views have
become almost totally opaque to the modern critic, he tries to explain why
substantial numbers of people in his period were prepared to stake all on
some version of the millenarian hope, while admitting that even at the time
some deviant millenarians appeared mad enough to their fellows to be put in
asylums. The key is found in some enduring features of popular culture; a
persistence of wild seventeenth-century millenarianism right through the
eighteenth century, long-standing convictions that the world was overrun by
spirits, old habits of interpretation in which correspondences and signatures
bulked large. If continuities will not in themselves explain a history, they
may explain why for many people a demand for cataclysmic social change
should be cast in this form, even as the institutions millenarians created
open the possibility that they may have recruited people psychologically in
need of the services they offered. Brushing aside the question of truth with
the cavalier assurance of a liturgical reformer, Professor Harrison proposes
to use millenarianism as a window into the mind not of the inarticulate, but
of the not very articulate. Popular culture is used to explain millenarianism;
millenarianism to illumine popular culture. On all these matters he has
many good things to say, and since he sets out plainly what it is he wants to
explain, his book will have an enduring value as being much the most
convenient compendium of material on Southcottianism.
    Where so much is good, it may seem unreasonable to ask for a somewhat
different bias in the book; but it seems to me not certain that popular
culture is illuminated by assuming that it operated by processes altogether
different from official culture, here conceived as a tradition standing alongside it. Popular millenarianism could not have existed without the Bible, a
major portion of 'official tradition', and Professor Harrison's religious
seekers tended to have a distaste for official religion based on first-hand
experience. Attitudes to death, changing only very slowly, were common to
both, and it may be that the bewildering kaleidoscope of counters from
culture at various levels which creates such confusion in Professor Harrison's
story was almost equally characteristic of what may be misunderstood as an
official 'tradition'. The Bible, a constant indeed, was itself an unresolved
tension of religious approaches to the human predicament of varied dates,
character and social reference. Why, to put it plainly, was Methodism, in
which so many of Professor Harrison's gallery dabbled, very unmillenarian,
while sects of Calvinist derivation proved a seedbed for views of his kind?
And why does he never say that since one of the principal cardboard
characters in the official scenario was the downfall of the Pope, the dire
troubles of the Papacy in the 1770s were bound to revive this kind of
speculation? Most of what he describes was lunacy, but was perhaps arrived

at by processes not very different from those by which official culture operated. Perhaps a more useful point of comparison than those which Professor Harrison adopts would have been Württemberg, where apocalyptic expectations entered deeply into popular pietism, and popular pietism became deeply rooted in the official church. If Bengel was a spokesman for a 'country' opposition to a baroque and catholic court, expectations of the end became part of the stock-in-trade of those with institutions to maintain. Perhaps after all official culture was less 'traditional' than it liked to make out.

University of Durham   W.R. WARD

H.M. Brown, *The Catholic Revival in Cornish Anglicanism: A Study of the Tractarians of Cornwall 1833–1906*, published by the author, St. Winnow Vicarage, Lostwithiel, PL22 OLF, 1980, pp. iii + 105, 16 plates, price £2.95; Michael Sparrow, *One Hundred Not Out: A Century of Work at St. Faith's Mission, Landport*, published by the author, St. Faith's Centre, Fyning Street, Portsmouth, 1979, pp. 52, 22 plates, price £1.00 + postage and packing.

It is probably symptomatic of our secular society that relatively few local historians take a serious interest in church history, and most contributions take the form of decidedly antiquarian church guides. It is a pleasure therefore to welcome two new booklets which are not antiquarian exercises, though both are written by clergymen with a close personal involvement in the subject about which they write.

Canon Brown's is the more substantial of the two booklets. Very little work has been done on the parochial impact of the Oxford Movement, which was greater in Cornwall than in some other parts of the country. That being so, it is a pity that Canon Brown could not perhaps have provided, in some respects, a more exhaustive study. Part of the problem is lack of organisation. Canon Brown has succeeded in giving a rather impressionistic picture of what the background was, the actual events and their significance. He would have done better if he had separated the main themes from the detailed evidence, and, in order to illustrate the latter, concentrated on a few typical parishes. An appendix listing all those parishes with Tractarian or ritualist incumbents (and Canon Brown is very haphazard in his definition of the many varieties of Anglican high churchmanship) would have been a useful bonus, particularly as the index is so inadequate. One wonders also about the wisdom of breaking the study in 1906, which was very much in the middle of the last great orgy of ritualism, rather than continuing to about 1930 which is a more realistic terminal date. However, these are perhaps rather specialist criticisms, and the general student of local ecclesiastical history will find Canon Brown's booklet a useful addition to the available literature.

Fr. Sparrow's subject is more limited, the study of two mission churches in the parish of St. Mary's, Portsea, which from 1878 until the inter-war period was regarded as a model of what other Anglican, urban, working-class parishes ought to be. It is, however, a very much more polished work than one has come to expect of the *genre*, and one very much hopes that the author will find time to write the more general study of mission churches in Portsmouth that he rightly advocates. For a number of very specific local reasons these mission churches had a much longer life in Portsmouth than in many other urban communities, where they either became independent parish churches fairly quickly, or ceased to function within a generation.

Kent Archives Office   NIGEL YATES

David Roberts, *Paternalism in Early Victorian England*, Croom Helm, London 1979, pp. x + 337, price £14.95.

Piccadilly Circus used to be known as the Hub of the Empire. Many Imperialists, contrary to Marxist theory, devoted themselves to the expansion of the British Empire out of Christian concern for the souls of the heathen and out of paternalist secular concern for the provision of at least the basic necessaries to satisfy the subject races' bodily needs. I suppose few travelling around what, by a supreme irony, (since its dedication was far from erotic), has become known as Eros connect the statue with the man whose life's work it was erected to commemorate. The seventh Earl of Shaftesbury, earnest, evangelical emancipator of the chimney boys was the very archetype of a paternalist; in the current terminology he would undoubtedly be termed a 'wet'. The Tory paternalists of the nineteenth century combined opposition to political reform, with opposition to the rootless new industrialists and their laissez faire factory system, and with opposition to the growing passion for 'equality' by the undermining of the landed class system. They were essentially defending the vestiges of the theory of feudalism — the system of reciprocal duties, of fealty and allegiance to the lord, who gave protection and aid to his tenants and vassals. It was a system based on property — a stake in the country. But though property brought privileges, it brought corresponding duties, if only for defence of property: Burke wrote 'the great must submit to the dominion of prudence and virtue or else none will submit to the dominion of the great'. Paternalism embraced mediaevalist romantics like Sir Kenelm Digby, as well as the down to earth merchant-manufacturer Tories like Sadler and Oastler; both High Church paternalists and more wide-ranging evangelicals, the latter of whom like F.D. Maurice gave birth to Christian Socialism, that curious contradiction in terms — since Christian redemption depends on individual good works, whereas their collectivisation financed by others robs the charitable intent of any virtue. As Southey said: 'There is no other means whereby nations can be reformed than by that which alone individuals can be regenerated'.

United in opposition to levelling, in the words of Dr. Arnold: 'Equality is the dream of a madman or the passion of a fiend'; united also in their belief in the 'unalterable relations which Providence has ordained' they believed in a 'community of subordination', where the lower orders were subordinate to their temporal masters, who were in turn subordinate to God in Heaven. They were opposed to the growth of society to an inhuman scale which the industrial revolution made inevitable; they looked to the parish as the centre of good works and opposed the centralising tendencies of bureacracy. In the words of Oastler: 'If there is an excellence in the English constitution it is that it leave the inhabitants of every locality to manage its own affairs'. They believed in property and the self-regulation of laws; they believed, with Burke, that whilst 'Government can prevent much evil it can do little positive good'. They believed like Dr. Johnson that 'most schemes of political improvement are very laughable things'. Coleridge put it thus: 'I have no faith in Act of Parliament Reform; let us become better people'. Some of the paternalists had interesting ideas — like J.M. Ludlow's adaptation of Adam Smith to fit the administration of charity; he wanted Parliament to grant money to all faiths so that each could create its own clerisy, which would compete with each other to do the most Christian work in the creation of a paternal society. Taken together the Paternalists, in spite of oddities, had much to say which was coherent and logical.

This book is excellently researched and well-written; the author has not simply theorised about his subject, he has taken the various manifestations of paternalism and treated them to an interesting examination e.g. paternalism in the early Victorian novel, the patriarchy of Sussex, the clergy of the Church of England, the new industrial magnates. Out of this straw he has made his bricks, which he has then assembled into the edifice of his theory. This book is a useful contribution to the literature of that period when the 'Condition of England' question was the dominant concern.

Hatfield Polytechnic NEIL HAMILTON

John Hoare, *Sussex Railway Architecture,* Harvester Press, Hassocks 1979, pp109, 100 plates, price £6.50.

This book sets out to describe and analyse a stylistically minor art form, yet one which proliferates nationally as the legacy of a series of Victorian enthusiasms. For his purpose, Sussex is convenient, largely the purlieu of the London, Brighton and South Coast Railway Company; on the other hand, it must be said that few of the stations he devotes much of the book to draw much in the way of inspiration from local vernacular examples. It is a collection which illustrates amply the Victorians' diffusion of architectural and constructional models through a variety of experiments (some singularly amateur) in their adaptation to uses far from their original intention — gothic schoolrooms became minor stations, Italianate villas booking halls. In many senses the book is a joyful exploration, a useful companion to countryside meanderings, alas no longer as easy by rail as was once the case; it is a singular irony that we can only visit many of his examples by using forms of transport which have superseded the railways. Useful as it is, the book has severe flaws. Like so many works written for railway enthusiasts it must often appear opaque to the ordinary reader. The author has chosen a chronological narrative style where often a place-related or analytical approach to building types would have been much clearer. There is only one map, overcrammed and without chronological information, so that many of the textual references are lost. There are no plans reproduced in a work that seeks to bridge the gap between architectural history and industrial archaeology and we are often without a sense of dimension. There are many very good photographs but their use is one of the saddest features of the book. It looks as if it was designed to be in 2 parts, text and pictures, and a not very sympathetic art editor has welded them together without much concern for the relationship between the two. The worst example of this is Chapter 4, on the South Eastern Railway Company; this only served the far eastern parts of Sussex, yet the accompanying pictures are taken from Petworth and Chichester, well to the west. Few of the pictures in the book appear near the text which refers to the buildings and there is no cross-referencing between illustrations and text. Finding one's way round the book is as difficult as reading a badly prepared railway timetable. It is a pity; John Hoare writes with enthusiasm, he knows his materials and places and he has been let down badly by the presentation.

University of Sussex   JOHN LOWERSON

E.W. Gadd, *Victorian Logs,* K.A.F. Brewin Books, Studley 1979, pp. xxii + 196, 14 plates, price £7.95; *Trowbridge in Pictures 1812–1914,* ed. Michael Lansdown and Michael Marshman for West Wiltshire Branch of the Historical Association, Trowbridge 1979, 122 plates with commentary[no pagination], price £3.50; Christopher Hibbert, *London: The Biography of a City,* Penguin Books, London 1980, pp. xii + 290, 178 plates, 5 maps, price £4.95.

Eric Gadd's book is not a detailed analysis of Victorian school log books in general. It is a discussion of the log books of one school in particular, the Northam National Boys' and Girls' Schools, Southampton, for fifteen years between 1863 and 1877. The author has transcribed the two school log books for these years and sets the scene locally and nationally in a discursive introduction.

The book will doubtless be enjoyed by the many students of Southampton's history. Mr. Gadd's style is chatty, too chatty for this present writer who does not care to see the author's personal recollections intrude into the text albeit bracked. Nor does she care for such statements as 'the Prince of Wales (to be denied kingship for nearly forty years) marries the beautiful Princess Alexandra of Denmark *and goes his merry way*' or 'Peel, *father of the British Bobby,* had died a dozen years before . . .' It is for these sorts of reasons and for a rather simplistic analysis of events in the introductory chapters, curiously not numbered, which make it difficult to recommend this book as a serious contribution to the history of education. However Brewin Books are to be commended for venturing into the field of records publication. Only thus can archival material be made available to a wider readership.

Trowbridge in Pictures, like *Victorian* Logs will be of most interest to its local readership, those people who know Trowbridge or were brought up there, whose eyes will alight on details that will escape the reader who is not familiar with the geography of the town which was the home of Bowyer's pork sausages and was once described as 'the Manchester of the West'. For as the authors tell us 'no other town in the West of England clothing district, and few if any in the south of England, could show the same concentration of industry as existed in the centre of Trowbridge'. These photographs remind us of Trowbridge's former eminence in the textile trade. Other topics covered include the churches, the garrison, public utilities, transport, major events and personalities and 'buildings that have gone'. Such catalogues of destruction make depressing reading. It is tempting to speculate that our current fascination for collections of photographs of long-vanished street scenes and rural idylls reflects a growing awareness of what has been lost and an increasing sense of unease as a standard uniformity of design has been stamped upon our towns and cities.

London: The Biography of a City is a lushly illustrated version published by Penguin Books of Christopher Hibbert's original book first produced in hardback in 1969. It does not claim to be more than what it is: a popular introduction to the history of a city which more than most cities in the western world has generated strong passions in the breast of man, from William Dunbar in the late 15th century who sighed after 'the flower of cities all!' and Dr. Johnson who professed that 'when a man is tired of London, he is tired of life; for there is in London all that life can afford', to William Cobbett who animadverted upon 'the great wen . . . the monster' and Sir Arthur Conan Doyle who in *A Study in Scarlet* alluded to London as 'that great cesspool'. 'The flower of cities' and 'that great cesspool': London was and perhaps still is all of these things.

Portsmouth City Records Office   SARAH PEACOCK

James E. Cronin, *Industrial Conflict in Modern Britain*, Croom Helm, London 1979, pp242, 10 figs, price £4.95.

'Trade cycle theory' is a phrase with rather an antique ring nowadays but is one, which in the post-Keynesian era we shall hear a lot more of. Cronin seeks to produce for us a 'strike cycle theory'. His theory is interesting although his style of writing does its best to diminish it, characterised as it is by the academic pomposity of the Royal 'we' when he means 'I' and by the mind-numbing jargon of sociology which has the unfortunate affect of nearly supplanting the human story to be unfolded by mechanistic pseudo-science.

The book is remarkable in its sub-Marxian controversialism e.g. 'the balance of power in modern industry is sharply skewed in favour of management', a view which scarcely conforms to the experience of managers in the unionised sector of our economy, and a view which liberal economic historians would reject on theoretical grounds as well.

The author does well when he attacks some prevailing theories e.g. the myth of the 'making of the English working class' as something that can be dated to specific decades or periods of social development; as Cronin rightly says, 'the working class is being made, unmade and remade incessantly' and 'social conflict is not the manifestation of some fixed and undifferentiated quantum of discontent that expresses itself in one form or another at different points in time.' But Cronin does less well in attempting to put a new theory in the place of these. Let the final sentence of the book stand as its epitaph: 'the strike (is) the fundamental statement of the humanity and intelligence of the working class.'

Hatfield Polytechnic   NEIL HAMILTON

F.A. Youngs, *Guide to the Local Administrative Units of England, Southern England,* Royal Historical Society, London 1979, pp. xx + 830, n.p.

This is an enormously useful volume which should find a place on the shelves of every local record office, town public library or academic institution. It is divided into four parts. The first part lists all parishes on a county-by-county basis, covering the whole of Southern England, the home counties, East Anglia, Gloucestershire and Oxfordshire. At the beginning of each county list there is a 'sequence' of administrative units, both civil and ecclesiastical, showing how units have been divided and united over the years. The entries for each parish then show to which administrative units they belonged at various dates: hundreds, poor law unions, parliamentary constituencies, archdeaconries and rural deaneries, and so on. The second part lists all the civil administrative units in each county, though dating is not detailed until the nineteenth century. The third part lists parliamentary constituencies and their boundaries. The fourth part lists dioceses and their subdivisions. There is an exhaustive list of sources.

The volume is extremely clearly laid out, and the work involved in compiling it must have been immense. One can have nothing but admiration for and gratitute to the compiler for providing both scholars and the general public with a first-class work of reference, and gratitude too to the Royal Historical Society for underwriting the costs of publication at a time of appalling inflation in the printing industry.

Kent Archives Office   NIGEL YATES

Cornwall Record Office: A Brief Introduction to Sources, Truro 1979, pp. ii + 31, price 50p + 15p postage and packing.

This booklet was originally compiled as a brief guide for schools wishing to use original documents for local studies and has now been reproduced for sale to the general public. It is therefore necessary to bear in mind its primary purpose for it introduces the young student to all the various types of local archives be they connected with local government, the church, of all denominations, private estate or business. With special reference to Cornwall it gives a useful summary of the series of documents a record producing authority would have compiled — and then it gives a brief indication of what has in fact survived and is to be found in the County Record Office. It is however to be regretted that the necessity to be brief has curtailed so severely greater precision of covering dates and names of places. In particular one questions the desirability to separate artificially the civil from the ecclesiastical parish records as the complete separation of the two has only come in comparatively modern times. All the same any student of a specific subject will find this booklet a useful guide to sources, though perhaps not so useful if he wishes to delve into the history of a particular place. Perhaps most helpful of all to students of all ages — who don't always know where to start looking or indeed realise the need to consult printed sources as well as original material — are the references to other relevant general material, such as directories and guide books, and the mention of where they can be seen if not held by the Record Office. Useful too are the cross references in the text and the selective bibliography given at the end. It does not pretend to be exhaustive but it does provide a start for the inquisitive to proceed further.

Portsmouth City Records Office   M.J. HOAD

Annual Review of Periodical Literature

The articles listed in this review were mostly published in 1977. Archaeological, geographical or sociological articles have been included only in cases where they appear to be of substantial interest to the local or regional historian. Although this review aims to be as complete as possible, it is obvious that useful articles will have been missed, and the Review Editor will be glad to be informed of such articles which can then be referred to in subsequent reviews.

Abbreviations

AC	*Archaeologia Cantiana*
AP	*Avon Past*
BAJ	*Berkshire Archaeological Journal*
BIHR	*Bulletin of the Institute of Historical Research*
DH	*Devon Historian*
DP	*Dorset Past*
HM	*Hampshire Magazine*
HR	*Hatcher Review*
JEH	*Journal of Ecclesiastical History*
JRIC	*Journal of the Royal Institute of Cornwall*
JTH	*Journal of Transport History*
LDLHSP	*Leatherhead and District Local History Society Proceedings*
LH	*Local Historian*
LPS	*Local Population Studies*
OC	*Old Cornwall*
PAR	*Portsmouth Archives Review*
SAC	*Sussex Archaeological Collections*
SANH	*Somerset Archaeology and Natural History*
SDNQ	*Somerset and Dorset Notes and Queries*
Spire	*Annual Report of Friends of Salisbury Cathedral*
TBGAS	*Transactions of Bristol and Gloucestershire Archaeological Society*
TDA	*Transactions of the Devonshire Association*
WANHSB	*Wiltshire Archaeological and Natural History Society Bi-Annual Bulletin*
WF	*Wiltshire Folklife*
WI	*Wealden Iron*

(1) Before 1500

The late C.A.F. Meekings, in an article edited by R.F. Hunnisett, traces the early history of Netley Abbey in Hampshire, with particular attention to the acquisition of its temporalities, in *JEH* xxx 1-38.

W.F. Proudfoot, mindful of the fact that 'gavelkind was a form of tenure found chiefly in Kent and was there so usual that land was presumed to be held in gavelkind unless the contrary was proved', traces the history of the manor and chantry of Scotgrove and shows how, 'by a quirk of history, much information about the long defunct manor of Scotgrove is available in the pages of *Robinson on Gavelkind,* this because Scotgrove was the subject of a leading case in that field which came before the Court of Common Pleas in the reign of Edward II', in *AC* xciv 7–26.

S. Lay and R. Isles describe medieval deer parks in Avon in *AP* i 5-12, and J.D. Wilson describes those in Dorset in *DP* i 6–10.

W.J. Blair discusses and largely calendars various groups of documents relating to the district around Leatherhead, including the surviving pre-1500 court rolls of the manor of Packenesham Magna, in *LDLHSP* iv 3–18, 30–8.

Cecil Plaxton contributes a brief account of St. Edmund of Abingdon's career as treasurer of Salisbury Cathedral and prebendary of Calne, between 1222 and 1234, before his consecration as archbishop of Canterbury, in *Spire* xlix 9–11.

S.P. Pistono throws further light on the piratical activities of two well-known Devon shipmen in the reign of Henry IV, in *TDA* cxi 145–63.

(2) 1500–1750

N.I. Orme has compiled biographies of two early 16th century schoolmaster-musicians in *SNDQ* xxxi 19–26, and pays particular attention to the hitherto neglected chantry certificate of 1548, and appends a comprehensive list of chantries in Devon and their priests, in *TDA* cxi 75–123.

G. Finch examines population changes in Hartland, Devon, in the 16th and 17th centuries in *DH* xix 12–22.

Peter Webb analyses the careers of John and Jasper Horsey, two Tudor opportunists, in *DP* i 28–32.

Irvine Gray prints what has survived of the presentments for Gloucestershire of the Domesday of Inclosures of 1517 in *TBGAS* xcvii 75–80.

M.J. Kitch surveys the personnel of the Chichester Cathedral chapter between 1521 and 1558, and shows that the chapter contributed little to the spiritual life of the cathedral or diocese, or to diocesan administration, in *SAC* cxvi 277–92.

Jeremy Goring chronicles the short-lived restoration of the canons of Bayham Abbey after its suppression in 1525, discussing its wider causes, both local and national, and pointing out that it took place, like the

Peasants' Revolt and Cade's Rebellion, at the Whitsun holiday season, in *SAC* cxvi 1–10

Dom Frederick Hockey publishes the first post-dissolution account of the Domus Dei of Portsmouth from a manuscript in the Public Record Office in *PAR* iv 2–11.

Katherine Wyndham examines the extent of the royal estate in Somerset in the mid-16th century in *BIHR* lii 129–37 and the initial purchasers of these lands in *SANH* cxxiii 65–74.

B.G. Awty provides provisional identifications of some French immigrant ironworkers in the Wealden area in the 1540s in *WI* xvi 2–11

John Buxted discusses the circle of 'learned and ingeniose' poets, including Sir Philip Sydney, Edward Dyer, Fulke Greville and Samuel Daniel, patronised by Mary Herbert, Countess of Pembroke, at Wilton between 1577 and 1621, in *HR* viii 15–21.

John Farrant describes John Norden's manuscript description of Sussex in 1595, the first such account of the county, in *SAC* cxvi 269–75.

Colin Brent continues his study of rural employment and land tenure in East Sussex between 1560 and 1640 in *SAC* cxvi 41–55.

J.H. Bettey describes the circumstances of the dismissal of the steward at Cranborne by the Earl of Salisbury in 1625 in *SDNQ* xxx 365–7 and analyses the marketing of agricultural produce in Dorset during the seventeenth century in *DP* i 1–5.

Pamela Stewart uses presentments for the subdean of Salisbury's visitations to give a picture of parish life in 17th century Salisbury in *HR* viii 22–7.

N. Caplan explains the distribution of Roman Catholics in Sussex in the late 17th and 18th centuries, and attempts to establish their numbers, in *SAC* cxvi 19–29.

M.J. Dobson discusses the value of the original Compton census returns of 1676 for the demographer and historian with respect to the deanery of Shoreham, covering over thirty parishes in West Kent, the recent discovery of which in Lambeth Palace Library fills a missing gap in the Kent returns and completes 'the picture of the geography of dissent in 17th century Kent', in *AC* xciv 61–73.

J.R. Holman analyses the Bristol apprenticeship registers between 1675 and 1726 and shows that apprenticeship was a significant factor attracting people into Bristol and accounting for its population growth since large numbers remained in the city on completion of their apprenticeship, in *TBGAS* xcvii 85–92.

E.G. Thomas provides a similar analysis of apprenticeship and settlement in Portsmouth in the late 17th and early 18th centuries from the surviving parish papers in the City Records Office in *PAR* iv 12–24.

Michael Trinick assembles the contemporary evidence and traces surviving fittings of the Great House at Stowe, 'the noblest house in the West of England', built by the Grenvilles in 1679 and demolished in 1739, in *JRIC* viii 90–108.

M.G. Smith shows how Bishop Trelawney of Exeter insisted on the proper maintenance of church fabric between 1689 and 1707 in *TDA* cxi 13–30.

Kenneth Rogers describes new documentary evidence about the owners of Maggot Castle, an 18th century mansion, now destroyed, in the Wiltshire parish of Urchfont, in *WANHSB* xxv 7–8.

(3) After 1750

C.W. Chalklin, in a study of prison building in Berkshire between 1766 and 1820, shows a fivefold increase in expenditure, active involvement of the justices of the peace, and concludes that, compared to other southern counties with greater resources and population, Berkshire was very interesting for the number and variety of prisons and for the methods of raising capital and organising the building process, in *BAJ* lxix 61–71.

John Webb provides a detailed account of performances and personnel at the Portsmouth theatre between 1771 and 1774 from Sir Frederic Madden's notes on the account book, once in his possession but now lost, in *PAR* iv 44–60.

G.J. Davies describes the shipping using the port of Weymouth between 1775 and 1783 in *SDNQ* xxxi 1–4

Sue Farrant, in a study of the changing structure of landownership in the lower Ouse valley in Sussex between 1780 and 1840, shows how smaller units gave way to larger ones, both in the size of the estates and the size of farms, in *SAC* cxvi 261–8.

B.F. Hills, having examined contemporary naval records at the Public Record Office and the National Maritime Museum, details and analyses the ships that were built at Sandwich for the Royal Navy by Andrew and Thomas Hills between 1781 and 1813, in *AC* xciv 195–230.

Osamu Saito compares statistics relating to occupations from Cardington in Bedfordshire and Corfe Castle in Dorset in two surviving lists of inhabitants for 1782 and 1790 respectively, and in the evidence of the 1851 census, in *LPS* xxii 14–29

T.G. Holt discusses the contemporary evidence concerning the building and furnishing of a chapel for Roman Catholic worship at Lulworth in Dorset by Thomas Weld during the late 18th century in *DP* i 33–41.

J.A. Vickers summarises the principal events in the history of early Methodism in Hampshire in *PAR* iv 25–43.

A.L. Macfie introduces the Pattenden Diaries, covering the period 1797-1819 in which a Dover draper and stocking-seller recorded those 'daily remarks and occurences' which he deemed to be of interest, providing thereby 'a graphic record of life in Dover during a critical period in its history' in *AC* xciv 139–47.

R.G. Swann discusses Carters, a firm of dyers and cleaners in Southampton from 1837 to 1941, in *HM* xix (5) 77.

Peter Stainer examines the extent of the copper ore trade in Devon and Cornwall in the 19th century in *JTH* v 18–35

J.R. Goddard describes Mormon activity in the Steeple Ashton area of Wiltshire, and the pattern of Mormon emigration to Utah in the mid-19th century, in *WF* iii (1) 34–7.

Bruce Coleman discusses the patterns of religious practice in Devon revealed by the 1851 census of religious worship in *DH* xviii 3–7.

T. Boyle describes the riots between English and foreign navvies during the construction of the Mark Beech railway tunnel in 1866 in *SAC* cxvi 11–18.

J.F. James describes the fitting of water turbines in Dorset water mills during the late 19th and early 20th centuries in *SDNQ* xxx 419–20.

C.J. Wrigley considers the attitude of William Barnes, the Dorset poet, towards the social problems of his time, in *DP* i 19–27.

G. Burke analyses the effectiveness of the poor law and private charitable relief in the exceptional circumstances caused by the collapse of the mining industry in West Cornwall between 1870 and 1880 in *JRIC* viii 148–59.

Pamela Horn discusses the significance of the Berkshire Agricultural and General Workers' Union in a rural community in the 1890's in *LH* vi 353–9.

J.D. Osborne sketches the career of a Wiltshire man, Stephen Reynolds (1881–1919), whose novels reflect with great accuracy life in a Sidmouth fisherman's house in the early years of this century, in *TDA* cxi 49–57.

Percy Trollope recollects the life of a keeper at Horningsham on the Longleat estate in the early years of this century in *WF* ii (3) 40–8.

Arthur Wakelin contributes the first part of an account of the life and early career of Arthur Whitlock, a shepherd of Pitton, near Salisbury, who died in 1943, in *WF* iii (1) 3–13.

BRISTOL RECORD SOCIETY

Volume XXXIII *Calendar of the Bristol Apprentice Book 1532-1565 Part II 1542-1552* edited by Elizabeth Ralph and Nora M. Hardwick

The first part of the Apprentice Book was published by the Society in 1948. The new volume covers a period of ten years during which some 1800 enrolments were made.

The volume is issued free to all who have paid the subscription for 1980 (£3.00). Price to non-members, £9.00 (postage and packaging 90p extra).

Recent publications include *The Overseas Trade of Bristol in the Sixteenth Century* (vol. XXXI) and *The Great White Book of Bristol* (vol. XXXII).
The Accounts of the Constables of Bristol Castle in the Thirteenth Century will be published in 1981 and *The Papers of the Smyths of Ashton Court to 1642* in 1982.

The first of a new series of Occasional Papers *Radicalism in Bristol in the Nineteenth Century* by David Large will be published later this year. Price £1.20 including postage.

Annual subscription to the Society £3.00.
Details of publications and membership from David Large, Hon. Secretary, Department of History, University of Bristol.

VOL. XV, No. 65   APRIL 1981

ARCHIVES

Journal of the British Records Association

The Use of Archives and Written Records in Meteorological Research: by Gordon Manley

Three Charters of Bury St Edmunds Abbey in Corpus Christi College, Cambridge: by Catherine P. Hall

Access to Archives in France: by M. Duchein

The IXth International Congress on Archives, London, 1980: by Kathryn M. Thompson

'Archives in the North West Region': British Records Association Liverpool Conference 1980: by Margaret and John Post

The Emmison Retirement Gift: A Brief Account of its Work: by W.J. Smith

Report and Comment   **Reviews**   **Works Received**
Published twice yearly   Honorary Editor: A.S. Cook

Articles, publications for review or notice, and enquiries from intending contributors should be sent to the Editor, *Archives,* at India Office Library and Records, 197 Blackfriars Road, London SE1 8NG. Enquiries about subscriptions and requests for single copies should be sent to British Records Association, The Charterhouse, Charterhouse Square, London EC1M 6AU.

Annual subscription: £8.00 (£10.00 for subscriptions through agents or booksellers); free to subscribing members of the Association (details sent on request).

HAMPSHIRE STUDIES

Based upon intensive research and opening up many new areas of investigation, this book will undoubtedly establish itself as a standard work much in demand by all concerned with the history of the area, and of interest in many respects to students of the past generally.

The Origins of Portsmouth
By Margaret Hoad
The Portsmouth Map of 1545/6
By Paul Harvey
Hampshire and the Catholic Revival in the 1580s
By E.S. Washington
Ship Money in Hampshire
By Patricia Haskell
The Navy and Portsmouth under the Commonwealth
By John Marsh
A Seventeenth-Century Merchant's Account Book
By James Thomas

Prize Office and Prize Agency at Portsmouth 1689-1748
By John Bromley
Young Antiquaries: Lake Allen and Frederic Madden
By John Webb (Joint Editor)
Victorian Church Attendance: The Local Evidence
By Nigel Yates (Joint Editor)
The Portsmouth Corset Industry in the Nineteenth Century
By Ray Riley
The Parliamentary Representation of Portsmouth 1885-1918
By Sarah Peacock (Joint Editor)

Price £12.00 from City Record Office, 3 Museum Road, Portsmouth PO1 2LE. Please make cheques/postal orders payable to Portsmouth City Council.

Vol. LIII No. 128   *November 1980*   *Price £4.00*

BULLETIN OF THE
INSTITUTE OF HISTORICAL RESEARCH

Edited by F. M. L. Thompson

Articles

The king and the princes in 11th-century France.	Elizabeth M. Hallam
Richard I and Berengaria of Navarre.	J. Gillingham
The bishop of London's city soke.	Pamela Taylor
Enacting clauses and legislative initiative, 1559-71.	G.R. Elton
Venetian law and order: a myth?	A.D. Wright
The social and economic structure of an early modern suburb: the Tything at Worcester.	I. Roy and S. Porter
Grenville's Election Act, 1770.	P. Lawson
Whiggery and the dilemma of Reform: Liberals, Radicals and the Melbourne administration, 1835-9.	I.D.C. Newbould

Notes and Documents

The foundation of Oseney abbey.	D. Postles
The execution of Hastings: a neglected source.	C.H.D. Coleman
Van der Delft's message: a reappraisal of the attack on Protector Somerset.	J.S. Berkman
Charles I on innovation: a confidential directive on an explosive issue.	Joyce L. Malcolm
The earl of Bedford's notes of the Short Parliament of 1640.	Esther S. Cope
A poet, a plotter and a postmaster: a disputed polemic of 1668.	S.K. Roberts
Lloyd George's Liberal supporters in December 1916: a note.	J.M. McEwen

UNIVERSITY OF LONDON: INSTITUTE OF HISTORICAL RESEARCH
SENATE HOUSE, LONDON, WC1E 7HU

Roman Mosaics in Britain

A Catalogue of Mosaics and their Schemes David S. Neal

So often accidental discoveries of mosaics have caused damage to them, and lack of time and money have prevented the opportunity for preservation. It is a sad reflection that of the 88 mosaics illustrated in this volume 35 are lost or only small areas of them survive. It is an even sadder fact that of about 1,000 mosaics recorded since the seventeenth century most are destroyed.

In this volume, David Neal of the Department of the Environment presents his illustrations along with a catalogue of their schemes. The result of many years work, this book assimilates a vast collection of previously published work to become a definitive study of Romano-British mosaics and their schemes.

Published in collaboration with the Society for Promotion of Roman Studies as a dual edition. When appearing under the Society's imprint this forms volume one of the Britannia Monograph Series.

208pp (including 76pp plates)
+ 6pp colour plates
This volume includes colour
MICROFICHE (16mm) in a
pocket at the back of the book)
containing 83 illustrations.
297mm × 210mm
ISBN 0 904387 64 X   £9.95   *limp bound only*   *June*

Roman Gloucestershire Alan McWhirr

This is the first general account of life in Gloucestershire when Britain was part of the Roman Empire. At that time the area amounted to a significant part of the province of *Britannia*, possessing two major cities, Gloucester and Cirencester, and a host of well-appointed villas farming the land around them.

Besides the two urban centres there were other major settlements at Dorn, Bourton-on-the-Water, Lower Slaughter, Dymock, Wycomb, Kingscote and extensive occupation in the Fairford/Lechlade region. There are plans of each of these sites and details of the latest discoveries.

The evidence is reviewed for both agriculture and other activities which took place in the countryside, including pottery making, tile and brick production, stone quarrying and iron extraction. The making and laying of mosaics, many of which have been found, is examined as are other items which reflect the artistic taste of the local people. Death and burial customs are discussed in the light of excavations of 450 skeletons from the cemetery at Cirencester.

Approx. 224pp illustrated 219mm × 157mm
case edition ISBN 0 904387 63 1   £7.95
paper edition ISBN 904387 60 7   £3.95 *June*
Alan Sutton Publishing Limited, 17a Brunswick Road, Gloucester. GL1 1HG

BRISTOL BRANCH OF THE HISTORICAL ASSOCIATION

Pamphlets on Bristol History

Hon. General Editor   Patrick McGrath
Assistant General Editor   Peter Harris

The Branch has published 47 pamphlets on aspects of Bristol's history from prehistoric to modern times.

Three new pamphlets will be published in 1981:

No. 48 *Electricity in Bristol 1863-1948* by Peter Lamb (July)

No. 49 *The Streets of Bristol* by Elizabeth Ralph (September)

No. 50 *Bristol and the Civil War* by Patrick McGrath (November)

The price of these pamphlets will be 60p each (73p post-free). Orders to Peter Harris, 74, Bell Barn Road, Stoke Bishop, Bristol 9. Details of pamphlets still in print will be sent on request.

NEW PUBLICATION

THE EXCAVATION OF THE ROMAN CLASSIS BRITANNICA FORTS AT DOVER 1970-1977
by BRIAN PHILP

FORMAT:

272mm x 210mm; 260 pages; 70 pages of line-drawings; 30 half-tone plates; six large pullouts; rigid case-binding, with gold blocking on spine.

CONTENTS:

This, the third major research report in the Kent Monograph Series, includes chapters on earlier discoveries at Dover, the battle to save the forts from destruction; the unfinished early fort; the defensive wall and ditches of the main fort; two major gatehouses; two internal granaries and twelve other major internal buildings; some 50 sets of drains, sewers and externally the aqueduct and the forecourt podium. Specialists reports cover coins, samian, stamped tiles, intaglios, figurines, small finds, building materials, coarse pottery, mortaria and animal bones.

PRICE: £9.80 per volume. Postage/delivery and packing £1.20 per volume extra.

Cheques and Postal orders made payable to K.A.R.U.

Send remittance to CIB HQ, Dover Castle, Kent.

SUSSEX RECORD SOCIETY

The Sussex Record Society was founded in 1901 by a small but distinguished group of men which included Lewis Andre, Francis Barchard, A.W. Beckett, Somers Clark, the Rev. Canon Cooper, L.F. Salzman, Charles Thomas-Stanford, H. Wagner and others. The membership totalled 100 in the first year including three Institutional Members. With the death of Dr Salzman in 1971 the Society lost the last of its founders; he was also Vice-President and Literary Director and, till shortly before his death, Hon. Secretary.

The aims of the Society have remained the same throughout the eighty years of its life, "to transcribe and publish documents relating to the County". During those years seventy-two volumes have been published including a Jubilee Volume of Sussex Views of the late 18th Century after water-colour drawings by H.S. Grimm and J. Lambert. The last volume issued in 1979 was "Accounts of the Roberts Family of Boarzall, Sussex, c. 1568-1582", Edited by Professor Robert Tittler.

Publications include Marriage Licences, Parish Registers, Post-mortem Inquisitions, Medieval Custumels, Churchwarden's Presentments, the Chartularies of Lewes Priory and Chichester Cathedral, Manor Surveys and Terriers &c. Many of these volumes are now out-of-print but a price list of available titles will be sent on request.

Our next volume (No. 72 in the general series) will be "An Illustrated Catalogue of Printed Maps of Sussex 1575-1900" by David Kingsley and should be published in the autumn of this year. Volume 73 "Correspondence between the Dukes of Richmond and Newcastle 1732-1750", edited by Mr. T.J. McCann, will be available in 1982.

Membership   Ordinary Members £6 per year
Institutional Members £8 per year
(Each member receives a copy of our annual publication)

WRITE TO The Hon Secretary,
Sussex Record Society,
Barbican House,
Lewes, Sussex BN7 1YE

Corinium Museum

"One of the country's finest collections of antiquities from Roman Britain".

The Museum takes its name from the Roman town of Cirencester which was second only to London in size in the province of Britain.

The displays are arranged in chronological order from prehistory through the Roman period to Saxon and Medieval times. Here you can see beautiful mosaics, full scale reconstructions of a Roman kitchen, dining room and stone-mason's workshop, personal possessions, jewellery, pottery and coins.

To complement the permanent displays a regular programme of temporary exhibitions introduces other subjects and draws from the reserve collections. Disabled facilities.

Park Street, Cirencester, Glos.

Cirencester, Glos.

Cotswold Countryside Collection

A new museum housed in remaining buildings of the Northleach House of Correction, one of the group of 'country prisons' in Gloucestershire reflecting the advanced ideas of prison reform of Sir George Onesiphorus Paul, country squire and magistrate. Reconstructed displays in original cell block.

The Museum houses the Lloyd Baker collection of agricultural history representing the whole range of agricultural methods in the period of horse power. The climax is a unique exhibition of Gloucestershire harvest-wagons, beautiful in design and construction, prime examples of the craftsman's art.

A developing museum with seasonal opening arrangements

Details: tel. Cirencester (0285) 5611

Northleach, Glos.

Patronage Pedigree and Power

in Later Medieval England   Edited by Charles Ross

The Sense of Dynasty in the Reign of Henry VI   *R.A. Griffiths*
The Richmondshire Community of Gentry
   during the Wars of the Roses   *A.J. Pollard*
The Changing Role of the Wydevilles in Yorkist Politics to 1483   *Michael Hicks*
Baronial Councils in the Later Middle Ages   *Carole Rawcliffe*
Ruling Elites in the Reign of Henry VII   *Margaret Condon*
Japan and England during the fifteenth century: The Onin War
   and the Wars of the Roses   *K.R. Dockray*
Yorkist Propaganda: Pedigree, prophecy and
   'British History' in the Reign of Edward IV   *Alison Allan*
The First English Standing Army? Military
   Organization in Lancastrian Normandy   *Anne Curry*

Patronage the Crown and the Provinces

in Later Medieval England   Edited by Ralph A. Griffiths

Rumour, Propaganda and Popular Opinion during the
   Wars of the Roses   *Charles Ross*
The King's Burden?: the consequences of Royal Marriage
   in Fifteenth Century England   *Anne Crawford*
English Coastal Defence: some Fourteenth-century
   Modifications within the System   *J.R. Alban*
John Beaufort, Duke of Somerset and the French Expedition of 1443 *Michael Jones*
Herefordshire, 1413-61: some Aspects of Society and Public Order *Ailsa Herbert*
The Struggle for Power in Mid-fifteenth-century Devonshire   *Martin Cherry*
Urban Patronage and Patrons in the Fifteenth Century   *Rosemary Horrox*
Patronage and Promotion in the Late-medieval Church   *Robert W. Dunning*

The Crown and Local Communities

in England and France in the Fifteenth Century
Edited by J.R.L. Highfield and Robin Jeffs

Political Theory and Local Communities in Later
   Medieval France and England   *J.P. Genet*
The Centre, the Periphery, and the Problem of Power Distribution
   in Later Medieval France   *P.S. Lewis*
The Breton Nobility and their Masters from the Civil War of 1341-64
   to the Late Fifteenth Century   *Michael Jones*
The Crown, Magnates, and Local Government in
   Fifteenth-Century East Anglia   *Roger Virgoe*
London and the Crown 1451-61   *Caroline M. Barron*
The bonnes villes and the King's Council in
   Fifteenth-Century France   *B. Chavalier*
The Relations between the Towns of Burgundy and the
   French Crown in the Fifteenth Century   *André Leguai*
Local Reaction to the French Reconquest of Normandy:
   The Case of Rouen   *C.T. Allmand*
Dissension in the Provinces under Henry III, 1574-85   *Mark Greengrass*

Patronage Pedigree and Power, £7.95; Patronage the Crown and Provinces, £7.95;
The Crown and Local Communities, £8.95 (case) £4.95 (paper).

   If you wish to be put on our mailing list for fifteenth-century studies, please
write to the address below quoting classification reference 2413.

ALAN SUTTON PUBLISHING LIMITED
17a BRUNSWICK ROAD   GLOUCESTER GL1 1HG

THE COMPLETE PEERAGE
of England, Scotland, Ireland, Great Britain and the United Kingdom, Extant, Extinct or Dormant
G.E. COKAYNE

George Edward Cokayne's *The Complete Peerage* was first published in eight volumes between 1887–98. This was effectively replaced by *"a new edition, revised and much enlarged,"* and edited between 1910 and 1959 successively by Vicary Gibbs (Cokayne's nephew), H.A. Doubleday, Duncan Warrant, Lord Howard de Walden and Geoffrey H. White. This was in twelve volumes with volume twelve being issued in two parts. Volume thirteen was issued in 1940, not as part of the alphabetical sequence, but as a supplement covering creations between 1907 and 1938.

The 1981 reprint is being published in a reduced format to help reduce the production cost, and to meet objections of the shelf space required to house a full size set. It will be printed on matt cartridge and bound in waterproof buckram with attractive dust jackets. Library sleeves can be supplied if required.

1910–1959 edition specifications   1981 edition

Vol. 1   AB/Adam to Basing   **published 1910**
ed. by Vicary Gibbs.   xlpp, 504pp
Vol. II   Bass to Canning   **published 1912**
ed. by Vicary Gibbs & H.A. Doubleday   xpp, 662pp
Vol. III   Canonteign to Cutts   **published 1913   Vol. 1, 1874pp as 472pp**
ed. by Vicary Gibbs & H.A. Doubleday   xpp, 648pp

Vol. IV   Dacre to Dysart   **published 1916**
ed. by Vicary Gibbs & H.A. Doubleday   xpp, 774pp
Vol. V   Eardley to Goojerat   **published 1926**
ed. by H.A. Doubleday, Duncan Warrand & Lord Howard de Walden   xpp, 804pp
Vol. VI   Gordon to Hurstpierpoint   published 1926   Vol. 2, 2326pp as 584pp
ed. by H.A. Doubleday & Lord Howard de Walden   xiipp, 716pp

Vol. VII   Husee to Lincolnshire   published 1929
ed. by H.A. Doubleday & Lord Howard de Walden   xpp, 754pp
Vol. VIII Lindley to Moate   published 1932   Vol. 3, 1628pp as 408pp
ed. by H.A. Doubleday & Lord Howard de Walden   xpp, 854pp

Vol. IX   Moels to Nuneham   published 1936
ed. by H.A. Doubleday, Geoffrey H. White & Lord Howard de Walden xpp, 800pp, 174pp
Vol. X   Oakham to Richmond   published 1945   Vol. 4, 1982pp as 496pp
ed. by Geoffrey H. White   xivpp, 848pp, 136pp

Vol. XI   Rickerton to Sisonby   published 1949
ed. by Geoffrey H. White   viiipp, 748pp, 162pp
Vol. XII/1 Skelmersdale to Towton   published 1953   Vol. 5, 1796pp as 448pp
ed. by Geoffrey H. White   xpp, 816pp, 52pp

Vol. XII/2 Tracton to Zouche   published 1959
ed. by Geoffrey H. White with assistance of R.S. Lea   xpp, 964pp, 50pp
Vol. XIII Peers Created 1901 to 1938   published 1940   Vol. 6, 1672pp as 416pp

---

Pagination details as above. 248mm × 174mm
Photo-reduced – four pages to one page
ISBN 0 904387 82 8 (six vol. set)   £300.00

TO BE PUBLISHED BY ALAN SUTTON PUBLISHING LIMITED
DECEMBER 1981